THIRD EDITION

P9-EMN-897

GRAMMAR IN CONTEXT

SANDRA N. ELBAUM

HEINLE & HEINLE

THOMSON LEARNING ™

United States · Australia · Canada · Mexico · Singapore · Spain · United Kingdom

Vice President, Editorial Director ESL/EFL: Nancy Leonhardt
Production Editor: Michael Burggren
Acquisitions Editor: Eric Bredenberg
Developmental Editor: Thomas Healy
Marketing Manager: Charlotte Sturdy
Manufacturing Coordinator: Mary Beth Hennebury
Project Management: Michael Granger; Modern Graphics, Inc.

Composition: Modern Graphics, Inc.
Photo Research: Susan Van Etten
Illustration: Outlook/Anco
Cover/Text Designer: Linda Dana Willis
Cover Photography: Richard Glover/CORBIS
Printer: Von Hoffman Graphics

For permission to use material in this text, contact us:

web   www.thomsonrights.com
fax   1-800-730-2215
phone   1-800-730-2214

Heinle & Heinle Publishers
20 Park Plaza
Boston, MA 02116

UK/EUROPE/MIDDLE EAST:
Thomson Learning
Berkshire House
168-173 High Holborn
London, WC1V 7AA, United Kingdom

AUSTRALIA/NEW ZEALAND:
Nelson/Thomson Learning
102 Dodds Street
South Melbourne
Victoria 3205 Australia

CANADA:
Nelson/Thomson Learning
1120 Birchmount Road
Scarborough, Ontario
Canada M1K 5G4

LATIN AMERICA:
Thomson Learning
Seneca, 53
Colonia Polanco
11560 México D.F. México

ASIA (excluding Japan):
Thomson Learning
60 Albert Street #15-01
Albert Complex
Singapore 189969

JAPAN:
Thomson Learning
Palaceside Building, 5F
1-1-1 Hitotsubashi, Chiyoda-ku
Tokyo 100 0003, Japan

SPAIN:
Thomson Learning
Calle Magallanes, 25
28015-Madrid, España

Photo & Illustration Credits:
p. 1 © Susan Van Etten, **p. 2** © Lowell Georgia/Corbis, **p. 17** © Susan Van Etten, **p. 37** © Susan Van Etten, **p. 38** © Joseph Sohn: Chromo Sohn Inc./Corbis, **p. 38** © Susan Van Etten, **p. 53** © Tony Arruza/Corbis, **p. 53** © Jay Syverson/Corbis, **p. 75** © Flip Sghulke/Corbis, **p. 76** © Joseph Schwartz Collection/Corbis, **p. 89** © Bettmann/Corbis, **p. 89** © Lynn Goldsmith/Corbis, **p. 90** © Bettmann/Corbis, **p. 101** © Susan Van Etten, **p. 149** © Sandra Elbaum, **p. 160** © Kevin R. Morris/Corbis, **p. 163** © Neal Preston/Corbis, **p. 164** © Robert Holmes/Corbis, **p. 172** © Jennie Woodcock/Corbis, **p. 185** © Bettmann/Corbis, **p. 192** © Bettmann/Corbis, **p. 209** © Susan Van Etten, **p. 245** © R. W. Jones/Corbis, **p. 246** © Corbis, **p. 257** © Susan Van Etten, **p. 258** © Susan Van Etten, **p. 279** © Charles E. Rotkin/Corbis, **p. 315** © Kevin Fleming/Corbis, **p. 335** © Bettmann/Corbis, **p. 344** © Catherine Karnow/Corbis, **p. 356** © Gary Nolan/Corbis, **p. 371** © Bettmann/Corbis, **p. 391** © Jacques M. Chenet/Corbis, **p. 403** © Susan Van Etten, **p. 404** © Susan Van Etten, **p. 404** © Susan Van Etten, **p. 419** © Joseph Sohn; Chromo Sohn Inc./Corbis

Library of Congress Cataloging-in-Publication Data

Elbaum, Sandra N.
    Grammar in Context / Sandra Elbaum.—3rd ed.
        p. cm.
    Includes index.
    ISBN 0-8384-1268-8 (bk. 1 : pbk. : alk. paper)—ISBN 0-8384-1270-X (bk. 2: pbk. : alk. paper)—ISBN 0-8384-1272-6 (bk. 3: pbk. : alk. paper)
    1. English language—Grammar—Problems, exercises, etc.   2. English language—Textbooks for foreign speakers.   I. Title.
PE1112.E3642000
428.2′4—dc21

                                                              00-040822

ISBN 0-8384-1270-X

Printed in the United States of America
2 3 4 5 6 7 8 9   05 04 03 02 01

Contents

Lesson **3**

Lesson **4**

Lesson 5

Lesson 6

Lesson 7

Lesson 8

Lesson 9

Lesson 10

Lesson 11

Lesson 12

Lesson 13

Lesson 14

Lesson 15

Appendices

In loving memory of
Roberto Garrido Alfaro

Acknowledgments

I would also like to show my appreciation for the following teachers who reviewed **Grammar in Context:**

Caroline Cochran	Northern Virginia Community College, VA
Carol Dent	City College of San Francisco, Alemany Center, CA
Bill Griffith	Georgia Institute of Technology, GA
Kathi Jordan	Contra Costa College, CA
Ed Rosen	City College of San Francisco, CA
Rebecca Suarez	University of Texas, El Paso, TX
Ethel Tiersky	Truman College, IL
Karen Tucker	Georgia Institute of Technology, GA
Andrea Woyt	Truman College, IL
Anita Zednik	Northern Virginia Community College, VA

A special thanks to my family of friends for helping me get through it all: Jim M. Curran, Cornelius Hassell, Chay Lustig, Hal Mead, Alison Montgomery, Marilyn Orleans, Meg Tripoli, and Lydia York.

And many thanks to my students at Truman College, who have increased my understanding of my own language and taught me to see life from another point of view. By sharing their observations, questions, and life stories, they have enriched my life enormously.

A word from the author

It seems to me that I was born to be an ESL teacher. My parents immigrated to the U.S. from Poland as adults and were confused not only by the English language but by American culture as well. Born in the U.S., I often had the task as a child to explain the intricacies of the language and allay my parents' fears about the culture. It is no wonder to me that I became an ESL teacher, and later, an ESL writer who focuses on explanations of American culture in order to illustrate grammar. My life growing up in an immigrant neighborhood was very similar to the lives of my students, so I have a feel for what confuses them and what they need to know about American life.

ESL teachers often find themselves explaining confusing customs and providing practical information about life in the U.S. Often, teachers are a student's only source of information about American life. With **Grammar in Context, Third Edition,** I enjoy sharing my experiences with you.

Grammar in Context, Third Edition connects grammar with American cultural context, providing learners of English with a useful and meaningful skill and knowledge base. Students learn the grammar necessary to communicate verbally and in writing, and learn how American culture plays a role in language, beliefs, and everyday situations.

Enjoy the new edition of **Grammar in Context!**

Sandra N. Elbaum

Grammar in Context Unites Learners and Language

Students learn language in context, increasing their understanding and ability to use new structures.

Learning a language through meaningful themes and practicing in a contextualized setting promotes both linguistic and cognitive development. In **Grammar in Context,** grammar is presented in interesting and informative readings, and the language is subsequently practiced throughout the chapter. Students learn more, remember more and can use language more effectively when they learn grammar in context.

Students expand their knowledge of American topics and culture.

American themes add a historical and cultural dimension to students' learning. The readings in **Grammar in Context** help students gain insight into American culture and the way many Americans think and feel about various topics. Students gain ample exposure to and practice in dealing with situations such as finding an apartment, holiday traditions, and shopping, as well as practicing the language that goes with these situations. Their new knowledge helps them enjoy their stay or life in the U.S.

Students are prepared for academic assignments and everyday language tasks.

Discussions, readings, compositions and exercises involving higher level critical thinking skills develop overall language and communication skills. In addition to the numerous exercises in the student text and workbook, teachers will find a wealth of ideas in **Grammar in Context.** Students will have interesting, fulfilling, and successful experiences that they will take with them as they complete their ESL classes.

Students learn to use their new skills to communicate.

The exercises and Expansion Activities in **Grammar in Context** help students learn English while practicing their writing and speaking skills. Students work together in pairs and groups to find more information about topics, to make presentations, to play games, and to role-play. Their confidence to use English increases, as does their ability to communicate effectively.

Students enjoy learning.

If learning is meaningful, it is motivational and fun. Places, famous people, trends, customs, and everyday American activities all have an impact on our students' lives, and having a better understanding of these things helps them function successfully in the U.S. By combining rich, cultural content with clear grammar presentation and practice, **Grammar in Context** engages the student's attention and provides guidance in grammar usage and writing. And whatever is enjoyable will be more readily learned and retained.

Welcome to
Grammar in Context, Third Edition
Spanning language and culture

Students learn more, remember more and can use grammar more effectively when they learn language in context. **Grammar in Context, Third Edition** connects grammar with rich, American cultural context, providing learners of English with a useful and meaningful skill and knowledge base.

Grammar charts use simple and clear language taken from the readings to explain structures in context.

Language Notes refine students' understanding of the target structure.

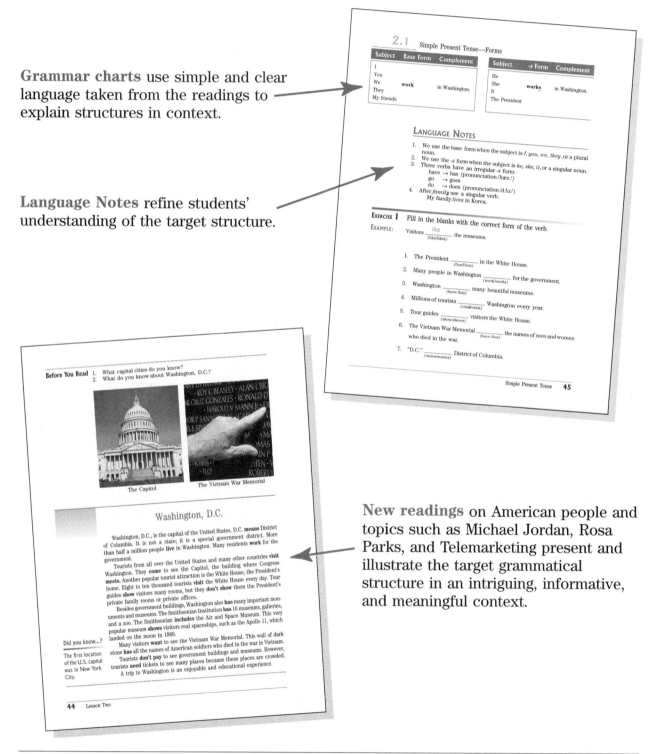

2.1 Simple Present Tense—Forms

Subject	Base Form	Complement
I		
You		
We	**work**	in Washington.
They		
My friends		

Subject	-s Form	Complement
He		
She	**works**	in Washington.
It		
The President		

LANGUAGE NOTES

1. We use the base form when the subject is *I, you, we, they,* or a plural noun.
2. We use the *-s* form when the subject is *he, she, it,* or a singular noun.
3. Three verbs have an irregular *-s* form:
   have → has (pronunciation /hæz/)
   go → goes
   do → does (pronunciation /dʌz/)
4. After *family* use a singular verb.
   My family *lives* in Korea.

EXERCISE 1 Fill in the blanks with the correct form of the verb.
EXAMPLE: Visitors __like__ the museums.
(like/likes)

1. The President _____ in the White House.
   (live/lives)
2. Many people in Washington _____ for the government.
   (work/works)
3. Washington _____ many beautiful museums.
   (have/has)
4. Millions of tourists _____ Washington every year.
   (visit/visits)
5. Tour guides _____ visitors the White House.
   (show/shows)
6. The Vietnam War Memorial _____ the names of men and women
   (have/has)
   who died in the war.
7. "D.C." _____ District of Columbia.
   (mean/means)

Simple Present Tense **45**

Before You Read 1. What capital cities do you know?
2. What do you know about Washington, D.C.?

The Capitol   The Vietnam War Memorial

Washington, D.C.

Washington, D.C., is the capital of the United States. D.C. **means** District of Columbia. It is not a state; it is a special government district. More than half a million people **live** in Washington. Many residents **work** for the government.

Tourists from all over the United States and many other countries **visit** Washington. They **come** to see the Capitol, the building where Congress **meets**. Another popular tourist attraction is the White House, the President's home. Eight to ten thousand tourists **visit** the White House every day. Tour guides **show** visitors many rooms, but they **don't show** them the President's private family rooms or private offices.

Besides government buildings, Washington also **has** many important monuments and museums. The Smithsonian Institution **has** 16 museums, galleries, and a zoo. The Smithsonian **includes** the Air and Space Museum. This very popular museum **shows** visitors real spaceships, such as the Apollo 11, which landed on the moon in 1969.

Many visitors **want** to see the Vietnam War Memorial. This wall of dark stone **has** all the names of American soldiers who died in the war in Vietnam. However, tourists **don't pay** to see government buildings and museums. Tourists **need** tickets to see many places because these places are crowded.

A trip to Washington is an enjoyable and educational experience.

Did you know...?

The first location of the U.S. capital was in New York City.

44 Lesson Two

New readings on American people and topics such as Michael Jordan, Rosa Parks, and Telemarketing present and illustrate the target grammatical structure in an intriguing, informative, and meaningful context.

A wide array of exercises keeps the classroom lively and targets a variety of learning styles.

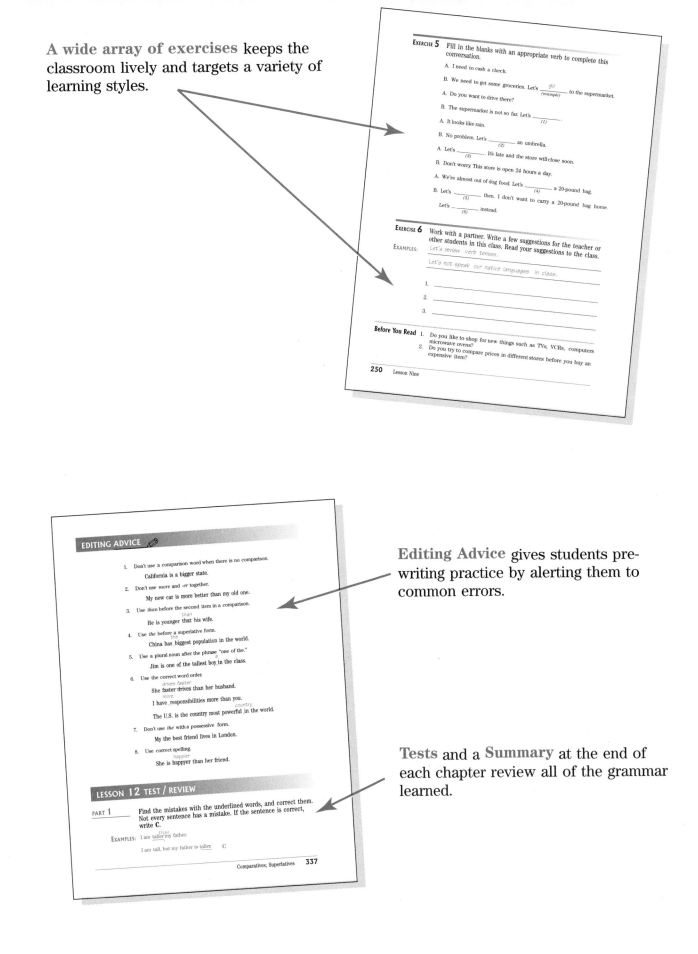

EXERCISE 5   Fill in the blanks with an appropriate verb to complete this conversation.

A. I need to cash a check.

B. We need to get some groceries. Let's ___go___ to the supermarket.
                                              (example)

A. Do you want to drive there?

B. The supermarket is not so far. Let's _____.
                                            (1)

A. It looks like rain.

B. No problem. Let's _____ an umbrella.
                      (2)

A. Let's _____. It's late and the store will close soon.
        (3)

B. Don't worry. This store is open 24 hours a day.

A. We're almost out of dog food. Let's _____ a 20-pound bag.
                                        (4)

B. Let's _____ then. I don't want to carry a 20-pound bag home.
        (5)
Let's _____ instead.
      (6)

EXERCISE 6   Work with a partner. Write a few suggestions for the teacher or other students in this class. Read your suggestions to the class.

EXAMPLES: *Let's review verb tenses.*

Let's not speak our native languages in class.

1. _____

2. _____

3. _____

Before You Read   1. Do you like to shop for new things such as TVs, VCRs, computers microwave ovens?
2. Do you try to compare prices in different stores before you buy an expensive item?

250   Lesson Nine

EDITING ADVICE

1. Don't use a comparison word when there is no comparison.
   California is a bigger state.

2. Don't use *more* and *-er* together.
   My new car is more better than my old one.

3. Use *than* before the second item in a comparison.
                            than
   He is younger that his wife.

4. Use *the* before a superlative form.
              the
   China has biggest population in the world.

5. Use a plural noun after the phrase "one of the."
                                     s
   Jim is one of the tallest boy in the class.

6. Use the correct word order.
       drives faster
   She faster drives than her husband.
      more
   I have responsibilities more than you.
                                  country
   The U.S. is the country most powerful in the world.

7. Don't use *the* with a possessive form.
   My the best friend lives in London.

8. Use correct spelling.
       happier
   She is happyer than her friend.

LESSON 12 TEST / REVIEW

PART 1   Find the mistakes with the underlined words, and correct them. Not every sentence has a mistake. If the sentence is correct, write C.

EXAMPLES: I am taller my father.
                     than

            I am tall, but my father is taller.   C

Comparatives; Superlatives   337

Editing Advice gives students pre-writing practice by alerting them to common errors.

Tests and a **Summary** at the end of each chapter review all of the grammar learned.

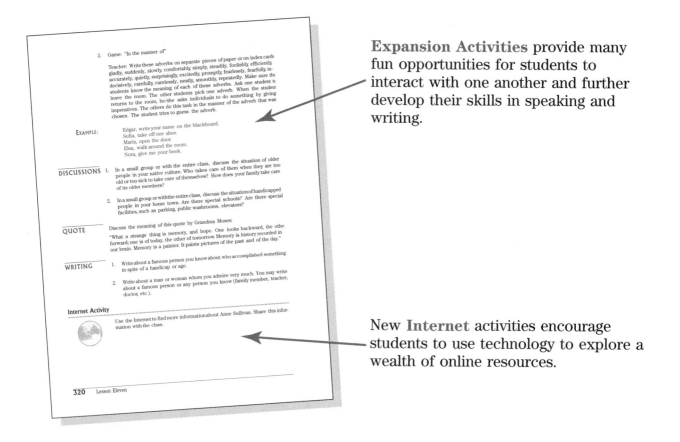

Expansion Activities provide many fun opportunities for students to interact with one another and further develop their skills in speaking and writing.

New **Internet** activities encourage students to use technology to explore a wealth of online resources.

More Grammar Practice Workbooks

Used in conjunction with **Grammar in Context** or as a companion to any reading, writing, or listening skills text, **More Grammar Practice** helps students learn and review the essential grammar skills to make language learning comprehensive and ongoing.

- Clear grammar charts

- Extensive exercises

- Great for in-class practice or homework

- Follows the same scope and sequence as **Grammar in Context, Third Edition**

GRAMMAR

The Simple Present Tense
Frequency Words

CONTEXT

Pets
Letter About American Customs

LESSON FOCUS

We use the simple present tense to talk about facts.
The U.S. *has* about 275 million people.
The U.S. *is* in North America.

We use the simple present tense to talk about regular activities, habits, or customs. We use frequency words to show how often an action happens.
Americans *often* wear shorts in the summer.
Americans *sometimes* say, "Have a nice day."

Before You Read

1. Do you like animals?
2. Do you have a pet?

Read the following article. Pay special attention to the verb *be* and other verbs in the simple present tense.

Pets

Americans **love** pets. About 60 percent of Americans **live** with one or more animals. About four in ten households **have** at least one dog. Three in ten households **own** at least one cat.

Americans **think** of their pets as part of the family: 79 percent of pet owners **give** their pets holiday or birthday presents,[1] and 33 percent of pet owners **talk** to their pets on the phone or through the answering machine. Many pet owners **sleep** with their dogs or cats. Many people **travel** with their pets. (It **costs** about $50 to fly with a pet.) Some hotels **allow** guests to bring their pets.

Americans **pay** a lot of money to keep pets. They **spend** $12 billion a year in vet[2] bills and pet supplies. There **are** schools, toys, hotels, restaurants, clothes, and cemeteries for pets. There **are** magazines for pet owners. There **are** hundreds of Web sites for pet owners.

Pets **are** a lot of fun. They **are** affectionate, too. People who **are** lonely **get** a lot of love from their animals. Medical research **shows** that contact with a dog or a cat can lower a person's blood pressure.

Pets **need** a lot of attention. Before you buy a pet, it's important to ask yourself these questions:

- **Are** you patient?
- **Are** you home a lot?
- If you **have** children, **are** they responsible?
- **Are** pets allowed where you live?

Unfortunately, some people **don't realize** that pets need a lot of care. Some people **see** a cute puppy or kitten, **buy** it, and later **abandon** it because they **don't want** to take care of it. It **is** important to understand that a pet **is** a long-term responsibility.

Labrador Retrievers

Did you know...?

The most common registered breed of dog in the U.S. is the labrador retriever.

[1] These statistics are from the American Animal Hospital Association, 1995.
[2] *Vet* is short for *veterinarian*. This is an animal doctor.

Examples	Explanation
I **am** patient. Dogs **are** friendly. My grandmother **is** lonely. It **is** important to choose the right pet. There **are** toys for dogs.	I → am you, we, they → are he, she, it, → is there → is or are
She **is not** home much. Some children **are not** responsible.	Negatives: am not, are not, is not

LANGUAGE NOTES

1. We can make a contraction with the subject pronoun and *am*, *is*, or *are*.

    I am → I'm   he is → he's
    you are → you're   she is → she's
    we are → we're   it is → it's
    they are → they're

2. We can make a contraction with most nouns and *is*.
    My grandmother**'s** lonely.
    Your dog**'s** beautiful.

3. We don't make a contraction with *is* if the noun ends in these letters: *s*, *se*, *ce*, *ze*, *sh*, *ch*, or *x*.
    A mouse *is* a small animal.
    A fo<u>x *is*</u> a relative of a dog.

fox

4. In writing, we don't make a contraction with a noun and *are*.
    My *children are* responsible.

5. In writing, we don't make a contraction with *there are*.
    There are many kinds of dogs.

6. The negative contractions are: *isn't* and *aren't*.
    She *isn't* home much.
    You *aren't* patient.
    There is no contraction for *am not*.

EXERCISE 1 Fill in the blanks with the correct form of *be*. Make a contraction wherever possible.

EXAMPLE: My dog<u> 's </u> very small.

1. You take care of your dog. You _____ responsible.

2. Pet ownership _____ a big responsibility.

3. My cat _____ soft.

4. Dogs _____ great pets because they _____ affectionate.

   They _____ also good protection for a house.

5. My dog _____ a member of my family.

6. Some cats _____ very affectionate. Other cats _____ very independent.

7. It _____ a big responsibility to own a pet.

8. Kittens and puppies _____ cute.

9. We _____ ready to get a pet.

10. Some people _____ lonely.

EXERCISE 2 Fill in the blank with the correct form of *be*. Then fill in the second blank with a negative form. Use contractions wherever possible.

EXAMPLE: Today<u> 's </u> my daughter's birthday. It <u> isn't </u> a holiday.

1. My daughter and I _____ at the pet shop. We _____ at home.

2. My husband _____ at work now. He _____ with me.

3. I _____ patient. My husband _____ patient.

4. This puppy _____ for my daughter. It _____ for my son.

5. My daughter _____ responsible. My son _____ responsible.

6. Dogs _____ good for protection. Cats _____ good for protection.

7. My daughter _____ excited. She _____ bored.

8. This _____ a lab.³ It _____ a small dog.

---

³ *Lab* is short for *labrador retriever.*

Examples	Uses
I **am** patient. The pet shop **is** located on the corner. The children **are** excited about the new puppy.	With a description (adjective) NOTE: Some words that end in *-ed* are adjectives: *tired, married, worried, interested, bored, excited, crowded, located*
This **is** a labrador. A labrador **is** a big dog.	With a classification or definition of the subject
My dog **is** in the yard.	With a location
My husband **is** from Guatemala.	With a place of origin
My dog **is** three (years old).	With age
The cat **is** hungry. The window is open. I **am** cold.	With physical states
There **are** toys for dogs. There **is** a dog restaurant near my house.	With *there*
It **is** ten o'clock now. It **is** warm today.	With time and weather.

LANGUAGE NOTES

Be cold means to feel a low temperature. *Have a cold* shows an illness.
Please bring me my sweater. *I'm cold.*
I'm sick. *I have a cold.*

EXERCISE 3 Fill in the blanks with the missing words.

EXAMPLE: My dog __'s__ hungry. He wants to eat.

1. Your son _____ responsible because he _____ only four
   (not)
   years _____ .

2. My aunt _____ married. Her dog _____ her only companion.
   (not)

3. In the U.S., there _____ cemeteries for pets.

4. Some cats _____ very affectionate.

5. My dog _____ thirsty. Put water in his dish.

6. This _____ a kitten. It _____ only two weeks _____.

7. Don't leave your dog in the car. _____ hot today.

8. My dog _____ cold in the winter. She needs a sweater.

9. _____ is a picture of my dog.

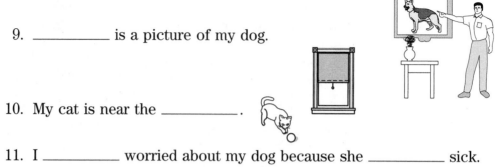

10. My cat is near the _____ .

11. I _____ worried about my dog because she _____ sick.

12. My vet's office _____ located about two miles from my house.

1.3 Questions with *Be*

Statement	*Yes/No* Question and Short Answer
Dogs are fun.	**Are dogs** affectionate? Yes, they are.
My dog is big.	**Is your dog** big? No, he isn't.
I am responsible.	**Am I** patient? Yes, you are.

Statement	*Wh-* Question
You are at home.	When **are you** at home?
My son isn't responsible.	Why **isn't your son** responsible?
You aren't patient.	Why **aren't you** patient?

LANGUAGE NOTES

1. In a statement, we put the subject before the verb *be*. In a question, we put *be* before the subject.
   The dog is big.
   Is the dog friendly?

2. If a short answer is negative, we can make a contraction with *be*. If a short answer is affirmative, we can't make a contraction.
   Is your dog small? No, he *isn't.* OR No, *he's not.*
   Is your dog friendly? Yes, he *is.* (NO CONTRACTION)

3. Most question words can contract with *is.* (EXCEPTION: *which is*)
   Where's your cat?
   What's your cat's name?
   Which is bigger, a Collie or a Lab? (NO CONTRACTION)

4. Some common questions with *be* are:
What's your name? My name is Linda.
What time is it? It's 4:32.
What color is the flag? It's red, white, and blue.
What kind of dog is this? It's a Lab.
What's this? It's a leash.
What's a Collie? It's a dog.
How are you? I'm fine.
How's the weather? It's sunny and warm.
How old is your daughter? She's 10 (years old).[4]
How tall are you? I'm five feet, three inches tall (or 5′3″).[5]
Where are you from? I'm from Mexico.

leash

EXERCISE 4 Read each question. Answer with a short answer. Do not make a contraction for a short answer after *yes*.

EXAMPLES: Is the teacher a native speaker of English?
Yes, she is.
Is the teacher near the door?
No, she isn't.

1. Are you from Africa?

2. Are you tired?

3. Is the teacher from your native country?

4. Are the students bored?

5. Are the windows of the classroom open?

6. Is the door open?

7. Are you an immigrant?

8. Is it warm in the classroom?

9. Is there a map in the classroom?

10. Is the school located near your house?

[4] It is not polite to ask an adult American about his or her age.
[5] For conversion to the metric system, see Appendix D.

Ask and answer. (You may work with a partner.)

EXAMPLE: Where are you from?
I'm from El Salvador.

1. What city are you from?

2. What color is the flag of your native country?

3. What time is it now in your hometown?

4. What sports are popular in your native country?

5. What pets are popular in your native country?

6. What kind of cars are popular in your native country?

7. What's the capital of your native country?

8. Who's the president (or leader) of your native country?

9. When's Labor Day in your native country?

10. What's a popular holiday in your native country?

EXERCISE **6**   Fill in the blanks in this phone conversation between Betty (B) and Alice (A).

B. Hello?

A. Hi. This ___is___ Alice.
        (example)

B. Hi, Alice. How _____?
                        (1)

A. I'm fine. This _____ a long distance call. I _____ at home
                    (2)   *(3 not)*
now.

B. Where _____?
                (4)

A. I'm at Disneyland.

B. What's Disneyland? _____ a city?
                            (5)

A. No, it _____. _____ a park in California.
            (6)   *(7)*

B. What kind of park _____?
                        (8)

A. It's a place for children to have fun. There _____ a lot of things
                                                    (9)
to do here.

B. _____ with you?
        (10)

A. My daughter _____ with me. We _____ here for her birthday.
                    (11)   *(12)*

B. How _____ she?
(13)

A. She _____ 10 _____ . She _____ very excited about
(14)   (15)   (16)
the trip.

B. Why _____ with you?
(17)

A. My husband isn't here because he _____ too busy. Anyway, he
(18)

_____ interested in Disneyland.
(19 not)

B. _____ the weather in California?
(20)

A. _____ sunny and warm. _____ warm in New York?
(21)   (22)

B. No. The weather here _____ terrible. _____ only 50° and
(23)   (24)
rainy. You _____ lucky to be in California.
(25)

A. Yes, I _____ . My daughter and I _____ tired now. And
(26)   (27)
we _____ hungry. I'll talk to you when I get home.
(28)

B. Thanks for calling. Bye.

1.4 The Simple Present Tense—Forms

Base Form	-S Form
I **love** animals.	My mother **loves** children.
We **love** animals.	My father **loves** children.
You **love** animals.	My family **loves** children.
My children **love** animals.	My dog **loves** children.
They **love** animals.	Everyone **loves** children.

LANGUAGE NOTES

1. The simple present tense has two forms: the base form and the *-s*
    form.
    love—loves
    want—wants

2. We use the *-s* form after *he, she, it,* singular nouns, *everyone, every-body, everything, no one, nobody, nothing,* and *family.*
3. We use the base form after *I, you, we, they,* and plural nouns.
4. Three verbs have an irregular *-s* form:
    have → has (pronunciation /hæz/)
    go → goes
    do → does (pronunciation: /dəz/)

5. For a review of the spelling and pronunciation of the -s form, see Appendix A.

EXERCISE 7 Fill in the blanks with the base form or the -s form.

EXAMPLE: Americans ___love___ pets.
                (love)

My son ___loves___ his new kitten.
            (love)

1. My girlfriend _____ her dog a present on his birthday.
                      (give)

2. People _____ affection from animals.
              (get)

3. Everyone _____ affection.
                (need)

4. It _____ a lot of money to have a pet.
        (cost)

5. Some pet owners _____ to their pets on the phone.
                        (talk)

6. My daughter _____ a puppy for her birthday.
                    (want)

7. My neighbor's dog _____ all the time.
                          (bark)

8. Some people _____ with their dogs.
                    (travel)

9. Forty percent of Americans _____ at least one dog.
                                  (have)

10. My brother _____ three dogs.
                    (have)

11. Dogs _____ their owners.
            (protect)

12. My family _____ animals.
                  (love)

13. Nobody _____ the dog's age.
                (know)

14. Everybody _____ that puppies and kittens are cute.
                  (think)

1.5 Negative Statements with the Simple Present Tense

Examples	Explanation
My neighbors **have** two dogs. They **don't have** a cat.	We use *don't* + the base form with *I, you, we, they,* or a plural noun.
My daughter **wants** a puppy. She **doesn't want** a kitten.	We use *doesn't* + the base form with *he, she, it,* or a singular noun.

LANGUAGE NOTES

1. *Don't* is the contraction for *do not*. *Doesn't* is the contraction for *does not*.
2. Always use the base form after *don't* and *doesn't*.

EXERCISE 8   Write the negative form of the underlined verb.

EXAMPLE: We <u>have</u> two cats. We _____*don't have*_____ a dog.

1. My cats <u>eat</u> special food. They _____ food from our table.

2. My cats <u>like</u> tuna. They _____ chicken.

3. One cat <u>sleeps</u> in my bed. She _____ alone.

4. I <u>buy</u> cat food. I _____ dog food.

5. My landlord <u>allows</u> cats. He _____ dogs.

6. My cats <u>need</u> attention. They _____ a lot of my time.

7. Some cats <u>go</u> outside. My cats _____ outside.

8. You <u>like</u> dogs. You _____ cats.

9. We <u>have</u> cats. We _____ children.

10. I <u>like</u> cats. My sister _____ cats.

EXERCISE 9   Check (√) the items that describe you. Make an affirmative or negative statement about yourself. Then ask a question. Another student will answer.

EXAMPLE: __√__ I speak Spanish.
A. I speak Spanish. Do you speak Spanish?
B. No, I don't. I speak Romanian.

EXAMPLE: _____ I live in a suburb.
A. I don't live in a suburb. Do you live in a suburb?
B. Yes, I do.

1. _____ I speak Spanish.

2. _____ I like American movies.

3. _____ I have a cell phone.

4. _____ I take the bus to school.

5. _____ I have a pet.

6. _____ I like cats.

7. _____ I like to wake up early.

8. _____ I have a CD player.

9. _____ I like to use computers.

10. _____ I know a lot about American history.

1.6   Questions with the Simple Present Tense

Wh- Word	Do/Does Don't/Doesn't	Subject	Verb	Complement	Short Answer
		My friend	**has**	a dog.	
		She	**doesn't have**	a cat.	
	Does	she	**have**	a Labrador?	No, she **doesn't.**
What kind of dog	**does**	she		**have**?	
Why	**doesn't**	she	**have**	a cat?	

LANGUAGE NOTES

We use the base form in questions.[6]

EXERCISE 10 Fill in the blanks to complete this conversation.

A. Do you ___*like*___ animals?
                   (example)

B. Yes, I _____. In fact, I love animals very much. I especially
              (1)
like dogs.

A. _____ you have a dog?
       (2)

B. No, I _____.
            (3)

A. If you love dogs, why _____ a dog?
                                    (4)

B. Because my landlord _____ dogs.
                          (5 not/permit)

A. _____ he permit cats?
       (6)

B. Yes, he _____.
               (7)

---

[6] You will see an exception to this rule in Lesson Four, "Questions About the Subject."

A. _____ a cat?
       (8 have)

B. Yes, I do, but I _____ to find a new home for my cat.
                         (9 need)

    _____ you know anyone who wants a cat?
         (10)

A. Why _____ your cat?
             (11)

B. I'm getting married in three months and my girlfriend _____

    _____ to live with cats.
        (12 not/want)

A. Why _____ to live with cats? Doesn't she
                (13)

    _____ them?
       (14)

B. She _____ them, but she's allergic to them. When she
           (15 like)

    _____ over, she _____ and _____ .
        (16 come)   (17 sneeze)   (18 cough)

    She _____ to come over any more.
           (19 not/want)

A. That's a big problem.

B. Yes, it is. I _____ to find a good home for my cat.
                     (20 need)

    _____ you want my cat?
         (21)

A. Sorry. My landlord _____ dogs or cats. Maybe you need
                          (22 not/allow)

    a new girlfriend.

B. I _____ so. I_____ her and she _____
       (23 not/think)   (24 love)   (25 love)
    me.

A. Well, I _____ you find a good home for your cat soon.
               (26 hope)

1.7   Wh- Questions with a Preposition

Preposition	Wh- Word	Do/Does	Subject	Verb	Preposition
With	whom	do	you	live?	
	Who	do	you	live	**with**?
On	what floor	does	he	live?	
	What floor	does	he	live	**on**?
	Where	do	you	come	**from**?

Language Notes

1. Putting the preposition before a question word is very formal. In conversation, most people put the preposition at the end.
    FORMAL: *With* whom do you live?
    INFORMAL: Who do you live *with*?

2. We omit *at* in a question about time.
    What time does the class begin?
    It begins *at* 3 o'clock.

3. For country of origin, you can use *be from* or *come from*.
    Where are you from?
    Where do you come from?

EXERCISE 11 Ask a question using the words given. Then use the words in parentheses ( ) to ask a *wh-* question whenever possible. Another student will answer.

EXAMPLE: you/eat in the cafeteria (with whom) OR (who . . . with)
A. Do you eat in the cafeteria?
B. Yes, I do.
A. Who do you eat with? OR With whom do you eat?
B. I eat with my friends.

1. you/live alone (with whom) OR (who . . . with)

2. you/go to bed early (what time)

3. the teacher/come to class on time (what time)

4. the teacher/come from this city (where . . . from)

5. you/practice English outside of class (with whom) OR (who . . . with)

6. you/think about your future (what else)

7. you/complain about English grammar (what else)

8. you/listen to the radio (what station)

9. the teacher/talk about spelling (what else)

10. you/interested in animals (what animals)

11. you/come from Mexico (where)

12. you/go to sleep at midnight (what time)

Wh- Word	*Do/Does*	Subject	Verb Phrase	Answer
What	**does**	vet	**mean**?	It means veterinarian or animal doctor.
How	**do**	you	**spell** vet?	V - E - T
How	**do**	you	**say** "dog" in Spanish?	"Perro"
How much	**does**	dog food	**cost**?	It costs about $10 a bag.

LANGUAGE NOTES

Mean, spell, say, and *cost* are verbs and should be in the verb position of a question.

EXERCISE 12 Fill in the blanks with the missing words.

EXAMPLE: What _____*does*_____ "vet" mean?

1. How _____ does the textbook cost?

2. How much _____ bananas cost this week?

3. How much _____ a phone call to your country _____ per minute?

4. I need to buy the textbook. How much _____?

5. I want to buy this computer. How _____?

6. What does "kitten" _____? It means baby cat.

7. I don't know the word "puppy." What does _____?

8. I don't know the word "cemetery." What _____?

9. In Spanish, we say "maestro" for teacher. How do _____ teacher in your language?

10. In Spanish, we say "estudiante" for student. How _____ student in your language?

11. In Spanish, we say "escuela" for school. How _____ in your native language?

12. I want to write your last name. How do you _____ your last name?

13. How _____ spell your first name?

14. How _____ the name of this college?

EXERCISE 13 Fill in the blanks to complete the questions.

A. How ___*is*___ your cousin Bill? I never see him.
   (example)

B. He's fine. But he doesn't live here anymore.

A. Where _____?
            (1)

B. He lives in L.A. now.

A. What _____?
          (2)

B. L.A. means Los Angeles. We say L.A. for short.

A. Where _____?
            (3)

B. L.A. is on the west coast. It's in California. I plan to visit him next month.

A. How much _____?
                    (4)

B. An airplane ticket to Los Angeles costs about $200.

A. Why _____ in L.A.?
          (5)

B. He lives in L.A. because he goes to school there now.

A. What college _____?
                      (6)

B. He goes to Los Angeles City College.

A. _____ California?
          (7)

B. Oh, he likes it very much.

A. _____ his address? I want to write to him.
          (8)

B. Yes, I have his address. He lives at 734 Sierra Avenue.

A. How _____ "Sierra"?
          (9)

B. S-I-E-R-R-A.

A. Sierra sounds like a Spanish word. What _____?
                                                (10)

B. It means "mountain." Many places in California have Spanish names. In fact, Los Angeles means "the angels."

1. Are some American customs strange for you? Which ones?
2. In your native culture, when you invite someone to a restaurant, who pays?

Read the following letter from Elena in the U.S. to Sofia in Russia. Pay special attention to the frequency words.

Letter About American Customs

Dear Sofia,

I want to tell you about life in the U.S. Some American customs are so strange for me.

Americans treat their pets like a member of the family. My friend Marianne lives alone but she has a dog, Sparky. She **always** carries a picture of Sparky in her wallet. She **often** buys toys for him, especially on his birthday. **Once a month**, she takes him to a dog groomer. The groomer gives him a bath and cuts his nails. When Marianne travels, she **sometimes** takes her dog with her. She **often** calls her dog on the telephone when she's not home and talks into the answering machine. Sparky even sleeps in bed with her.

Another strange custom is this: **Sometimes** Marianne invites me to go to a restaurant. When the check arrives, she **usually** starts to divide the bill in half. Or she says, "Your part is $10.95 and my part is $12.75." In our country, **whenever** I invite someone to a restaurant, I pay.

There's another strange custom. When Americans don't finish their meal in a restaurant, they **often** ask for a doggie bag. Even people who don't have a dog ask for a doggie bag. They take the food home and eat it later. But in Marianne's case, she **usually** likes to share her food with Sparky. She **often** orders a steak in a restaurant because Sparky likes a good steak.

There is another custom that is strange for me. Americans **often** ask, "How are you?" but they **rarely** wait for an answer. Marianne asks me this question **whenever** she sees me, but she **never** listens to my answer. If I start to say, "I don't feel well," she doesn't hear me and says, "That's nice." **Sometimes** I hear her ask other pet owners, "How's your dog?" or, "How's your cat?" She seems more interested in animals' health than in people's health.

I learn a lot about American customs from Marianne. If I don't understand something, she **always** explains it to me. But life is still strange for me here.

Please write me soon. How are you? I'm not American. I REALLY want to know the answer.

Your good friend,
Elena

1.9 Simple Present Tense—Uses

Examples	Uses of the Simple Present Tense
Sixty percent of Americans **have** a pet. Pets **need** attention.	To state a fact
Marianne **comes** from the U.S. Elena **comes** from Russia.	To show one's country or city of origin
Marianne **always** carries a picture of her dog in her wallet. She **often** buys toys for her dog. When Americans don't finish their meal in a restaurant, they **sometimes** ask for a doggie bag. **Whenever** we go to a restaurant, we divide the check.	To show a regular activity, a habit, or a custom

LANGUAGE NOTES

1. For place of origin, we use the simple present tense, not the past tense.
    I *come* from China. NOT: I *came* from China.

2. For a place of origin, we can also use *be from.*
    I *am from* China.

EXERCISE **14** Fill in the blanks with the correct form of the verb in parentheses ( ).

EXAMPLE: Marianne always _____*explains*_____ American customs to Elena.
                                   (explain)

1. Elena often _____ about American customs.
                      (think)

2. Marianne always _____ a picture of her dog in her wallet.
                          (carry)

3. They sometimes _____ in a restaurant.
                         (eat)

4. Marianne sometimes _____ for a doggie bag.
                             (ask)

5. She often _____ her food with her dog.
                   (share)

6. When the check _____, the two women usually _____
                        (arrive)   (divide)
   it.

7. Americans often _____, "How are you?"
                          (ask)

8. Sometimes they _____ for an answer.
                        (not/wait)

1.10 Frequency Words

Frequency Word		Example
always	100%	Elena **always** pays when she invites someone to a restaurant.
usually/generally	↑	Marianne **usually** (**generally**) divides the bill in half.
often/frequently		Americans **often** (**frequently**) ask, "How are you?"
sometimes/occasionally		Marianne **sometimes** (**occasionally**) invites me to a restaurant.
rarely/seldom/hardly ever	↓	Elena **rarely** (**seldom**) (**hardly ever**) eats in a restaurant.
never/not ever	0%	Marianne **never** waits for an answer to her question.
		She does**n't ever** wait for an answer.

EXERCISE 15 Fill in the blanks with an appropriate frequency word.

EXAMPLE: Americans ___*often*___ say, "Have a nice day."

1. I _____ say, "How are you?" when I meet a friend.

2. I'm _____ confused about American customs.

3. I _____ smile when I pass someone I know.

4. I _____ shake hands when I get together with a friend.

5. Americans _____ ask me, "What country are you from?"

6. I _____ celebrate my birthday in a restaurant.

7. I _____ buy birthday presents for my good friends.

8. If I invite a friend to a restaurant, I _____ pay for both of us.

9. I _____ ask for a "doggie bag" in a restaurant.

10. I _____ eat in fast-food restaurants.

EXERCISE 16 Fill in the blanks with an appropriate frequency word. (You may find a partner and compare your answers.)

EXAMPLE: People in my native country ___*rarely*___ ask, "How are you?"

1. Women in my native country _____ kiss their friends when they get together.

2. People in my native country _____ visit each other without calling first.

3. Men in my native country _____ do housework.

4. Most people in my native country _____ work hard.

5. Students in my native country _____ stand up when the teacher enters the room.

6. Married women in my native country _____ wear a wedding ring.

7. Married men in my native country _____ wear a wedding ring.

8. Women in my native country _____ wear shorts in the summer.

9. People in my native country _____ complain about the political situation.

10. People in my native country _____ eat in restaurants.

11. People in my native country _____ leave a tip in a restaurant.

12. People in my native country _____ take food home from a restaurant.

1.11 Position of Frequency Words

Subject	Frequency Word	Verb	Complement
I	**often**	ask	about American customs.
We	**rarely**	eat	in a restaurant.

Subject	Be	Frequency Word	Complement
I	am	**often**	confused about American customs.
We	are	**always**	interested in American customs.

LANGUAGE NOTES

1. Frequency words come after the verb *be* but before other verbs.

   I'*m often* confused about American customs.

   I *always ask* questions about American customs.

2. The following words can also come at the beginning of a sentence: *usually, generally, often, frequently, sometimes, occasionally.*
   I *usually* eat at home.
   Usually I eat at home.
   We *sometimes* talk about American customs in class.
   Sometimes we talk about American customs in class.
   Americans *often* ask, "How are you?"
   Often Americans ask, "How are you?"

EXERCISE **17** Add a frequency word to each sentence to make a **true** statement about yourself.

EXAMPLE: I drink coffee at night.
I never drink coffee at night.

1. I talk to my neighbors.

2. I pay my rent on time.

3. I'm busy on Saturdays.

4. I receive letters from my friends.

5. I call my family in my country.

6. I travel in the summer.

7. I speak English at home with my family.

8. I eat meat for dinner.

9. I go downtown.

10. I study in the library.

11. I eat cereal for breakfast.

12. I bring my dictionary to class.

EXERCISE 18 Add a verb (phrase) to make a **true** statement.

EXAMPLE: I/usually

I usually drink coffee in the morning.

OR   *I'm usually afraid to go out at night.*

1. I/rarely/on Sunday

_____

2. I/usually/on the weekend

_____

3. I/hardly ever

_____

4. I/sometimes/at night

_____

5. people from my native country/often

_____

6. people from my native country/seldom

_____

7. Americans/sometimes

_____

8. Americans/rarely

_____

9. women from my native country/hardly ever

_____

10. men from my native country/hardly ever

_____

1.12 Questions with *Ever*

Examples	Explanation

Do you **ever** eat in a restaurant?
  Yes, I **sometimes** do.
Does the teacher **ever** give surprise tests?
  No, he **never** does.
	We use *ever* in a *yes/no* question when we want an answer that has a frequency word.

Are you **ever** afraid to go out at night?
  Yes, I **sometimes** am.
Is the teacher **ever** late to class?
  No, he **never** is.
	In a short answer, the frequency word comes between the subject and the verb.

LANGUAGE NOTES

1. The verb after *never* is affirmative. We do not put two negatives together.
    Do Americans ever bow? No, they *never* do.

2. We can give a short answer with *yes* or *no* and the frequency word.
    Do you *ever* shake hands when you meet your friends?
    Yes, always.
    Do the students *ever* stand up when the teacher enters the room?
    No, *never*.

EXERCISE 19 Fill in the blanks with a frequency word to make a **true** statement about yourself. Then ask a question with *ever*. Another student will answer.

EXAMPLE: I ___*rarely*___ eat breakfast in a restaurant.
A. Do you ever eat breakfast in a restaurant?
B. No, I never do.

1. I _____ sleep with the light on.

2. I _____ watch TV in the morning.

3. I _____ take a bubble bath.

4. I _____ spend money on foolish things.

5. I'm _____ afraid to go out at night.

6. I'm _____ tired while I'm in class.

bubble bath

7. I _____ cry at a sad movie.

8. I _____ dream in English.

9. I _____ take off my shoes when I enter my house.

10. I _____ babysit for a member of my family.

11. I _____ eat fast food.

12. I _____ wear a watch.

13. I _____ use cologne or perfume.

14. I _____ fall asleep with the TV on.

15. I _____ fall asleep in class.

1.13 Frequency Expressions and Questions with *How Often*

Examples	Explanation
I eat in a restaurant **once a month**. **How often** do you eat in a restaurant? My mother writes to me **every week**. **How often** does your mother write to you? I walk my dog **three times a day**. **How often** do you walk your dog?	Expressions that show frequency are: • every day (week, month, year) • every other day (week, month, year) • from time to time • once in a while We can ask a question with *how often* when we want to know the frequency of an activity.
How often does the teacher review grammar? She reviews grammar **whenever** she has time.	We can show frequency with *whenever*.

LANGUAGE NOTES

Frequency expressions can come at the beginning of a sentence or at the end of a sentence.

I talk to my friend *every day.*
Every day I talk to my friend.
From time to time, I go to the theater.
I go to the theater *from time to time.*

EXERCISE 20 Ask a question with "How often do you...?" and the words given. Another student will answer.

EXAMPLES: eat in a restaurant
A. How often do you eat in a restaurant?
B. I eat in a restaurant once a week.

go downtown
A. How often do you go downtown?
B. I go downtown whenever I have a doctor's appointment.

1. need to renew your driver's license
2. shop for groceries
3. exercise
4. get a haircut
5. use your dictionary
6. water your plants

7. use public transportation
8. use the Internet
9. go to the post office
10. go to the dentist
11. watch the news on TV
12. go to the teacher's office

SUMMARY OF LESSON 1

1. Observe the simple present tense with the verb *be*.

> You **are** from California.
> You **aren't** from Massachusetts.
> **Are** you from Los Angeles? No, **I'm** not.
> Where **are** you from?

> She**'s** late.
> She **isn't** on time.
> **Is** she here?
> No, she **isn't**.
> Where **is** she?
> Why **isn't** she here?

2. Observe the simple present tense with other verbs.

BASE FORM
> They **have** a car.
> They **don't have** a bike.
> **Do** they **have** an American car?
> Yes, they **do**. OR No, they **don't**.
> What kind of car **do** they **have**?
> Why **don't** they **have** a foreign car?

-*S* FORM
> She **speaks** Spanish.
> She **doesn't speak** Portuguese.
> **Does** she **speak** English?
> Yes, she **does**. OR No, she **doesn't**.
> When **does** she **speak** English?
> Why **doesn't** she **speak** Portuguese?

3. Frequency words:

always	100%
usually/generally	↑
often/frequently	
sometimes/occasionally	
rarely/seldom/hardly ever	↓
never/not ever	0%

4. Questions with frequency words:
   Does he **ever** work at night? Yes, he sometimes does.
   How often does he work on Saturdays? Once a month.

EDITING ADVICE ✏

1. Do not use a contraction in a short affirmative answer.

   Are you happy in the U.S. Yes, ~~I'm~~ _I am_.

2. Do not make a contraction with a word that ends with *s*, *se*, *ce*, *ze*, *sh*, *ch*, or *x*.

   English~~'s~~ _is_ a difficult language.

3. Do not use *have* with age. Do not use *years* without *old*.

   My daughter ~~has~~ _is_ 10 years _old_.

4. Do not use *have* with *hungry, thirsty, hot, cold, afraid*.

   Please open the window. I ~~have~~ _am_ hot.

5. Don't forget the subject *it* with time and weather and impersonal expressions.

   _It i_ Is cold today.

   _It i_ Is important to know English.

6. Don't forget the verb *be*. Remember that some words that end in *-ed* are adjectives, not verbs.

   The college _is_ located downtown.

   _am_ I very tired.

7. Don't confuse *your* (possession) and *you're* (you are).

       You're
      ~~Your~~ a very good student.

8. Use correct word order in questions.

          are you
      Why ~~you are~~ late?

          doesn't your sister
      Why ~~your sister doesn't~~ drive?

9. In a contraction, be careful to put the apostrophe in place of the missing letter. Put the apostrophe above the line.

             isn't
      The teacher ~~is'nt~~ here today.

         doesn't
      He ~~doesn,t~~ know the answer.

10. There's no contraction for *am not*.

        I'm not
      ~~I amn't~~ sick today.

11. Don't repeat the subject with a pronoun.

      My brother ~~he~~ lives in Puerto Rico.

12. Don't use *be* with another present tense verb.

      I'~~m~~ come from Poland.

      We'~~re~~ have a new computer.

13. Use the *-s* form when the subject is *he, she, it, everyone,* or *family*.

             s
      My father live^ in New York.

             s
      Everyone know^ the answer.

             s
      My family live^ in Egypt.

14. Use *doesn't* when the subject is *he, she, it,* or *family*.

        doesn't
      He ~~don't~~ have a car.

15. Use the base form after *does*.

      He doesn't speak~~s~~ English.

      Where does he live~~s~~?

16. Don't forget to use *do* or *does* to form the question.

       does
Where ˄ your father works?

17. Don't put an object between *don't* or *doesn't* and the main verb.

       know your friend.
I don't ~~your friend know.~~

18. Use normal question formation for *spell*, *mean*, and *cost*.

       does "custom" mean?
What ~~means "custom"?~~

       do you
How ˄ spell "responsible"?

       does   *cost*
How much ~~costs~~ the newspaper ˄?

19. Use the correct word order with frequency words.

       sometimes goes
He ~~goes sometimes~~ to the zoo.

       I never
~~Never I~~ eat in a restaurant.

       am never
I ~~never am~~ late to class.

20. Don't put a frequency phrase between the subject and the verb.

       all the time
She ~~all the time~~ talks on the phone ˄.

21. Don't use *ever* in an affirmative answer.

Does he ever go to church?

       sometimes
Yes, ~~ever.~~

LESSON 1 TEST / REVIEW

PART 1   Find the mistakes with the underlined words and correct them. Not every sentence has a mistake. If the sentence is correct, write **C**.

EXAMPLES: Does your mother <u>speaks</u> Polish?

Where <u>do</u> they live?   **C**

1. How often <u>does</u> they go shopping?

2. I <u>don't need</u> help.

3. Why <u>you don't</u> answer my question?

4. How many languages <u>speaks your brother</u>?

5. My brother <u>don't</u> like American food.

6. Who does your sister <u>lives</u> with?

7. She <u>doesn't understand</u> your question.

8. She <u>doesn't pizza like</u>.

9. <u>How you spell</u> "occasion"?

10. What <u>means</u> "occasion"?

11. How much <u>costs the textbook</u>?

12. I <u>never am</u> bored in class.

13. I <u>never go</u> out at night.

14. <u>Do you ever</u> rent a video? Yes, often.

15. Does she ever wear jeans? No, <u>ever</u>.

16. <u>Sometimes I don't understand</u> Americans.

17. <u>What often</u> do you get a haircut?

18. <u>She every other day</u> writes a letter.

19. Everyone <u>need</u> love.

20. My family <u>live</u> in Colombia.

21. Is your father an engineer? Yes, <u>he's</u>.

22. <u>France's</u> a beautiful country.

23. I want to eat. I <u>am</u> hungry.

24. <u>Is</u> very hot today.

25. The college <u>located</u> on Main and Green.

26. <u>You're</u> my favorite teacher.

27. Why <u>the teacher isn't</u> here today?

28. My little brother <u>has 10 years</u>.

29. I <u>don't interested</u> in sports.

30. She <u>doesn't have</u> a cell phone.

31. I have my sweater, so I <u>amn't</u> cold.

32. <u>I'm have</u> a new TV.

33. <u>She's comes</u> from Mexico.

PART **2** Fill in the blanks with the affirmative form of the verb in parentheses ( ). Then write the negative form of the verb.

EXAMPLES: Elena _____*wants*_____ to write about strange American customs.
(want)

She _____*doesn't want*_____ to write about the weather.

1. Marianne _____ Elena.
(know)

She _____ Sofia.

2. Marianne _____ a dog.
(have)

Elena _____ a dog.

3. Elena _____ in the U.S.
(live)

Sofia _____ in the U.S.

4. Marianne _____ American.
(be)

Elena _____ American.

5. You _____ some American customs.
(understand)

You _____ all American customs.

6. American customs _____ strange for Elena.
(be)

American customs _____ strange for Marianne.

7. I _____ for an answer to "How are you?"
(wait)

Americans _____ for an answer.

8. Everyone _____ questions.
(ask)

Elena _____ "How are you?" if she's not interested in the answer.

Read each statement. Then write a *yes/no* question about the words in parentheses ( ). Write a short answer.

EXAMPLE: Elena lives in the U.S. (Marianne)
Does Marianne live in the U.S.? Yes, she does.

1. Marianne has a dog. (Elena) (no)

    _____

2. Elena and Marianne live in the U.S. (Sofia) (no)

    _____

3. Elena has an American friend. (Sofia) (no)

    _____

4. Americans often ask, "How are you?" (ever ask, "How's it going?") (yes/
    sometimes)

    _____

5. You live in the U.S. (in New York City) [Give a true answer about yourself.]

    _____

6. American customs are strange for Elena. (for Marianne) (no)

    _____

PART **4**

Read each sentence. Then write a *wh-* question about the word in parentheses ( ). An answer is not necessary.

EXAMPLE: Americans often ask, "How are you?" (why)
Why do they ask, "How are you?"

1. You spell "America" A-M-E-R-I-C-A. (How/spell/custom)

    _____

2. Elena lives in the U.S. (where/Sofia)

    _____

3. "Puppy" means baby dog. (kitten)

    _____

4. You say "How are you?" in English. You say "¿Cómo está usted?" in Spanish. (how/"how are you"/in Russian)

_____

5. "How are you?" is not a serious question in the U.S. (why)

_____

6. Marianne doesn't wait for an answer. (why)

_____

7. Elena writes to Sofia once a week. (Sofia/write to Elena)

_____

8. They divide the check in a restaurant. (why)

_____

9. Elena doesn't have a dog. (why)

_____

10. You pay for your friends in a restaurant. (why)

_____

EXPANSION ACTIVITIES

CLASSROOM ACTIVITIES

1. Put a check (√) to indicate which of the following are American customs and which are customs in your native culture. Discuss your answers in a small group or with the entire class. (If you don't have information about Americans, ask the teacher.)

Customs	Americans	People in my native culture
Students wear jeans to class.	√	
Students call their teachers by their first names.		
Students talk to each other during a test.		
Students write in their textbooks.		
Teachers stand in class.		
People talk a lot about politics.		
People drink a lot of soft drinks.		
Children watch TV a lot.		

(continued)

Customs	Americans	People in my native culture
Friends get together in coffeehouses.		
Most women wear makeup.		
People eat some foods with their hands.		
People are friendly with their neighbors.		
People say, "How are you?"		
Most people use credit cards.		
Men open doors for women.		
Young people give their seats to older people on the bus.		
People eat with chopsticks.		
Most people have a car.		
A lot of people wear gym shoes.		
People travel in the summer.		
Most people take off their shoes when they enter a house.		
Young adults live separately from their parents.		
People usually leave a tip in a restaurant.		
Most people know how to use a computer.		
People pay attention to the weather report.		
Most students study a foreign language.		

2. Fill in the blanks with a frequency word to tell how often you do these activities. Find a partner and discuss your activities with your partner.

EXAMPLE: I _*often*_ wear jeans to class.

a) I _____ write personal letters to my friends and family.

b) I _____ sit in the sun to get a suntan.

c) I _____ carry a personal stereo.

d) I _____ wear running shoes.

e) I _____ take off my shoes when I enter a house.

f) I _____ discuss politics with my friends.

g) I _____ wear sandals in warm weather.

h) I'm _____ friendly with my neighbors.

3. Work with a partner or in a small group. Tell if you think this animal is a good pet. Why or why not?

a) A snake

snake

b) A parakeet

parakeet

c) A rabbit

d) A lizard

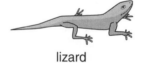

lizard

e) A turtle

turtle

f) A hamster

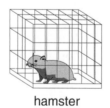

hamster

g) A cat

h) A dog

i) Tropical fish (Note: *Fish* can be singular or plural)

DISCUSSION

1. Do a lot of people you know have a pet? Do they treat their pet like a member of the family? Do you have a pet now? What kind?

2. Americans tip a waitress or waiter, a taxi driver, and a hair stylist. Discuss tipping customs in other countries.

PROVERBS

The following proverbs mention animals. Discuss the meaning of each proverb. Do you have a similar proverb in your native language?

1. You can't teach an old dog new tricks.

2. While the cat's away, the mice will play.

3. Man's best friend is his dog.

4. Curiosity killed the cat.

5. His bark is worse than his bite.

JOKE

A woman is outside of her house. A dog is near her. A man walks by and is interested in the dog. He wants to pet the dog. He asks the woman, "Does your dog bite?" The woman answers no. The man pets the dog and the dog bites him. He says, "You told me that your dog doesn't bite." The woman answers, "This is not my dog. My dog is in the house."

WRITING

1. Write a letter to a friend or relative in another country. Write about customs that are strange for you. Use the letter on pages 17–18 as your model.

2. Write a letter to an American who plans to visit your community or native country. Explain customs in your culture that the American will find strange.

3. Write about the advantages or disadvantages of owning a dog, a cat, or other pet.

OUTSIDE ACTIVITY

Go to the cafeteria. Observe what people are doing. Make note of any behavior that you think is strange. Talk about your observations with the class.

Internet Activities

1. Type in "pet" at a search engine. Find a Web site that advertises pet supplies. Make a list of all the unusual things Americans buy for their pets.

2. Find information about a breed of dog that you like. (Try the Web site of the American Kennel Club or AKC.)

GRAMMAR

The Present Continuous Tense
The Future Tense

CONTEXT

Sunday Afternoon in the Park
The Graying of America

LESSON FOCUS

We use the present continuous tense[1] to talk about
an action that is in progress now.

> We *are studying* Lesson Two now. The teacher *is explaining* the
> grammar now.

We use the future tense to talk about plans or
predictions about the future.

> We *will have* a test at the end of this lesson.
> We *are going to study* the past tense in Lesson Three.

[1] The present continuous is sometimes called the present progressive.

Before You Read
1. Do you like to go to the park? Do you like to sit in the sun?
2. Do you think elderly Americans are physically active?

Read the following article. Pay special attention to present continuous tense verbs.

Sunday Afternoon in the Park

Dear Fatima,

It's a beautiful Sunday afternoon and **I'm sitting** in the park now under a big, old tree. **I'm taking** a break from my studies to write you this letter. **I'm watching** Americans and their strange behaviors. I want to describe some of these behaviors to you. I want to know what you think of them.

I'm sitting in the shade, but most of the people **are sitting** in the sun.

A lot of people **are wearing** short-sleeved shirts and shorts. They**'re trying** to get a suntan. Don't they know that the sun is bad for the skin?

Most of the people **are sitting** alone. Some of them **are reading** magazines. One woman **is talking** on her cell phone. A man **is playing** Frisbee with his dog. He**'s throwing** it to the dog, and the dog **is running** to catch it. Why **isn't** he **playing** with a friend? Why **is** he **playing** with a dog? Another woman **is working** on a computer. Why **isn't** she **relaxing**? Some people **are listening** to a personal stereo. I don't think they**'re having** fun. Some people have a big boom box. They**'re playing** their music loud and **bothering** other people.

Most of the people in the park are young, but I see a few elderly people too. Two elderly men **are playing** tennis. Another elderly man **is jogging**. They seem to be in very good health. But I also see an elderly woman in a wheelchair. A young woman **is pushing** the wheelchair, but I don't think it's her daughter. Don't American children spend time with their parents when they are old and sick?

I**'m learning** a lot about American customs. In fact, I**'m keeping** a diary and **writing** my observations.

Please write to me soon and let me know what **is happening** back home.
Your friend,
Sarah

2.1 The Present Continuous Tense—Forms

Examples	Explanation
I **am taking** a break now. Some people **are listening** to the radio. A man **is playing** with his dog.	The present continuous tense uses *am, is, are* + verb + *-ing*.
Sarah**'s writing** a letter. She**'s sitting** in the park. We**'re learning** about American customs.	We can make a contraction with the subject pronoun and a form of *be*. Most nouns can also contract with *is*.[2]
Sarah **isn't** wearing a bathing suit. Most people **aren't** sitting in the shade.	To form the negative, put *not* after *is, am,* or *are*. We can make a contraction for *are not (aren't)* and *is not (isn't)*.
Sarah **is looking** at Americans and **writing** about her impressions.	When the subject is doing two or more things, don't repeat the *be* verb.

[2] See Lesson 1, page 3 for exceptions.

Language Notes

For a review of the spelling of the *-ing* form of verbs, see Appendix A.

Exercise 1   Fill in the blanks with the present continuous form of the verb in parentheses ( ). Use correct spelling.

Example: Sarah _____*is writing*_____ a letter.
(write)

1. Sarah _____ in the park.
(sit)

2. She _____ in the sun.
(not/sit)

3. She _____ Americans.
(watch)

4. She _____ to her friend.
(write)

5. A lot of people _____ bathing suits.
(wear)

6. Sarah _____ a bathing suit.
(not/wear)

7. One woman _____ on her cell phone.
(talk)

8. Another woman _____ on her computer.
(work)

9. A young woman _____ an elderly woman in a wheelchair.
(push)

10. Some people _____ to their personal stereos.
(listen)

11. Two elderly men _____ tennis.
(play)

12. An elderly man _____ .
(jog)

13. A young man _____ with his dog.
(play)

14. He _____ with a friend.
(not/play)

15. The dog _____ to catch a Frisbee.
(run)

16. We _____ about American customs.
(read)

17. I _____ in the blanks with the correct answers.
(fill)

18. We _____ the past tense now.
(not/study)

Examples	Uses
A man **is playing** with his dog. A woman **is talking** on her cell phone. Sarah **is writing** a letter.	To show that an action is in progress now, at this moment.
Sarah **is learning** about American customs. She **is keeping** a diary.	To show a long-term action that is in progress. It may not be happening at this exact moment.
A lot of people **are wearing** bathing suits. Sarah **is sitting** in the shade.	To describe a state or condition, using the following verbs: *sit, stand, wear, sleep.*

EXERCISE 2 Fill in the blanks with an affirmative or negative verb to make a **true** statement about what is happening now.

EXAMPLES: I ___*'m wearing*___ jeans now.
                   (wear)

The teacher ___*isn't writing*___ on the blackboard now.
                   (write)

1. The sun _____ now.
   (shine)

2. It _____ now.
   (rain)

3. I _____ my answers in my book.
   (write)

4. I _____ a pencil to write this exercise.
   (use)

5. We _____ this exercise together.
   (do)

6. The teacher _____ the students with this exercise.
   (help)

7. The teacher _____ a watch.
   (wear)

8. I _____ my dictionary now.
   (use)

9. We _____ possessive forms now.
   (practice)

10. I _____ jeans.
    (wear)

11. The teacher _____.
    (stand)

12. I _____ near the door.
    (sit)

EXERCISE 3 Write three sentences about being a student. Tell what is happening in your life as a student. (You may share your sentences with the class.)

EXAMPLES: I'm taking five courses this semester.
I'm staying with my sister this semester.
I'm majoring in math.

You may use these verbs: *learn, study, take courses, stay, live, major, plan.*

1. _____
2. _____
3. _____

EXERCISE 4 Write three sentences to tell which things in your life are changing. Then find a partner and ask your partner if he or she is experiencing the same changes.

EXAMPLES: I'm gaining weight. Are you gaining weight?
I'm planning to buy a house. Are you planning to buy a house?
My English pronunciation is improving. Is your pronunciation improving?

You may use the following verbs: *plan, get (become), learn, grow, gain, lose, improve, think about, change, start.*

1. _____
2. _____
3. _____

2.3 Questions with the Present Continuous Tense

Compare statements, questions, and short answers using the present continuous tense.

Wh- Word	Be (+ N't)	Subject	Be (+ N't)	Verb + -ing	Complement	Short Answer
		Sarah	is	writing	a letter.	
		She	isn't	writing	a composition.	
	Is	she		writing	to her family?	No, she isn't.
What	is	she		writing	about?	Her observations.
Why	isn't	she		writing	to her family?	

LANGUAGE NOTES

1. Don't use a contraction for a short *yes* answer.
    Is she writing a letter? Yes, *she is*. (NOT: Yes, *she's*.)

2. When the question is "What...doing?" we usually answer with another verb.
    What is Sarah *doing*? She's *writing* a letter.
    What are you *doing*? I'm *studying* verbs.

3. Informally, Americans often put the preposition at the end of a question. COMPARE:
    INFORMAL: What is Sarah writing *about*?
    FORMAL: *About* what is she writing?
    INFORMAL: Who are you talking *to*?
    FORMAL: *To* whom are you talking?

EXERCISE 5   Fill in the blanks to make *yes/no* questions about the reading on pages 38–39.

EXAMPLE: _Is Sarah reading a book?_ _____ No. She isn't reading a book.

1. _____ about American customs? Yes, she's learning about American customs.

2. _____ a bathing suit? No, she isn't. She's wearing a dress.

3. _____ in the sun? No, she isn't. She's sitting in the shade.

4. _____ with his friend? No, he isn't. He's playing with his dog.

5. _____ in her diary? Yes, she is. She's writing in her diary about American customs.

6. _____ tennis? Yes, they are. The elderly men are playing tennis.

7. _____ bathing suits? Yes, they are. Most people are wearing bathing suits.

8. _____ to get a suntan? No, she isn't. Sarah isn't trying to get a suntan.

Read each statement. Then write a question about the words in parentheses ( ). An answer is not necessary.

EXAMPLE: Sarah's writing something. (what)
What is she writing?

1. Sarah is watching Americans. (why)

2. Sarah isn't wearing a bathing suit. (why)

3. A man and a dog are playing with something. (what)

4. Some people aren't relaxing. (why)

5. Sarah is learning about American customs. (how)

6. Most people are sitting alone. (why)

7. A dog is running. (why)

8. Sarah isn't sitting in the sun. (why)

9. Sarah is writing to someone. (who . . . to)

10. Sarah is looking at someone. (who . . . at)

11. Sarah is writing about something. (what . . . about)

12. Two elderly men are playing. (what)

13. Some people are reading. (what)

14. Sarah is doing something. (what)

Contrasting the Simple Present and the Present Continuous

FORMS

Simple Present	Present Continuous
She sometimes **wears** a dress.	She**'s wearing** sunglasses now.
She **doesn't wear** shorts.	She **isn't wearing** shoes.
Does she ever **wear** a bathing suit?	**Is** she **wearing** a T-shirt?
No, she **doesn't**.	No, she **isn't**.
How often **does** she **wear** a dress?	What **is** she **wearing**?
Why **doesn't** she ever **wear** a bathing suit?	Why **isn't** she **wearing** shoes?

USE

Examples	Explanation
The President **lives** in the White House. I usually **study** in the library. Americans often **say**, "Have a nice day."	Use the simple present tense to talk about a general truth, a habitual activity, or a custom.
Sarah **is sitting** in the shade now. She **is writing** a letter to a friend. She **is learning** a lot about American customs.	Use the present continuous tense for an action that is in progress at this moment, or for a longer action that is in progress at this general time.

LANGUAGE NOTES

1. *Live* in the simple present shows a person's home. In the present continuous, it shows a temporary, short-term residence.
   > Sarah's family *lives* in Iran.
   > Sarah *is living* in a dorm this semester.

2. "What do you do (for a living)?" asks about a job. "What are you doing?" asks about an activity now.
   > What does she do for a living?
   > She's a nurse.
   > What is she doing?
   > She's waiting for the bus.

EXERCISE 7 The following statements of fact or custom use the simple present tense. Take out the frequency word to tell if these things are happening now to the subject in parentheses ( ). Use the present continuous tense.

EXAMPLES: Americans never study the difference between tenses. (we)
We're studying the difference between tenses now.

1. Americans often wear blue jeans. (I)

2. American men sometimes wear an earring. [Use the name of a man in this class.]

3. Americans rarely stand in class to answer the teacher's question. (I)

4. Americans sometimes make a mistake with English grammar. (I)

5. Americans often wear running shoes. (my teacher)

6. American students sometimes study a foreign language. (I)

7. American teachers sometimes sit behind the desk. (my teacher)

8. American students sometimes write in their textbooks. (I)

EXERCISE 8 Read the following statements of fact or custom. Take out the frequency word to write a question about now. Write a short answer.

EXAMPLE: The teacher usually corrects the homework.
Is the teacher correcting the homework now? No, he isn't.

1. The teacher often gives tests.

   _____

2. The students sometimes ask questions.

   _____

3. You sometimes use your dictionary.

   _____

4. The teacher often explains the grammar.

   _____

5. You usually listen to the teacher.

   _____

6. The teacher often uses the blackboard.

_____

7. You sometimes write the answers in your book.

_____

8. The students sometimes make mistakes.

_____

9. The teacher sometimes stands in class.

_____

10. You sometimes use a pencil.

_____

2.5   Nonaction Verbs

Action Verbs	Nonaction Verbs
Sarah **is watching** Americans in the park.	She **sees** some strange behaviors.
She **is learning** about American customs.	She **knows** that American customs are different.
Some people **are listening** to the radio now.	Sarah **hears** the noise.

LANGUAGE NOTES

1. We do not usually use the present continuous tense with certain verbs, called nonaction verbs. These verbs describe a state or condition, not an action. We use the simple present tense, even when we talk about now.

2. Nonaction verbs are:

believe	hear	matter	prefer	think
care	know	mean	remember	understand
cost	like	need	see	want
have	love	own	seem	

Fill in the blanks with the simple present or the present continuous tense of the verb in parentheses ( ).

EXAMPLES: Sarah <u>*doesn't understand*</u> all American customs.
(not/understand)
She <u>*is writing*</u> to her friend now.
(write)

1. Sarah lives in the U.S. so she _____ a little about American
   (know)
   customs now.

2. Sarah _____ to describe American behaviors to her friend.
   (want)

3. Some of the people in the park _____ lonely to Sarah.
   (seem)

4. One woman _____ on a cell phone.
   (talk)

5. She _____ .
   (not/relax)

6. Sarah _____ two elderly men.
   (see)

7. The elderly men _____ tennis.
   (play)

8. They _____ bathing suits.
   (not/wear)

9. Some people in the park _____ to get a suntan. They
   (want)
   _____ that the sun is bad for the skin.
   (not/care)

10. Sarah _____ American customs in her letter now.
    (describe)

11. Sarah _____ a break from her studies.
    (take)

12. She _____ to relax on Sundays.
    (need)

2.6 *Think, Have,* and the Sense Perception Verbs

Action	Nonaction
A) Sarah **is thinking** about her friend now.	F) Sarah **thinks** that many American behaviors are strange.
B) Sarah **is looking** at people in the park.	G) Women in bathing suits **look** strange to Sarah.
C) She **is smelling** the flowers.	H) The flowers **smell** nice.

(continued)

Action	Nonaction
D) Sarah **is having** new experiences in the U.S. E) She **is having** a sandwich for lunch.	I) She **has** a pen and paper in her hand. J) She **has** new American friends. K) My friend **has** a fever now.

LANGUAGE NOTES

1. *Think*, *have*, and the sense perception verbs (*look*, *taste*, *feel*, *smell*) can be both action and nonaction verbs, but the meaning is different.
2. When we think <u>about</u> something (sentence A), *think* is an action verb. When *think* means to have an opinion about something (sentence F), *think* is a nonaction verb.
3. When the sense perception verbs describe an action (sentences B and C), they are action verbs. When they describe a state (sentences G and H), they are nonaction verbs.
4. When *have* means to experience something or to eat or drink something (sentences D and E), it is an action verb. When *have* shows possession, relationship, or illness (sentences I, J, K), it is a nonaction verb.

EXERCISE 10 Fill in the blanks with the simple present or the present continuous form of the verb in parentheses ( ).

EXAMPLES: Some of the women in the park _____*are wearing*_____ bathing suits.
(wear)

Sarah never _____*wears*_____ a bathing suit.
(wear)

1. Sarah _____ in the park now.
   (sit)

2. She usually _____ in the shade because she _____
   (sit)   *(not/like)*
   the sun. She _____ the sun is bad for the skin.
   (think)

3. Sarah _____ much about American customs.
   (not/know)

4. Some people in the park _____ magazines. They _____
   (read)   *(not/talk)*
   to each other.

5. Sarah sometimes _____ a book in the park, but now she
   (read)

   _____ a letter.
   (write)

6. Some people _____ to a boom box. Sarah _____
   (listen)   (hear)
   the loud music, and she _____ it. But the people
                              (not/like)
   _____.
     (not/care)

7. Sarah _____ to describe American customs to her friend.
         (want)

8. Her friend _____ in the U.S.
              (not/live)

9. Sarah _____ some American customs.
         (not/like)

10. Some men on the beach _____ at the women in bathing
                              (look)
    suits now.

11. These women _____ strange to Sarah.
                    (look)

12. A young woman _____ care of an elderly woman.
                      (take)

13. The young woman _____ like the elderly woman's
                        (not/look)
    daughter.

14. Sarah _____ that some Americans _____
          (think)   (not/care)
    about their elderly parents.

15. Sarah _____ her parents and _____ to take
          (love)   (want)
    care of them when they're old.

16. Her parents are in their fifties and _____ her help now.
                                             (not/need)

2.7 Questions with the Simple Present and the Present Continuous

Compare statements and questions that use the simple present tense.

Wh- Word	Do/Does (+ N't)	Subject	Verb	Complement
		She	**watches**	TV.
When	**does**	she	**watch**	TV?
		My parents	**speak**	English.
What language	**do**	your parents	**speak?**	
		Your sister	**lives**	with someone.
With whom	**does**	she	**live?**	
Who	**does**	she	**live**	with?
		You	**don't like**	her.
Why	**don't**	you	**like**	her?

(continued)

Compare statements and questions that use the present continuous tense.

Wh- Word	Be (+ N't)	Subject	Be	Main Verb	Complement
		She	is	sitting.	
Where	is	she		sitting?	
		You	aren't	listening	to the music.
Why	aren't	you		listening	to the music?

EXERCISE 11 Use the words in parentheses ( ) to write a question. An answer is not necessary.

EXAMPLES: Sarah is watching Americans. (why)
Why is she watching Americans?

She wants to describe American behavior. (to whom)
To whom does she want to describe American behavior?

1. Sarah likes to sit in the park. (when)

   _____

2. She doesn't like to sit in the sun. (why)

   _____

3. She's very surprised by American customs. (why)

   _____

4. A man is playing Frisbee. (with whom) OR (who...with)

   _____

5. The people in the park seem strange to Sarah. (why)

   _____

6. Some people are wearing shorts. (what/Sarah/wear)

   _____

7. The sun is bad for the skin. (why)

   _____

8. An elderly man is jogging. (where)

   _____

9. A woman is talking on a cell phone. (who...to)

   _____

10. Two men are playing tennis. (where)

_____

11. Elderly people need exercise. (why)

_____

12. A young woman is pushing an elderly woman's wheelchair. (why)

_____

EXERCISE 12 This is a phone conversation between two friends, Patty (P) and Linda (L). Fill in the blanks with the missing words. Use the simple present or the present continuous tense.

P. Hello?
L. Hi, Patty. This is Linda.

P. Hi, Linda. What _____*are you doing*_____ now?
                     (you/do)

L. Not much. _____ to meet for coffee?
             (1 you/want)

P. I can't. I _____ . I _____ dinner in
          (2 cook)   *(3 have)*

   the oven now, and I _____ for it to be finished.
                       (4 wait)

   What _____?
        (5 you/do)

L. I _____ for a test. But I _____ to take
      (6 study)   *(7 want)*

   a break now. Besides, I _____ to talk to someone. I
                     (8 need)

   usually _____ to my roommate when I _____
         (9 talk)   *(10 have)*

   a problem, but she _____ some friends in New York
              (11 visit)

   now.

P. We can talk while I _____ dinner. It _____
             (12 prepare)   *(13 sound)*

   like something serious _____ .
           (14 happen)

L. My boyfriend and I _____ to get married.
            (15 plan)

P. That's wonderful! Congratulations!

L. There's one small problem. My parents _____ the
                 (16 not/like)

   idea.
P. They don't? Why not?
L. Well, as you know, I'm a Christian. And he's a Moslem.

P. That _____.
   (17 not/matter)

L. It _____ to my family. And to his parents too.
   (18 matter)

   We _____ about getting married without telling our
   (19 think)
   parents.

P. I _____ that's such a good idea.
   (20 not/think)

L. I _____ what else to do.
   (21 not/know)

P. I'll call you later and we can talk more about it. I _____
   (22 hear)
   my husband coming in the door, and dinner is almost ready.

L. Thanks for listening. Talk to you later.

Before You Read
1. In your native culture, who takes care of people when they get old?
2. Do old people in your native culture get a lot of respect?

Read the following article. Pay special attention to future tense verbs.

The Graying of America

The overall population of the U.S. is growing slowly. At the end of the twentieth century, the American population was 273 million. By the middle of this century, it **is going to be** 394 million. Even though this is not a big growth, one group is growing very fast—the elderly (65 years old and over). There are two reasons for this sudden rise in the number of older Americans. First, life expectancy is increasing. In 1900, when the life expectancy was 47, 1 in 25 Americans was elderly. In 1990, with a life expectancy of 79 for women and 73 for men, 1 in 8 was elderly.

The second reason for this growth is the aging of the "Baby Boomers." In the 18 years after World War II, from 1946 to 1964, a large number of babies were born—75 million. The people born during this period, known as the Baby Boomers, are now middle aged and **will** soon **be** elderly. The average age of the population **is going to increase** as the Baby Boomers get older and live longer. The median age of Americans in 1970 was 28; in 1995 it was 35.8. By 2050, it **will be** 40.3. In the middle of the twenty-first century, 1 in 5 Americans **will be** elderly.

What does this mean for America? First, more and more middle-aged people **are going to have** the responsibility of taking care of parents and other older relatives. They **will become** the "sandwich" generation, taking care of their parents as well as their children. For taxpayers, this means that they **are going to pay** more as one-fifth of the population uses one half of the resources.

It **will be** interesting to see how America **will handle** these changes.

Did you know...?

There are 72,000 Americans today who are 100 years old or older. By the year 2050, this number will probably be 834,000.

2.8 The Future Tense with *Will*

Examples	Explanation
People **will live** longer. They **will need** help from their children. There **will be** more elderly people in 50 years.	We use *will* + the base form to form the future tense.
I'll be 75 years old in 2050. You**'ll take** care of your parents.	We can contract *will* with the subject pronouns: *I'll, you'll, he'll, she'll, it'll, we'll, they'll.*
The population **will not** go down. I **won't** live with my children.	To form the negative, put *not* after *will*. The contraction for *will not* is *won't.*

Compare statements, questions, and short answers using *will*.

Wh- Word	Will Won't	Subject	Will Won't	Verb	Complement	Short Answer
		She	will	live	with her daughter.	
		She	won't	live	alone.	
	Will	she		live	with her son?	Yes, she **will**.
Where	will	she		live?		
Why	won't	she		live	alone?	

LANGUAGE NOTES

1. You can put a frequency word between *will* and the main verb.
    I will *always* help my parents.
2. Do not make a contraction for a short *yes* answer.
    Will you buy a new car soon? Yes, I *will*. (NOT: Yes, I'll.)

EXERCISE 13 Fill in the blanks with an appropriate verb in the future tense. Use *will*.

EXAMPLE: In the future, people _____*will live*_____ longer.

1. The population of old people _____ .

2. There _____ more older people by the middle of the twenty-first century.

3. Where _____ you _____ when you are old?

4. _____ your children _____ care of you?

5. How old _____ you _____ in 2050?

EXERCISE 14 A mother (M) is worried about her son (S), who is going away to college. Fill in the blanks to complete this conversation. Use the future with *will*.

M. I'm worried about you. You _____*will be*_____ alone for the first time
                                    (example)
in your life.

S. Don't worry, Mom. I _____ alone. There _____
                              (1)   *(2)*
a lot of people on campus.

M. Who _____ your clothes for you?
          (3)

S. I'll wash them myself.

M. What _____?
          (4)

S. I'll eat the food in the dorm.

M. Make sure you eat a lot of fruits and vegetables.

S. Don't worry. I _____ .
(5)

M. When _____ ?
(6)

S. My classes will begin next week.

M. What _____ this week?
(7)

S. This week I _____ my new roommate. He's from Germany.
(8)

M. When _____ ?
(9)

S. He'll probably arrive tomorrow. This week I _____ my
(10)
suitcases and set up my computer. Also I _____ my books
(11)
at the bookstore. I _____ a map of the campus and learn
(12)
how to get around.

M. _____ enough money?
(13)

S. Yes, I'll have enough money. Remember, I have your credit card. But

I _____ only _____ it for necessary things.
(14)   (15)

M. _____ call me once a week?
(16)

S. Yes, I _____ you. And I _____ you e-mail too.
(17)   (18)

M. _____ home for the holidays?
(19)

S. Yes, I _____ . I'll come home for Thanksgiving and Christ-
(20)
mas. But I won't come home for Labor Day.

M. Why _____ for Labor Day?
(21)

S. Because I won't have enough time.

M. Drive carefully.

S. I will.

M. I _____ you.
(22)

S. I'll miss you too, Mom.

The Future Tense with *Be Going To*

Examples	Explanation
People **are going to live** longer. They **are going to need** help from their children. There **are going to be** more elderly people in 50 years.	We use *be going to* + the base form to form the future tense.
I'm **not** going to live with my children.	To form the negative, put *not* after *am, is, are*.

Compare statements, questions, and short answers with *be going to*.

Wh- Word	*Be* (+ *N't*)	Subject	*Be* (*Not*)	*Going to*	Verb	Complement	Short Answer
		She	is	going to	live	with her daughter.	
		She	isn't	going to	live	alone.	
	Is	she		going to	live	with her son?	No, she **isn't**.
Where	is	she		going to	live?		
Why	isn't	she		going to	live	with her son?	

LANGUAGE NOTES

1. In informal speech, *going to* before another verb often sounds like "gonna." In formal English, we don't write "gonna." Listen to your teacher's pronunciation of *going to* in the following sentences.
    Where's he going to live?
    (Where's he "gonna" live?)
    He's going to live in a dorm.
    (He's "gonna" live in a dorm.)

2. Only *going to* before another verb sounds like "gonna." We don't pronounce "gonna" at the end of a sentence or before a noun.
    Where is he going?
    He's going to the bookstore.

3. We often shorten *going to go* to *going*.
    He's *going to go* to the supermarket.
    He's *going* to the supermarket.

4. We use the preposition *in* with the future tense to mean *after*.
    He's going return *in* an hour.

EXERCISE 15 Fill in the blanks with an appropriate verb in the future tense. Use *be going to*.

EXAMPLE: <u>Are</u> your children <u>going to take care of</u> you?

1. The cost of health care _____ .

2. People _____ higher taxes.

3. How old _____ your daughter _____ in 2050?

4. _____ you _____ care of your elderly parents?

5. A lot of people _____ over 100 years old in 2050.

EXERCISE 16 Fill in the blanks to tell what is going happen.

EXAMPLE: My running shoes are very old. I need new shoes. <u>I'm going to buy</u> a new pair.

1. The sky is getting very cloudy and dark. It looks like it _____

   _____ .

2. Now it's raining. I need to go out. I _____ an umbrella with me.

3. I'm hungry. I _____ dinner.

4. My friend is arriving today at 4 o'clock. I _____ her at the airport.

5. We're almost finished with this lesson. The teacher _____ us a test soon.

6. The government needs more money. It _____ taxes.

7. My grandparents' apartment is too big for them. They _____

   _____ to a smaller apartment.

8. My grandfather is almost 65 and still working. He _____ soon and just relax.

9. My friends are coming over tomorrow, and my house is dirty.

   I _____ the house today.

10. My brother is going to Puerto Rico for vacation. He _____ me a postcard.

EXERCISE 17 Do you have questions for the teacher about this semester, next semester, or his or her life in general? Write three questions to ask the teacher about the near or distant future.

EXAMPLES: *What time are you going to leave today?*

When are you going to give us a test?

Are you going to retire soon?

1. _____

2. _____

3. _____

2.10 *Will* vs. *Be Going To*

Uses	*Will*	*Be Going To*
Prediction	My father always exercises and eats well. I think he **will live** a long time.	I think my father **is going to live** a long time.
Fact	The sun **will set** at 6:43 tonight. The population of older people **will increase**.	The sun **is going to set** at 6:43 tonight. The population of older people **is going to increase**.
Scheduled event	The movie **will begin** at 8 o'clock.	The movie **is going to begin** at 8 o'clock.
Plan		My grandfather **is going to move** to Florida next year. I **am going to return** to my native country in three years.
Promise	I **will** always **take** care of you, Mom.	
Offer to help	A: This box is heavy. B: **I'll carry** it for you.	

LANGUAGE NOTES

1. Use either *will* or *be going to* for predictions, facts about the future, and scheduled events. *Will* is more formal than *be going to*.
2. When we have a plan to do something, we usually use *be going to*.
3. When we make a promise or offer to help, we usually use *will*.

4. We sometimes use the present continuous tense with a future meaning. We can do this with planned events in the near future. We do this especially with verbs of motion.

My grandmother *is moving* into a retirement home on Friday.
I'*m helping* her move on Friday.

EXERCISE 18 Choose *will* or *be going to* to fill in the blanks. In some cases, both are possible.

EXAMPLE:

1. A. Where are you going?

   B. I'm going to the park this afternoon. I ___*am going to meet*___ my
      (example: meet)
   friend and play tennis with her. I have to return some videos to the video store, but I don't have time.

   A. Give them to me. I _____ that way.
      (pass)

   I _____ them for you.
      (return)

2. A. I have to go to the airport. My sister's plane _____
      (arrive)
   at four o'clock this afternoon.

   B. I _____ with you. I _____ in the car while
      (go)   (stay)
   you go into the airport. That way, you _____
                                              (not/have to)
   pay for parking.

3. A. My sister's birthday is next week.

   B. _____ her a birthday present?
      (you/give)

   A. Of course, I _____ .

   B. What _____ her?
           (you/give)

   A. She loves the theater. I _____ her tickets to a play.
                                  (buy)

   B. How old _____?
                 (be)

   A. She _____ 21 years old.
             (be)

4. Teacher: Next week we _____ our midterm test.
                            (have)

   Student: _____ hard?
              (it/be)

   Teacher: Yes, but I _____ you prepare for it.
                          (help)

---

5. Wife: I won't have time to pick up the children this afternoon. I have to work late.

   Husband: Don't worry. I _____ them up.
   (pick)

   Wife: I won't have time to cook either.

   Husband: Just relax. I _____ dinner tonight.
   (prepare)

6. Man: I want to marry you.

   Woman: But we're only 19. We're too young.

   Man: I _____ 20 in April.
   (be)

   Woman: But you don't even have a job.

   Man: I _____ a job.
   (find)

   Woman: Let's wait a few years.

   Man: I _____ for you forever. I _____ you.
   (wait) *(always/love)*

7. A. Do you want to watch the football game with me on Saturday?

   B. I can't. My brother _____ . I _____ him.
   (move) *(help)*

   A. Do you need any help?

   B. We need boxes. Do you have any?

   A. No, but I _____ for boxes. I _____
   (look) *(go)*

   to the supermarket this afternoon. I _____ boxes
   (get)

   there. I _____ them to your house.
   (bring)

   B. Thanks.

8. A. I'm so excited. I _____ a puppy.
   (get)

   B. That's a big responsibility. You're never home. How _____

   _____ care of it?
   (take)

   A. My cousin lives with me now. She doesn't have a job. She

   _____ me take care of the dog.
   (help)

   B. What about your landlord? Is it OK with him?

   A. I _____ him.
   (not/tell)

B. You have to tell him. He _____ if you have a dog.
(know)

You _____ take the dog out three times a day.
(have to)

And the dog _____ .
(bark)

2.11   The Future Tense + Time/*If* Clause

Examples	Explanation
When my parents **are** old, I **will take** care of them. After they **retire**, they **will move** to a warm climate. If my brother **isn't** home by six o'clock, I'm **going to eat** without him. I'm **going to do** the homework before I **go** home.	We use the future tense only in the main clause; we use the simple present tense in the time clause and *if* clause.

LANGUAGE NOTES

Use a comma if the time or *if* clause is before the main clause.

When my parents are old, I'll take care of them. (Use a comma.)

I'll take care of my parents when they're old. (Don't use a comma.)

EXERCISE 19 Connect the sentences using *if* or the time word in parentheses ( ).

EXAMPLE: I will retire. I will play golf. (when)

When I retire, I will play golf. OR *I will play golf when I retire.*

1. I will retire. I'm not going to live with my children. (when)

_____

2. I will be old. I will take care of myself. (when)

_____

3. My parents will need help. I'll take care of them. (if)

_____

4. I won't be healthy. I'll live with my children. (if)

_____

5. I won't have money. I will get help from the government. (if)

_____

6. My parents will die. I'll move to another city. (after)

_____

7. I will get a pension. I won't need to depend on my children. (if)

_____

8. I'll retire. I'm going to save my money. (before)

_____

EXERCISE 20 Think about a specific time in your near future (when you graduate, when you get married, when you have children, when you find a job, when you return to your native country, when you are old). Write three sentences to tell what will happen at that time. Find a partner who is close to your age. Compare your answers to your partner's answers.

EXAMPLE: *When I have children, I won't have as much free time as I do now.*

When I have children, I'm going to have a lot more responsibilities.

When I have children, my parents will be very happy.

1. _____

2. _____

3. _____

EXERCISE 21 A foreign student (F) is talking to an American (A) about getting old. Fill in the blanks with the correct form of the verb to complete this conversation. In many cases, you can use either *be going to* or *will*.

F. How's your grandfather?

A. He's OK. I ___*'m going to visit*___ him this afternoon.
                    (visit)

F. How's he doing?

A. He's in great health. Next week he _____ to Hawaii to
                                              (1 go)
   play golf.

F. How old is he?

A. He _____ 78 next month. Did I tell you? In June, he
       (2 be)

   _____ married to a widow he met in the retirement
       (3 get)

   home.

F. That seems so strange to me. Why _____ that?
                                         (4 he/do)

A. Why not? They like each other, and they want to be together.

F. What _____ when he's no longer able to take care of
        (5 you/do)

   himself?

A. We never think about it. He's in such great health that we think

   he _____ healthy forever. I think he _____
       (6 be)   (7 outlive³)

   us all.

F. But he _____ help as he gets older.
           (8 probably/need)

A. We _____ that bridge when we come to it.⁴ Do you have
       (9 cross)

   plans for your parents as they get older?

F. They're in their 50s now. But when they _____ older,
                                              (10 be)

   they _____ with me and my wife. In our country, it's an
        (11 live)

   honor to take care of our parents.

A. That sounds like a great custom. But I think it's better when older
   people are independent. I'm glad that Grandpa doesn't depend on us.

   And when I _____ old, I _____ care of myself.
               (12 be)   (13 take)

   I don't want to depend on anyone.

F. You _____ your mind when you _____ elderly.
       (14 change)   (15 be)

A. Maybe. I have to catch my bus now. Grandpa is waiting for me.

   I _____ you later.
      (16 see)

F. Wait. I have my car. I _____ you to your grandfather's
                           (17 drive)

   place.

A. Thanks.

---

³ To *outlive* means to live longer than other people.
⁴ This expression means *We'll worry about that problem when the problem happens, and not before.*

EXERCISE 22 This is a conversation between two co-workers. They are talking about retirement. Fill in the blanks with the correct form and tense of the verb in parentheses ( ).

A. I hear you're going to retire this year.

B. Yes. Isn't it wonderful? I _____*will be*_____ 65 in September.
    _(be)_

A. What _____ after you _____?
    (1 you/do)   _(2 retire)_

B. I'm trying to sell my house now. When I _____ my house,
    (3 sell)

    I _____ to Florida and buy a condo.
    (4 move)

A. What _____ in Florida?
    (5 you/do)

B. I _____ a sailboat and spend most of my time on the
    (6 buy)
    water.

A. But a sailboat is expensive.

B. When I _____ 65, I _____ to use my savings.
    _(7 be)_   _(8 start)_

    Also, I _____ a lot of money when I _____
    (9 get)   _(10 sell)_

    my house. What _____ when you _____?
    (11 you/do)   _(12 retire)_

A. I'm only 45 years old. I have another 20 years until I _____.
    (13 retire)

B. Now is the time to start thinking about retirement. If

    you _____ your money for the next 20 years, you
    (14 save)

    _____ a comfortable retirement. But if you
    (15 have)

    _____ about it until the time _____,
    (16 not/think)   _(17 come)_

    you _____ enough money to live on.
    (18 not/have)

A. I _____ about it when the time _____. I'm
    (19 worry)   _(20 come)_
    too young to worry about it now.

B. If you _____ until you _____ 65 to think about
    (21 wait)   _(22 be)_

    it, you _____ a poor, old man. On Monday morning when
    _(23 be)_

    we _____ at work, I _____ you to a woman
    _(24 be)_   _(25 introduce)_

who can explain the company's savings plan to you. After you

_____ to her, I'm sure you _____ your mind
    (26 talk)   *(27 change)*

about when to worry about retirement.

SUMMARY OF LESSON 2

Uses of Tenses

Simple Present Tense	
General truths, facts	Sixty percent of Americans **have** a pet. The United States **has** 50 states.
Regular activities, habits, customs	I always **drink** coffee in the morning. Sometimes I **study** in the library.
Place of origin	Linda **comes** from Mexico. Maria **comes** from Guatemala.
In a time clause or in an **if** clause of a future statement	When I **get** home, I'll do my homework. If I **pass** this course, I'll go on to the next level.
With nonaction verbs	She **knows** the answer. I **hear** the music.

Present Continuous (with action verbs only)	
Now	We**'re comparing** verb tenses now. I**'m looking** at page 66 now.
A long action in progress at this general time	Sarah **is learning** about American customs. She**'s keeping** a diary in the U.S.
A plan in the near future	I**'m driving** to California next week. My sister **is going** with me.
A descriptive state	She**'s wearing** shorts. She**'s sitting** in the park.

Future		
A plan		**I'm going to buy** a new car next month.
A fact	The number of old people **will increase**.	The number of old people **is going to increase**.
A prediction	I think you **will be** rich someday.	I think you **are going to be** rich someday.
A promise	I **will** always **love** you.	
An offer to help	Relax. **I'll cook** tonight.	
A scheduled event	Registration **will begin** on August 18.	Registration **is going to begin** on August 18.

EDITING ADVICE ✎

1. Always include *be* in a present continuous tense verb.

   She ^is^ working now.

2. Don't use the present continuous tense with a nonaction verb.

   I ~~am~~ lik~~ing~~ ^e^ your new car.

3. Don't use *be* with another verb for the future.

   I will ~~be~~ go back to my native country in five years.

4. Include *be* in a future sentence that has no other verb.

   He will ^be^ angry.

   There will ^be^ a party soon.

5. Don't combine *will* and *be going to*.

   He will ~~going to~~ leave.   *OR He's going to leave.*

6. Use the future tense with an offer to help.

   The phone's ringing. I ^'ll^ get it.

7. Don't use the future tense after a time word or *if*.

   When they ~~will~~ go home, they are going to watch TV.

   If I ~~will~~ *am* be late, I'll call you.

8. Use a form of *be* with *going to*.

   He *is* going to help me.
   ∧

9. Use correct word order in questions.

   When ~~you will~~ *will you* go back to your native country?

   Why ~~she isn't~~ *isn't she* going to buy a new car?

LESSON 2 TEST / REVIEW

PART **1**   Find the mistakes with the underlined words, and correct them. Not every sentence has a mistake. If the sentence is correct, write **C**.

EXAMPLES: You can't move this sofa alone. <u>I'll help</u> you.   C
Where <u>will you ~~be~~ live</u> when you are old?

1. He <u>sitting</u> near the door.

2. What <u>will you do</u> after you graduate?

3. I'm <u>going to buy</u> a new car soon.

4. He's listening to the radio. <u>He's hearing</u> the news.

5. <u>She going to leave</u> on Friday.

6. <u>I'll going to watch</u> TV tonight.

7. <u>I going to do</u> my homework when I get home.

8. What <u>you going to do</u> tonight?

9. <u>I'm leaving</u> for New York on Friday.

10. There <u>will</u> a test on Friday.

11. I <u>will be know</u> English well in a few years.

12. If you don't eat dinner, you <u>will hungry</u> later.

13. She <u>won't leave</u> her family.

14. If you need something, let me know. I <u>get</u> it for you.

15. Why <u>won't you</u> tell me about your problem?

16. She's looking at the report. She <u>sees</u> the problem now.

17. Why <u>she isn't</u> going to visit her grandmother?

18. I'll cross that bridge when I <u>come</u> to it.

PART 2

Mary (M) is talking to her friend Sue (S) on the phone. Fill in the blanks with the correct tense and form. Use the simple present, present continuous, or future.

S. Hi, Mary.

M. Hi, Sue. How are you?

S. Fine. What are you doing?

M. I _____*am packing*_____ now. We _____ next Saturday.
        (pack)   *(1 move)*

S. Oh, really? Why? You _____ such a lovely apartment now.
                                   (2 have)

M. Yes, I know we do. But I _____ a baby in four months, so we
                             (3 have)

   _____ a bigger apartment when the baby _____.
        (4 need)   *(5 arrive)*

S. But your present apartment _____ an extra bedroom.
                                      (6 have)

M. Yes. But my husband _____ to have an extra room for an
                             (7 always/like)

   office. He usually _____ a lot of work home. He _____
                  (8 bring)   *(9 need)*
   a place where he can work without noise.

S. Do you need help with your packing?

M. Not really. Bill and I _____ home this week to finish the
                           (10 stay)

   packing. And my mother _____ me now too.
                           (11 help)

S. I _____ over next Saturday to help you move.
       (12 come)

M. We _____ professional movers on Saturday. We don't want to
         (13 use)
   bother our friends.

S. It's no bother. I _____ to help.
              (14 want)

M. Thanks. There probably _____ a few things you can help me
                                (15 be)

with on Saturday. I have to go now. I _____ Bill. He
                                            (16 hear)

_____ me. He _____ me to help him in the basement.
   (17 call)   (18 want)

I _____ you back later.
    (19 call)

S. You don't have to call me back. I _____ you on Saturday. Bye.
                                         (20 see)

PART 3 Fill in the blanks with the negative form of the underlined verb.

EXAMPLE: Mary is busy. Sue ____*isn't*____ busy.

1. Sue is talking to Mary. She _____ to her husband.

2. Mary is going to move to a bigger apartment. She _____
   to a house.

3. Mary's husband needs an extra room. He _____ a
   big room.

4. Sue will go to Mary's house on Saturday. She _____
   tomorrow.

5. Mary will move the small things. She _____ the
   furniture.

6. Her new apartment has an extra room. Her old apartment _____

   _____ an extra room.

PART 4 Write a *yes/no* question about the words in parentheses ( ).
Then write a short answer based on the conversation in Part 2
on pages 69–70.

EXAMPLE: Sue is busy. (her husband)
         Is her husband busy? Yes, he is.

1. Sue's husband is helping her pack. (her mother)

   _____

2. Her husband works in an office. (at home)

   _____

3. Her present apartment has an extra room for an office. (for the baby)

_____

4. Professional movers will move the furniture. (her friends)

_____

5. Mary is staying home this week. (her husband)

_____

6. Mary's going to have a baby. (Sue)

_____

PART 5   Write a *wh-* question about the words in parentheses ( ). An answer is not necessary.

EXAMPLE: Mary's packing now. (why)
Why is Mary packing?

1. They're going to move to a bigger apartment. (why)

_____

2. Her husband needs an extra bedroom. (why)

_____

3. She doesn't want her friends to help her move. (why)

_____

4. She's going to have a baby soon. (when)

_____

5. Bill is calling Mary now. (why)

_____

6. They'll use professional movers. (when)

_____

EXPANSION ACTIVITIES

1. Check (√) the activities that you plan to do soon. Form a group of 5–7 students. Ask questions about the items another student checked.

EXAMPLE:

√ move
When are you going to move?
Why are you moving?
Are your friends going to help you?
Are you going to rent a truck?
Where are you going to move to?

a. ___ send an e-mail

b. ___ visit a friend

c. ___ invite guests to my house

d. ___ buy something new

e. ___ take a vacation

f. ___ celebrate a birthday or holiday

g. ___ go to a concert or sporting
event

h. ___ transfer to another college

i. ___ move

j. ___ take the citizenship test

k. ___ start a new job

l. ___ have an out-of-town visitor

m. ___ get married

2. Check (√) your predictions about the future. Form a small group and discuss your predictions with your group. Give reasons for your beliefs.

a. ___ People are going to have fewer children than they do today.

b. ___ People will live longer.

c. ___ People will have a healthier life.

d. ___ People are going to be happier.

e. ___ People will be lonelier.

f. ___ People will be more educated.

g. ___ Everyone is going to have a computer.

h. ___ There will be a cure for cancer and other serious illnesses.

i. ___ There will be a cure for the common cold.

1. Give the list in the above Classroom Activity 2 to an American. Find out his or her predictions. Report to the class something interesting that the American told you.

2. Keep a small notebook and a pen with you at all times for a week. Write down all the behaviors of other people that seem strange to you. Observe food, clothes, shopping, recreation, relationships between males and females, relationships between parents and children, behaviors of small children, behaviors on public transportation, behaviors at school, etc. Write what people are doing as you are observing.

EXAMPLE: A woman is standing on the bus. No one is giving her a seat.
People are eating chicken with their fingers.

Internet Activities

1. Find a Web site for the elderly. Find out what kinds of products and services are available for senior citizens. Search under "senior citizens" or try the National Council of Senior Citizens (NCSC) or American Association of Retired Persons (AARP).

2. Look for a life expectancy calculator on the Internet. Calculate how long you will probably live.

3. On the Internet, look for *Time* magazine's article of November 8, 1999, called "Beyond 2000." Look for *Time's* February 21, 2000 issue, called "Visions of the 21st Century." What do these articles predict for the future?

Lesson Three

GRAMMAR
The Simple Past Tense
Habitual Past with *Used To*

CONTEXT
Martin Luther King, Junior
Discrimination and Segregation

LESSON FOCUS
We use the simple past tense to talk about an action
that started and finished in the past.
> I *listened* carefully. I *understood* the explanation.

Used to + a base form shows habitual past actions.
> I *used to have* a dog. Now I have a cat.

Martin Luther King, Jr. 1929–1968

75

1. In your native country, does the government give equality to everyone?
2. Is there one group of people that has a harder life than other groups? Which group? What kind of problems do these people have?

Read the following article. Pay special attention to simple past-tense verbs and *used to* + base form.

Martin Luther King, Junior[1]

Today all people in the United States have equal rights under the law. But this **was** not always the case, especially for African-Americans.[2] Even though slavery in the U.S. **ended** in 1865, blacks **continued** to suffer inferior treatment. The government **did** little to improve the lives of African Americans.

Life for black people **was** especially hard in the South. Many businesses there **used to have** signs in their windows that **said:** "Blacks Not Allowed." Public restrooms **used to have** signs that **said:** "Whites Only." Black children **had to go** to separate, and often inferior, schools. Buses **used to reserve** the front seats for white people. African Americans **had** to stand or sit in the back of the bus. Martin Luther King, Jr., a black minister living in Montgomery, Alabama, **wanted** to put an end to discrimination.[3]

One evening in December of 1955, Rosa Parks, a 42-year-old African American woman, **got** on a bus in Montgomery, Alabama, to go home from work. She **was** tired when she **sat** down. When some white people **got** on the crowded bus, the bus driver **ordered** Ms. Parks to stand up. Ms. Parks **refused** to leave her seat. The bus driver **called** the police and they **came** and **arrested** Ms. Parks.

Did you know...?

Martin Luther King, Jr., was interested in the ideas of Mahatma Gandhi of India. He studied and used Gandhi's technique of nonviolent protest.

[1] When a father and son have the same name, the father uses *senior* (Sr.) after his name; the son puts *junior* (Jr.) after his name.
[2] *African-Americans*, whose ancestors came from Africa as slaves, are sometimes called "blacks."
[3] Discrimination means giving some people lower treatment than others.

When Martin Luther King, Jr., **heard** about her arrest, he **told** African Americans in Montgomery to boycott the bus company. People who **used to ride** the bus to work **decided** to walk instead. One year later, as a result of the boycott, the Supreme Court outlawed discrimination on public transportation.

During his life, King **organized** many more peaceful protests. He **was** in jail many times because of his activities, but this **did not stop** him. In 1963, he **led** a peaceful demonstration in Washington, D.C., where he **gave** his most famous speech. He **said**, "I have a dream that my four little children will one day live in a nation where they will not be judged by the color of their skin, but by the content of their character."

In 1964, Congress **passed** a new law that officially **gave** equality to all Americans. This law **made** discrimination in employment and education illegal. King **won** the Nobel Peace Prize[4] for his work in creating a better world.

In 1968, King **went** to Memphis, Tennessee, to support striking city workers. A great tragedy **occurred** there. King was shot and killed. He **was** only 39 years old.

In 1983, Martin Luther King's birthday (January 15) **became** a national holiday.

3.1 Past of *Be*

Examples	Explanation
Life **was** hard for black people. King **was** in jail for his protests. Many African-Americans **were** part of the protest. Before 1964, laws **were** different.	The past of the verb *be* has two forms: *was* and *were*. I, he, she, it → was we, you, they → were
There **was** a bus boycott in 1955. There **were** many people in Washington in 1963.	After *there*, use *was* or *were* depending on the noun that follows. Use *was* with a singular noun. Use *were* with a plural noun.
King **wasn't** born in Alabama. African-Americans **weren't** happy with the segregation laws.	To make a negative statement, put *not* after *was* or *were*. The contraction for *was not* is *wasn't*. The contraction for *were not* is *weren't*.
King **was born** in 1929.	Always use a form of *be* with *born*.
King **was** married to Coretta Scott. He **was** not worried about his safety.	Use *be* with adjectives that end in *-ed*: *crowded, tired, bored, interested, worried, married, divorced, allowed, permitted.*

(continued)

[4] This is a prize given once a year for great work in literature, science, and world peace.

Wh- Word	Was/Were Wasn't/Weren't	Subject	Was/Were	Complement	Short Answer
		King	**was**	a great leader.	
		He	**wasn't**	happy with the laws.	
	Was	he		from the North?	No, he **wasn't**.
Where	**was**	he		from?	
Why	**wasn't**	he		happy with the laws?	

EXERCISE 1 Fill in the blanks with the correct word(s).

EXAMPLE: Martin Luther King, Jr., _____*was*_____ a great American.

1. Martin Luther King, Jr., _____ born in Georgia.

2. He (not) _____ born in Alabama.

3. He and his father _____ ministers.

4. He _____ tired of discrimination of African-Americans.

5. African-Americans (not) _____ allowed to enter some restaurants in the South.

6. There _____ discrimination in public transportation.

7. _____ discrimination in employment? Yes, there

   _____ .

8. Rosa Parks was a citizen of Montgomery, Alabama. _____ an African-American? Yes, she was.

9. She was tired and took a seat on the bus. Why _____ tired?

10. African-Americans weren't allowed to sit down on a crowded bus in

    Montgomery. Why _____ to sit down?

11. King was in jail. Why _____ in jail? He _____ in jail for protesting unfair laws.

12. How old _____ when he was killed? He was 39.

13. _____ small at the time? Yes, his children were small.

Simple Past Tense of Regular Verbs

Examples	Explanation
Martin Luther King, Jr., **lived** in the South. He **organized** peaceful protests. In 1964, Congress **passed** a new law. In 1968, someone **killed** King.	For regular verbs, the simple past tense ends in -ed. BASE FORM PAST FORM live lived organize organized pass passed kill killed
King **lived** in the South. He **didn't live** in the North.	Use the past form in affirmative statements. Use *didn't* + the base form in negative statements.
He **wanted to change** certain laws. Rosa Parks **refused to stand up**.	The verb after *to* does not use the past form.

LANGUAGE NOTES

1. The past form is the same for all persons.
   I worked.   He worked.   They worked.   You worked.

2. We often use *ago* with the simple past tense.
   Slavery ended over 100 years *ago*.
   King died more than 30 years *ago*.
   We studied about him a few minutes *ago*.

3. For a review of the spelling and pronunciation of the -ed past form, see Appendix A.

EXERCISE **2**   Fill in the blanks with the simple past tense of the verb in parentheses ( ).

EXAMPLE: King _____*lived*_____ in the south.
                           (live)

1. Slavery _____ in 1865, but discrimination _____ .
                  (end)   *(continue)*

2. King _____ equality for all people.
             (want)

3. King _____ as a minister.
             (work)

4. In many places, the law _____ whites from blacks.
                               (separate)

5. Black children _____ separate schools.
                     (attend)

6. King _____ these laws.
   (dislike)

7. The bus driver _____ Rosa Parks to stand up, but she
   (order)

   _____ .
   (refuse)

8. The bus driver _____ the police.
   (call)

9. The police _____ Ms. Parks.
   (arrest)

10. King _____ a peaceful protest.
    (organize)

11. In 1964, Congress _____ the law.
    (change)

12. In 1968, a great tragedy _____ . Someone _____
    (occur)   _(kill)_

    King.

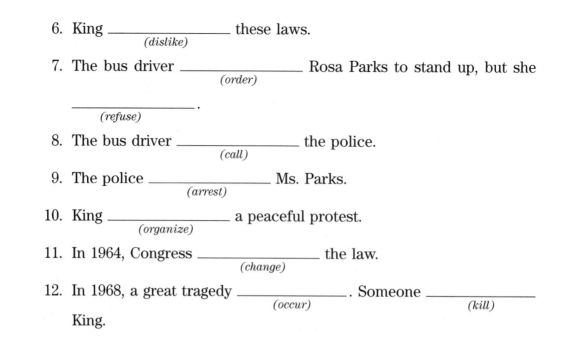

3.3   Simple Past Tense of Irregular Verbs

Examples	Explanation
Rosa Parks **got** on the bus and **sat** down. The police **came**. King **gave** a famous speech in Washington, D.C., in 1963.	Many past-tense verbs are irregular. They do not have an *-ed* ending.
Some African-Americans **stood** up for white people. Rosa Parks **didn't stand** up.	Use the past form in affirmative statements. Use *didn't* + the base form in negative statements.

LANGUAGE NOTES

The following is a list of irregular past tenses. For an alphabetical list of irregular verbs, see Appendix M.

Verbs with no change				Final *d* changes to *t*	
beat	fit	put	spit	bend—bent	send—sent
bet	hit	quit	split	build—built	spend—spent
cost	hurt	set	spread	lend—lent	
cut	let	shut			

(continued)

Verbs with Vowel Changes

feel—felt	mean—meant*	dig—dug	sting—stung
keep—kept	sleep—slept	hang—hung	strike—struck
leave—left	sweep—swept	spin—spun	swing—swung
lose—lost	weep—wept	stick—stuck	win—won

awake—awoke	speak—spoke	begin—began	sing—sang
break—broke	steal—stole	drink—drank	sink—sank
choose—chose	wake—woke	forbid—forbade	spring—sprang
freeze—froze		ring—rang	swim—swam
		shrink—shrank	

bring—brought	fight—fought	blow—blew	grow—grew
buy—bought	teach—taught	draw—drew	know—knew
catch—caught	think—thought	fly—flew	throw—threw

arise—arose	rise—rose	bleed—bled	meet—met
drive—drove	shine—shone	feed—fed	read—read**
ride—rode	write—wrote	flee—fled	speed—sped
		lead—led	

sell—sold	tell—told	find—found	wind—wound

mistake—mistook	take—took	lay—laid	say—said***
shake—shook		pay—paid	

swear—swore	wear—wore	bite—bit	light—lit
tear—tore		hide—hid	slide—slid

become—became	fall—fell	
come—came	hold—held	
eat—ate		
forgive—forgave	run—ran	
give—gave	sit—sat	
lie—lay	see—saw	

forget—forgot	shoot—shot	stand—stood
get—got		understand—understood

Miscellaneous Changes

be—was/were	go—went	hear—heard
do—did	have—had	make—made

*There is a change in the vowel sound. *Meant* rhymes with *sent*.
**The past form of *read* is pronounced like the color *red*.
***Said* rhymes with *bed*.

Fill in the blanks with the past tense of the verb in parentheses ( ).

EXAMPLE: King _____*fought*_____ for the rights of all people.
(fight)

1. King _____ born in 1929.
(be)

2. King _____ a minister.
(become)

3. He _____ married in 1953.
(get)

4. He _____ a job in a church in Montgomery, Alabama.
(find)

5. African-Americans _____ a hard time, especially in the South.
(have)

6. Rosa Parks was tired and _____ down on the bus.
(sit)

7. Some white people _____ on the bus.
(get)

8. The bus driver _____ Parks to stand up.
(tell)

9. Police _____ and arrested Parks.
(come)

10. King _____ about her arrest.
(hear)

11. In 1963, he _____ a beautiful speech in Washington, D.C.
(give)

12. Many people _____ to see King in Washington in 1963.
(go)

13. King _____ an important prize for his work.
(win)

14. A man _____ King in 1968.
(shoot)

3.4 Negatives and Questions with the Simple Past Tense

Compare affirmative statements, negative statements, questions, and short answers with the simple past tense.

Regular Verb

Wh- Word	Did Didn't	Subject	Verb	Complement	Short Answer
		King	**wanted**	equality.	
		He	**didn't want**	segregation.	
	Did	he	**want**	violence?	No, he **didn't**.
Why	**did**	he	**want**	equality?	
Why	**didn't**	he	**want**	violence?	

(continued)

Irregular Verb

Wh- Word	Did Didn't	Subject	Verb	Complement	Short Answer
		Black children	**went**	to separate schools.	
		They	**didn't go**	to school with white children.	
	Did	they	**go**	to good schools?	No, they **didn't**.
Where	**did**	they	**go**	to school?	
Why	**didn't**	they	**go**	to school with white children?	

LANGUAGE NOTES

Use the past form in affirmative statements. Use *did* + the base form in negatives and questions.[5]

EXERCISE 4   Write the negative form of the underlined words.

EXAMPLE: Slavery <u>ended</u> in 1865. Discrimination ___*didn't end*___.

1. King <u>lived</u> in the South. He _____ in the North.

2. King <u>wanted</u> equality for everyone. He _____ separate schools for blacks and whites.

3. He <u>thought</u> about the future of his children. He _____ about his own safety.

4. He <u>believed</u> in peace. He _____ in violence.

5. He <u>became</u> a minister. He _____ a politician.

6. He <u>was</u> in jail for his protests. He _____ in jail for a crime.

7. African-Americans <u>had</u> to stand on a crowded bus. White people _____ to stand.

8. African-Americans <u>rode</u> the buses in Montgomery before 1955. They _____ the buses after the arrest of Rosa Parks.

9. King <u>went</u> to Memphis in 1968. His wife _____ there.

10. He <u>died</u> violently. He _____ peacefully.

[5] For an exception to this rule, see Lesson Four, "Questions About the Subject."

Exercise 5 A student is interviewing her teacher about Martin Luther King, Jr. Fill in the blanks with the correct form of the verb.

S. Do you remember Martin Luther King, Jr.?

T. Of course I do. I _____*saw*_____ him on TV many times when
   (example: see)

   I _____ young.
   (1 be)

S. _____ him on TV when he was in Washington, D.C.?
   (2 see)

T. Yes, I _____. I remember his famous speech in Washington
   (3)

   in 1963.

S. What _____ about?
   (4 speak)

T. He _____ about equality for everyone.
   (5 speak)

S. _____ to Washington?
   (6 a lot of people/go)

T. Oh, yes. 250,000 _____ to Washington.
   (7 go)

S. Do you remember when he died?

T. I was in high school when he _____. The principal
   (8 die)

   _____ to our class and _____ us the news.
   (9 come)   *(10 tell)*

S. What _____ when you heard the news?
   (11 do)

T. At first we _____ it. Then we all started to
   (12 not/believe)

   _____. We _____ home from school and
   (13 cry)   *(14 go)*

   _____ the news on TV.
   (15 watch)

S. Where _____ he when he died?
   (16 be)

T. He _____ on the balcony of a hotel in Memphis when a
   (17 be)

   man _____ and _____ him. It was terrible.
   (18 come)   *(19 shoot)*

   But we should remember King for his life, not his death. We celebrate
   Martin Luther King, Jr.'s birthday.

S. Really? I _____ that. When is it?
   (20 not/know)

T. He _____ born on January 15. We don't have school on
   (21 be)

   that date.

S. _____ a holiday right after he died?
       (22 this date/become)

T. No. It _____ a holiday in 1985.
       (23 become)

S. How do you remember so much about King?

T. I _____ a paper on him when I was in college.
       (24 write)

EXERCISE 6   A woman wrote a story about the major events in her life. Fill in the blanks with the correct form of the verb in parentheses ( ).

My name is Irina Katz. I ___*was born*___ in 1938 in the former Soviet
       (born)

Union in a small Ukrainian town. I _____ there until 1941. In
       (1 live)

1939 World War II _____ . In 1941 the German army
       (2 start)

_____ my country, and my father _____ into the
(3 invade)   *(4 go)*

army. My family _____ to leave our city. We _____
       (5 have)   *(6 go)*

to Uzbekistan. After the war _____ , my family _____
       (7 end)   *(8 return)*

to Ukraine, to the city of Lvov. My father _____ back from the
       (9 come)

army as a disabled soldier. In 1989 we _____ permission to leave
       (10 get)

our country.

There _____ a few circumstances that _____
       (11 be)   *(12 lead)*

to our decision to leave our country. First, we _____ that we
       (13 think)

would have more opportunities in the U.S. My family is Jewish and we

_____ discrimination. Second, we _____ to get
(14 suffer)   *(15 want)*

away from a bad political situation. It _____ not easy to make
       (16 be)

this decision. My father _____ to leave because he
       (17 not/want)

_____ sick. However, my married daughter _____
(18 be)   *(19 move)*

to the U.S. with her family in 1987. I _____ her very much. In
       (20 miss)

1988 my father _____ , and then we _____ that
       (21 die)   *(22 realize)*

we _____ no reason to stay. However, it _____ very
       (23 have)   *(24 be)*

---

hard to leave behind our way of life, friends, and jobs and go to a place where the future would be uncertain.

After we _____ Ukraine, we _____ to Vienna,
              (25 leave)   (26 go)

Austria, and then to Rome, Italy. We _____ permission to come
                                        (27 get)

to America, but some of our friends _____ permission.
                                        (28 not/receive)

We _____ to Chicago. When I _____ my daughter
     (29 come)   (30 see)

at the airport, we both _____ to cry. I _____ happy
                          (31 start)   (32 be)

to be with my family again.

At first, everything _____ very difficult for me because
                        (33 be)

I _____ English. My children _____ English quickly,
   (34 not/understand)   (35 learn)

and they _____ jobs. I _____ to study English at
           (36 find)   (37 begin)

Truman College. Unfortunately, I _____ English when I was in
                                    (38 not/study)

my country. I _____ German.
                (39 study)

Even though it _____ difficult to start a new life, I know
                  (40 be)

we _____ the right decision to come to the U.S.
     (41 make)

EXERCISE 7   Write the negative form of the underlined verb.

EXAMPLE: I lived in a small town as a child. I ___*didn't live*___ in a city.

1. I was born in Ukraine. I _____ in Russia.

2. My father went into the army. My brother _____ into the army.

3. We got permission to leave the country in 1989. We _____ permission to come directly to the U.S.

4. There were a lot of opportunities for our children in the U.S. There

   _____ a lot of opportunities for them in Ukraine.

5. Our oldest daughter moved to the U.S. in 1987. We _____ to the U.S. at that time.

6. My father died in 1988. He _____ during the war.

7. It was hard to leave our country. It _____ easy to leave our friends and jobs behind.

8. We left behind our friends. We _____ a good political situation.

9. We received permission to come to the U.S. Some of our friends _____ permission.

10. My children learned English quickly. I _____ English quickly.

11. I studied English in the U.S. Unfortunately, I _____ English in Ukraine.

EXERCISE 8 Read each statement. Then write a *yes/no* question about the word(s) in parentheses ( ). Write a short answer.

EXAMPLE: Irina came to the U.S. (to Los Angeles)
Did she come to Los Angeles? No, she didn't.

1. Irina was born in 1938. (in Moscow)

   _____

2. She lived in a small town before the war. (after the war)

   _____

3. The German army invaded Poland. (Ukraine)

   _____

4. Her family returned to Ukraine. (to their hometown)

   _____

5. She lived in Lvov until 1989. (her daughter)

   _____

6. It was hard for Irina to leave her family. (her job)

   _____

7. She went to Vienna. (to Rome)

   _____

8. She got permission to come to America. (all her friends)

   _____

9. Her children learned English quickly. (Irina)

   _____

EXERCISE 9 Read each statement. Then write a *wh-* question about the word(s) in parentheses ( ). An answer is not necessary.

EXAMPLE: Irina was born in 1938. (where)
Where was she born?
_____

1. She left her town in 1941. (why)
_____

2. The war began in 1939. (when/the war/end)
_____

3. The German army invaded her country. (when)
_____

4. Her family went to Uzbekistan in 1941. (where/after the war)
_____

5. She wanted to leave her country in the 1980s. (why)
_____

6. She had several reasons for leaving her country. (how many)
_____

7. Her father died. (when)
_____

8. Her future was uncertain in the U.S. (why)
_____

9. She came to the U.S. in 1989. (when/her daughter)
_____

10. She saw someone in the Chicago airport. (whom)
_____

11. She didn't understand English at first. (why)
_____

EXERCISE 10 Check (√) the things you did this past week. Exchange books with another student. Ask the other student about the items he or she checked.

EXAMPLE: √ I made a long-distance phone call.
A. I made a long-distance phone call.
B. Who(m) did you call?
A. I called my father in Mexico.
B. How long did you talk?
A. We talked for about 15 minutes.

1. ___ I made a long-distance phone call.
2. ___ I shopped for groceries.
3. ___ I met someone new.
4. ___ I got together with a friend.
5. ___ I wrote a letter.
6. ___ I bought some new clothes.
7. ___ I went to the bank.

8. ___ I read something interesting (a book, an article).
9. ___ I went to the post office.
10. ___ I did exercises.
11. ___ I got a letter.
12. ___ I went to an interesting place.

Before You Read
1. Are you a baseball fan? Do you see many African-Americans on baseball teams?
2. Do you see many TV programs with African-American characters?
3. Do you know the people in these photos?

Jackie Robinson (1919–1972)

Bill Cosby

Read the article on the following page. Pay special attention to *used to*.

Discrimination and Segregation

Segregation, or separation of the races, **used to be** part of American life. Many hotels, schools, and restaurants **used to be** for whites only. And many professions **used to be** limited to whites. One example of this was in major league baseball. African-Americans, unable to join the major leagues, **used to have** a separate league. That finally changed in 1947, when the manager of the Brooklyn Dodgers saw African-American Jackie Robinson play baseball and invited him to join his team. Even though Robinson was a great player, he suffered insults and even death threats.

Another profession where African-Americans suffered discrimination was in acting. They appeared in movies and on TV, but they **used to play** servants and slaves. Their characters were often lazy, stupid, or superstitious. In 1984, *The Cosby Show*, starring Bill Cosby, changed the image of African-Americans on TV. This popular show was about an upper-middle-class African-American family.

Another area where African-Americans suffered discrimination was in music. Marian Anderson, a talented opera star, performed all over the U.S. and Europe. But in 1939, when a concert hall in Washington, D.C., found out that their performer was going to be a black woman, the performance was canceled.

Even though laws today prohibit discrimination, many African-Americans still feel it in their everyday life.

Marian Anderson (1902–1993)

3.5 Habitual Past with *Used To*

Examples	Explanation
African-Americans **used to have** their own baseball leagues. On TV and in movies, blacks **used to play** servants.	*Used to* + a base form shows a habit or custom over a past period of time. This custom no longer exists.
Some restaurants **didn't use to** serve African-Americans.	For negatives, omit the *d*.

LANGUAGE NOTES

1. *Used to* is for past habits or customs. It is not for an action that happened once or a few times.

   > Many restaurants *used to* serve white people only. (This happened over a period of time.)

   > In 1946, the manager of the Dodgers *invited* Robinson to play for his team. (This happened in 1947 only.)

2. We don't pronounce the *d* in *used to*.

EXERCISE 11 Tell which of the following you used to do when you were a child.

EXAMPLE: cry a lot
            I used to cry a lot.
            OR
            I didn't use to cry a lot.

1. enjoy school	9. tell lies
2. obey my parents	10. read mystery stories
3. attend religious school	11. live on a farm
4. play with dolls	12. eat a lot of candy
5. play soccer	13. live with my grandparents
6. fight with other children	14. believe in Santa Claus
7. draw pictures	15. watch a lot of TV
8. have a pet	16. read comic books

EXERCISE 12 Name something. Practice *used to*.

EXAMPLE: Name something you used to know when you were in elementary school.

            I used to know the names of all the presidents (but I don't know them anymore).

1. Name something you used to do when you were a child.

2. Tell what kind of stories you used to enjoy when you were a child.

3. Name something you used to believe when you were a child.

4. Name something you used to like to eat when you were a child.

5. Tell about some things your parents, grandparents, or teachers used to tell you when you were a child.

6. Tell about some things you used to do when you were younger.

EXERCISE 13 A young man is comparing how his life used to be five years ago and how his life is now. Complete his statements.

EXAMPLE: I used to _____*be lazy*_____. Now I'm hard-working.

1. I used to _____. Now I save my money.

2. I used to _____. Now I'm a serious student.

3. I used to _____. Now I live alone.

4. I used to _____. Now I almost never watch TV.

5. I used to _____. Now I come home after work and study.

6. I used to _____. Now I have short hair.

7. I used to _____. Now I have a car and drive everywhere.

8. I used to _____. Now I'm on a diet and I'm losing weight.

9. I used to _____. Now I make my own decisions.

10. I used to _____. Now I use my credit card for most of my purchases.

EXERCISE 14 Write sentences comparing the way you used to live in your native country with the way you live now. Share your sentences with a partner or with the entire class.

EXAMPLES: *I used to live with my whole family. Now I live alone.*

I used to work in a restaurant. Now I'm a full-time student.

I didn't use to speak English at all. Now I speak English pretty well.

Ideas for sentences:
school   job   hobbies   apartment/house   family life   friends

1. _____

2. _____

3. _____

4. _____

5. _____

1. Simple Past Tense
    Be

    > He **was** at work yesterday.
    > He **wasn't** at home.
    > **Was** he on time? Yes, he **was**.
    > Where **was** he yesterday?
    > Why **wasn't** he at home?

    Regular Verb

    > She **worked** last Friday.
    > She **didn't work** last Saturday.
    > **Did** she **work** last night?
    > Yes, she **did**.
    > When **did** she **work**?
    > Why **didn't** she **work** last Saturday?

    Irregular Verb

    > He **bought** a new car.
    > He **didn't buy** an American car.
    > **Did** he **buy** a Toyota?
    > Yes, he **did**.
    > Where **did** he **buy** his car?
    > Why **didn't** he **buy** an American car?

2. Habitual Past with *Used To*

    > I **used to** live on a farm. Now I live in a city.
    > I **used to** walk to work. Now I drive.

EDITING ADVICE

1. Use *was/were* with *born*.

    > *was*
    > He born in Germany.
    > ^

2. Don't use *was/were* with *die*.

    > He ~~was~~ died two years ago.

3. Don't use a past form after *to*.

    > *leave*
    > I decided to ~~left~~ early.

    > I wanted to go home and ~~watched~~ TV.

The Simple Past Tense; Habitual Past with *Used To*   **93**

4. Don't use *was* or *were* to form a simple past tense.

   went
   He ~~was go~~ home yesterday.

5. Use *there* when a new subject is introduced.

   There w
   ~~Was~~ a big earthquake in 1906.

6. Use a form of *be* before an adjective. Remember, some *-ed* words are adjectives.

   were
   They ‸excited about their trip to America.

7. Don't use *did* with an adjective. Use *was/were*.

   were
   Why ~~did~~ you afraid?

8. Use the correct word order in a question.

   didn't you
   Why ~~you didn't~~ return?

9. Use *did* + the base form to form a question.

   did   buy
   What kind of car ‸you ~~bought~~?

10. Use the base form after *didn't*.

    He didn't work~~ed~~ yesterday.

11. Don't forget the *d* in *used to*.

    d
    She use‸ to live in Miami.

12. Don't add the verb *be* before *used to* for habitual past.

    I~~'m~~ used to play soccer in my country.

LESSON 3 TEST / REVIEW

PART **1**   Write the past form of the following verbs.

EXAMPLE: draw _____drew_____

1. eat _____   3. give _____   5. send _____

2. put _____   4. write _____   6. listen _____

7. read _____	12. find _____	17. make _____
8. take _____	13. stand _____	18. hear _____
9. bring _____	14. leave _____	19. feel _____
10. talk _____	15. sit _____	20. fall _____
11. know _____	16. go _____	21. get _____

PART **2**   Find the mistakes with the underlined words, and correct them. Not every sentence has a mistake. If the sentence is correct, write **C**.

EXAMPLES: She ~~losed~~ *lost* her umbrella.
Did she lose her glove?   C

1. My mother borned in Italy.

2. Why you didn't eat breakfast?

3. Did you studied English in your country?

4. When arrived your uncle?

5. Were a lot of people at the airport last night.

6. Why was you late?

7. Did you afraid of the robber?

8. I enjoyed the concert.

9. Last night I read an interesting article.

10. My grandmother was died ten years ago.

11. They decided to drove to New York.

12. I excited about my trip to London last year.

13. What did she do about her problem?

14. Why he wasn't happy?

15. Where you bought your coat?

16. She use to live in Miami.

Write the negative form of the underlined word.

EXAMPLE: Rosa Parks lived in Alabama. She _____*didn't live*_____ in Washington.

1. She was tired when she got out of work. She _____ sick.

2. She went to work by bus. She _____ to work by car.

3. The bus driver told African-Americans to stand. He _____ white Americans to stand.

4. Some African-Americans stood up. Rosa Parks _____ up.

5. The police came to the bus. They _____ to her house.

6. They took her to jail. They _____ her to her house.

7. Martin Luther King, Jr. organized a protest. Rosa Parks _____ a protest.

8. Slavery ended in 1865. Discrimination _____ in 1865.

9. King believed in peaceful protest. He _____ in violence.

10. King spoke about brotherhood. He _____ about violence.

PART 4 Write a question beginning with the word given. (An answer is not necessary.)

EXAMPLE: Martin Luther King, Jr. lived in the South.

Where _____*did he live?*_____

1. King became a minister.

Why _____

2. King was born in Georgia.

When _____

3. King didn't like segregation.

Why _____

4. Black children went to separate schools.

Why _____

5. Some restaurants didn't permit black people to eat there.

Why _____

6. King was in jail many times because of his protests.

   How many times _____

7. King won the Nobel Prize.

   When _____

8. Rosa Parks worked in Montgomery.

   Where _____

9. She was tired.

   Why _____

10. She went home by bus.

    How many times _____

11. She lived in the South.

    Where _____

12. She didn't want to obey the law.

    Why _____

13. The police took her to jail.

    Why _____

PART 5

Write two sentences with *used to* comparing your life in your native country with your life in the U.S.

1. _____

2. _____

EXPANSION ACTIVITIES

CLASSROOM ACTIVITIES

1. Check (√) the sentences that are true for you. Find a partner and exchange books. Give each other more information about the things you checked. Ask each other questions about these activities.

   a) _____ I bought a CD in the past week.

   b) _____ I worked last Saturday.

   c) _____ I rode a bike this past week.

d) ＿＿ I went to a party last weekend.

e) ＿＿ I got a driver's license in the past year.

f) ＿＿ I took a trip in the past year.

g) ＿＿ I got married in the last two years.

h) ＿＿ I found a job this month.

i) ＿＿ I spent more than $50 today.

j) ＿＿ I received some money this week.

k) ＿＿ I was born in March.

l) ＿＿ I ate pizza in the past month.

m) ＿＿ I bought a car in the past year.

n) ＿＿ I came to the U.S. alone.

2. Who did it?

Teacher: Pass out an index card to each student.

Students: Write something you did last weekend. It can be something unusual or something ordinary. (Examples: I went fishing. I baked a pie. I did my laundry.)

Teacher: Collect the cards. Pull out one card at a time and read the sentence to the class. The students have to guess who wrote the card.

3. Who used to do it?

Teacher: Pass out an index card to each student.

Students: Think of some things you used to be, wear, do, etc. when you were in high school. Think of things that other students would not guess about you. Write two or three of these things on the card.

Teacher: Collect the cards. Pull out one card at a time and read the sentences to the class. The students have to guess who wrote the card.

EXAMPLES:
I used to hate studying a foreign language.
I used to have very long hair.
I used to be a terrible student.

4. Bring in a picture of yourself when you were younger. Describe yourself at that time and compare yourself to now.

EXAMPLE:
I used to play soccer all day with my friends. Now I don't have time for it.

5. Fill in the blank. Discuss your answers in a small group or with the entire class.

Before I came to the U.S., I used to believe that ＿＿＿＿＿＿＿＿＿＿
＿＿＿＿＿＿＿＿＿＿, but now I know it's not true.

DISCUSSION   In a small group or with the entire class, discuss the following:

1. Changes in daily life: Compare how life used to be when you were younger with how it is now.

2. Fashions: Talk about different styles or fashions in the past.

EXAMPLE: In the 1960s, men used to wear their hair long.

WRITING   Choose one of the following topics to write a short composition.

1. Write a paragraph or paragraphs telling about your childhood.

2. Write a paragraph or paragraphs to tell about changes in your native country. Compare how life used to be with how it is now.

3. If you are married, write a paragraph or paragraphs comparing your life as a married person with your life as a single person.

4. Write a short composition about your life. Use the composition in Exercise 6 as your model. Answer the following questions as part of your composition.

    a. Where were you born?

    b. What was your life like in your native country?

    c. Why did you decide to leave your native country?

    d. What happened immediately after you left your native country?

    e. How was your life in your first few months in the U.S.?

OUTSIDE ACTIVITY   Interview an American. Ask this person to tell you about changes he or she sees in American society. Ask this person to compare how he or she used to live with how he or she lives now. Report some interesting information to the class.

Internet Activities

1. Find information about one of the people below. Tell the class why this person was (or is) famous.

   George Wallace   James Earl Ray

   Jesse Jackson   Jesse Owens

   Malcolm X   Nat Turner

   John Wilkes Booth   Rodney King

   Mohandas Gandhi

2. At a search engine, type in "I Have a Dream" to find Martin Luther King, Jr.'s most famous speech.

GRAMMAR

Subject and Object Pronouns
Possessive Forms
Reflexive Pronouns

CONTEXT

An American Wedding
His Story/Her Story

LESSON FOCUS

We use subject and object pronouns to take the
place of subject and object nouns.

Steve likes Debbie because *she* is good to *him*.

We can use possessive forms to show ownership or
relationship.

Steve's wedding was big. *My* wedding was small.

If the subject and the object of the sentence are the
same, we use a reflexive pronoun for the object.

I see *myself*.   They can take care of *themselves*.

1. Where do people get married in your native culture?
2. What kind of clothes do the bride and groom wear in your native culture?
3. At what age do people usually get married in your native culture?

Read the following article. Pay special attention to object pronouns.

An American Wedding

Many American young couples consider their wedding to be one of the most important days of their life. They save for **it** and often spend a year planning for **it**: finding a place, selecting a menu, buying a wedding dress, ordering invitations and sending **them** to friends and relatives, choosing bridesmaids and ushers, selecting musicians, and much more.

veil

bride   groom   bouquet

When the day arrives, the groom doesn't usually see the bride before the wedding. It is considered bad luck for **him** to see **her** ahead of time. The guests wait with excitement to see **her** too. When the wedding begins, the groom enters first. Then the bridesmaids and ushers enter. When the bride finally enters, everyone turns around to look at **her**. Often the bride's father or both her parents walk **her** down the aisle to the groom's side.

During the ceremony, the bride and groom promise to love and respect each other for the rest of their lives. They answer questions about love and respect by saying "I do." The groom's "best man" holds the rings for **them** until they are ready to place **them** on each other's fingers. At the end of the ceremony, the groom lifts the bride's veil and kisses **her**.

There is a party after the ceremony. People make toasts, eat dinner, and dance. The bride and groom usually dance the first dance alone. Then guests join **them**.

Before the bride and groom leave the party, the bride throws her bouquet over her head, and the single women try to catch **it**. It is believed that the woman who catches **it** will be the next one to get married.

The newlyweds[1] usually take a trip, called a honeymoon, immediately after the wedding.

Did you know...?

The average cost of a wedding in the U.S. with 200 guests is $15,000. These costs include the bridal dress, the flowers, the rings, the dinner, the cake, the invitations, the reception hall, the musicians, the photographer, and the limousine.

---

[1] For a short time after they are married, the bride and groom are called *newlyweds*.

4.1 Subject and Object Pronouns

Examples	Explanation
The bride wears a veil. The groom lifts **it** to kiss **her**.	We use object pronouns to take the place of nouns that follow the verb.
When the bride enters, everyone turns around to look at **her**.	An object pronoun can follow a preposition.

LANGUAGE NOTES

1. The object pronouns are: *me, you, him, her, it, us, them*. Compare subject and object pronouns:

		Examples:		
Subject	Object	S	V	O
I	me	You	love	me.
you	you	I	love	you.
he	him	She	loves	him.
she	her	He	loves	her.
it	it	I	love	it.
we	us	They	love	us.
they	them	We	love	them.

2. We use *them* for plural people and things.
    Do you know the bride's parents? Yes, I know *them*.
    Do you like the flowers? Yes, I like *them*.

EXERCISE 1 Fill in the blanks with an object pronoun in place of the underlined word.

EXAMPLE: The groom doesn't walk down the aisle with the bride. Her father walks with ____*her*____.

1. The bride doesn't enter with the groom. He waits for _____, and she goes to _____ .

2. The groom takes the ring. He puts _____ on the bride's hand.

3. The bride wears a veil. The groom lifts _____ to kiss _____ .

4. The bride doesn't throw the bouquet to all the women. She throws _____ to the single women only.

5. People make toasts to <u>the bride and groom</u>. They wish _____ health and happiness.

6. <u>The groom</u> promises to love the bride, and the bride promises to love _____ .

7. The bride and groom receive <u>gifts</u>. They usually open _____ at home.

Say and *Tell*

Examples	Explanation
The bride and groom **say** "I do." The newlyweds **said** "thank you" to the guests.	We *say* something. We *say* something to someone.
The newlyweds **told** their friends about their honeymoon. They **told** the musicians to start the music.	We *tell* someone something. We *tell* someone to do something.

LANGUAGE NOTES

1. *Say* and *tell* have the same meaning, but we use them differently. We say something. (*Say* has a direct object.) We tell someone something. (*Tell* has an indirect object and a direct object.)
    COMPARE:
    The teacher *said* the answer.
    The teacher *told* us the answer.

2. We use *tell* in a few expressions without an indirect object:
    tell the truth   tell a secret
    tell a lie   tell time
    tell a story   tell (all) about something

3. There are other verbs like *tell* that have an indirect object and a direct object. For verbs followed by an indirect and a direct object, see Appendix I.

	INDIRECT OBJECT	DIRECT OBJECT
I gave	the newlyweds	a present.
They sent	the guests	thank-you notes.

EXERCISE 2 Fill in the blanks with the correct form of *say* or *tell*.

EXAMPLES: The teacher usually ___*says*___ hello when he enters the room.

The teacher ___*told*___ the class about the meeting.

1. The teacher _____ us her name on the first day of class.

2. The teacher tries to _____ the students' names correctly.

3. Don't _____ your classmates the answers during a test.

4. If you know that you're going to be absent, _____ the teacher.

5. Children shouldn't _____ a lie.

6. Some people _____ a prayer before they go to bed.

7. You must _____ the truth in court.

8. I had to _____ goodbye to many friends before I left my country.

9. When you need to interrupt a conversation, you should _____, "Excuse me."

10. Some people can't _____ no.

11. He _____, "Sit down."

12. The teacher _____ us to write a short composition.

4.3 Possessive Forms of Nouns

We use possessive forms to show ownership or relationship.

Noun	Ending	Examples
Singular Noun: bride groom	Add apostrophe + **s**	The **bride's** dress is white. The **groom's** tuxedo is black.
Plural noun ending in **-s**: parents guests	Add apostrophe only	She got married in her **parents'** house. The **guests'** coats are in the coat room.
Irregular Plural Noun: men women	Add apostrophe + **s**	The **men's** suits are black. The **women's** dresses are beautiful.
Names that end in **s**: Charles	Add apostrophe only OR Add apostrophe + **s**	Do you know **Charles'** wife? OR Do you know **Charles's** wife?

LANGUAGE NOTES

1. We use the possessive form for people and other living things.
   Jack's wife is very nice.
   The *dog's* name is Pee-Wee.
2. For inanimate objects, we usually use "the _____ of _____."
   The name of the church is Saint Mary's.
3. We can use a possessive noun and a possessive adjective together.
   My mother's brother lives in Washington, D.C.

EXERCISE 3 Fill in the blanks to make the possessive form of the noun.

EXAMPLE: The bride___'s___ grandfather looked very handsome.

1. The groom_____ mother is very nice.

2. The bride_____ flowers are beautiful.

3. The bridesmaids_____ dresses are blue.

4. They invited many guests to the wedding. They didn't invite the guests_____ children.

5. The women_____ dresses are very elegant.

6. Charles_____ sister was a bridesmaid.

7. The newlyweds_____ picture is in the newspaper.

8. Do you know the children_____ names?

EXERCISE 4 Fill in the blanks with the two nouns in parentheses ( ). Put them in the correct order. Use the possessive form of one of the nouns, except with non-living things.

EXAMPLES: _____The dog's name_____ is Pee-Wee.
   (name/the dog)

I don't like the _____color of your car._____
   (your car/color)

1. The _____ lives far away.
   (bride/grandmother)

2. The _____ are not very big.
   (offices/teachers)

3. The _____ are very small.
   (windows/the rooms)

4. The _____ are in the basement.
   (children/toys)

5. The _____ is King College.
   (name/this school)

6. Barbara and Sally are _____.
   (names/women)

7. I'm studying English in _____.
   (Mr. Harris/class)

8. My _____ is not very far.
   (house/parents)

4.4 Possessive Adjectives

We can use possessive adjectives to show possession. Compare the subject pronouns and the possessive adjectives.

Subject Pronoun	Possessive Adjective	Examples
I	my	I'm wearing **my** white dress.
you	your	You're wearing **your** new dress.
he	his	He's wearing **his** blue suit.
she	her	She's wearing **her** new necklace.
it	its	The church has **its** own reception hall.
we	our	We're attending **our** cousin's wedding.
they	their	The newlyweds opened **their** gifts.

LANGUAGE NOTES

Be careful with *his* and *her*.

I have a married brother. *His* wife is very nice.

The bride looks beautiful. *Her* father looks proud.

EXERCISE 5 Fill in the blanks with a possessive adjective.

EXAMPLE: I love ____*my*____ parents.

1. I have one sister. _____ sister got married five years ago.

2. She loves _____ husband very much.

3. He's an accountant. He has _____ own business.

4. They have one child. _____ son's name is Jason.

5. They bought a house last year. _____ house isn't far from my house.

6. My sister and I visit _____ parents once a month. They live two hours away from us.

7. My sister said, "My car isn't working this week. Let's visit them in _____ car."

8. You don't know what's in a book by looking at _____ cover.

EXERCISE 6 Fill in the blanks with a possessive adjective.

A. What are you going to wear to ___*your*___ sister's wedding?
(example)

B. I'm going to wear _____ new blue dress.
(1)

A. Did your sister buy a new dress for her wedding?

B. No, she's going to borrow _____ best friend's dress.
(2)

A. Will the wedding be at your house?

B. Oh, no. We live in an apartment. _____ apartment is too small.
(3)
We're going to invite over 200 guests. The wedding is going to be at a church. Afterward, we're going to have a dinner in a restaurant.

The restaurant has _____ own reception hall.
(4)

A. Are the newlyweds going on a honeymoon after the wedding?

B. Yes. They have friends who have a cottage.

They're going to stay at _____ friends'
(5)
cottage in the country for a week.

A. Is the groom's mother a nice woman?

cottage

B. I don't know _____ mother. I'll meet her at the wedding for the
(6)
first time.

4.5 Questions with *Whose*

Whose + Noun	Auxiliary Verb	Subject	Verb	Answer
Whose dress	did	the bride	borrow?	She borrowed her sister's dress.
Whose last name	will	the bride	use?	She'll use her husband's last name.
Whose flowers	are	those?		They're the bride's flowers.

LANGUAGE NOTES

Whose + a noun asks a question about possession.

EXERCISE 7 Write a question with *whose*. The answer is given.

EXAMPLE: _Whose flowers are these_____? They're the bride's flowers.

1. _____? That's my father's car.

2. _____? Those are my brothers' toys.

3. _____? I listen to the Beatles' music.

4. _____? I'm using my friend's bike.

5. _____? I like my mother's cooking.

6. _____? The bride borrowed her sister's dress.

4.6 Possessive Pronouns

Examples	Explanation
You forgot your book today. You can borrow **mine**.	*Mine* = my book
My car is old. **Yours** is new.	*Yours* = your car

LANGUAGE NOTES

1. When we use a possessive pronoun, we omit the noun.
   COMPARE: Her dress is white.
   Your dress is blue. OR *Yours* is blue.

2. Compare the three forms below:

Subject Pronoun	Possessive Adjective	Possessive Pronoun
I	my	mine
you	your	yours
he	his	his
she	her	hers
it	its	—
we	our	ours
they	their	theirs
who	whose	whose

Subject and Object Pronouns; Possessive Forms; Reflexive Pronouns   **109**

3. After a possessive noun, we can omit the noun.
   The groom's parents look happy.
   The bride's parents do too. OR The *bride's* do too.

4. *Whose* can be a possessive adjective or a possessive pronoun.
   This is my coat.
   Whose coat is that? OR *Whose* is that?

EXERCISE 8 In each sentence below, choose either the possessive pronoun or the possessive adjective.

EXAMPLE: Can I borrow ((your,) yours) car?

1. (My, Mine) is in the shop.

2. My sister has a car, but (her, hers) car needs a new battery.

3. My parents have a car. (Their, Theirs) doesn't have air conditioning.

4. My wife and I have a car. (Our, Ours) car is a Chevy.

5. Your car is old. (My, Mine) car is new.

6. My car has a new battery. (Your, Yours) has an old battery.

7. My parents have an American car. (Your, Yours) parents have a Japanese car.

EXERCISE 9 Fill in the blanks with *I, I'm, me, my,* or *mine.*

1. _____ a student.

2. _____ live in an apartment near school.

3. _____ apartment is on the first floor.

4. _____ parents often visit _____.

5. They don't have a computer. They use _____.

EXERCISE 10 Fill in the blanks with *we, we're, us, our,* or *ours.*

1. _____ classroom is large.

2. _____ study English here.

3. _____ foreign students.

4. The teacher helps _____ learn English.

5. The teacher brings her book, and we bring _____.

EXERCISE 11 Fill in the blanks with *you, you're, your,* or *yours*. Pretend you are talking directly to the teacher.

1. _____ the teacher.

2. _____ come from the U.S.

3. My first language is Polish. _____ is English.

4. _____ pronunciation is very good.

5. We see _____ every day.

EXERCISE 12 Fill in the blanks with *he, he's, his,* or *him*.

1. I have a brother. _____ name is Paul.

2. _____ married.

3. _____ has four children.

4. My apartment is small. _____ is big.

5. I see _____ on the weekends.

EXERCISE 13 Fill in the blanks with *she, she's, her,* or *hers*.

1. I have a sister. _____ name is Marilyn.

2. I visit _____ twice a week.

3. _____ lives in a suburb.

4. _____ a teacher. _____ husband is a doctor.

5. My children go to private school. _____ go to public school.

EXERCISE 14 Fill in the blanks with *it, it's,* or *its*.

1. The school has a big library. _____ comfortable and clean.

2. _____ has many books and magazines.

3. _____ hours are from 8 a.m. to 8 p.m.

4. I use _____ every day.

5. _____ on the first floor.

Fill in the blanks with *they, they're, them, their,* or *theirs.*

1. My parents rent _____ apartment.

2. My apartment is small, but _____ is big.

3. _____ very old now.

4. _____ live in a suburb.

5. I visit _____ on the weekends.

4.7 Questions About the Subject

Compare these statements and related questions:

Wh- Word	Do/Does Did	Subject	Verb	Complement
What	does	The bride	throws	something.
		she	throw?	
		Someone	caught	the bouquet.
		Who	caught	the bouquet?
What	did	The guests	brought	something.
		they	bring?	
		Some guests	brought	gifts.
		How many guests	brought	gifts?
Why	do	Some women	try	to catch the bouquet.
		they	try	to catch the bouquet?
		Which women	try	to catch the bouquet?
		Something	happened	next.
		What	happened	next?

LANGUAGE NOTES

1. Questions about the subject are different from other questions. They don't include *do, does,* or *did.*

2. We usually answer a subject question with a subject and an auxiliary verb.
   Who wears a white dress? The bride *does.*
   Who caught the bouquet? The bride's cousin *did.*
   How many people came to the wedding? One hundred fifty people
        did.

3. *What happened* is a subject question. We usually answer with a different verb.

    What happened after the wedding?
    The bride and groom *went* on a honeymoon.

4. After *who*, use the **-s** form for the simple present tense. After *how many*, use the base form. After other questions, use either the base form or the **-s** form.

    Who *has* the prettiest dress?
    How many people *want* to dance?
    Which woman *has* the prettiest dress?
    Which women *have* the prettiest dresses?

5. In a question about the object, *whom* is very formal. Informally, many Americans say *who*.

    FORMAL: *Whom* did your brother marry?
    INFORMAL: *Who* did your brother marry?

EXERCISE **16** Use the simple present tense of the verb in parentheses ( ) to ask a question about this class. Any student may volunteer an answer.

EXAMPLES: Who (ride) a bike to school?
A. Who rides a bike to school?
B. I do.

How many students (have) the textbook?
A. How many students have the textbook?
B. We all do.

1. Who (explain) the grammar?

2. How many students (speak) Spanish?

3. Who usually (sit) near the door?

4. What usually (happen) after class?

5. Who (want) to repeat this course?

6. Who (need) help with this lesson?

7. Who (have) a computer?

8. How many students (live) in a dorm?

9. Who (have) a cell phone?

10. Who (live) alone?

EXERCISE 17 Use the simple past tense of the verb in parentheses ( ) to ask a question. Any student may volunteer an answer.

EXAMPLE: Who (buy) a used textbook?
              A. Who bought a used textbook?
              B. I did.

    1. Who (move) last year?

    2. Who (understand) the explanation?

    3. Who (take) a trip recently?

    4. Who (bring) a dictionary to class today?

    5. Who (pass) the last test?

    6. Which students (come) late today?

    7. Which student (arrive) first today?

    8. How many students (do) today's homework?

    9. How many students (study) English in their countries?

  10. How many students (bring) a cell phone to class?

EXERCISE 18 Read each statement. Then write a question about the words in parentheses ( ). No answer is necessary.

EXAMPLE: Someone takes the bride to the groom. (who)
              Who takes the bride to the groom?

    1. Someone dances the first dance. (who)

    2. Someone holds the rings. (who)

    3. Two people say "I do." (how many people/"congratulations")

    4. The bridesmaids sometimes wear matching dresses.[2] (which woman/ a white dress)

    5. The bride pays for her white dress. (who/the bridesmaids' dresses)

---

[2] *Matching dresses* are all the same color.

EXERCISE 19 Read each statement. Then write a question about the words in parentheses ( ). Some of the questions are about the subject. Some are not. No answer is necessary.

EXAMPLES: The bride wears a white dress. (what/the groom)

What does the groom wear?

The bride enters last. (who/first)

Who enters first?

1.   The bride throws the bouquet. (when)

_____

2.   Some women try to catch the bouquet. (which women)

_____

3.   The groom puts the ring on the bride's finger. (on which hand) OR (which hand . . . on)

_____

4.   The band plays music. (what kind of music)

_____

5.   Someone dances with the bride. (who)

_____

6.   Guests give presents. (what kind of presents)

_____

7.   Some people cry at the wedding. (who)

_____

8.   There's a dinner after the ceremony. (what/happen/after the dinner)

_____

EXERCISE 20 In the conversation below, two women are talking about their families. Fill in the blanks to complete the questions. Some of the questions are about the subject. Some are about the object.

A. How do you have time to work, go to school, and take care of a family?

B. I don't have to do everything myself.

A. Who _____helps you_____ ?
        (example)

B. My husband helps me.

A. I usually cook in my house. Who _____?
                                        (1)

B. Sometimes my husband cooks; sometimes I cook. We take turns.

A. I usually clean. Who _____?
                            (2)

B. I usually clean the house.

A. How many _____?
                (3)

B. I have five children.

A. How many _____?
                (4)

B. Three children go to school. The younger ones stay home.

A. Do you send them to public school or private school?

B. One of my sons goes to private school.

A. Which _____?
            (5)

B. The oldest does. He's in high school now.

A. It's hard to take care of so many children. How do you find the time to go to class?

B. As I said, my husband helps me a lot. And sometimes I use a babysitter.

A. I'm looking for a sitter. Who(m) _____?
                                        (6)

B. I recommend our neighbor, Susan. She's 16 years old, and she's very good with our children.

A. Maybe she's too busy to help me. How many families _____ _____?
                                                                            (7)

B. I think she works for only one other family. I'll give you her phone number. If she's not busy, maybe she can work for you too.

A. Thanks. I can use some help.

EXERCISE 21 Fill in the blanks with *who, whom, who's*, or *whose*.

1. _____ your English teacher? Cindy Kane is my teacher.
2. _____ do you live with? I live with my sister.
3. _____ has the right answer? I have the right answer.
4. There's no name on this book. _____ is it?
5. _____ parents speak English? My parents do.

4.8 Reflexive Pronouns—Forms

Subject	Verb	Reflexive Pronoun
I	see	myself.
You	see	yourself.
He	sees	himself.
She	sees	herself.
It	sees	itself.
We	see	ourselves.
You	see	yourselves.
They	see	themselves.

LANGUAGE NOTES

If the subject and object are the same, we use a reflexive pronoun as the object. COMPARE:

I see you. (object pronoun)
I see myself. (reflexive pronoun)

Before You Read
1. What kind of problems do married people usually have?
2. How can married people solve their problems?

Read the following stories. Pay special attention to reflexive pronouns.

His Story/Her Story

Frank and Sylvia are like many American couples. They have problems balancing their relationship, their children, their careers, their families, and other responsibilities. Read each one's story.

Sylvia's story:

Now that I'm married, I don't have time for **myself** anymore. We used to spend time with each other. Now that we have kids, we never have time for **ourselves**. We both work, but Frank doesn't help me with housework or with the kids. I have to do everything all by **myself**. My husband only thinks of **himself**. When he wants something, like a new CD player or new software, he buys it. He never buys me flowers or other presents anymore. I tell **myself** that he still loves me, but sometimes I'm not so sure. Sometimes I think the problem is his fault, but sometimes I blame **myself**.

Frank's story:

Sylvia never has time for me anymore. We used to do things together. Now I have to do everything **myself**. If I want to go to a movie, she says that she's too busy or too tired or that the kids are sick. I rarely go to the movies, and if I do, I go by **myself**. It seems that all I do is work and pay bills. Other married people seem to enjoy **themselves** more than we do. She says she wants me to help her with the housework, but she really prefers to do everything **herself** because she doesn't like the way I do things. She wants us to see a marriage counselor, but I don't like to tell other people about my problems. I like to solve my problems **myself**.

4.9 Using Reflexive Pronouns

Examples	Explanation
Sylvia sometimes blames **herself**. (D.O.) I tell **myself** that he loves me. (I.O.) He only thinks of **himself**. (O.P.)	A reflexive pronoun can be a direct object (D.O.), an indirect object (I.O.), or the object of a preposition (O.P.)
He goes to the movies **by himself**. She has to do everything **all by herself**.	We often use a reflexive pronoun to mean alone. We often add (*all*) *by* before the reflexive pronoun.

LANGUAGE NOTES

1. After an imperative, use *yourself* or *yourselves*.
   Enjoy *yourself*.
   Here's $50. Buy *yourselves* a nice present.
   Be good to *yourself*.

2. We use reflexive pronouns in a few idiomatic expressions:
   When you are a guest in someone's house and the host wants you to feel comfortable, he may say, "Make *yourself* at home."
   When you are invited to take food at the dinner table, the hostess may say, "Help *yourself*."

EXERCISE 22 Fill in the blanks with the correct reflexive pronoun.

EXAMPLE: Sylvia and Frank are talking about ___*themselves*___ .

1. I don't have enough time for _____ .

2. Are both of you serious or can you laugh at _____?

3. They can't solve the problem by _____ .

4. Frank doesn't like to talk about _____ .

5. What does Sylvia tell _____?

6. We sometimes blame _____ for our problems.

7. Do you ever go to the movies by _____?

8. Maybe you expect too much of marriage, Frank. Don't be so hard on _____ .

9. I have to take care of the children. They can't take care of _____ .

10. We have a new electric coffee maker. It turns _____ on in the morning.

11. We enjoyed _____ on our honeymoon.

12. A. Did your mother teach you to cook or did you teach _____ _____?

    B. I taught _____ .

13. A. My parents have a great marriage.

    B. Don't compare _____ to your parents. Times are different.

14. Don't just look at the problems. Give _____ credit for the good things you do too.

EXERCISE 23 Write two sentences telling about things you like to do by yourself. Write two sentences telling about things you don't like to do by yourself.

EXAMPLES:

I like to shop by myself.

I don't like to eat by myself.

_____

_____

_____

_____

EXERCISE 24 Answer these questions.

1. Do you like to talk about yourself in class?

2. Do you ever do something special for yourself? What do you do?

3. What kind of problems do most married people have today? Do you think American married couples have the same problems as couples in your native country?

4. Do you think married couples can solve their problems by themselves? At what point should they go to a marriage counselor?

5. Do you think married people should spend most of their time together, or should they spend time by themselves?

6. Do you think young people are realistic about marriage? How can they prepare themselves for the reality of marriage?

7. Some people go on TV in the U.S. and talk about themselves and their personal problems. Does this happen in your native country?

8. What do you think Sylvia and Frank should do?

EXERCISE 25 Combination Exercise. Fill in the blanks with the correct pronoun or possessive form.

Frank and Sylvia used to do a lot of things together. _____*They*_____
                                                         (example)

went to movies, went out to restaurants, and took vacations together. But

now _____ are always too busy for each other. _____
         (1)   *(2)*

have two children and spend most of _____ time taking care
                                          (3)

of _____ .
      (4)

Frank and Sylvia bought a house recently and spend _____
                                                        (5)

free time taking care of _____. It's an old house and needs a
                              (6)
lot of work.

When Frank and Sylvia have problems, _____ try to solve
                                                (7)
_____ by _____. But sometimes Sylvia goes
       (8)   (9)
to _____ mother for advice. Frank never goes to _____
        (10)   (11)
mother. He doesn't want to bother _____ with _____
                                         (12)   (13)
problems. Frank often complains that Sylvia cares more about the kids and

the house than about _____.
                            (14)

Sylvia wants to go to a marriage counselor, but Frank doesn't want to

go with _____. He always says to Sylvia, "We don't need a
              (15)
marriage counselor. We can solve _____ problems by _____.
                                        (16)   (17)
You just need to pay more attention to _____. If you want to
                                               (18)
see a counselor, you can go by _____. I'm not going." Sylvia
                                      (19)
feels very frustrated. She thinks that the marriage isn't going to get better

by _____.
        (20)

SUMMARY OF LESSON 4

1.   Pronouns and Possessive Forms

Subject Pronoun	Object Pronoun	Possessive Adjective	Possessive Pronoun	Reflexive Pronoun
I	me	my	mine	myself
you	you	your	yours	yourself
he	him	his	his	himself
she	her	her	hers	herself
it	it	its	—	itself
we	us	our	ours	ourselves
you	you	your	yours	yourselves
they	them	their	theirs	themselves
who	whom	whose	whose	—

Examples:

Robert and Lisa are my friends.
They come from Canada.
I like **them**.
My country is small. **Theirs** is big.
Their children are grown.
They live by **themselves**.

Who has a new car?
With **whom** do you live? (FORMAL)
Who do you live with? (INFORMAL)
Whose book is that?
This is my dictionary. **Whose** is that?

2. Possessive Form of Nouns

Singular Nouns
the **boy's** name
my **father's** house
the **child's** toy
the **man's** hat
Charles' wife/**Charles's** wife

Plural Nouns
the **boys'** names
my **parents'** house
the **children's** toys
the **men's** hats

3. *Say* and *Tell*

He **said** his name.
He **told** me his name.

He **said** goodbye to his friends.
He **told** them to write often.

4. Questions About the Subject

Simple Present:
Someone knows the answer.
Who knows the answer?
How many students know the answer?
Which student knows the answer?
Which students know the answer?

Simple Past:
Someone killed Martin Luther King, Jr.
Who killed King?
Which man killed King?
What happened to this man?

EDITING ADVICE

1. Don't confuse *you're* (you are) and *your* (possessive form).

    You're
    ~~Your~~ late.

    Your
    ~~You're~~ class started ten minutes ago.

2. Don't confuse *he's* (he is) and *his* (possessive form).

    He's
    ~~His~~ married.

    His
    ~~He's~~ wife is a friend of mine.

3. Don't confuse *it's* (it is) and *its* (possessive form).

This college is big. ~~Its~~ a state university.
It's

~~It's~~ library has many books.
Its

4. Don't confuse *his* (masculine possessor) and *her* (feminine possessor).

   My sister loves ~~his~~ son.
   her

   My brother loves ~~her~~ daughter.
   his

5. Don't confuse *my* and *mine*.

   I don't have ~~mine~~ book today.
   my

6. Don't confuse *they're* and *their*.

   ~~They're~~ last name is Williams.
   Their

7. Use the correct pronoun (subject or object).

   I have a daughter. I love ~~she~~ very much.
   her

8. For a compound subject, use "another person and I." Don't use *me* in the subject position.

   My father and ~~me~~ like to go fishing.
   I

   ~~Me and my father~~ like to go fishing.
   My father and I

9. For a compound object, use "another person and me." Don't use *I* in the object position.

   My parents gave my brother and ~~I~~ a present.
   me

10. Don't use *the* with a possessive form.

    ~~The~~ my wife's mother is very nice.
    M

11. Don't use an apostrophe to make a plural form.

    They invited many ~~guest's~~ to the wedding.
    guests

12. Don't use an auxiliary verb in a question about the subject.

    Who ~~does~~ speak Spanish?
    s

13. Don't separate *whose* from the noun.

   Whose ˇis this (book?)

14. Don't confuse *whose* and *who's*.

   Whose
   ~~Who's~~ coat is that?

15. Use the correct word order for possession.

   My wife's mother
   ~~Mother my wife~~ helps us a lot.

16. Put the apostrophe after the **s** of a plural noun that ends in **s**.

   parents'
   My ~~parent's~~ house is small.

17. The **s** in a possessive pronoun is not for a plural.

   Theirs parents live in Canada.

18. Don't use a form of *be* with *what happened*.

   What ~~was~~ happened to your new car?

LESSON 4 TEST / REVIEW

PART 1   Find the mistakes with the underlined words, and correct them. Not every sentence has a mistake. If the sentence is correct, write C.

EXAMPLES: The bride's ~~the~~ parents are very proud.
   They are going to get married in their parents' house.   C

1. Do you like the bridesmaid's dresses?

2. The groom puts the ring on the brides' left hand.

3. The bride throws his bouquet to the single women.

4. The groom dances with her new wife.

5. When will they open their friends gifts?

6. They're car has a sign that says "Just Married."

7. The groom's friend's often make a party for him before the wedding.

8. <u>Your</u> wedding was very beautiful.

9. She married <u>his best friend's</u> brother.

10. <u>Her husband's mother's</u> friend is wearing a beautiful dress.

11. Do you like your mother-in-law? I don't like <u>mother my husband</u>.

12. The <u>womens'</u> dresses are very elegant.

13. <u>My sister's the wedding</u> will be in March.

14. Your name is different from your <u>husband's</u> name.

15. She visits <u>hers</u> parents once a week.

16. The groom graduated from college. <u>His</u> an accountant now.

17. <u>Our</u> friends invited <u>my wife and me</u> to <u>their</u> wedding.

18. <u>My wife and me</u> went to a beautiful wedding.

19. Who <u>did get</u> married in a church?

20. <u>Whose mother</u> is that? I think it's <u>mother the bride</u>.

21. How many people <u>brought</u> gifts to the wedding?

22. <u>Who throw</u> the bouquet at an American wedding? The bride does.

23. <u>Theirs</u> dresses are green. <u>Mine</u> is black.

24. <u>The your</u> wedding was lovely.

25. What <u>was happened</u> after the wedding?

<u>PART 2</u>   Choose the correct word to complete each sentence.

EXAMPLE: Do you like _____*c*_____ neighbors?

a. you   b. you're   c. your   d. yours

1. Where do your parents live? _____ live in Colombia.

   a. My   b. Mine   c. Mine's   d. Mines

2. _____ coat is that?

   a. Whose   b. Who's   c. Who   d. Whom

Subject and Object Pronouns; Possessive Forms; Reflexive Pronouns   **125**

3. _____ is usually white.

    a. The bride's dress   c. The brides' dress
    b. Dress the bride   d. The dress of bride

4. My sister's daughter is 18. _____ son is 16.

    a. His   b. Her   c. Hers   d. Her's

5. What's _____?

    a. the name your son   c. the name your son's
    b. your son's name   d. your the son's name

6. Look at those dogs. Do you see _____?

    a. they   b. its   c. them   d. it's

7. We have your phone number. Do you have _____?

    a. us   b. our   c. ours   d. our's

8. What is _____?

    a. that building name   c. the name of that building
    b. the name that building   d. the name's that building

9. _____

    a. Whose is this sweater?   c. Who's is this sweater?
    b. Whose sweater is this?   d. Who's sweater is this?

10. _____ knows the correct answer?

    a. Who   b. Whom   c. Whose   d. Who's

11. They have my address, but I don't have _____.

    a. their   b. them   c. they're   d. theirs

12. We did it by _____.

    a. self   b. oneself   c. ourself   d. ourselves

13. They can help _____.

    a. theirself   b. theirselves   c. themself   d. themselves

14. I know _____ very well.

    a. myself   b. mineself   c. meself   d. self

15. My teacher speaks Spanish. My _____ teacher doesn't.

    a. husbands   b. husbands'   c. husband's   d. the husband's

Fill in the blanks with *said* or *told*.

1. She _____, "Excuse me."

2. She _____ them to study.

3. She _____ him the truth.

4. She _____ hello to her neighbor.

5. She _____ the answers.

6. She _____ us about her trip.

7. She _____ an interesting story.

8. She _____ them her name.

PART **4**

Complete the question. Some of these questions ask about the subject. Some do not. (The answer is underlined.)

EXAMPLES: What _____*does the bride wear*_____?
The bride wears a white dress and a veil.

Who _____*usually cries at the wedding*_____?
The bride's mother usually cries at the wedding.

1. When _____?
She throws the bouquet at the end of the wedding party.

2. Which women _____?
The single women try to catch the bouquet.

3. On which hand _____?
The groom puts the ring on the bride's left hand.

4. Whom _____?
The groom kisses the bride.

5. Whose _____?
The bride's ring has a diamond.

6. Whose _____?
The bride uses her husband's last name.

7. Who _____?
A professional photographer took pictures at my wedding.

8. Whose _____?
I borrowed my sister's dress.

9. Whose _____, yours or your sisters?
   My sister's wedding was bigger.

10. How many people _____?
    Over 250 people came to the wedding.

11. Who _____?
    The bride and groom cut the cake.

PART 5   Fill in the blanks with a reflexive pronoun.

EXAMPLE: She likes to talk about _____herself_____.

1. I made the cake all by _____.

2. The bride made her dress _____.

3. They prepared _____ financially before getting married.

4. We helped _____ to another piece of cake.

5. The groom bought _____ a new pair of shoes.

6. All of you should help _____ to more cake and coffee.

7. Did you go to the wedding by _____ or did your wife go with you?

EXPANSION ACTIVITIES

CLASSROOM ACTIVITIES

1. Form a small group. The group should have people from different countries, if possible. Talk about weddings and marriages in your native countries.

   a. Who chooses a husband for a woman?

   b. Who pays for the wedding?

   c. What happens at the wedding?

   d. What happens after the wedding?

   e. Do the guests bring gifts to the wedding? What kind of gifts do they give? Where do the bride and groom open the gifts?

   f. How many people attend a wedding?

   g. Where do people get married?

   h. Do people dance at a wedding?

i. Who takes pictures?

j. What color dress does the bride wear?

k. At what age do people usually get married?

2. In a small group, interview one person who is married. Ask this person questions about his or her wedding.

EXAMPLES:
Where did you get married?
How many people did you invite?
How many people came?
Where did you go on your honeymoon?

3. According to an American tradition, the bride should wear:
Something old,
Something new,
Something borrowed,
Something blue.
Do you have any traditions regarding weddings in your native country?

4. Do you have a video of a wedding in your family? If so, can you bring it to class and tell the class about it? The teacher may have a video of an American wedding to show the class.

5. Write some advice for newlyweds in each of the following categories. Discuss your sentences in a small group.

home	problem solving
children	mother-in-law
housework	money
careers	time together/time apart
family obligations	

WRITING

1. Write about a typical wedding in your native country, or describe your own wedding.

2. Write about a problem you once had or have now. Tell what you did (or are doing) to help yourself solve this problem or how others helped you (or are helping you).

Internet Activities

1. Do a search on "bridal registry" on the Internet. Make a list of the types of wedding gifts people give in the U.S.

2. Do a search on "weddings" on the Internet. Find out how Americans plan for a wedding.

GRAMMAR

Singular and Plural
Noncount Nouns
There + Be
Quantity Words

CONTEXT

Pilgrims, American Indians, and Thanksgiving
Taking the Land from the American Indians

LESSON FOCUS

Some nouns have a singular and plural form. These are called count nouns.

I ate one *apple*. She ate two *apples*.

Some nouns have no plural form. These are called noncount nouns.

I ate some *soup*. I drank some *water*.

We can use *there + be* to introduce count and noncount nouns.

There are some apples on the table.
There's some milk in the refrigerator.

We can use quantity words with count and noncount nouns.

I bought *a little* coffee. I bought *a few* bananas.

The Mayflower

1.   What do you know about American Thanksgiving?
2.   Do you have a day of thanks in your native culture?

Read the following article. Pay special attention to singular and plural nouns.

Pilgrims, American Indians,[1] and Thanksgiving

Pilgrims

squash

Americans celebrate Thanksgiving on the fourth Thursday in November. At this time, they get together with family and **friends**, eat a traditional big **meal**, and give thanks for all the good **things** in their **lives**. What is the origin of this special day?

In 1620, a group of 120 **men**, **women**, and **children** left England for America on a ship called the Mayflower. They came to America in search of religious **freedom**. They started their new life in a deserted[2] Indian village in what is now the state of Massachusetts. But half of the Pilgrims did not survive their first cold, hard winter. In the spring, two American **Indians** found the **people** from England in very bad condition. They didn't have enough **food**, and they were in bad **health**. Squanto, an English speaking American Indian, stayed with them for several **months** and taught them how to survive in this new place. He brought them deer **meat** and animal **skins**; he showed them how to grow **corn** and other **vegetables**; he showed them how to use **plants** as **medicine**; he explained how to use **fish** for fertilizer[3]—he taught them many **skills** for survival in their new land.

By the time their second fall arrived, the Pilgrims had enough **food** to get through their second winter. They were in better **health**. They decided to have a thanksgiving **feast**[4] to celebrate their good **fortune**. They invited Squanto and neighboring Indian **families** of the Wampanoag tribe to come to their dinner. The Pilgrims were surprised when 90 Indians showed up. The Pilgrims did not have enough **food** for so many people. Fortunately, the Indian **chief** sent some of his people to bring food to the celebration. They brought five **deer**, **fish**, **beans**, **squash**, corn **bread**, **berries**, and many wild **turkeys**. The feast lasted for three **days**. There was a short time of **peace** and **friendship** between the Indians and the Pilgrims.

Now on Thanksgiving Day in the U.S., we eat some of the traditional **foods**, such as **turkey**, **sweet potatoes**, and **cranberries**, that the Indians shared with the Pilgrims.

---

[1] The natives of America are called American Indians, Indians, or Native Americans.
[2] *Deserted* means empty of people.
[3] We put fertilizer in the earth to help plants grow. Fertilizer is made of natural things.
[4] A *feast* is a large dinner.

Regular Noun Plurals

Word Ending	Example Noun	Plural Addition	Plural Form
Vowel	bee banana	+ s	bees bananas
s, ss, sh, ch, x, z	church dish box watch class	+ es	churches dishes boxes watches classes
Voiceless consonants	cat lip month	+ s	cats lips months
Voiced consonants	card pin	+ s	cards pins
Vowel + y	boy day	+ s	boys days
Consonant + y	lady story	$\cancel{y}$ + ies	ladies stories
Vowel + o	video radio	+ s	videos radios
Consonant + o	potato hero	+ es	potatoes heroes
EXCEPTIONS: photos, pianos, solos, altos, sopranos, autos, avocados			
f or fe	leaf knife	**f** + ves	leaves knives
EXCEPTIONS: beliefs, chiefs, roofs, cliffs, chefs, sheriffs			

(continued)

Irregular Noun Plurals

Singular	Plural	Examples	Explanation
man woman mouse tooth foot goose	men women mice teeth feet geese	**Men** and **women** came to America from England.	Vowel change
sheep fish deer	sheep fish deer	The Indians brought five **deer**.	No change
child person	children people (or persons) NOTE: *People* is more commonly used than *persons*.	The Pilgrims brought their **children** to America. Many **people** came to the celebration.	Different word form
	pajamas clothes pants/slacks (eye)glasses scissors	Your **clothes** are dirty. My **glasses** are broken.	No singular form
news politics		The **news** is not good. **Politics** is interesting for me.	Singular form ends in -s. No plural form.

LANGUAGE NOTES

1. We use the plural to talk about more than one. Regular noun plurals end in -s or -es. Some noun plurals are irregular.
    > One hundred twenty *men*, *women*, and *children* came from England. Two *Indians* found these people.
2. Exact numbers use the singular form.
    > The U.S. has over 270 *million* people.
3. Inexact numbers use the plural form.
    > *Millions* of Indians live in America.
    > *Hundreds* of Europeans came to America in the 1600s.
    > My grandfather is in his *seventies*.
4. We use the plural form in the following expressions: *one of* (*the, my, his, her*, etc.).
    > One of the *Indians* spoke English.
5. We use a singular noun and verb after *every*.
    > Every *person needs* love and attention.
6. Don't make an adjective plural.
    > We have many *good* things in our lives.

EXERCISE 1   Write the plural form of each noun.

EXAMPLE: hour ___*hours*___

1. American _____
2. family _____
3. leaf _____
4. child _____
5. deer _____
6. city _____
7. language _____
8. cloud _____
9. potato _____
10. valley _____

11. butterfly _____
12. man _____
13. fish _____
14. wolf _____
15. donkey _____
16. fox _____
17. country _____
18. month _____
19. goose _____
20. woman _____

EXERCISE 2   Find the mistakes with the underlined words, and correct them. Not every sentence has a mistake. If the sentence is correct, write **C**.

EXAMPLES:

men
Five man left early.

is
Mathematics are my favorite subject.

I saw two deer in the forest.   *C*

1. She has two childrens.

2. One of her daughter is a doctor.

3. Eleven millions peoples died in the war.

4. The news are on TV at 6 o'clock.

5. His pants is very expensive.

6. Five women in this class speak French.

7. Every students want to pass this course.

8. Math is one of my favorite subject in school.

9. Everyone want to have a good life.

10. Many Americans own a home.

11. Hundreds of people saw the accident.

12. My mother is in her sixties.

EXERCISE 3 Fill in the blanks with the correct form of the word in parentheses ( ).

EXAMPLE: _____Americans_____ celebrate Thanksgiving in November.
          (American)

1. One hundred twenty _____ came to America on the
   (person)
   Mayflower.

2. _____, _____, and _____ came to
   (Man)   *(woman)*   *(child)*
   America on the Mayflower.

3. They had very hard _____ in America.
   (life)

4. _____ of Indians lived in America before the arrival of
   (Million)
   the Pilgrims.

5. Squanto taught the Pilgrims _____ to live in America.
   (skill)

6. He stayed with the Pilgrims for several _____.
   (month)

7. Indians used _____ for fertilizer.
   (fish)

8. Many Indian _____ came to celebrate with the Pilgrims.
   (family)

9. They brought five _____ and many wild _____.
   (deer)   *(turkey)*

10. The feast lasted for three _____.
    (day)

5.2 Using the Singular and Plural for Generalizations

Examples	Explanation
A child needs love. Children need love.	When we make a generalization, we say that something is true of the noun in general.
A big city has a lot of traffic. Big cities have a lot of traffic.	To make a generalization, we use a singular noun after *a* or *an*, or the plural noun with no article.

EXERCISE 4 Make a generalization about the following nouns. Use the plural form. (You may work with a partner.)

EXAMPLE: American teachers _____are very informal.____

1. American children _____

2. American colleges _____

3. Buses in this city _____

4. Elderly Americans _____

5. American cities _____

6. American doctors _____

7. American women _____

8. American men _____

EXERCISE 5 Make a generalization about these professions. Use the singular form. (You may work with a partner.)

EXAMPLE: A taxi driver _____ *has a dangerous job.* _____

1. A teacher _____

2. A doctor _____

3. A nurse _____

4. A garbage collector _____

5. A lawyer _____

6. A musician _____

7. A librarian _____

8. A movie star _____

9. An accountant _____

10. A newspaper reporter _____

5.3 Noncount Nouns

There are several types of noncount nouns:

Group A. Nouns that have no distinct, separate parts. We look at the whole.			
milk	wine	bread	electricity
oil	yogurt	meat	lightning
water	pork	butter	thunder
coffee	poultry[5]	paper	cholesterol
tea	soup	air	blood
Group B. Nouns that have parts that are too small or insignificant to count			
rice	hair	sand	
sugar	popcorn	corn	
salt	snow	grass	

(continued)

---

[5] Poultry includes domestic birds that we eat, such as chickens and turkeys.

Group C. Nouns that are classes or categories of things. The members of the category are not the same.

money or cash (nickels, dimes, dollars) fruit (cherries, apples, grapes)
food (vegetables, meat, spaghetti) makeup (lipstick, rouge, eye shadow)
furniture (chairs, tables, beds) homework (compositions, exercises, reading)
clothing (sweaters, pants, dresses) jewelry (necklaces, bracelets, rings)
mail (letters, packages, postcards, fliers)

Group D. Nouns that are abstractions

love	happiness	nutrition	music	information
life	education	intelligence	art	nature
time	experience	unemployment	work	help
truth	crime	pollution	health	noise
beauty	advice	patience	trouble	energy
luck	knowledge	poverty	fun	friendship

Group E. Subjects of study

history grammar biology
chemistry geometry math (mathematics*)

*NOTE: Even though *mathematics* ends with *s*, it is not plural.

LANGUAGE NOTES

1. We classify nouns into two groups: count nouns and noncout nouns. A count noun is something we can count. It has a singular and plural form. We can put a number before a count noun.

   one potato   five potatoes
   one apple   ten apples

2. A noncount noun is something we don't count. It has no plural form. We cannot put a number before a noncount noun. With a noncount noun, we use a unit of measure, which we can count.

   one cup of coffee   five cups of coffee

3. Count and noncount nouns are grammatical terms, but they are not always logical. Rice is very small and is a noncount noun. Beans and peas are also very small but are count nouns.

4. Some nouns can be either count or noncount. *Food* and *fruit* can be count nouns when they mean categories of food or fruit. COMPARE:

   She eats a lot of *fruit* every day. (noncount noun)
   Oranges and grapefruits are *fruits* that contain vitamin C. (count noun)
   She bought a lot of *food* for the party.
   Traditional *foods* on Thanksgiving are turkey and sweet potatoes. (count noun)
   For a list of nouns that can be count or noncount, see Appendix G.

5. When referring to whole turkeys or other birds, these words are count nouns. When referring to a part of the bird, these are noncount nouns.

The Indians brought many *turkeys* to the feast.
We eat *turkey* on Thanksgiving.

6. Some nouns that have a plural form in other languages are noncount in English. *Advice, information, knowledge, equipment, furniture,* and *homework* are always noncount nouns in English.

EXERCISE 6 Go back to the article about Indians, Pilgrims, and Thanksgiving on page 132. Mark the nouns in the article with **C** for count noun or *NC* for noncount noun.

EXAMPLES: Indians = *C*
freedom = *NC*

EXERCISE 7 Decide if the noun in parentheses ( ) is count or noncount. If it is a count noun, change it to the plural form. If it is a noncount noun, do not use the plural form.

EXAMPLE: *Education* is expensive in an American college.
(*Education*)

Besides the tuition, you have to pay for your *books* .
(*book*)

1. American Indians have a lot of respect for _____ . They
(*nature*)

love _____, _____, _____, and
(*flower*)   (*tree*)   (*bird*)

_____ .
(*fish*)

2. Thanksgiving is a celebration of _____ and _____ .
(*peace*)   (*friendship*)

3. On Thanksgiving, Americans eat a lot of _____ and sometimes
(*food*)

gain weight.

4. Squanto gave the Pilgrims a lot of _____ about planting
(*advice*)

_____ and other _____ . He had a lot of
(*corn*)   (*vegetable*)

_____ about the land.
(*knowledge*)

5. The Pilgrims didn't have any _____ with American food.
(*experience*)

6. On the first Thanksgiving, Indians brought _____,
(*meat*)

_____, _____, and _____ .
(*bean*)   (*bread*)   (*berry*)

7. The Pilgrims celebrated because they had a lot of good

_____ .
(*fortune*)

8. American Indians use _____ for _____ .
(*plant*)   (*medicine*)

9. My friends went to the Southwest last summer. They bought American Indian _____, such as _____ and
(jewelry)   (ring)

_____.
(necklace)

10. Do you have a lot of _____ about American
(information)

_____?
(holiday)

5.4 Quantities with Count and Noncount Nouns

Ways we see noncount nouns:

By container	By portion	By measurement	By shape or whole piece	Other
a bottle of water	a slice (piece) of bread	an ounce of sugar	a loaf of bread	a piece of mail
a carton of milk	a piece of meat	a quart of oil	an ear of corn	a piece of furniture
a jar of pickles	a piece of cake	a pound of meat	a piece of fruit	a piece of advice
a bag of flour	a strip of bacon	a gallon of milk	a head of lettuce	a piece of information
a can of soda (pop)	a piece (sheet) of paper	a pint of cream	a candy bar	a work of art
a cup of coffee	a slice of pizza		a roll of film	a homework assignment
a glass of water	a scoop of ice cream		a tube of toothpaste	
a bowl of soup			a bar of soap	

LANGUAGE NOTES

1. We cannot put a number before a noncount noun. With a noncount noun, we use a unit of measure, which we can count.
   one cup of coffee   five cups of coffee

2. For a list of conversions from the American system of measurement to the metric system, see Appendix D.

EXERCISE 8 Fill in the blanks with a specific quantity.

EXAMPLE: I drink three ____*glasses of*____ water a day.

1. You should take a few _____ film on your vacation.

2. I'm going to buy two _____ meat to make dinner for the family.

3. _____ milk is heavy to carry.

4. She drinks two _____ coffee every morning.

5. Buy _____ bread for dinner.

6. He eats _____ fruit a day.

7. Some Americans carry a _____ water with them.

8. I ate two _____ cake.

9. Let me give you _____ advice before you apply to colleges.

10. How many _____ gas did you buy at the gas station?

Before You Read 1. Who were the original inhabitants of your native country?
2. Are there any ethnic minorities in your native country? Do they have the respect of the majority population?

Read the following article. Pay special attention to *there* + a form of *be*.

Taking the Land from the Native Americans

Before the arrival of Europeans, **there were** between 10 and 16 million Native Americans in America. Today **there are** fewer than 2 million. What happened to these natives of America?

The friendship between the Indians and Europeans did not last for long. As more English people came to America, they did not need the help of the Indians, as the first group of Pilgrims did. The white people started to take the land away from the Indians. As Indians fought to keep their land, many of them were killed. Also, **there were** many deaths from diseases that Europeans brought to America. In 1830, President Andrew Jackson took the Indians' lands and sent them to live on reservations. Indian children had to learn English. Often they were punished for speaking their own language. As a result, **there are** very few Indians today who speak the language of their ancestors.[6]

Today **there are** about 500 tribes in the U.S., each with its own traditions. **There are** about 300 reservations, but only 22 percent of American Indians live on this land. **There is** a lot of unemployment and poverty on many reservations. As a result, many Indians move to big cities to find work. Many return to their reservations only for special celebrations such as Pow-Wows, when Indians wear their traditional clothing and dance to traditional music.

Did you know...?

Many place names in the U.S. are American Indian names. Chicago, for example, comes from an Indian word meaning smelly onion.

[6] *Ancestors* are grandparents, great-grandparents, etc.

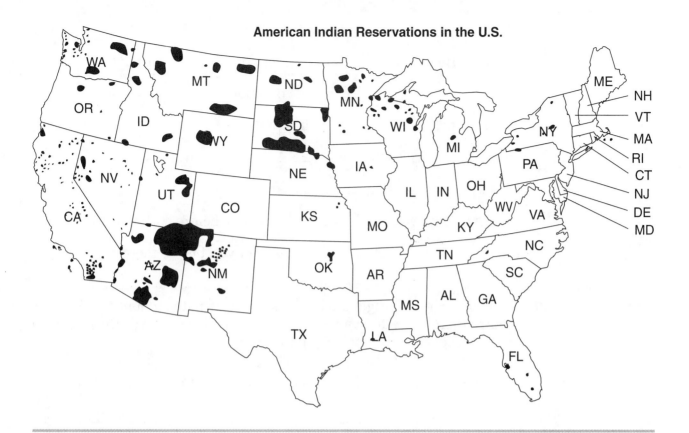

American Indian Reservations in the U.S.

5.5   *There* + A Form of *Be*

	There	*Be*	Article/Quantity	Noun	Place/Time
COUNT	There	is	a	reservation	in Wyoming.
	There	are	about 500	Indian tribes	in the U.S.
	There	are	a lot of	jobs	in a big city.
	There	will be	some	rain	tomorrow.
NONCOUNT	There	is	a lot of	unemployment	on some reservations.
	There	was		peace	at first.

LANGUAGE NOTES

1. We use *there* + a form of *be* to introduce a new noun, either count or noncount. A sentence that begins with *there* often gives a place or a time.
2. If two nouns follow *there*, use a singular verb (*is*) if the first noun is singular. Use a plural verb (*are*) if the first noun is plural.

   > There *is one* Korean student and three Mexican students in this class.

There *are three* Mexican students and one Korean student in this class.

3. In conversation, you will sometimes hear *there's* with plural nouns.
   INFORMAL: *There's* a lot of reservations in California.
   FORMAL: *There are* a lot of reservations in California.

4. After we introduce a noun with *there*, we can continue to speak of this noun with a pronoun.
   There are over 500 tribes of Native Americans in the U.S. *They* each have their own traditions.
   There is a Navajo reservation in Arizona. *It's* very big.
   There's a Navajo woman in my chemistry class. *She* comes from Arizona.

5. Observe the word order in questions with *there*.
   Is there unemployment on some reservations? Yes, there is.
   Are there any reservations in California? Yes, there are.
   How many Navajo Indians *are there* in Arizona?

6. We don't use a specific noun after *there*.
   WRONG: There's the Sears Tower in Chicago.
   RIGHT: The Sears Tower is in Chicago.
   WRONG: There's Paris in France.
   RIGHT: Paris is in France.

EXERCISE 9   Fill in the blanks with the correct form and tense.

EXAMPLE: There ___*are*___ a lot of Indians in Oklahoma.

1. There _____ a lot of reservations in California.

2. There _____ more American Indians 200 years ago than there

   _____ today.

3. In the beginning, there _____ peace between the Indians and the Pilgrims.

4. Later there _____ wars between the Indians and the white people who took their land.

5. _____ _____ enough food to eat at the first Thanksgiving? Yes, there was.

6. How many people _____ _____ at the first Thanksgiving celebration?

7. Next week there _____ _____ a test on noncount nouns.

8. How many questions _____ _____ _____ on the test?

EXAMPLE: There was a war _in my country from 1972 to 1975._

1. There will be a test _____

2. There are a lot of problems _____

3. There's a lot of snow _____

4. There are a lot of people _____

5. There is a lot of crime _____

6. There are a lot of reservations _____

7. There was a presidential election _____

8. There are a lot of students _____

9. There was a war in my country _____

5.6 Quantity Expressions—Overview

We can use quantity expressions to talk about the quantity of count and noncount nouns.

Examples
There are about **two million** American Indians today.
The Pilgrims had **very little** food during the first winter.
The American Indians had **a lot of** knowledge about the land.
The Pilgrims didn't have **much** knowledge about the land.
Many Indians died from disease.
Some Indians today live on reservations.
Very few Indians today speak their native language.

EXERCISE **11** Fill in the blanks to complete these statements.

EXAMPLE: There are 500 _____tribes_____ of American Indians in the U.S.

1. Before the arrival of the white people from Europe, there were at

    least _____ American Indians.

2. After the first cold winter in America, the Pilgrims didn't have much _____ .

3. Many Pilgrims _____ during the first winter.

4. Some _____ helped the Pilgrims.

5. The Indians taught them many _____ to help them survive.

6. The second year in America was much better. They had a lot of _____ .

7. As more white people came to America, many _____ lost their land.

8. Many Indians can't find work on their reservations. There is a lot of _____ on a reservation.

5.7 *Some, Any, A, No*

	Singular Count	Plural Count	Noncount
Affirmative	There's **a** clock in the kitchen.	There are (**some**) windows in the kitchen.	There's (**some**) rice in the kitchen.
Negative	There isn't **a** clock in the kitchen. There's **no** clock in the kitchen.	There aren't (**any**) windows in the kitchen. There are **no** windows in the kitchen.	There isn't (**any**) rice in the kitchen. There's **no** rice in the kitchen.
Question	Is there **a** clock in the kitchen?	Are there (**any**) windows in the kitchen?	Is there (**any**) rice in the kitchen?

LANGUAGE NOTES

1. We use *a* or *an* with singular count nouns.
2. We can use *some* for affirmative statements, with both noncount nouns and plural count nouns. *Some* can be omitted.
   I have *some* time.
   I have time.

3. We can use *any* for questions and negatives, with both noncount nouns and plural count nouns. *Any* can be omitted.
   Do you have *any* change?
   Do you have change?

4. *Some* can also be used in questions.
   Do you have *some* change?

5. Use an affirmative verb before *no*. COMPARE:
      There *is no* time.
      There *is no** answer to your question.
      There *isn't any* time.
      There *isn't an* answer to your question.
   **NOTE: Don't use the indefinite article after *no*.

6. You will sometimes see *any* with a singular count noun.
      Which pen should I use for the test? You can use *any* pen.
   Any, in this case, means whichever you want. It doesn't matter which pen.

EXERCISE 12 Use *there* + the words given to tell about your hometown. (If you use *no*, delete the article.) You can add a statement to give more information.

EXAMPLES: a mayor
There's a mayor in my hometown. He's a young man.

a subway
There's no subway in my hometown.

1. a university
2. a subway
3. an English language newspaper
4. an airport
5. a soccer team

6. a river
7. a jail
8. an art museum
9. an English language institute
10. a cemetery

EXERCISE 13 Fill in the blanks with *some, any, a, an,* or *no*.

EXAMPLES: I have ____*some*____ money in my pocket.

Do you have ____*any*____ time to help me?

Do you have ____*a*____ new car?

I have ____*no*____ experience as a babysitter.

1. Do you have _____ questions about this exercise?

2. Do you have _____ dictionary with you?

3. Did you have _____ trouble with the homework?

4. If we have _____ extra time, we'll go over the homework.

5. The teacher can't help you now because he has _____ time.

6. The teacher can't help you now because he doesn't have _____ time.

7. I'm confused. I need _____ answer to my question.

8. I have _____ questions about the last lesson. Can you answer them for me?

9. I understand this lesson completely. I have _____ questions.

10. I understand this lesson completely. I don't have _____ questions.

11. I work hard all day and have _____ energy late at night.

12. I don't have _____ computer.

5.8 *A Lot Of, Much, Many*

	Plural Count	Noncount
Affirmative	He has **many** friends. He has **a lot of** friends.	He has **a lot of** time.
Negative	He doesn't have **many** friends. He doesn't have **a lot of** friends.	He doesn't have **much** time. He doesn't have **a lot of** time.
Question	Does he have **many** friends? Does he have **a lot of** friends? How **many** friends does he have?	Does he have **much** time? Does he have **a lot of** time? How **much** time does he have?

LANGUAGE NOTES

1. *Much* is rare in affirmative statements. It is more common to use *a lot of* in affirmative statements.
2. In conversation, *of* is often pronounced /ə/. Listen to your teacher pronounce the above sentences.
3. When the noun is omitted, we say *a lot*, not *a lot of*.
   Do you get *a lot of* mail?
   No, I don't get *a lot*.
4. In conversation, many people say "lots of" or "plenty of" for both noncount and plural count nouns:
   He has *lots of time*. He has *plenty of friends*.

EXERCISE 14 Fill in the blanks with *much, many,* or *a lot (of).* Avoid *much* in affirmative statements. In some cases, more than one answer is possible.

EXAMPLES: You don't need _____*much*_____ time to do this exercise.

I have _____*a lot of (or many)*_____ friends.

1. Busy people don't have _____ free time.

2. Was there _____ snow last winter?

3. _____ American Indians prefer to live in big cities.

4. There's _____ crime in a big city.

5. There isn't _____ traffic in a small town.

6. There aren't _____ schools in a small town.

7. How _____ coffee do you drink in the morning?

8. I like coffee, but I don't drink _____ because it keeps me awake at night.

9. There are _____ Japanese cars in the U.S.

10. How _____ students in this class come from Korea?

5.9 *A Lot Of* vs. *Too Much/Too Many*

A lot of = Large quantity No problem is presented	*Too much/many* = Excessive quantity A problem is presented
A lot of American Indians live in Oklahoma.	My friend left the reservation because there was **too much** unemployment and she couldn't find a job.
I have **a lot of** homework.	I don't have time to talk to you. I have **too much** homework.
I have **a lot of** cousins.	I have no time to study. I have **too many** family responsibilities.

LANGUAGE NOTES

1. *A lot of* has a neutral tone. It shows a large quantity but doesn't present a problem. *Too much* or *too many* usually presents a problem or has a complaining tone.

2. Use *too much* with noncount nouns. Use *too many* with count nouns.
   I have *too much* work.
   I have *too many* responsibilities.

3. We can put *too much* at the end of a verb phrase.
   She can't buy that car because it costs *too much*.

EXERCISE 15 Use *a lot of, too much*, or *too many* to fill in the blanks in the story below. In some cases, more than one answer is possible.

Coleen Finn

My name is Coleen Finn. I'm a Ho-chunk Indian. My tribal land is in Wisconsin. But I live in Chicago because there is ___too much___ unemployment on my tribal land, and I can't find a good job there. There are _____ opportunities in Chicago, and I found a job as a
(1)
secretary in the English Department at Truman College. I like my job very much. I have _____ responsibilities and I love the challenge.
(2)

I like Chicago, but I miss my land, where I still have _____
(3)
relatives and friends. I often go back to visit them whenever I get tired of

life in Chicago. My friends and I have _____ fun together, talking,
(4)
cooking our native food, walking in nature, and attending Indian ceremonies,

such as Pow-Wows. I need to get away from Chicago once in a while to feel

closer to nature. Even though there are _____ nice things about
(5)
Chicago, there are _____ cars and trucks in the big city and
(6)
there is _____ pollution. A weekend with my tribe gives me
(7)
time to relax and smell fresh air.

EXERCISE 16 Fill in the blanks after *too* with *much* or *many*. Then complete the statement.

EXAMPLE: If I drink too ___*much*___ coffee, ___*I won't be able to sleep tonight.*___

1. If I try to memorize too _____ words, _____

2. If I make too _____ mistakes on my homework, _____

_____

3. If I spend too _____ money on clothes, _____

4. If I drink too _____ coffee, _____

5. If I spend too _____ time with my friends, _____

6. If I stay up _____ late, _____

5.10 *A Few, Several, A Little*

Count	Noncount
I have **a few** questions.	I need **a little** help.
I have **several** mistakes on my composition.	I need **a little** more time.

LANGUAGE NOTES

1. Use *a few* or *several* with count nouns.
2. Use *a little* with noncount nouns.

EXERCISE 17 Fill in the blanks with *a few, several,* or *a little.*

EXAMPLES: He has ___*a few*___ problems with his car.

He has ___*a little*___ experience as a teacher.

1. Every day we study _____ grammar.

2. We do _____ exercises in class.

3. I have _____ knowledge about computers.

4. _____ students are absent today.

5. I have _____ cash with me.

6. I have _____ dollars in my pocket.

7. I bought _____ furniture for my apartment.

8. I have _____ chairs in my living room.

9. I had _____ mistakes on my composition.

10. I need _____ help with my composition.

5.11 *A Few* vs. *Few; A Little* vs. *Little*

Positive Emphasis	Negative Emphasis
I have **a few** good friends. I'm happy.	I have **few** good friends. I'm lonely.
I have **a little** money. Let's go to the cafeteria and get something to eat.	I have **very little** money. I can't buy anything today.
There are **a few** American Indian students in my biology class.	**Few** young American Indians speak the language of their ancestors.

LANGUAGE NOTES

1. When we omit **a** before *few* and *little*, we are emphasizing the negative quantity. We are saying the quantity is not enough.

2. We often use *very few* or *very little* to emphasize a negative quantity.

3. Whether something is enough or not enough does not depend on the quantity. It depends on the perspective of the person.
   Is the glass half empty or half full?

   ☺ One person may say the glass is half full. He sees something positive about the quantity of water in the glass: The glass has *a little* water.

   ☹ Another person may say the glass is half empty. He sees something negative about the quantity of water in the glass: The glass has *(very) little* water.

EXERCISE 18 Fill in the blanks with *a little*, *very little*, *a few*, or *very few*.

EXAMPLES: He has ___a little___ extra money. He's going to buy a sandwich.

He has ___very little___ extra money. He can't buy anything.

1. I have _____ food in my refrigerator. Let's make dinner at my house.

2. In some countries, people have _____ food, and many people are starving.[7]

3. That worker has _____ experience. He probably can't do that job.

4. That worker has _____ experience. He can probably do that job.

5. I eat _____ meat every day because I want protein in my diet.

6. I want to bake cookies, but I can't because I have _____ sugar in the house.

7. When there is _____ rain, plants can't grow.

8. Tomorrow there may be _____ rain, so you should take an umbrella.

9. Twenty-five years ago, home computers were very rare. _____ people had a home computer.

10. Before I bought my computer, I talked to _____ people about which computer to buy.

11. There are _____ monkeys in the zoo. Let's go to see them.

12. There are _____ gray whales in the world. These animals are an endangered species.[8]

13. If you want to study medicine, I can give you a list of _____ good medical schools in the U.S.

whale

14. _____ high schools teach Latin. It is not a very popular language to study anymore.

15. I want to say _____ words about my country. Please listen.

16. My father is a man of _____ words. He rarely talks.

17. English is the main language of _____ countries.

18. Women are still rare as political leaders. _____ countries have a woman president.

---

[7] To *starve* means to suffer or die from not having enough food.
[8] An *endangered species* is a type of living thing that is becoming more and more rare. The species is in danger of disappearing completely if it is not protected.

EXERCISE 19 Ask question with *"Are there . . . ?"* and the words given about another student's hometown. The other student will answer with an expression of quantity. Practice count nouns.

EXAMPLE: museums
A. Are there any museums in your hometown?
B. Yes. There are a lot of (a few, three) museums in my hometown.
OR
No. There aren't any museums in my hometown.

1. department stores   6. open markets
2. churches   7. hospitals
3. synagogues   8. universities
4. skyscrapers   9. mosques
5. supermarkets   10. bridges

EXERCISE 20 Ask a question with *"Are there any . . . ?"* or *"Are there many . . . ?"* and the words given about another student's native country. The other student will answer with an expression of quantity. Practice count nouns.

EXAMPLE: single mothers
A. Are there many single mothers in your country?
B. There are very few.

1. homeless people   5. American businesses
2. working women   6. nursing homes
3. fast-food restaurants   7. rich people
4. factories   8. good universities

EXERCISE 21 Ask a question with *"Is there . . . ?"* and the words given about another student's native country. The other student will answer with an expression of quantity. Practice noncount nouns.

EXAMPLE: petroleum/in your native country
A. Is there much petroleum in your native country?
B. Yes. There's a lot of petroleum in my native country.
OR
No. There isn't much petroleum in my native country.

In Your Native Country   In Your Hometown
1. petroleum   5. traffic
2. industry   6. rain
3. agriculture   7. pollution
4. tourism   8. noise

Singular and Plural; Noncount Nouns; *There + Be*; Quantity Words   **153**

EXERCISE 22 Ask a student a question with *"Do you have . . . ?"* and the words given. The other student will answer. Practice both count and noncount nouns.

EXAMPLE: American friends
A. Do you have any American friends?
B. Yes. I have many (or a lot of) American friends.
   OR
   No. I don't have many American friends.

EXAMPLE: free time
A. Do you have a lot of free time?
B. Yes. I have some free time.
   OR
   No. I have very little free time.

1. problems in the U.S.

2. American friends

3. relatives in New York

4. time to relax

5. brothers and sisters (siblings)

6. experience with computers

7. questions about American customs

8. trouble with English pronunciation

9. information about points of interest in this city

10. knowledge about computer programming

EXERCISE 23 Cross out the phrase that doesn't fit and fill in the blanks with an expression of quantity to make a **true** statement about your native country. Discuss your answers.

EXAMPLE: ~~There's~~/There isn't ___much___ unemployment in my native country.

1. There's/There isn't _____ opportunity to make money in my native country.

2. There are/There aren't _____ divorced people in my native country.

3. There are/There aren't _____ foreigners in my native country.

4. There's/There isn't _____ freedom in my native country.

5. There are/There aren't _____ American cars in my native country.

6. There are/There aren't _____ political problems in my native country.

7. There is/There isn't _____ unemployment in my native country.

8. There is/There isn't _____ crime in my hometown.

SUMMARY OF LESSON 5

1. Study the words that we use before count and noncount nouns.

Singular Count	Plural Count	Noncount
a tomato	some tomatoes	some coffee
no tomato	no tomatoes	no coffee
	any tomatoes (with questions and negatives)	any coffee
	a lot of tomatoes	a lot of coffee
	many tomatoes	much coffee (with questions and negatives)
	a few tomatoes	a little coffee
	several tomatoes	
	How many tomatoes?	How much coffee?

2. Sentences with *There*
   Count
   > **There's a** Vietnamese student in this class.
   > **There are** some Chinese students in this class.

   Noncount
   > **There's** some rain in my hometown in the winter.
   > How much rain **is there** in the spring?

3. *Too Much/Too Many/A Lot Of*
   - *A lot of* + count or noncount noun (no problem is presented)
     > She's a healthy woman. She gets **a lot of** exercise.
     > She walks **a lot of** miles.
   - *Too much* + noncount noun (a problem is presented)
     > She doesn't qualify for financial aid because her parents make **too much** money.
   - *Too many* + count noun (a problem is presented)
     > There are **too many** students in the class. The teacher doesn't have time to help everyone.

1. Some plural forms are irregular and don't take -s.

   She has two childrens.

2. Use a singular noun and verb after *every*.

   Every ~~children~~ need^s love.

   Every ~~children~~ need love.
   (with "s" inserted above "need" and a caret under it)

3. Use the plural form after *one of*.

   One of my sister^s is a lawyer.

4. Don't use *a* or *an* before a plural noun.

   (some)
   She bought a new socks.

5. Don't put *a* or *an* before a noncount noun.

   some OR *a piece of*
   I want to give you ~~an~~ advice.

6. A noncount noun is always singular.

   a lot of
   I have ~~many~~ homeworks to do.

   pieces of
   She bought three furnitures.

7. Use *there* to introduce a noun.

   There a
   Are a lot of people in China.

8. Be careful with *there* and *they're*. They sound the same.

   There
   ~~They're~~ are many problems in the world.

9. Don't use a specific noun after *there*.

   T   *is*
   ~~There's~~ the Golden Gate bridge in San Francisco.

10. Include *of* with a unit of measure.

    of
    He bought three rolls film.

11. Omit *of* after *a lot* when the noun is omitted.

    I have a lot of time, but my brother doesn't have a lot ~~of~~.

12. Use *a little/a few* for a positive meaning. Use *little/few* for a negative meaning.

    He can't help you because he has a little time. *(very)*

13. Don't use *too much* or *too many* if the quantity doesn't present a problem.

    He's a lucky man. He has ~~too many~~ friends. *a lot of*

14. Don't use a double negative.

    He doesn't have ~~no~~ money. *any*
    or He has no money.

LESSON 5 TEST / REVIEW

PART 1   Find the mistakes with the underlined words, and correct them. Not every sentence has a mistake. If the sentence is correct, write **C**.

EXAMPLES: How ~~many~~ <u>milks</u> did you drink? *much*

    How <u>much</u> time do you have?   **C**

1. He doesn't have <u>no</u> job.

2. One of my <u>friend</u> moved to Montana.

3. I can't go out tonight because I have <u>too much</u> work.

4. Three <u>womens</u> came into the room.

5. I had a lot of friends in my country, but in the U.S. I don't have <u>a lot of</u>.

6. <u>A lot of American</u> own a computer.

7. A person can be happy if he has <u>a few</u> good friends.

8. I have <u>much</u> information about my country.

9. Every <u>workers</u> in the U.S. pays taxes.

Singular and Plural; Noncount Nouns; *There + Be*; Quantity Words   **157**

10. Are there <u>any</u> mistakes in this sentence?

11. My mother gave me a lot of <u>advices</u>.

12. You need <u>a luck</u> to win the lottery.

13. <u>There's the White House</u> in Washington, D.C.

14. I can help you on Saturday because I'll have <u>too much</u> time.

15. <u>Are</u> a lot of students in the cafeteria, and I can't find a seat.

16. A few of my <u>teacher</u> speak English very fast.

17. Did you buy <u>a new furniture</u> for your apartment?

18. Some <u>man</u> are very polite.

19. I have <u>many</u> problems with my landlord.

20. Did you have <u>much fun</u> at the party?

21. I have <u>a</u> new dishes in my kitchen.

22. Several <u>students</u> in this class speak French.

23. I have a dog. I don't have <u>any</u> cat.

24. <u>Many</u> people like to travel.

25. He doesn't need <u>any</u> help from you.

26. I have <u>a little</u> time. I can help you.

27. I have <u>a little</u> time. I can't help you.

28. He bought three <u>pounds meat</u>.

29. How <u>much</u> apples did you eat?

30. How many <u>cup of coffees</u> did you drink?

31. <u>They're are</u> four Mexican students in the class.

32. I want to give you <u>an</u> advice about your education.

Fill in the blanks with the singular or plural form of the word in parentheses ( ).

EXAMPLE: The Pilgrims didn't have a lot of ___*experience*___ with American land.
$\qquad$ *(experience)*

1.   The Indians had many _____ with white _____
$\qquad$ *(war)* $\qquad$ *(person)*
over their lands.

2.   Some _____ have a big problem with _____ and
$\qquad$ *(reservation)* $\qquad$ *(unemployment)*
_____ . There aren't enough _____ for everyone.
$\qquad$ *(poverty)* $\qquad$ *(job)*

3.   My father gave me a lot of _____ . He told me that there are
$\qquad$ *(advice)*
more _____ in big _____ than on the reservations.
$\qquad$ *(job)* $\qquad$ *(city)*

4.   We like to visit the art museum. We like to see the _____
$\qquad$ *(sculpture)*
and _____ by famous _____ . We like all kinds
$\qquad$ *(painting)* $\qquad$ *(artist)*
of _____ .
$\qquad$ *(art)*

5.   My brother likes all kinds of _____ . He has a large collection
$\qquad$ *(music)*
of _____ and _____ .
$\qquad$ *(CD)* $\qquad$ *(tape)*

PART **3**   Fill in the blanks with an appropriate measurement of quantity. In some cases, several answers are possible.

EXAMPLE: I bought a ___*loaf*___ of bread.

1.   I drank a _____ of tea.

2.   She drank a _____ of milk.

3.   I usually put a _____ of sugar in my coffee.

4.   There's a _____ of milk in the refrigerator.

5.   I'm going to buy a _____ of furniture for my living room.

6.   The teacher gave a long homework _____ .

7.   My father gave me an important _____ of advice.

8.   I took three _____ of film on my vacation.

9.   I need a _____ of paper to write my composition.

10.   We need to buy a _____ of soap.

Read this composition by an American Indian. Choose the correct words to complete the composition.

My name is Joseph Falling Snow. I'm (*an*, ⓐ, *any*) Native American from a Sioux[9] reservation in South Dakota. I don't live in South Dakota anymore because I couldn't find (*a*, *any*, *no*) job. There's (*a little*, *a few*, *very little*, *very few*) work on my reservation. There's (*much*, *a lot of*, *many*) poverty. My uncle gave me (*a*, *an*, *some*, *any*) good advice. He told me to go to Minneapolis to find (*a*, *an*, *some*) job. Minneapolis is a big city, so there are (*much*, *many*, *any*) job opportunities here. It was easy for me to find a job as a carpenter. I had (*no*, *not*, *any*) trouble finding a job because I have (*a lot of*, *many*, *much*) experience.

My native language is Lakota, but I know (*any*, *a few*, *very few*) words in my language. Most of the people on my reservation speak English. (*A few*, *Any*, *A little*) older people still speak Lakota, but the language is dying out as the older people die.

(*A few*, *A little*, *Few*, *Little*) times a year, I go back to the reservation for a Pow-Wow. We wear our native costumes and dance our native dances. It gets very crowded at these times because (*much*, *any*, *a lot of*) people from our reservation and nearby reservations attend this celebration. We have (*much*, *many*, *a lot of*) fun.

[9] *Sioux* is pronounced /su/.

CLASSROOM ACTIVITIES

1. Work with a partner. Imagine that you have to spend a few weeks alone on a deserted island. You can take 15 things with you. What will you need to survive? Give reasons for each item.

EXAMPLE:
> I'll take a lot of water because I can't drink ocean water. It has salt in it.

2. Complete the following sentence in as many ways as you can. Compare your answers with a partner or in a small group.

Happiness is _____.

EXAMPLES:
> Happiness is sleeping until ten o'clock in the morning.
> Happiness is helping an elderly person.
> Happiness is an air conditioner on a hot day.

3. Complete the following sentence in as many ways as you can. Compare your answers with a partner or in a small group.

Life is _____.

EXAMPLES:
> Life is too short.
> Life is a gift.

4. Game: Where am I? Teacher: Write these words on separate index cards: at the airport, downtown, at the library, at a supermarket, at a department store, on the highway, at the zoo, at church, at the beach, at home, on an elevator, on a bus, on an airplane, at the post office, in the school cafeteria. Students: One student picks an index card with a place name and says, "Where am I?" Other students have to guess where he/she is by asking questions.

EXAMPLES:
> Are you indoors or outdoors?
> Are there a lot of cars in this place?
> Is it noisy in this place?
> Are there a lot of people in this place?

5. Find a partner. Take something from your purse, pocket, book bag, or backpack. Say, "I have _____ with me." Then ask your partner if he or she has this. If you're not sure if the item is a count or noncount noun, ask the teacher.

EXAMPLES:
> I have a comb in my pocket. Do you have a comb in your pocket?
> I have some makeup in my purse. Do you have any makeup in your purse?
> I have some money from my country in my pocket. Do you have any money from your country?

DISCUSSION

Read the following quotes and discuss what they mean to you.

1. Once I was in a big city and I saw a very large house. They told me it was a bank and that the white men place their money there to be taken care of, and that by and by they got it back with interest. We are Indians and we have no such bank. When we have plenty of money or blankets, we give them away to other chiefs and people, and by and by they return them with interest, and our hearts feel good. Our way of giving is our bank.

   —Chief Maquinna, Nootka tribe

2. Treat the earth well. It was not given to you by your parents; it was loaned to you by your children.

3. "Today is a time of celebrating for you—a time of looking back to the first days of white people in America. But it is not a time of celebrating for me. It is with a heavy heart that I look back upon what happened to my people. When the Pilgrims arrived, we, the Wampanoags, welcomed them with open arms, little knowing that it was the beginning of the end. . . . Let us always remember, the Indian is and was just as human as the white people." From a speech by a Wampanoag Indian given on Thanksgiving in 1970 in Massachusetts, at the 350th anniversary of the Pilgrim's arrival in America.

WRITING

1. Write about an ethnic minority in your native country. Where and how do they live? Use expressions of quantity.

2. Write a paragraph telling about the advantages or disadvantages of living in this city. You may write about pollution, job opportunities, weather, traffic, transportation, and crime. Use expressions of quantity.

Internet Activities

1. Search for American Indian Web sites. Find the names and locations of three tribes.

2. Search for more information about the Pilgrims. Why did they leave England? Where did they go before coming to America?

GRAMMAR
Adjectives
Noun Modifiers
Adverbs
Too and *Enough*

CONTEXT
Exercise, Diet, and Weight
Overweight Children

LESSON FOCUS

An adjective describes a noun.
> I ate an *excellent* dinner.

A noun can also describe a noun.
> I need a *soup* spoon.

An adverb describes a verb (phrase).
> They prepared the dinner *lovingly*.

We can use *too* and *enough* with adjectives, adverbs, and nouns.
> The soup is *too* hot to eat.
> The soup has *too* much salt.
> I don't have *enough* time to prepare dinner.

Read the following article. Pay special attention to adjectives, noun modifiers, and adverbs.

Exercise, Diet, and Weight

Americans are **concerned** about their weight. Everyone knows that it's important to eat **well** and exercise **regularly**. We see **beautiful, thin** fashion models and want to look like them. We see commercials for **exercise** machines showing **fit, thin** people exercising. **Health** clubs are full of people trying to get in shape. Sales of **diet** colas and low-calorie foods indicate that Americans want to be **thin**. However, 50 percent of Americans are **overweight**. Why is this so?

First, today's lifestyle does not include enough **physical** activity. When the U.S. was an agricultural society, farmers ate a **big, heavy** meal, but they burned off the calories by doing **hard physical** labor. Today, most people don't get enough exercise. Instead of walking, Americans drive almost everywhere, even when the trip is close to home. When people get home from work, they're usually too **tired** to exercise **regularly**. After dinner, they just watch TV. They have no chance to burn off calories.

Another reason why Americans don't lose weight is that they eat **poorly**. They are influenced by commercials and ads for **fatty** foods, **soft** drinks, candy, and **sugary** cereals that look **good**. Even though most people know that these foods aren't **healthy**, many don't have enough time to eat a **well-balanced** diet. It's **easy** to stop at a **fast-food** restaurant to pick up a **greasy** burger and fries. These foods are **high** in fat, carbohydrates, sodium, and calories. People eat them **quickly** and in **large** quantities—triple burgers, **extra-large** colas, **large** orders of fries.

Eating a high-fat diet and not getting enough exercise will result in **heart** disease for many people.

Did you know...?

Thirty-five percent of the money Americans spend on food is spent outside the home.

Examples	Explanation
We ate a **big** meal. I don't like to eat **fatty** foods.	An adjective describes a noun. An adjective can come before a noun.
Fast food is **inexpensive**. Models are **thin**. You look **healthy**. Burgers taste **delicious**.	An adjective can come after the verb *be* and the sense-perception verbs: *look, seem, sound, smell, taste, feel*.
Are you **concerned** about your weight? I'm **tired** after work. The health club is **located** near my house.	Some *-ed* words are adjectives: *tired, worried, crowded, located, married, divorced, excited, disappointed, finished, frightened*.
He did exercises and got **tired**. I ran for three miles and got **thirsty**. If you eat too much candy, you're going to **get** sick.	An adjective can follow *get* in these expressions: *get tired, get worried, get hungry, get sleepy, get thirsty, get married, get divorced, get sick, get angry*. In these expressions, *get* means *become*.

LANGUAGE NOTES

1.   We do not make adjectives plural.
     a *thin* model   *thin* models
     a *big* glass   *big* glasses

2.   *Very*, *quite*, and *extremely* can come before adjectives.
     You are *very* healthy.
     They are *extremely* tired.

3.   Conversational words that come before adjectives are *pretty, sort of, kind of,* and *real.*
     I was *kind of* tired after work.
     We had a *real* delicious meal.
     I had a *pretty* hard day.

4.   After an adjective, we can substitute a singular noun with *one* and a plural noun with *ones.*
     Do you want a big pizza or a small *one*?
     The first lessons were easy. The last *ones* are hard.

EXERCISE 1   Fill in the blanks with an appropriate word.

EXAMPLE: Burgers and fries are _____*high*_____ in calories.

1. Fries are cooked in oil. They are very _____.

2. I ate a terrible meal and I got _____.

3. Do you want a large cola or a small _____?

4. She's very _____ about her children's health because they prefer candy to fruit.

5. I didn't sleep at all last night. I'm very _____ today.

6. Have a piece of fresh apple pie. I just had a piece. It _____ good.

EXERCISE 2   Find the mistakes with the underlined words and correct them. Not every sentence has a mistake. If the sentence is correct, write C.

EXAMPLE: I'm very <u>excite</u> about my trip to Italy.   *excited*

He <u>got sleepy</u> while he was driving and had to stop.   C

1. I didn't get enough sleep last night and I'm very <u>tire</u> today.

2. She has two <u>wonderfuls</u> children and a <u>great</u> husband.

3. This T-shirt is too small for me. I need a <u>big</u>.

4. This turkey sandwich tastes <u>quite good</u>.

5. When did you <u>get marry</u>?

6. The park was very <u>crowded</u>.

7. The park <u>located</u> near the lake.

8. You look <u>beautiful</u> today.

Examples	Explanation
Do you have an **exercise machine**? A **farm worker** gets a lot of exercise. Some people eat at a **fast-food restaurant**. I joined a **health club**.	A noun can modify (describe) another noun. The second noun is more general than the first. An exercise machine is a machine. A leg exercise is an exercise.
I bought new **running** shoes. Do you ever use the **swimming** pool?	Sometimes a gerund describes a noun. It shows the purpose of the noun.
My five-year-**old** son prefers candy to fruit. **Potato** chips have a lot of grease. My new shoes are in the **shoe** box.	The first noun is always singular. A five-year-old son is a son who is five **years** old.
Do you have your **driver's** license? I can't understand the **owner's** manual for my new VCR.	Sometimes a possessive form describes a noun.

LANGUAGE NOTES

When a noun describes a noun, the first noun usually receives the greater emphasis in speaking. Listen to your teacher pronounce the following:

I wear my *running* shoes when I go to the *health* club and use the *exercise* machines.

EXERCISE 3 Fill in the blanks by putting the words in parentheses ( ) in the correct order. Remember to remove the *s* from plural noun modifiers.

EXAMPLES: People need a ___*winter coat*___ in December.
(coat/winter)

He bought a ___*beautiful car.*___
(beautiful/car)

1. In the supermarket, we put our things in a _____
(cart/shopping)

2. I need a _____ to stir my tea.
(tea/spoon)

3. To fry eggs, you need a _____
(pan/frying)

4. A _____ drives a taxi.
(taxi/driver)

5. The school is closed during _____.
   (spring/break)

6. She took a _____.
   (vacation/very/long)

7. A _____ has a _____.
   (factory/worker) *(hard/job)*

8. Many _____ use robots.
   (factories/automobiles)

9. _____ buy their _____ at the _____.
   (college/students) *(books/text)* *(store/books)*

10. I had a _____ with my boss.
    (meeting/pretty/long)

11. Some people prefer to shop in a _____ store.
    (food/health)

12. Does your building have a _____?
    (swimming/pool)

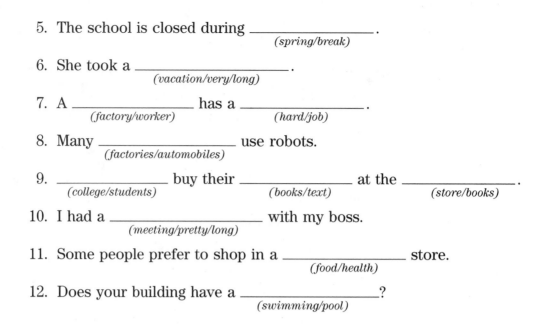

6.3   Adverbs of Manner

Examples	Explanation
I choose my food **carefully**. Some people eat **poorly**.	An adverb of manner tells how or in what way a person does something. We form most adverbs of manner by putting *-ly* at the end of an adjective.
Do you eat **well**?	The adverb for *good* is *well*.
He worked **hard** and came home **late**. Don't eat so **fast**.	Some adverbs of manner do not end in *-ly*. The adjective and adverb are the same.

LANGUAGE NOTES

1. Some adjectives end in *-ly: lovely, early, friendly, lively, ugly, lonely*. They have no adverb form. We use an adverbial phrase to describe the action.

    She is a friendly person.
    She behaves *in a friendly manner*.
    He is a lively person.
    He danced *in a lively way*.

2. *Hard* and *hardly* are both adverbs, but they have completely different meanings.

    He worked very *hard*. = He put a lot of effort into his work.
    He *hardly* worked. = He did very little work.

3. *Late* and *lately* are both adverbs, but they have completely different meanings.
> He came home *late*. He missed dinner.
> *Lately*, he never comes home on time. (*Lately* means "recently.")

4. An adverb of manner usually follows the verb phrase.
> She ate her lunch *quickly*.
> You speak English *well*.

5. *Very*, *extremely*, and *quite* can come before an adverb.
> They work *very slowly*.
> She drives *extremely well*.
> You speak English *quite fluently*.

EXERCISE 4   Write the adverb form of the word in parentheses ( ). Then check (√) the activities that you do in this way. Make statements telling how you do these activities.

EXAMPLES: √ shop ___carefully___
                          (careful)

I shop carefully. I always try to buy healthy food for my family.

____ dance ___well___
                (good)

I don't dance well. I never learned.

1. ____ answer every question _____
                                    (honest)

2. ____ drive _____
              (fast)

3. ____ cook _____
              (good)

4. ____ talk _____
              (constant)

5. ____ work _____
              (hard)

6. ____ study _____
               (hard)

7. ____ speak Spanish _____
                       (fluent)

8. ____ type _____
              (fast)

9. ____ type _____
              (accurate)

10. ____ choose my food _____
                          (careful)

---

11. ____ live _____
    (dangerous)

12. ____ love _____
    (passionate)

13. ____ meditate _____
    (quiet)

14. ____ sleep _____
    (sound¹)

15. ____ learned a second language _____
    (easy)

16. ____ lived _____ in my country
    (comfortable)

Adjective vs. Adverb

Adjective	Adverb
Jim looks **serious**. (*Serious* describes Jim.)	Jim is looking at his mistakes **seriously**. (*Seriously* tells how he is looking at his mistakes.)
The music sounds **good**. (*Good* describes the music.)	The singer sings **well**. (*Well* describes the singing.)
Your composition looks **good**. (*Good* describes the composition.)	You wrote it **well**. (*Well* describes how you wrote it.)
My father got **angry**. (*Angry* describes my father.)	He spoke **angrily** to his children. (*Angrily* tells how he spoke.)

LANGUAGE NOTES

1. An adjective describes a noun. An adverb describes a verb (phrase).
2. Use an adjective after the following verbs if you are describing the subject. Use an adverb if you are telling how the action (the verb) is done:

    smell   sound   seem   feel

    taste   look   appear

    She looks *happy*.
    She is looking at the contract *carefully*.

3. Use an adjective, not an adverb, in expressions with *get*.
    He got *sleepy* after drinking a glass of warm milk.
    He got *hungry* after working all morning.

¹ When a person sleeps *soundly*, she doesn't wake up easily.

4. For health, use *well*.
>He's sick. He doesn't look *well* today.
>In conversational English, people often use *good* for health.
>>He's sick. He doesn't look *good* today.

5. Use the adjective, not the adverb, in the expression *as usual*.
   COMPARE:
>>As *usual*, he worked last Saturday.
>>He *usually* works on Saturday.

6. An adverb can come before an adjective in phrases such as these:

completely right	extremely important	pleasantly surprised
well known	perfectly clear	absolutely wrong

EXERCISE 5 Fill in the blanks with the correct form of the word—adjective or adverb.

Last week I had my first job interview in the U.S. I wanted to do ___*well*___. A _____ (1 good) friend of mine told me about a résumé service. He told me that this service helps you prepare your résumé _____ (2 careful). I wanted my résumé to look _____ (3 professional). I never wrote a résumé before, so I used this service. I wanted to have a _____ (4 perfect) résumé.

A few days before the interview, I worked very _____ (5 hard) to prepare answers to possible questions. The night before the interview, I chose my clothes _____ (6 careful) and ironed them. I wanted to appear _____ (7 neat). My friend told me that it's best to look _____ (8 conservative), so I chose my dark-blue suit. I went to bed _____ (9 early), as _____ (10 usual), but I didn't sleep _____ (11 good) because I was _____ (12 extreme/nervous).

The interview was _____ (13 difficult) because I had trouble answering many of the questions. The interviewer was _____ (14 friendly), but she didn't speak _____ (15 clear). I couldn't understand her pronunciation. I could _____ (16 hard) understand some of the questions.

I probably won't get this job. But it was _____ (17 good) practice to have this interview. It prepared me _____ (18 good) for the next interview.

Read the following article. Pay special attention to *too* and *enough*.

Overweight Children

In the United States, at least one in five children is overweight. Over the past 20 years, this number has increased by more than 50 percent. Why are so many children overweight?

First, many children don't get **enough** physical exercise. Only one-third of children who live within a mile of their school walk to school. When children get home from school, they spend **too much** time watching TV and playing video games. The average American child spends 24 hours a week watching TV. In addition, many children have unhealthy eating habits. Children eat **too much** food that is high in calories and fat. Eight percent of the calories children take in are from sodas.

Genetics is also a factor. Children with overweight parents may be at risk for becoming overweight. However, if families develop good eating and exercise habits early, they can prevent their children from becoming overweight.

6.5 *Too* and *Enough*

Too + Adjective/Adverb *Too* + *Much/Many* + Noun	Adjective/Adverb + *Enough*	*Enough* + Noun
I'm **too tired** to exercise. It's never **too late** to change your habits. Children eat **too much food** that is high in calories. They spend **too many hours** in front of the TV.	A diet of colas and burgers is not **good enough**. I walked **quickly enough** to raise my heart rate.	Children don't get **enough exercise**. I don't have **enough time** to exercise.

LANGUAGE NOTES

1. *Too* indicates a problem. The problem is stated or implied.

2. Put *too* before the adjective or adverb: *too old, too tired, too slowly, too dangerously.*

3. Use *too much* before noncount nouns. Use *too many* before count nouns.
too much time	*too many calories*
too much grease	*too many sodas*

4. *Too much* can come at the end of the sentence.
   He got sick because he ate *too much.*

5. Put *enough* after the adjective or adverb. Put *enough* before the noun.
   old enough, tall enough, slowly enough
   enough money, enough time, enough books

6. An infinitive phrase can follow a phrase with *too* and *enough.*
   He's too young *to understand* life.
   You're old enough *to drive.*

7. *Too good to be true* shows a positive surprised reaction.
   I just won a million dollars. It's *too good to be true.*

EXERCISE 6   Fill in the blanks to complete these statements.

EXAMPLE: People drive everywhere. They don't _____*walk*_____ enough.

    1. Children eat too _____, so they get fat.

    2. Children shouldn't drink so much soda because it contains too many

      _____ .

---

3. Most Americans don't get enough _____ .

4. Many people say, "I don't have enough _____ to do all the things I need to do."

5. Some students have too _____ responsibilities and can't handle all of them.

6. _____ takes too much time, so I rarely do it.

7. _____ costs too much, so I don't have one.

8. It's never too _____ to change your bad habits.

9. His clothes don't fit him anymore because he got too

   _____ .

10. You're never too old to _____ .

EXERCISE 7 Read the conversation between a husband (H) and a wife (W). Fill in the blanks with *too* or *enough* plus the word in parentheses ( ).

H. I'm tired of my job. Let's retire and go live in Hawaii.

W. But we're only 57 years old. We're ___*too young*___ to retire.
    (young)

H. I'd like to buy a very big house with a swimming pool.

W. But our house is _____ for us. Besides, we don't have
    (1 big)

   _____ for a bigger house.
   (2 money)

H. And I'd like to travel around the world.

W. But that's _____ .
    (3 expensive)

H. And I'd like our daughter to go with us.

W. She's 23 years old! She's _____ to make her own decisions.
    (4 old)

H. And I'd like to spend the next 50 years on a sailboat.

W. The next 50 years? You're kidding! We don't have _____ .
    (5 time)
   We're already 57 years old!

H. I'm just dreaming. You take me _____ .
    (6 seriously)

EXERCISE 8 Complete each statement with an infinitive.

EXAMPLES: I'm too young ___*to retire*___.

I'm not strong enough ___*to move a piano.*___.

1. I'm not too old _____.

2. I'm too young _____.

3. I'm not tall enough _____.

4. I have enough money _____.

5. I don't have enough time _____.

6. I don't speak English well enough _____.

EXERCISE 9 Use the words given to write questions to ask another student. The other student will answer.

EXAMPLES: old enough

Are you old enough to retire soon?

too tired

Are you too tired to do the homework?

1. too busy _____

2. too hard _____

3. enough time _____

4. strong enough _____

5. enough experience _____

EXERCISE 10 Fill in the blanks with *too, too much*, or *too many*. A person is complaining about the big city where she lives.

EXAMPLE: This city has ___*too much*___ crime.

1. It's _____ noisy.

2. It's _____ dirty.

3. There are _____ people.

4. There's _____ traffic.

5. There's _____ unemployment.

6. There's _____ pollution.

7. It's _____ big.

8. Life is _____ fast.

9. There are _____ problems.

10. Apartments are _____ expensive.

Subject	Verb	*Very/Too*	Adjective/Adverb
My grandmother	is	**very**	old, but she's in great health.
My 14-year-old brother	is	**too**	old to get into the movie theater at half price.
I	was	**very**	tired, but I went to work.
I	was	**too**	tired to exercise after work.
She	drives	**very**	slowly.
She	drives	**too**	slowly for highway traffic. She might get a ticket.

LANGUAGE NOTES

Don't confuse *very* and *too*. *Too* always indicates a problem in a specific situation. The problem can be stated or implied. *Very* is a neutral word.

EXERCISE 11 Fill in the blanks with *too* or *very*.

EXAMPLES: My sister is ___*very*___ beautiful.

I'm ___*too*___ short to touch the ceiling.

1. My grandfather is in _____ good health. He runs five miles a day.

2. I'm _____ sick to go to work today. I'll just stay in bed.

3. I can't believe I won first prize. It's _____ good to be true!

4. She found a great job. She's _____ happy.

5. She should be in an easier English class. This class is _____ hard for her.

6. That meal was delicious. You're a _____ good cook.

7. He is a _____ good person. He always helps his friends and neighbors.

8. My son is only six years old. He's _____ young to stay home alone.

9. Yesterday I saw a _____ beautiful sunset.

10. I can't reach those boxes on that shelf. It's _____ high for me.

1. Adjectives and Adverbs

ADJECTIVES	ADVERBS
She has a **beautiful** voice.	She sings **beautifully**.
She has a **late** class.	She arrived **late**.
She is a **good** driver.	She drives **well**.
She looks **serious**.	She looked at the contract **seriously**.
As **usual**, she woke up early.	She **usually** wakes up early.

2. Adjective Modifiers and Noun Modifiers

ADJECTIVE MODIFIER	NOUN MODIFIER
a **new** machine	an **exercise** machine
old shoes	**running** shoes
a **short** vacation	a **two-week** vacation
a **valid** license	a **driver's** license

3. *Very/Too/Enough/Too Much/Too Many*

He's **very** healthy.
He's **too** young to retire.
You're old **enough** to understand life.
I have **enough** money to take a vacation.
I can't go to the movies with you. I have **too much** homework.
She doesn't eat ice cream because it has **too many** calories.
One of my neighbors bothers me because she talks **too much**.

EDITING ADVICE

1. Adjectives are always singular.

   I had two importants meetings last week.

2. Certain adjectives end with *-ed*.

   He was tire*d* after his trip.

3. Put an adjective before the noun.

   She is a *very intelligent girl* ~~girl very intelligent~~.

4. Use *one(s)* after an adjective to take the place of a noun.

   He has an old dictionary. She has a new *one*.

---

5. Put a specific noun before a general noun.

   She made a ~~call phone~~. [*phone call*]

6. A noun modifier is always singular.

   She took a three-weeks vacation.

7. An adverb describes a verb. An adjective describes a noun.

   The teacher speaks English fluent. [*ly*]

   The teacher looks ~~seriously~~.

8. Don't put the *-ly* adverb between the verb and the object.

   He opened (carefully) the envelope.

9. Adverbs of manner that don't end in *-ly* follow the verb phrase.

   He (late) came home.

10. *Too* indicates a problem. If there is no problem, use *very*.

    Your father is ~~too~~ intelligent. [*very*]

11. *Too much/too many* is followed by a noun. *Too* is followed by an adjective or adverb.

    She's too ~~much~~ old to take care of herself.

12. Put *enough* after the adjective.

    He's ~~enough old~~ to get married. [*old enough*]

13. Don't use *very* before a verb.

    He ~~very~~ likes his job. [*very much*]

14. Don't confuse *hard* and *hardly*.

    I'm tired. I worked ~~hardly~~ all day.

PART 1

Find the mistakes with the underlined words, and correct them. Not every sentence has a mistake. If the sentence is correct, write C.

EXAMPLES: When did you get your ~~license~~ driver's? *license*

He gets up early and walks the dog.   C

1. Do you know where I can find the shoes department in this store?

2. She doesn't feel well today.

3. The language English is very different from my language.

4. I'm very tire because I worked hard all week.

5. Your answer seems wrongly.

6. My grandfather is too much old to work.

7. I don't like red apples. I like yellows ones.

8. The singer's voice sounds sweet.

9. I wrote carefully my name.

10. She bought a car very expensive.

11. I'm too happy to meet you.

12. He stayed in the library late to finish his class project.

13. She looked beautiful when she got marry.

14. You speak English very fluently.

15. He's not old enough to work.

16. I like your new shoes very much.

17. He hardly speaks a word of English. He just came to the U.S.

18. She's going to take her driving test. She looks nervously.

19. I'm completely surprised by the news of your marriage.

20. I very like your new apartment.

21. If you spend <u>too much</u> time in front of the TV, you'll get fat.

22. You have <u>too many</u> friends. You're a lucky person.

PART **2**   Fill in the blanks with the correct form, adjective or adverb, of the word in parentheses ( ).

EXAMPLES: She has ___*clear*___ pronunciation. She pronounces very ___*clearly*___ .
                            (clear)   *(clear)*

1. You need to find time to eat _____ . Don't eat food that is
                                       (good)

    _____ for you.
      (bad)

2. Don't drive _____ . It's important to arrive _____ .
                (fast)   *(safe)*

3. I can't understand you. Could you speak more _____ , please?
                                            (slow)

4. Some people learn languages _____ .
                                (easy)

5. Some people think that math is _____ , but it's
                                      (hard)

    _____ for me.
      (easy)

6. As _____ , we will have a test at the end of the lesson.
          (usual)

7. She spoke _____ , and I couldn't hear her _____ .
               (soft)   *(good)*

8. I need to learn English _____ .
                           (quick)

9. Do you exercise _____ or are you _____ ?
                     (regular)   *(lazy)*

10. You seem _____ today.
                (tired)

11. I'm very _____ .
          (busy)

12. She works very _____ , but she's _____ with her job.
                (hard)   *(happy)*

13. She is a _____ woman. She's very _____ .
                (lovely)   *(friendly)*

14. John sounds _____ , but he's not angry. He just talks
                    (angry)

    _____ .
      (loud)

15. You speak English _____ well. You have _____
                        (extreme)   *(perfect)*

    pronunciation. Everything you say is _____ _____ .
                                        (absolute)   *(clear)*

EXPANSION ACTIVITIES

CLASSROOM ACTIVITIES

1. Make a list of things that you ate in your native country that you don't eat in the U.S. Make a list of things that you eat in the U.S. that you didn't eat in your native country. Form a small group and compare your lists.

Things I eat in the U.S. that I didn't eat before:	Things I ate in my native country that I don't eat now:

2. Make a list of lifestyle changes for you and your family in the U.S. Find a partner from a different country, if possible. Compare your lists with your partner's lists. Which of these activities affect your health?

Things I do (or don't do) in the U.S.:	Things I did (or didn't do) in my native country:
EXAMPLES:	EXAMPLES:
I watch TV more often.	I hardly ever watched TV.
I shop once a week.	I shopped almost every day.
My children play with video games.	My children usually played outside.

3. Bad habits. Make a list of bad habits that you or someone in your family has.

EXAMPLES: I don't get enough exercise.
My daughter talks on the phone too much.

4. Game: One student thinks of the name of a food. Other students try to guess what it is by asking questions.

Sample questions:
Is it a fruit?
Is it soft?
Do people eat it for breakfast?
Is it good for your health?

5. Take something from your purse, pocket, or bag, but don't show it to anyone. Describe it. Another student will try to guess what it is.

6. Game: "In the manner of"
Teacher: Write these adverbs on separate pieces of paper or on index cards: gladly, suddenly, slowly, comfortably, simply, steadily, foolishly, efficiently, accurately, quietly, surprisingly, excitedly, promptly, fearlessly, fearfully, indecisively, carefully, carelessly, neatly, smoothly, repeatedly. Make sure the students know the meaning of each of these adverbs. Ask one student to leave the room. The other students pick one adverb. When the student returns to the room, he/she asks individuals to do something by giving imperatives. The others do this task in the manner of the adverb that was chosen. The student tries to guess the adverb.

EXAMPLES:
Edgar, write your name on the blackboard.
Sofia, take off one shoe.
Maria, open the door.
Elsa, walk around the room.
Nora, give me your book.

7. In some colleges, students evaluate teachers. Work with a partner and write an evaluation form for teachers at this college or for another profession you are familiar with.

EXAMPLES:

	Strongly Agree	Agree	Disagree	Strongly Disagree
1. Begins class promptly.				
2. Treats students with respect.				
3. Explains assignments clearly.				

1. In a small group or with the entire class, discuss what kind of food you usually eat. Do you think people eat healthful food in your native culture?

2. Americans often say, "You are what you eat." What do you think this means?

1. Think of a place in this city (a museum, a government office, a park, a shopping center, the airport, etc.). Write a brief description of this place.

2. Write a paragraph about your hometown (or a specific place in your hometown). Use descriptions.

3. Write a short composition comparing food in your native country to food in the U.S.

4. Write a short composition telling how your eating and exercise habits are different in the U.S.

Internet Activities

1. In a search engine, type in "food guide pyramid" to see what the U.S. Department of Agriculture recommends as a healthy daily diet. Or you can find the pyramid and more information about food by going to the U.S. Department of Agriculture Web site. Fill out the form called "How to Rate Your Diet." Bring a copy of the pyramid to class.

2. At a search engine, type in "height weight." Find a copy of a height/weight chart. Print it. See if you are the right weight for your height.

3. Find a conversion chart from the metric system to the English system. See how much you weigh in pounds.

Lesson Seven

GRAMMAR
Time Words and Time Clauses
The Past Continuous Tense

CONTEXT
Ellis Island
Albert Einstein

LESSON FOCUS
We use time words to introduce words and clauses of time.

> I studied German *for* ten years.
> I studied German *when* I lived in my country.

We use the past continuous tense to show the relationship of a longer past action to a shorter past action.

> She *was driving* to work when she had a flat tire.
> I *was climbing* a tree when I fell and broke my arm.

Ellis Island, New York

1. Are you the first member of your family to come to the U.S.?
2. How did you or your family come to the U.S.?
3. Was the process of entering the country difficult for you? How was it difficult?

Read the following article. Pay special attention to time words.

Ellis Island

For many years, Ellis Island, an island in New York harbor, was the main door through which millions of immigrants entered the United States. **From** the time it opened **in** 1892 **until** the time it closed **in** 1924, the U.S. Bureau of Immigration used Ellis Island to receive and process new arrivals. **During** this time, 12 million foreigners passed through this door with the hope of becoming Americans. They came from Italy, Poland, Russia, Germany, China, and many other countries. Sometimes more than 10,000 people passed through the registry room in one 24-hour period. New arrivals often waited **for** many hours **while** inspectors checked to see if they met legal and medical standards. Most did not speak English, and they were tired, hungry, and confused. Two percent (250,000 people) did not meet the requirements to enter the U.S. and had to return to their countries.

After Congress passed an immigration law that limited the number and nationality of new immigrants, immigration slowed down and Ellis Island was closed as an immigration processing center. It remained abandoned **until** 1965, **when** President Lyndon Johnson decided to restore it as a monument. Restoration of Ellis Island was finished **by** 1990. Now visitors to this monument can see the building as it looked **from** 1918 **to** 1920. In addition, they can see a wall with the names of many of those who passed through on their way to becoming American citizens.

Did you know...?

The largest number of immigrants in the U.S. between 1820 and 1996 came from Germany. The largest number between 1991 and 1996 came from Mexico.

7.1 *When, While, Until*

Examples	Explanation
When my grandfather arrived, he passed through Ellis Island. **Until** he came to the U.S., he lived in Poland. Ellis Island was closed **until** 1990. **When** it opened, visitors could see the history of immigration.	*When* means "at that time" or "after that time." *Until* means "before that time."

(continued)

Examples	Explanation
New arrivals waited **while** inspectors checked their documents. **While** they waited, they were often tired, confused, and hungry.	*While* means "during that time."

LANGUAGE NOTES

We can sometimes use *when* in place of *while*.

> *While* (or *when*) he was on the ship coming to America, he thought about his uncertain future.
>
> *While* (or *when*) I was in Paris, I studied French.

EXERCISE 1   Fill in the blanks with *when, while,* or *until.* In some cases, more than one answer is possible.

EXAMPLE: My grandfather came to the U.S. ___*when*___ he was 25 years old.

1. _____ he lived in Poland, he had a hard life.

2. _____ he left Poland, he didn't speak English at all.

3. _____ he was at Ellis Island, he had to wait for hours. He was

    nervous _____ he waited.

4. He was nervous _____ he got permission to enter the country. Then he felt more relaxed.

5. _____ he passed the inspection, he entered the country.

6. In Poland, he didn't study English. He didn't speak a word of English

    _____ he started to work in the U.S. Then he learned a little.

7. _____ he worked, he saved money to bring his wife and children to America.

8. My grandmother couldn't come to the U.S. _____ my grandfather had enough money to send for her and their children.

9. My grandfather lived in the U.S. _____ he died in 1968.

EXERCISE 2   Add a main clause to complete each statement.

EXAMPLE: Before I got to class today, ___*I finished all my homework.*___

1. While I was in high school, _____
2. When I finished high school, _____
3. When I left my country, _____
4. Until I came to this city/school, _____
5. When I arrived in the U.S., _____
6. Until I came to America, _____

EXERCISE 3   Finish the time expression to complete each statement.

EXAMPLE: I stayed in my country until ___*a civil war broke out.*___

1. I decided to come to the U.S. when _____
2. I found my apartment/house after _____
3. I enrolled in this English class after _____
4. I didn't understand English until _____
5. I got married/found a job/bought a car (*choose one*) when _____
_____

EXERCISE 4   Name something you never . . . until you came to the U.S.

EXAMPLE: Name something you never had.
I never had a car until I came to the U.S.

1. Name something you never did.
2. Name something or someone you never heard of.
3. Name something you never saw.
4. Name something you never thought about.
5. Name something you never had.
6. Name something you never ate.
7. Name something you never knew.

7.2   *When* and *Whenever*

Examples	Explanation
When she read the book, she learned a lot about American history.	*When* means "at that time" or "after that time."
Whenever she reads, she uses glasses.	*Whenever* means any time or every time.

LANGUAGE NOTES

With the general present, *when* and *whenever* have about the same meaning.

> *Whenever* I have free time, I like to play tennis.
> *When* I have free time, I like to play tennis.

EXERCISE 5   Add a main clause to complete each statement. Use the general present.

EXAMPLE: Whenever I take a test, ___*I feel nervous.*___

1. Whenever I feel sad or lonely, _____

2. Whenever I get angry, _____

3. Whenever I need advice, _____

4. Whenever I receive a present, _____

5. Whenever I get a letter from my family, _____

6. Whenever I'm sick, _____

7. Whenever the weather is bad, _____

8. Whenever the teacher explains the grammar, _____

_____

EXERCISE 6   Finish each sentence with a time clause.

EXAMPLES: I feel nervous ___*before I take a test.*___

I feel nervous ___*whenever I have to speak in class.*___

1. I feel relaxed _____

2. I get angry _____

3. I get bored _____

4. I can't concentrate _____

5. I'm happy _____

6. I'm in a bad mood _____

7. I sometimes daydream[1] _____

8. Time passes quickly for me _____

[1] To *daydream* means to dream while you are awake. Your mind does not stay in the present moment.

Time Word	Examples	Explanation
for	My grandfather waited at Ellis Island **for** many hours.	*For* tells how long.
in	Ellis Island closed **in** 1924. I'll go back to my country **in** two years. He finished the test **in** ten minutes.	Use *in* with a specific year or month. Use *in* to mean after or within a period of time.
during	He thought about his future **during** his trip to the U.S. **During** his interview, he answered many questions.	Use *during* with an activity.
by	Restoration of Ellis Island was finished **by** 1990. Please finish the test **by** 8:30.	*By* means no later than.
ago	One hundred years **ago**, new arrivals passed through Ellis Island.	*Ago* means before now.

LANGUAGE NOTES

1. Compare *before* and *ago*.
   She got married *before* she graduated.
   She got married three years *ago*.

2. Compare *during* and *for*.
   She fell asleep *during* the movie.
   She slept *for* two hours.

3. Compare *after* and *in*.
   I'll come back *in* an hour.
   I'll come back *after* I go to the post office.

4. Compare *before* and *by*.
   I have to return my library books *before* Friday. (Friday is not included.)
   I have to return my library books *by* Friday. (Friday is included.)

EXERCISE 7 Choose the the correct time word to fill in the blanks.

EXAMPLE: He lived with his parents (*during* (until) *by*) he was 19 years old.

1. (*When* *During* *Whenever*) he was a child, he lived with his grandparents.

2. (*During* *For* *While*) several years, he lived with his grandparents.

3. (*For   While   During*) his childhood, he lived with his grandparents.

4. (*While   Until   When*) he got married, he lived with his grandparents. Then he found an apartment with his wife.

5. (*Whenever   While   When*) he was ten years old, his grandparents gave him a bike.

6. (*While   During   Whenever*) he was in elementary school, he lived with his grandparents.

7. She worked for her father (*during   while   whenever*) she was in college.

8. She worked for her father (*for   during   while*) her free time.

9. She worked for her father (*during   whenever   when*) she was single.

10. She worked for her father (*for   during   while*) three years.

11. She worked for her father full time (*while   when   during*) her summer vacation.

12. She worked for her father (*when   until   while*) she got married. Then she quit her job to take care of her husband and children.

13. She worked for her father 12 years (*before   ago   after*).

14. (*Until   Whenever   During*) her husband needs help in his business, she helps him out.

15. She can't help you now. She's busy. She'll help you (*by   ago   in*) an hour.

16. Please finish this exercise (*by   in   until*) 8:30.

17. Please finish this exercise (*by   before   until*) you go home. The teacher wants it today.

18. Please finish this exercise (*in   after   by*) ten minutes.

19. He'll retire (*after   in   by*) two years.

20. He'll retire (*when   while   until*) he's sixty-five years old.

21. He'll work (*when   while   until*) he's sixty-five years old. Then he'll retire.

22. I'm not going to eat dinner (*when   while   until*) my wife gets home. Then we'll eat together.

The Past Continuous Tense

Examples	Explanation
In 1998, I **was living** in the U.S. In 1998, my parents **were living** in the Ecuador.	To form the past continuous tense, we use *was* or *were* + verb-*ing*. I, he, she, it → *was* you, we, they → *were*
In 1998, I **wasn't living** in my country. My parents **weren't living** with me.	To form the negative, put *not* after *was* or *were*. The contraction for *was not* is *wasn't*. The contraction for *were not* is *weren't*.

Before You Read
1.   What famous immigrants to the U.S. do you know?
2.   Did anyone from your native culture become famous in the U.S.?

Read the following article. Pay special attention to past continuous and simple past tense verbs.

Albert Einstein

Of the many immigrants who came to the U.S., one will always be remembered throughout the world: Albert Einstein. Einstein changed our understanding of the universe. When people think of the word "genius," Einstein's name often comes to mind. However, in Einstein's early years, he was not successful in school or at finding a job.

Did you know...?

After Einstein died, Princeton University kept his brain in a jar to study how the brain of a genius is different from an ordinary brain.

Einstein was born in Germany in 1879 of Jewish parents. He loved math and physics, but he disliked the discipline of formal German schooling. Because of his poor memory for words, his teachers believed that he was a slow learner. Einstein left school before receiving his diploma and tried to pass the exam to enter the Swiss Polytechnic Institute, but he failed on his first attempt. On his second attempt, he passed. He graduated in 1900. He **was planning** to become a teacher of physics and math, but he could not find a job in this field. Instead, he went to work in a patent office as a third class technical expert from 1902 to 1909. While he **was working** at this job,he **wrote** in his spare time. In 1905, when he was only 26 years old, he published three papers that explained the basic structure of the universe. His theory of relativity explained the relationship of space and time. Einstein was finally respected for his brilliant discovery. He returned to Germany to accept a research position at the University of Berlin. However, in 1920, while he **was lecturing** at the university, anti-Jewish groups often **interrupted** his lectures, saying they were "un-German."

In 1920, Einstein visited the United States for the first time. During his visits, he talked not only about his scientific theories, but also about world peace. While he **was visiting** the U.S. again in 1933, the Nazis **came** to power in Germany. They took his property, burned his books, and removed him from his university job. The U.S. offered Einstein a home. In 1935, he became a permanent resident of the U.S., and in 1940, he became a citizen. He received many offers of jobs from all over the world, but he decided to accept a position at Princeton University in New Jersey. He lived and worked there until he died in 1955.

7.5   The Past Continuous Tense—Forms

Compare statements, questions, and short answers using the past continuous tense.

Wh-Word	Was/Wasn't Were/Weren't	Subject	Was/Wasn't Were/Weren't	-ing Form	Complement	Short Answer
		Einstein	**was**	**living**	in the U.S.	
		He	**wasn't**	**living**	in Germany.	
	Was	he		**living**	in New Jersey?	Yes, he **was.**
Where	**was**	he		**living?**		
Why	**wasn't**	he		**living**	in Germany?	
		Who	**was**	**living**	in Germany?	

EXERCISE 8 Fill in the blanks with the correct form.

EXAMPLE: In 1889, Einstein was _____studying_____ in the Swiss Polytechnic Institute.

1. Einstein _____ plan_____ to become a teacher.

2. He _____ _____ to become a doctor.

3. In 1907, he _____ _____ in a patent office.

4. In 1933, he was _____ the U.S.

5. What _____ he do_____ in the U.S.?

6. _____ he planning to go back to Germany? Yes, he _____.

7. Where _____ you _____ in January, 1999?

8. _____ you sleep_____ at midnight last night?

   No, I _____ .

9. Why _____ _____ sleeping? I wasn't sleeping because I wasn't tired.

10. Who _____ _____ TV at 9:15 last night?

7.6 The Past Continuous Tense—Uses

Examples	Explanation
Einstein **was working** in a patent office in 1905.	We use the past continuous tense to show what was in progress at a specific moment in the past. 1905 ↓ ←-------x-------| -------------→ |was working| ↑
Einstein **was living** in Switzerland when he **developed** his theory of relativity. While Einstein **was visiting** the U.S., the Nazis **took** his property. Einstein **was living** in New Jersey when he **died**.	We use the past continuous tense with the simple past to show the relationship of a longer past action to a shorter past action. developed ↓ ←-------x-------| -------------→ |was living| ↑

LANGUAGE NOTES

1. You can show the relationship of a longer past action to a shorter past action two ways:

- Use *when* + the simple past with the shorter action.
- Use *while* + the past continuous with the longer action.
  COMPARE:
  Einstein was living in Switzerland *when* he *developed* his theory of relativity.
  Einstein developed his theory of relativity *while* he *was living* in Switzerland.

2. If the time clause precedes the main clause, separate the two clauses with a comma.

MAIN CLAUSE	TIME CLAUSE
He was living in New Jersey	when he died.

TIME CLAUSE	MAIN CLAUSE
While he was living in New Jersey,	he worked at Princeton University.

3. In a question with two clauses, only the verb in the main clause is in a question form.
   Where *was Einstein living* when the Nazis *took* his home?

4. We don't use the continuous form with the verb *be*, but it can have a continuous meaning.
   While she *was* at work, her husband called.
   While Einstein *was* in Switzerland, he developed his theory.

EXERCISE 9 Tell if the following things were happening in January, 1999.

EXAMPLE: go to school
             I was (not) going to school in January, 1999.

1. work   4. live in the U.S.
2. go to school   5. live with my parents
3. study English

EXERCISE 10 Ask a question with "What were you doing?" at these specific times. Another student will answer.

EXAMPLE: at 6 o'clock this morning
             A. What were you doing at 6 o'clock this morning?
             B. I was sleeping.

1. at 10 o'clock last night   4. at this time yesterday
2. at 4 o'clock this morning   5. at this time last year[2]
3. at 5 o'clock yesterday afternoon

---

[2] *At this time last year* does not refer to a specific hour, but is very general.

EXERCISE 11 Decide which of these two verbs has longer action. Fill in the correct tense (simple past or past continuous) of the verb in parentheses ( ) and *when* or *while*.

EXAMPLES: She __*was taking*__ a shower __*when*__ the telephone __*rang*__.
(take)   (ring)

It __*started*__ to rain __*while*__ I __*was walking*__ to
(start)   (walk)
school.

1. _____ the teacher _____ on the blackboard,
(write)

   she _____ the chalk.
   (drop)

2. He _____ and _____ his arm _____
   (fall)   (break)

   he _____ a tree.
   (climb)

3. Mary _____ in a department store _____ she
   (shop)

   _____ her purse.
   (lose)

4. I _____ my homework _____ my friend
   (do)

   _____ over.
   (come)

5. She _____ her husband _____ she _____
   (meet)   (attend)
   college.

6. _____ I _____ to work, I _____
   (drive)   (run)

   out of gas.³

7. _____ he _____ at the airport, his friends
   (arrive)

   _____ for him.
   (wait)

8. They _____ dinner _____ someone
   (eat)

   _____ on the door.
   (knock)

9. _____ I _____ a test, my pencil point
   (take)

   _____.
   (break)

10. The baby _____ me _____ I _____
    (interrupt)   (talk)
    to a friend.

³ To *run out of* means to use up everything.

196   Lesson Seven

11. I _____ my tooth _____ I _____
    (break)   (eat)
    a nut.

12. I _____ an old friend _____ I _____
    (meet)   (walk)
    in the park.

13. She _____ dinner _____ the smoke alarm
    (cook)
    _____ off.[4]
    (go)

14. He _____ snow _____ he _____
    (shovel)   (lose)
    his glove.

15. I _____ a fuse _____
    (blow)
    I _____ .
    (iron)

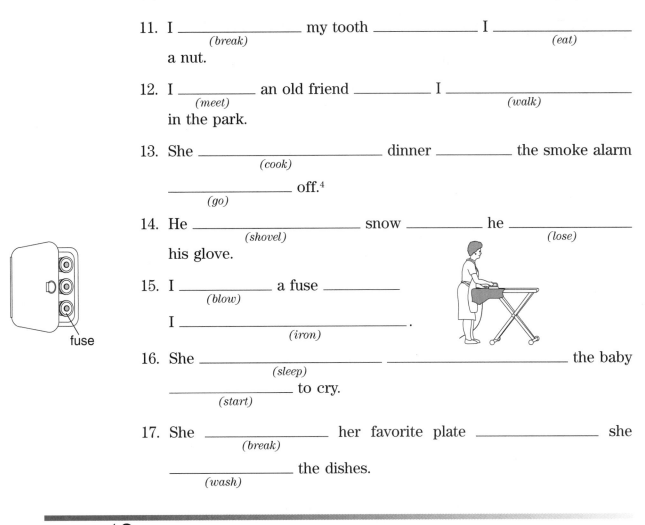

fuse

16. She _____ _____ the baby
    (sleep)
    _____ to cry.
    (start)

17. She _____ her favorite plate _____ she
    (break)
    _____ the dishes.
    (wash)

EXERCISE 12 Fill in the blanks with the simple past or the past continuous
form of the verb in parentheses ( ) in the following
conversations.

Conversation 1, between a wife (W) and husband (H)

W. Look what I found today! Your favorite watch!

H. Where ___*did you find*___ it?
          (example: find)

W. In your top drawer. I _____ away your socks when
                          (1 put)

   I _____ it.
     (2 find)

H. I wonder how it got there.

W. Probably while you _____ something in that drawer,
                        (3 put)

   it _____ off your wrist.
      (4 fall)

[4] When an alarm *goes off*, it starts to sound.

Time Words and Time Clauses; The Past Continuous Tense   **197**

Conversation 2, between a wife (W) and husband (H)

H. What happened? I _____ TV when I _____
(1 watch) _(2 hear)_
a loud crash in the kitchen.

W. I _____ to get something off the top shelf when
(3 try)

I _____ a vase.
(4 drop)

H. Why didn't you ask me to help you?

W. You _____ TV, and I _____ to disturb
(5 watch) _(6 not/want)_
you.

Conversation 3, between a son (S) and mother (M)

S. I _____ through some old boxes when I _____
(1 look) _(2 find)_
this picture of you and Dad when you were young. By the way,

how _____ you _____ Dad?
(3 meet)

M. One day I _____ in the park when he _____
(4 walk) _(5 stop)_
me to ask what time it was. We _____ to talk, and then
(6 start)

he _____ me to go out with him.
(7 ask)

S. Did you get married right away?

M. No. At that time, there was a war going on. We _____ for
(8 date)

about five months when he _____ drafted.[5] He had to
(9 get)

serve in the army. While he _____ in the army,
(10 serve)

he _____ me a beautiful letter. He asked me to marry
(11 write)
him as soon as he returned from military service.

S. Did you marry him when he _____ home?
(12 get)

M. Not right away. When he _____ home, I _____
(13 come) _(14 study)_

at the university, and I wanted to graduate first. We _____
(15 get)

married ten days after my graduation.

[5] When a person *gets drafted,* the government chooses him to serve in the military.

Was/Were going to (THE PLAN)	*but . . .* (WHY THE PLAN DIDN'T HAPPEN)
Einstein **was going to** return to Germany,	but the Nazis came to power.
I **was going to** buy a new car,	but I lost my job.
I **was going to** call you,	but I lost your phone number.

LANGUAGE NOTES

We use *was/were going to* + the base form to describe a plan that we didn't carry out. It means the same thing as *was/were planning to*.

I *was going to* call you, but I lost your phone number.

I *was planning to* call you, but I lost your phone number.

EXERCISE 13 Fill in the blanks to tell what prevented a plan from happening.

EXAMPLE: I was going to call you, but ___*I got busy and forgot about it.*___

1. We were going to have a picnic, but _____

   _____

2. I was going to finish that book last night, but _____

   _____

3. We were going to buy a house, but _____

   _____

4. They were going to leave for vacation on Monday, but _____

   _____

5. She was going to marry her boyfriend, but _____

   _____

6. They were going to drive to Canada, but _____

   _____

7. I was going to cook dinner, but _____

   _____

Examples	Explanation
(A) She **was eating** dinner when he arrived.	In sentence (A), the man's arrival happened during the time of the woman's dinner.
(B) She **ate** dinner when he arrived.	In sentence (B), the woman ate dinner after the arrival of the man.
(C) Einstein **was living** in the U.S. when he died. (D) Einstein **lived** in the U.S. when he lost his German citizenship.	In sentence (C), his death occurred during the time he was living in the U.S. In sentence (D), he started to live in the U.S. after he lost his German citizenship.
(E) While my son **did** his homework, I **cooked** dinner. (F) While my son **was doing** his homework, I **was cooking** dinner.	*While* can connect two past actions that happened in the same time period. You can use either the simple past (E) or the past continuous (F) in both clauses.

EXERCISE 14 A fable is an old story that teaches us a lesson about life. Fables often use animals to represent people. Here is a fable about an ant and a grasshopper. Fill in the blanks with the past or past continuous of the verb in parentheses ( ) to complete this story. In some cases, you may use either tense.

grasshopper

ant

During the summer, the ant ___was working (or worked)___ very hard
(work)

trying to gather the food that she would need for the long, cold winter. While the ant _____ (1 work), her neighbor, the grasshopper, _____ (2 have)

a good time. He _____ (3 sing) and _____ (4 enjoy) himself all summer.

When winter _____ (5 come), the ant had plenty of food to eat. However,

the grasshopper _____ (6 have) nothing to eat. The grasshopper _____ (7 go)

to the ant's house one day to ask for food. The ant _____ (8 prepare)

a delicious meal when he _____ (9 hear) the grasshopper knock on the door.

When she _____ (10 open) the door, the grasshopper _____ (11 say),

"Please give me some food." The ant asked him, "What _____ you

_____ (12 do) all summer while I _____ (13 work)?" The grasshopper

_____ (14 reply), "I _____ (15 sing) all summer." "Then go and dance now,"

the ant _____ (16 tell) him.

7.9 Time with Present Participles

Examples

Einstein left high school **before he finished** his studies.
Einstein left high school **before finishing** his studies.
After Einstein left high school, he studied mathematics and physics.
After leaving high school, Einstein studied mathematics and physics.

LANGUAGE NOTES

When the main clause and the time clause have the same subject, we can delete the subject of the time clause and use a present participle (verb + -ing.)

EXERCISE 15 Change these sentences. Use a present participle after the time word.

EXAMPLE: After ~~Einstein entered~~ *entering* the university, ~~he~~ *Einstein* developed his theory.

1. Einstein passed an exam before he entered the university.

2. He left high school before he received his diploma.

3. After Einstein developed his theory of relativity, he became famous.

4. He became interested in physics after he received books on science.

5. After Einstein came to the U.S., he got a job at Princeton.

6. Before you begin a test, you should read the instructions carefully.

7. You shouldn't talk to another student while you are taking a test.

8. After children finish kindergarten, they go to first grade.

SUMMARY OF LESSON 7

1. Time Words

Time Word	Examples
When	**When** immigrants came to America, they passed through Ellis Island.
While	They waited **while** inspectors checked their health.
Until	Ellis Island remained closed **until** 1990.
Before	**Before** 1920, many immigrants came to America.
After	**After** 1920, Congress limited the number of immigrants.
From . . . to	**From** 1892 **to** 1924, Ellis Island was an immigrant processing center.
During	**During** this time, 12 million immigrants passed through Ellis Island.
For	New arrivals had to wait **for** hours.
In	**In** 1905, Einstein wrote about relativity.
	We will finish the test **in** an hour.
By	Restoration of Ellis Island was finished **by** 1990.
Ago	One hundred years **ago**, new arrivals passed through Ellis Island.

2. Uses of the past continuous tense:
   A. To describe a past action that was in progress at a specific moment:
      He **was sleeping** at 6 o'clock this morning.
      Where **were** you **living** in December 1991?
   B. With the past tense, to show the relationship of a longer past action to a shorter past action:
      He **was sleeping** when the telephone **rang**.
      While she **was eating** lunch in the park, it **started** to rain.
      Martin Luther King, Jr., **was standing** on the balcony of a motel when a man **shot** and **killed** him.
   C. To show past intentions:
      I **was going to call** you, but I lost your phone number.
      She **was going to cook** dinner, but she didn't have time.

1. Put the subject before the verb in all clauses.

    the teacher entered
    When ~~entered the teacher~~, the students stood up.

2. Use *when*, not *while*, if the action has no duration.

    When
    ~~While~~ she spilled the milk, she started to cry.

3. Don't confuse *during* and *for*.

    for
    He watched TV ~~during~~ 3 hours.

4. Don't confuse *until* and *when*.

    when
    She will eat dinner ~~until~~ her husband comes home.

5. Don't confuse *before* and *ago*.

    ago
    They came to the U.S. three years ~~before~~.

6. After a time word, use an *-ing* form, not a base form.

    finding
    After ~~find~~ a job, he bought a car.

LESSON 7 TEST / REVIEW

PART 1   Find the mistakes with the underlined words, and correct them. Not every sentence has a mistake. If the sentence is correct, write C.

EXAMPLES: She came to the U.S. two weeks ~~before~~.   *ago*

While I <u>was walking</u> in the park, I saw my friend.   C

1. When he arrived, he <u>ate</u> dinner with his family.

2. After <u>leaving</u> my country, I went to Thailand.

3. When <u>arrived the teacher</u>, the students had a test.

4. I graduated <u>until</u> I finished all my courses.

5. While she <u>was washing</u> the dishes, she dropped the glass.

6. <u>While</u> she dropped the glass, it broke.

7. He studied English <u>until</u> he became fluent.

8. She served dinner <u>when</u> her guests arrived.

9. Einstein lived in the U.S. <u>until he died</u>.

10. They went home <u>until</u> the movie was over.

11. I'll be back <u>in</u> ten minutes.

12. <u>During</u> three weeks, he was on vacation.

13. Please return your library books <u>by</u> Friday.

14. She found a job three weeks <u>before</u>.

15. He was sick <u>for</u> a week.

16. I ate dinner an hour <u>ago</u>.

17. Einstein was in the U.S. <u>during</u> the Second World War.

18. I <u>was going to</u> call you, but I lost your phone number.

PART **2**   Fill in the blanks with the simple past or the past continuous form of the verb in parentheses ( ).

EXAMPLE: He ____*was walking*____ to his car when he ____*lost*____ his glove.
    (walk)   *(lose)*

1. What _____ at 4 p.m. yesterday afternoon? I tried
    (you/do)
    to call you, but you weren't home.

2. She _____ in Paris when the war _____.
    (live)   *(start)*

3. I _____ your necklace while I _____ for my
    (find)   *(look)*
    watch.

4. She _____ a house three years ago.
    (buy)

5. He _____ his wife while he _____ in a restaurant.
    (meet)   *(work)*

6. When my grandfather _____ to America, he _____
    (come)   *(find)*
    a job in a factory.

7. When he _____ at Ellis Island, his uncle _____
    (arrive)   *(wait)*
    for him.

8. While she _____ the computer, it _____ .
      (use)   (crash)

9. He _____ dinner when the fire _____ .
      (cook)   (start)

10. I _____ my car and _____ to the radio
      (drive)   (listen)

    when I _____ that John F. Kennedy, Jr. died.
            (hear)

PART 3   Fill in the blanks with an appropriate time word. Choose *when,*
whenever, while, until, before, after, by, ago, in, for, or *during.*
In some cases, more than one answer is possible.

EXAMPLE: I will continue to work ____*until*____ I am 65 years old. Then I will retire.

1. _____ it snows, there are a lot of traffic accidents.

2. I was walking to my friend's house _____ it started to rain. I
   was glad I had my umbrella with me.

3. _____ I was driving to school, I was listening to the radio.

4. _____ I finished my homework last night, I watched the news
   on TV.

5. I got my visa _____ coming to the U.S.

6. He must stay in his country _____ he gets permission to come
   to the U.S.

7. _____ he dropped his glasses, they broke.

8. We have to finish this lesson _____ 10 o'clock.

9. He found a job two months _____ .

10. He found a job three weeks _____ coming to the U.S.

11. He found a job _____ April.

12. It's 7:50. The movie will begin _____ ten minutes at 8:00.

13. _____ the movie began, everyone became quiet.

14. _____ she was watching the sad movie, she started to cry.

15. Einstein was 61 years old _____ he became a U.S. citizen.

16. Einstein lived in the U.S. _____ 22 years.

EXPANSION ACTIVITIES

CLASSROOM ACTIVITIES

1. Check (√) what was true for you before coming to the U.S. Find a partner and compare your list to your partner's list. Discuss any related information.

EXAMPLE:

    __√__ I studied English.
Student A: I studied English for one year before coming to the U.S.
Student B: I didn't study English before coming to the U.S.

1. ____ I studied American history.
2. ____ I studied English.
3. ____ I finished college.
4. ____ I bought new clothes.
5. ____ I had a clear idea about life in the U.S.
6. ____ I was afraid about the future.
7. ____ I read about this city.
8. ____ I had a map of this city.

2. Form a small group. Turn to the person next to you and say a year or a specific time of the year. The person next to you tells what was happening in his or her life at that time.

EXAMPLES:

1996
I was living with my parents.
January, 1999
I was studying to be a nurse in my country.

DISCUSSION

1. In a small group or with the entire class, discuss your experience of immigration. Was the process difficult? How did you feel during the process?

2. Einstein is often called a genius. Can you think of any other famous people who are geniuses?

3. In a small group or with the entire class, discuss the meaning of the fable in Exercise 14. What do you think this fable teaches us? Do you know anyone like the grasshopper or the ant in this fable?

WRITING

1. Write a short fable like the one in Exercise 14.

2. Write a paragraph about the changes that took place after a major historical event in your country or elsewhere in the world.

EXAMPLES:

After the communists took over in Cuba . . .
After the Khmer Rouge took power in Cambodia . . .
After the coup failed in the former Soviet Union . . .
After the president of my country was assassinated . . .

3. Write about the life of a famous person who interests you.

4. Write about how you met your spouse or how your father and mother met.

1. Most people remember what they were doing when they heard shocking news. Do you remember what you were doing when you heard the news that John Kennedy, Jr. died in a plane crash in July, 1999? Do you remember what you were doing when you heard that Princess Diana died in a car crash in August, 1997? Ask an American, "What were you doing when you heard the news?" You can ask an older American, "What were you doing when you heard the news that President Kennedy was killed in November, 1963?"

2. Is there a famous event in your native country that most people remember well? What was it? Ask people from your country what they were doing when this event happened. Report your findings to the class.

Internet Activity

Look for the Ellis Island Web site. Find out what time the museum is open. See what names are on the wall of the museum. Is your family's name on the wall?

Lesson Eight

GRAMMAR

Modals
Related Expressions

CONTEXT

An Apartment Lease
Tenants' Rights
The New Neighbors
At a Garage Sale

LESSON FOCUS

The modal auxiliaries are: *can, could, should, will, would, may, might, must.*

> She *can* swim well.
> I *must* return my library books.

Related expressions are: *be supposed to, be able to, have to, have got to, be allowed to, be permitted to, had better.*

> She *is able to* swim well.
> I *have to* return my library books.

Overview of Modals and Related Expressions

List of Modals	Facts About Modals

can
could
should
will
would
may
might
must
	1. The base form follows a modal. Never use an infinitive after a modal.
	    You **must pay** your rent. (NOT: You must to pay your rent.)
	
	2. Modals never have an *-s*, *-ed*, or *-ing* ending.
	    He **can** go. (NOT: He cans go.)
	
	3. To form the negative, put *not* after the modal.
	    You **should not** leave now.
	
	4. You can make a negative contraction with some modals.
	    can't couldn't shouldn't won't wouldn't mustn't
	    Don't make a contraction for *may not* or *might not*.
	
	5. Some verbs are like modals in meaning: *have to, be able to, be supposed to, be permitted to, be allowed to, had better.*
	    He **must** sign the lease. = He **has to** sign the lease.
	
	    I **must** pay my rent by the first of the month. = I'm **supposed to** pay my rent by the first of the month.
	
	    He **can** pay the rent. = He **is able to** pay the rent.

Before You Read

1. Do you live in an apartment? Do you have a lease? Did you understand the lease when you signed it?
2. Do renters in your hometown usually have to sign a lease?

Read the following article. Pay special attention to modals and related expressions.

An Apartment Lease

When people rent an apartment, they often **have to** sign a lease. A lease is an agreement between the owner (landlord[1]) and the renter (tenant). A lease states the period of time of the rental, the amount of the rent, and rules the renter **must** follow. Some leases contain the following rules:

Did you know...?

In the U.S., renters pay about 26 percent of their income on rent.

- Renters **must** not have a waterbed.
- Renters **must** not have a pet.
- Renters **must** not change the locks without the owner's permission.
- Renters **must** pay a security deposit.

[1] A *landlord* is a man. A *landlady* is a woman.

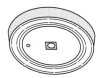
smoke detector

The renter **does not have to** agree to all the terms of the lease. He can ask for changes before he signs. A pet owner, for example, can ask for permission to have a pet by offering to pay a higher security deposit.

Owners also have to follow rules. They **must** provide heat during the winter months. In most cities, they **must** put a smoke detector in each apartment and in the halls.

Many owners ask the renter to pay a security deposit, in case there are damages. When the renter moves out, the owner **is supposed to** return the deposit plus interest if the apartment is in good condition. If there is damage, the owner **can** use part or all of the money to repair the damage. However, he **may** not keep the renter's money for normal wear and tear (the normal use of the apartment).

When the lease is up, the owner **can** offer the renter a new lease or he can ask the renter to leave. The owner **is supposed to** give the renter notice (usually at least 30 days) if he wants the renter to leave.

An owner **can't** refuse to rent to a person because of sex, race, religion, nationality, or disability.

8.2 Statements and Questions with Modals

Compare affirmative statements and questions using a modal.

Wh- Word	Modal (+ *n't*)	Subject	Modal	Verb (base form)	Complement	Short Answer
		He	**can**	have	a cat in his apartment.	
		He	**can't**	have	a dog.	
	Can	he		have	a waterbed?	No, he **can't**.
What	**can**	he		have	in his apartment?	
Why	**can't**	he		have	a dog?	
		Who	**can**	have	a dog?	

EXERCISE 1 Fill in the blanks to complete these statements and questions.

EXAMPLE: I can have a cat in my apartment, but I _____*can't*_____ have a dog.

1. I can't have a dog. Why _____ a dog?

2. You should _____ the lease before you sign it.

3. Why _____ before I sign it?

4. We must pay a security deposit. How much _____ pay?

5. My landlord says I must not _____ a waterbed in my apartment.

6. The landlord must _____ a smoke detector in each apartment.

7. If you damage something, the landlord can _____ some or all of your money to repair the damage.

8. How much money must _____ if I break a window?

9. _____ change the locks? No. You can't change the locks.

10. Why _____ change the locks?

11. The landlord can't _____ to rent to you because of your race or nationality.

12. _____ refuse to rent to me because of my religion? No, he can't.

8.3 _Must, Have To, Have Got To, Be Supposed To_

Formal or Official	Informal	Explanation
The landlord **must** give you a smoke detector.	He **has to** give you a smoke detector. OR He**'s got to** give you a smoke detector. OR He**'s supposed to** give you a smoke detector.	Legal obligation
You **must** leave the building immediately. It's on fire!	You **have to** leave the building immediately. OR You**'ve got to** leave the building immediately.	Urgency
	My apartment is too small. We **have to** move. OR We**'ve got to** move.	Personal necessity

LANGUAGE NOTES

1. We use _must_ in formal situations to describe rules and laws. It has an official tone. Avoid using _must_ for personal necessities. It sounds too strong. _Have to_ and _have got to_ are more common.

    Student to teacher: I _have to_ leave early today. My son is sick.

2. _Be supposed to_ is much more common than _must_ in reporting a rule. The creator or enforcer of the rule can say _must_. Someone who reports the rule usually says _be supposed to, have to,_ or _have got to_.

    TEACHER TO STUDENT: You _must_ write five compositions this semester.

STUDENT TO STUDENT: The teacher says we*'re supposed to* write five compositions this semester. (OR: We *have to* write five compositions.)

PARENT TO TEENAGER: You *must* be home by 11 p.m.

TEENAGER TO FRIEND: I*'m supposed to* be home by 11 p.m. (OR: I*'ve got to* be home by 11 p.m.)

3. In fast, informal speech, *have to* is often pronounced "hafta." *Has to* is pronounced "hasta." *Got to* is often pronounced "gotta." Listen to your teacher pronounce the sentences in the preceding box.

4. We don't usually use *have got to* for questions and negatives.

5. *Must* has no past form. The past of both *must* and *have to* is *had to*.

    At the end of my lease last May, I *had to* move.

    I *had to* find a bigger apartment.

EXERCISE 2 Fill in the blanks with *must* for rules and laws. Fill in the blanks with *have to* or *have got to* for personal necessities.

EXAMPLES: The landlord _____*must*_____ give you heat in cold weather.

It's too hot in here. I _____*have to*_____ open a window.

1. To get a driver's license, you _____ take an eye exam.

2. Our apartment is too small for our family. We _____ move.

3. My stove doesn't work. I _____ talk to the landlord about it.

4. You _____ sign the lease with a pen. A pencil is not acceptable.

5. We _____ buy a new sofa. Our old one looks terrible.

6. I _____ cook dinner for my family tonight. It's my turn.

7. The landlord _____ return your security deposit if you leave your apartment in good condition.

8. The landlord _____ give you notice if he wants you to leave at the end of your lease.

9. I _____ ask the landlord about the laundry room.

10. I'm looking for a new apartment. I _____ buy the newspaper and look at the "for rent" section.

EXERCISE 3 Finish these sentences to talk about personal necessity.

EXAMPLE: I always go to bed so late and then I'm tired the next morning. I've got to
go to bed earlier.

1. I won't have time to watch TV tonight. I've got to _____.

2. I can't talk to you now. I've got to _____.

3. I don't feel well. I have to _____.

4. I'm reading a novel, and I don't know the meaning of several words.
   I have to _____.

5. I'm gaining weight. I've got to _____.

6. We're going to have a test on modals next week. We've got to
   _____.

7. English is so important in the U.S. We've got to _____.

8. I eat too much junk food. I have to _____ or I'm
   going to get fat.

EXERCISE 4 Make a list of personal necessities you have.

EXAMPLE: *I have to change the oil in my car every three months.*

1. _____

2. _____

3. _____

EXERCISE 5 Make a list of things you had to do last weekend.

EXAMPLE: *I had to do my laundry.*

1. _____

2. _____

3. _____

EXERCISE 6 Make these sentences less formal by changing from *must* to *be supposed to*.

EXAMPLE: You must wear a seat belt.
You're supposed to wear your seat belt.

1. You must carry your driver's license with you when you drive.

2. The teacher must give a final grade at the end of the semester.

3. Your landlord must give you notice if he wants you to leave.

4. You must stop at a red light.

5. We must put money in the parking meter during business hours.

6. The landlord must give me a smoke detector.

7. We must write five compositions in this course.

8. We must bring our books to class.

EXERCISE 7 Finish these statements. Use *be supposed to*.

EXAMPLE: I *'m supposed to pay my rent* _____ on the first of the month.

1. Pets are not permitted in my apartment. I (not) _____ a pet.

2. The landlord _____ us heat in the winter months.

3. The tenants _____ before they move out.

4. The landlord _____ a smoke detector in each apartment.

5. I _____ my rent on the first of each month.

6. My stove isn't working. My landlord _____ it.

7. We're going to move out next week. Our apartment is clean and in good condition. The landlord _____ our security deposit.

EXERCISE 8   Write three sentences to tell what you are supposed to do for this course. (You may work with a partner.)

EXAMPLE: *We're supposed to write three compositions this semester.*

1. _____

2. _____

3. _____

8.4   *Can, Could, May, Be Able To, Be Permitted To, Be Allowed To*

Modal	Alternate expression	Explanation
I **can** pay up to $800 a month for an apartment.	**It is possible** for me to pay $800 a month.	Possibility
I **can't** understand the lease.	I **am not able to** understand the lease.	Ability
I **can't** have a pet in my apartment.	I **am not permitted to** have a pet. I **am not allowed to** have a pet.	Permission
The landlord **may not** keep my deposit for no reason.	The landlord **is not permitted to** keep my deposit. The landlord **is not allowed to** keep my deposit.	Permission
I **couldn't** speak English five years ago, but I can now.	I **wasn't able to** speak English five years ago, but I am able to now.	Past ability
I **could** have a dog in my last apartment, but I **can't** have one in my present apartment.	I **was permitted to** have a dog in my last apartment, but I **am not permitted to** have one in my present apartment.	Past permission

LANGUAGE NOTES

1. The negative of *can* is *cannot* (one word). The contraction is *can't*.
2. *Can* is not usually stressed in affirmative statements. Sometimes it is hard to hear the final *t*, so we must pay attention to the vowel sound to hear the difference between *can* and *can't*. Listen to your teacher pronounce these sentences:

I can gó. /kɪn/
I cán't go. /kænt/
In a short answer, we pronounce *can* as /kæn/.
Can you help me later?
Yes, I can. /kæn/

3. We use *can* in the following common expression:
    I *can't afford* a bigger apartment. I don't have enough money.

4. The past of *can* is *could*.
    I *can* control the heat in my present apartment.
    I *couldn't* control the heat in my last apartment.

EXERCISE 9 Fill in the blanks with an appropriate permission word to talk about what is or isn't permitted at this school.

EXAMPLES: We ___*aren't allowed to*___ bring food into the classroom.

We ___*can*___ leave the room without asking the teacher for permission.

1. We _____ eat in the classroom.

2. Students _____ talk during a test.

3. Students _____ use their dictionaries when they write compositions.

4. Students _____ write a test with a pencil.

5. Students _____ repeat a course a second time.

6. Students _____ sit in any seat they want.

7. Students _____ use their textbooks during a test.

8. Students _____ make a copy of their textbooks.

EXERCISE 10 Complete each statement.

EXAMPLE: The landlord may not ___*refuse to rent*___ to a person because of his or her nationality.

1. The tenants may not _____ the locks without the landlord's permission.

2. Each tenant in my building has a parking space. I may not _____

    _____ in another tenant's space.

3. Students may not _____ during a test.

---

4. I took my camera to the art museum last week, but I couldn't use it.

   There was a sign that said, "You may not _____ the artwork."

5. Teacher to students: "You don't need my permission to leave the room.

   You may _____ the room if you need to."

6. Some teachers do not allow cell phones in class. In Mr. Klein's class,

   you may not _____ during class.

7. My teacher says that after we finish a test, we may _____

   _____. We don't have to stay in class.

8. Some teachers do not allow food in the classroom. My teacher says

   we may not _____ in the classroom.

EXERCISE 11 Write statements to tell what is or is not permitted in this class, in the library, at this school, or during a test. If you have any questions about what is permitted, write a question for the teacher. (You may work with a partner.)

EXAMPLES:
We aren't allowed to talk in the library.

May we use our textbooks during a test?

_____

_____

_____

EXERCISE 12 Write three sentences telling about what you couldn't do in a classroom or school in your native country that you can do in an American school or classroom.

EXAMPLE:
In my country, I couldn't call a teacher by his first name, but I

can do it here.

1. _____

2. _____

3. _____

EXERCISE 13 Write three sentences telling about something that was prohibited in your native country that you can do in the U.S.

EXAMPLE: *I couldn't criticize the political leaders in my country, but I can*

do it now.

1. _____

2. _____

3. _____

Before You Read

1. What are some complaints you have about your apartment? Do you ever tell the landlord about your complaints?
2. Is your apartment warm enough in the winter and cool enough in the summer?

Read the following conversation. Pay special attention to *should* and *had better*.

Tenants' Rights

brochure

A. My apartment is always too cold in the winter. I've got to move.
B. You don't have to move. The landlord is supposed to give enough heat.
A. But he doesn't.
B. You **should** talk to him about this problem.
A. I did already. The first time I talked to him, he just told me I **should** put on a sweater. The second time I said, "You**'d better** give me heat or I'm going to move."
B. You **shouldn't** get so angry. That's not the way to solve the problem. You know, there are laws about heat. You **should** get information from the city so you can know your rights.
A. How can I get information?
B. Tomorrow morning, you **should** call the mayor's office and ask for a brochure about tenants' rights. When you know what the law is exactly, you **should** show the brochure to your landlord.
A. And what if he doesn't want to do anything about it?
B. Then you **should** report the problem to the mayor's office.
A. I'm afraid to do that.
B. Don't be afraid. You have rights. Maybe you **should** talk to other tenants and see if you can do this together.

Examples	Explanation
You **should** talk to the landlord about the problem. You **should** get information about tenants' rights. You **shouldn't** get so angry.	For advice, use *should*. *Should* = It's a good thing. *Shouldn't* = It's a bad thing.
You **had better** give me heat, or I'm going to move. You **had better not** miss the final exam, or you might fail the course.	For a warning, use *had better (not)*. Something bad can happen if you don't follow this advice.

LANGUAGE NOTES

1. The contraction for *had* (in *had better*) is *'d*.
    I'd   you'd   he'd   she'd   we'd   they'd

2. Americans sometimes don't pronounce the *'d*. You will hear Americans say, "You better be careful."

3. Remember, *must* is very strong and is not for advice. It is for rules and laws.
    COMPARE:
    Your landlord *must* give you a smoke detector.
    You *should* check the battery in the smoke detector occasionally.

EXERCISE 14 Fill in the blanks.

EXAMPLE: The students don't understand the lesson. The teacher should ___explain___
it again.

1. I can see you don't understand modals. You should _____ before the next test.

2. My mother is probably lonely. I should _____ more often.

3. You don't have enough gas in your tank. You should _____ very soon.

4. I always go to bed so late, and I feel terrible the next morning. I should _____ earlier.

5. I work at a desk all day. Now I'm gaining weight. I should _____ _____ .

6. It's going to get colder this afternoon. When you go out, you should _____ with you.

7. You're taking too many classes and you don't have enough time to study. Next semester you shouldn't _____ .

8. Children shouldn't lie. They should _____ to their parents.

EXERCISE 15 Give advice using *should*.

EXAMPLE: My landlord is going to raise the rent by 20 percent.
You should move.

1. My next-door neighbors play their stereo loud all the time. I can't sleep at night.

2. My landlady doesn't give us enough heat in the winter.

3. I can't understand my lease.

4. I broke a window in my apartment.

5. My landlord doesn't want to return my security deposit.

6. I have a job interview early tomorrow morning.

7. Some students talk in the library, and other students can't study.

8. My son doesn't want to do his homework. He just wants to be on the Internet all day.

EXERCISE 16 Fill in the blanks to complete the statement.

EXAMPLES: You'd better *take an umbrella* _____, or you're going to get wet.
You'd better fill up your gas tank right away, or *you're going to run* _____ *out of gas.*

1. Your stove is dirty. You'd better _____,
   or your landlord will keep your deposit.

2. He'd better _____, or he'll lose his job.

3. They'd better _____, or they'll fail this course.

4. He'd better put enough postage on that letter, or _____
   _____

5. The class starts in 5 minutes. We'd better hurry, or _____

_____

6. My passport is ready to expire. I _____,
or I won't be able to travel this summer.

7. The teacher said, "No talking during a test." We _____

_____, or the teacher will get angry.

8. I forgot my driver's license. Before I get into my car, I _____

_____, or I can get a ticket.

 8.6 Negatives of Modals and Related Expressions

Examples	Explanation
You **must not** change the locks without the landlord's permission. You **must not** take the landlord's smoke detector with you when you move.	Use *must not* for prohibition. These things are against the law or rule. *Must not* has an official tone.
I **can't** have a dog in my apartment. I **may not** have a waterbed in my apartment.	Use *cannot* or *may not* to show no permission. The meaning is about the same as *must not*. (*May not* is more formal than *cannot*.)
The landlord **is not supposed to** keep your security deposit. You **are not supposed to** talk to another student during the test. You **are not supposed to** park at a bus stop.	Use *be not supposed to* for prohibition. These things are against the law or rule. When reporting a rule, people use *be not supposed to* more than *must not*. Remember, *must not* has an official tone.
My landlady offered me a new lease. I **don't have to** move when my lease is up. The janitor takes out the garbage. I **don't have to** take it out.	These things are not necessary, not required. A person can do something if he wants, but he has no obligation to do this thing.
You **shouldn't** get angry. If you turn on the air-conditioning, you **shouldn't** leave the windows open. You **shouldn't** watch so much TV.	*Shouldn't* is for advice, not for rules.
You**'d better not** play your music so loud, or your neighbors will complain to the landlord.	*Had better not* is for a warning.

LANGUAGE NOTES

1. Remember, in affirmative statements, *have to, must,* and *be supposed to* have a very similar meaning. (Remember, *must* sounds more official.)

2. In negative statements, *must not, not have to,* and *shouldn't* have very different meanings.
   COMPARE:
   I *don't have to pay* my rent with cash. I can use a check.
   I *must not pay* my rent late.
   You *don't have to use* the elevator. You can use the stairs, if you like.
   There's a fire in the building. You *must not use* the elevator.

EXERCISE 17 Practice using *must not* for prohibition. (Use *you* in the impersonal sense.)

EXAMPLE: Name something you must not do.
            You must not steal.

1. Name something you must not do on the bus.

2. Name something you mustn't do during a test.

3. Name something you mustn't do in the library.

4. Name something you must not do in the classroom.

5. Name something you mustn't do on an airplane.

EXERCISE 18 Tell if you have to or don't have to do the following. For affirmative statements, you can also use *have got to*.

EXAMPLES: work on Saturdays
             I have to work on Saturdays. OR I've got to work on Saturdays.

             wear a suit to work
             I don't have to wear a suit to work.

1. speak English every day

2. use a dictionary to read the newspaper

3. pay rent on the first of the month

4. type my homework

5. work on Saturdays

6. come to school every day

7. pay my rent in cash

8. use public transportation

9. talk to the teacher after class

10. cook every day

EXERCISE 19 Answer these questions about your native country.

1. In your native country, does a citizen have to vote?

2. Do men have to serve in the military?

3. Do schoolchildren have to wear a uniform?

4. Do divorced men have to support their children?

5. Do people have to get permission to travel?

6. Do students have to pass an exam to get their high school or university diploma?

7. Do students have to pay for their own books?

8. Do citizens have to pay taxes?

9. Do people have to make an appointment to see a doctor?

10. Do young people have to show an ID to enter nightclubs?

EXERCISE 20 Fill in the blanks with *don't have to* (to show that something is not necessary) or *must not* or *be not supposed to* (to show that something is prohibited).

EXAMPLES: You ___*don't have to*___ bring your dictionary to class.

You ___*aren't supposed to*___ bring food into the computer lab.

1. You _____ talk to another student during a test.

2. You _____ drive through a red light.

3. You _____ speak English perfectly to become an American citizen. It's enough to speak simple English.

4. Resident aliens _____ become American citizens if they don't want to.

5. You _____ steal.

6. People over 17 years of age _____ attend school in the U.S. They can leave school if they want.

7. U.S. citizens _____ vote if they don't want to.

8. A U.S. citizen _____ support an enemy of the United States.

9. You _____ marry an American citizen to become a citizen of the U.S.

10. My lease says that I _____ have a dog in my apartment.

EXERCISE 21 Students (S) are asking the teacher (T) questions about the final exam. Fill in the blanks with the negative form of *have to, should, must, had better, can, may, be supposed to.* (In some cases, more than one answer is possible.)

S. Do I have to sit in a specific seat for the test?

T. No, you ___*don't have to*___ . You can choose any seat you want.
   (example)

S. Is it OK if I talk to another student during a test?

T. No. Absolutely not. You _____ talk to another student
   (1)
   during a test.

S. Is it OK if I use my book?

T. Sorry. You _____ use your book.
   (2)

S. What if I don't understand something on the test? Can I ask another student?

T. You _____ talk to another student, or I'll think you're
   (3)
   getting an answer. Ask me if you have a question.

S. What happens if I am late for the test? Will you let me in?

T. Of course I'll let you in. But you _____ come late.
   (4)
   You'll need a lot of time for the test.

S. Do I have to bring my own paper for the final test?

T. If you want to, you can. But you _____ bring paper.
   (5)
   I'll give you paper if you need it.

S. Must I write the test with a pen?

T. You can use whatever you want. You _____ use a
   (6)
   pen.

S. How long will the test take? The full period?

T. Probably not. You can use the full period, but you probably won't need so much time. Let me give you some advice: if you see an item that is difficult for you, go on to the next item. You

_____ spend too much time on a difficult item, or
(7)

you won't finish the test.

S. Can I bring coffee into the classroom?

T. The school has a rule about eating or drinking in the classroom.

You _____ bring food into the classroom.
(8)

S. If I finish the test early, must I stay in the room?

T. No, you _____ stay. You can leave.
(9)

Before You Read 1. Are people friendly with their neighbors in your community?
2. Do you know any of your neighbors now?

Read the following conversation. Pay special attention to *must*.

Two women meet for the first time in the hallway of their building and have this conversation.

The New Neighbors

L. Hi. You **must be** the new neighbor. I saw the moving truck out front this morning. Let me introduce myself. My name is Lisa. I live downstairs of you.

P. Nice to meet you, Lisa. My name is Paula. We just moved in.

crib

L. I saw the movers carrying a crib upstairs. You **must have** a baby.

P. We do. We have a ten-month-old son. He's sleeping now. Do you have any kids?

L. Yes, I have a 16-year-old-daughter and an 18-year-old son.

P. It **must be** hard to raise teenagers.

L. Believe me, it is! I **must spend** half my time worrying about where they are and what they're doing. My daughter talks on the phone all day. She **must spend** half of her waking hours on the phone with her friends. They're always whispering to each other. They **must have** some big secrets.

P. I know what you mean. My brother has a teenage daughter.

L. Listen, I don't want to take up any more of your time. You **must be** very busy. I just wanted to bring you these cookies.

P. Thanks. That's very nice of you. They're still warm. They **must be** right out of the oven.

L. They are. Maybe we can talk some other time when you're all unpacked.

8.7 *Must* for Conclusions

Examples	Explanation
The new neighbors have a crib. They **must have** a baby. Paula just moved in. She **must be** very busy. The teenage girls whisper all the time. They **must have** secrets.	*Must*, in these examples, shows a conclusion based on information we have or observations we make. *Must*, in these examples, talks about the present only, not the future.
I didn't see Paula's husband. He **must not** be home. Her daughter whispers on the phone. She **must not** want her parents to hear her conversation.	For a negative deduction, use *must not*. Do not use a contraction.

EXERCISE 22 A week later, Paula goes to Lisa's apartment and notices certain things. Use *must* + base form to show Paula's conclusions about Lisa's life.

EXAMPLE: There is a cat box in the kitchen.
            Lisa must have a cat.

Lisa's family

1. There are pictures of Lisa and her two children all over the house. There is no picture of a man.

2. There is a nursing certificate on the wall with Lisa's name on it.

3. There are many different kinds of coffee on a kitchen shelf.

4. There are a lot of classical music CDs.

5. In Lisa's bedroom, there's a sewing machine.

6. In the kitchen, there are a lot of cookbooks.

7. There's a piano in the living room.

8. In the bookshelf, there are a lot of books about modern art.

9. On the kitchen calendar, there's an activity filled in for almost every day of the week.

10. There are pictures of cats everywhere.

Family Calendar			
This Week	MOM	Joey	Ann
Sunday	Church social dinner at Molly's		
Monday	Carpool to school	Dentist 3:30	
Tuesday	Art Class 11:00		Start science project
Wednesday	Take cat to Vet	Report Due	
Thursday	Carpool to school		School play rehersal
Friday	PTA Meeting		Library with Lisa
Saturday		baseball game School Dance	piano lesson

EXERCISE 23

Many people get vanity license plates that tell something about their profession, hobbies, or families. Often words are abbreviated: M = am, U = you, 4 = For, 8 = the "ate" sound. Words are often without vowels. If you see the following license plates, what conclusion can you make about the owner? (You may work with a partner and get help from the teacher.)

EXAMPLES: EYEDOC ___*The owner must be an eye doctor.*___

1. I TCH ENGLSH _____

2. I LV CARS _____

3. I M GRANDMA _____

4. MUSC LVR _____

5. I LV DGS _____

6. TENNIS GR8 _____

7. I SK8 _____

8. CRPNTR _____

9. BSY MOM _____

10. SHY GUY _____

11. DAD OF TWO _____

12. RMNTIC GAL _____

13. NO TIME 4 U _____

14. CITY GAL _____

15. LDY DOC _____

16. LUV GLF _____

17. MXCAN GUY _____

18. I M GD COOK _____

19. ALWAYS L8 _____

20. WE DANCE _____

8.8 *Will* and *May/Might*

Examples	Explanation
My lease **will** expire on April 30.	Certainty about the future
My landlord **might** raise my rent at that time. I **may** move.	Possibility or uncertainty about the future
The teacher isn't here today. She **may** be sick. OR She **might** be sick.	Possibility or uncertainty about the present

LANGUAGE NOTES

1. *May* and *might* are modals. They both have about the same meaning: possibility or uncertainty, similar to the meaning of *maybe*. *Maybe* is an adverb. It usually comes at the beginning of the sentence.
   COMPARE:

   Maybe I will move.   I *may* move.
   Maybe he doesn't understand.   He *might* not understand.
   Maybe she is sick.   She *may* be sick.

2. We don't use a contraction for *may not* and *might not*.

EXERCISE 24 The following sentences contain *maybe*. Take away *maybe* and use *may* or *might* + base form.

EXAMPLE: Maybe your neighbors will complain if your music is loud.
Your neighbors might complain if your music is loud.

1. Maybe my sister will come to live with me.

2. Maybe she will find a job in this city.

3. Maybe my landlord will raise my rent.

4. Maybe I will get a dog.

5. Maybe my landlord won't allow me to have a dog.

6. Maybe I will move next year.

7. Maybe I will buy a house soon.

8. Maybe I won't stay in this city.

9. Maybe I won't come to class tomorrow.

10. Maybe the teacher will review modals if we need more help.

EXERCISE 25 Fill in the blanks with a possibility.

EXAMPLES: If you don't pay your rent on time, *you might have to pay a late fee.*

If I make a lot of noise in my apartment, *the neighbors may complain.*

1. When my lease is up, _____

2. If I don't clean my apartment before I move out, _____

_____

3. If a person doesn't graduate from high school, _____

_____

4. If I don't study for the next test, _____

5. If we don't register for classes early, _____

_____

6. If I don't pass this course, _____

EXERCISE 26 Fill in the blanks with possibilities.

EXAMPLE: One student isn't here today. She may _be out of town._

1. My neighbor's name is Robert T. Harris. His middle name might
   _____ or it might _____.

2. A. The school is getting a new teacher. Her name is Terry Karson.
      Do you know anything about her?

   B. Why do you say "her"? The new teacher may _____.
      Terry is sometimes a man's name.

3. A. I need a stamp. Do you have one?

   B. Let me look. I might _____.

4. A. Do you know where the nearest post office is?

   B. No, I don't. Ask the teacher. She might _____.

5. A. I don't have change for the vending machines. Do you have change
      for a dollar?

   B. Let me look in my pocket. I may _____.

6. A. Where is Linda Sanchez from?

   B. I don't know. That's a Spanish name. She might _____
      or she might _____.

7. A. Where's the dog? I can't find him.

   B. Did you look under the bed? He may _____.
      Or he may _____.

8. A. Do we have any more soda?

   B. Look in the refrigerator.

   A. I can't find any.

   B. We may not _____.

Before You Read
1. People often have a garage sale or an apartment sale before they move. At this kind of sale, people sell things that they don't want or need anymore. Did you ever buy anything at this kind of sale?
2. At a garage sale, it is usually not necessary to pay the asking price. You can bargain[2] with the seller. Can you bargain on prices in your native country? In a store? Where?

This is a conversation at a garage sale between a seller (S) and a buyer (B). Read the conversation. Pay special attention to modals and related expressions.

[2] When a buyer *bargains* with the seller, the buyer makes an offer lower than the asking price and hopes that he or she and the seller will agree on a lower price.

At a Garage Sale

S. I see you're looking at my microwave oven. **May** I help you with it?

B. Yes. I'm interested in buying one. Does it work well?

S. It's only two years old, and it's in perfect working condition. **Would you like** to try it out?

B. Sure. **Could** you plug it in somewhere?

S. I have an outlet right here. **Why don't we** boil a cup of water so you can see how well it works.

A few minutes later . . .

outlet

B. It seems to work well. **Would** you tell me why you're selling it, then?

S. We're moving next week. Our new apartment already has one.

B. How much do you want for it?[3]

S. $80.

B. **Will** you take $60?

S. **Can** you wait a minute? I'll ask my wife.

A few minutes later . . .

S. My wife says she'll let you have it for $65.

B. OK. **May** I write you a check?

S. I'm sorry. **I'd rather** have cash.

B. **Would** you hold it for me for an hour? I can go to the supermarket and cash a check.

S. **Could** you leave me a small deposit? Ten dollars, maybe?

B. Yes, I can.

S. Fine. I'll hold it for you, then.

8.9   Using Modals for Politeness

To ask permission	Explanation
May **Can** } I write you a check? **Could**	*May* and *could* are considered more polite than *can* by some speakers of English.

(continued)

---

[3] We ask "How much is it?" when the price is fixed. We ask "How much do you want for it?" when the price is negotiable. You can bargain for it.

To request that another person do something	Explanation
Can **Could** **Will** **Would** } you plug it in?	For a request, *could* and *would* are softer than *can* and *will*.

To express a want or desire	Explanation
Would you **like** to try out the microwave oven? Yes, I **would like** to see if it works. **I'd like** a cup of coffee.	*Would like* has the same meaning as *want*. *Would like* is softer than *want*. The contraction for *would* after a pronoun is *'d*.

To express preference	Explanation
Would you **rather** pay with cash or by credit card? **I'd rather** pay by credit card (than with cash).	We use *or* in questions with *would rather*. We use *than* in statements.

LANGUAGE NOTES

1. Modals are often used to make direct statements more polite.
    COMPARE:

    Plug it in. (VERY DIRECT)
    Would you plug it in, please? (MORE POLITE)

    Give me a deposit. (VERY DIRECT)
    Could you give me a deposit, please? (MORE POLITE)

    I want to buy the microwave. (DIRECT)
    I'd like to buy the microwave. (MORE POLITE)

2. We can make a suggestion by using a negative question form.
    COMPARE:

    Go to the supermarket and cash a check. (DIRECT)
    Why don't you go to the supermarket and cash a check? (MORE POLITE)

    Let's boil a cup of water. (DIRECT)
    Why don't we boil a cup of water? (MORE POLITE)

EXERCISE 27 Change each request to make it more polite. Practice *may, can, could + I?*

EXAMPLES: I want to use your phone.
              May I use your phone?

              I want to borrow a quarter.
              Could I borrow a quarter?

1. I want to help you.   3. I want to leave the room.
2. I want to close the door.   4. I want to write you a check.

EXERCISE 28 Change these commands to make them more polite. Practice *can, could, will, would + you?*

EXAMPLES: Call the doctor for me.
              Would you call the doctor for me?

              Give me a cup of coffee.
              Could you give me a cup of coffee, please?

1. Repeat the sentence.   3. Spell your name.
2. Give me your paper.   4. Tell me your phone number.

EXERCISE 29 Make these sentences more polite by using *would like*.

EXAMPLES: Do you want some help?
              Would you like some help?

              1.   I want to ask you a question.

              2.   The teacher wants to speak with you.

              3.   Do you want to try out the oven?

              4.   Yes. I want to see if it works.

EXERCISE 30 Make each suggestion more polite by putting it in the form of a negative question.

EXAMPLES: Plug it in.
              Why don't you plug it in?

              Let's eat now.
              Why don't we eat now?

1. Take a sweater.   3. Turn left here.
2. Let's turn off the light.   4. Let's leave early.

EXERCISE 31 Make a statement of preference using *would rather*.

EXAMPLE: work indoors/outdoors
I'd rather work indoors than outdoors.

   1.   live in the U.S./in my native country

   2.   live in the city/in a suburb

   3.   get up early/sleep late[4]

   4.   take a relaxing vacation/an active vacation

   5.   live in a house/a condo

   6.   read a story/write a composition

EXERCISE 32 Ask a question with the words given. Another student will answer.

EXAMPLE: eat Chinese food/Italian food
A. Would you rather eat Chinese food or Italian food?
B. I'd rather eat Italian food.

   1.   read fact/fiction

   2.   watch funny movies/serious movies

   3.   listen to classical music/popular music

   4.   visit Europe/Africa

   5.   own a large luxury car/a small sports car

   6.   watch a soccer game/take part in a soccer game

   7.   write a letter/receive a letter

   8.   cook/eat in a restaurant

EXERCISE 33 This is a conversation between a seller (S) and a buyer (B) at a garage sale. Make this conversation more polite by using modals and other polite expressions in place of the underlined words.

              May I help you?
S. ~~What do you want~~?

B. I'm interested in that lamp. Show it to me. Does it work?

S. I'll go and get a light bulb. Wait a minute.

---

[4] *Sleep late* means to wake up late in the morning

A few minutes later . . .

B. <u>Plug it in</u>.

S. You see? It works fine.

B. How much do you want for it?

S. This is one of a pair. I have another one just like it. They're $10 each.

I <u>prefer to sell</u> them together.

B. <u>Give them both to me for $15</u>.

S. I'll have to ask my husband. (*A few seconds later*) My husband says he'll sell them to you for $17.

B. Fine. I'll take them. Will you take a check?

S. I <u>prefer to</u> have cash.

B. I only have five dollars on me.

S. OK. I'll take a check. <u>Show me some identification</u>.

B. Here's my driver's license.

S. That's fine. Write the check to James Kucinski.

B. <u>Spell your name for me</u>.

S. K-U-C-I-N-S-K-I.

SUMMARY OF LESSON 8

Modal	Example	Explanation
can	I **can** stay in this apartment until March.	Permission
	I **can** type 75 words per minute.	Ability
	You **can't** park here. It's a bus stop.	Prohibition
	Can I borrow your pen?	Asking permission
	Can you turn off the light, please?	Request
should	You **should** be friendly with your neighbors.	A good idea
	You **shouldn't** leave the air conditioner on. It wastes electricity.	A bad idea
may	**May** I borrow your pen?	Asking permission
	You **may** leave the room.	Permission
	You **may not** talk during a test.	Prohibition
	It **may** rain tomorrow.	Future possibility
	The landlord **may** have an extra key.	Present possibility

Modal	Example	Explanation
might	It **might** rain tomorrow.	Future possibility
	The landlord **might** have an extra key.	Present possibility
must	A driver **must** have a license.	Rule or law
	You **must not** steal.	Prohibition
	My neighbor has a cat box. She **must** have a cat.	Conclusion
would	**Would** you help me move?	Request
would like	I **would like** to use your pen.	Want
would rather	I **would rather** live in the city than in the suburbs.	Preference
could	In my country, I **couldn't** say bad things about our country's leaders.	Past permission
	Before I came to the U.S., I **couldn't** speak English.	Past ability/inability
	Could you help me move?	Request
	Could I borrow your car?	Asking permission
have to	She **has to** leave.	Personal necessity
	He **had to** leave work early yesterday.	
have got to	She **has got to** see a doctor.	Personal necessity
not have to	You **don't have to** come back after the final exam, but you can if you want to.	No necessity
had better	You **had better** study, or you're going to fail the test.	Warning
be supposed to	I **am supposed to** pay my rent by the fifth of the month.	Reporting a rule
	We**'re not supposed to** have dog in our apartment.	
be able to	The teacher **is able to** use modals correctly.	Ability
be permitted OR allowed to	We**'re not allowed to** park here overnight.	Permission
	We**'re not permitted to** park here overnight.	

1. After a modal, we use the base form.

   I must ~~to~~ study.

   I can help~~ing~~ you now.

2. A modal has no ending.

   He can~~s~~ cook.

3. We don't put two modals together. We change the second modal to another form.

   have to
   She will ~~must~~ take the test.

4. Don't forget *to* after *be permitted, be allowed, be supposed, be able.*

   to
   We're not permitted ^ talk during a test.

5. Don't forget *be* before *permitted to, allowed to, supposed to, able to.*

   am
   I ^ not supposed to pay my rent late.

6. Use the correct word order in a question.

   should I
   What ~~I should~~ do about my problem?

7. Don't use *can* for past. Use *could* + a base form.

   couldn't go
   I ~~can't went~~ to the party last week.

8. Don't forget *would* before *rather.*

   'd
   I ^ rather live in Canada than in the U.S.

9. Don't forget *had* before *better.*

   'd
   You ^ better take a sweater. It's going to get cold.

10. Don't forget *have* before *got to.*

    've
    It's late. I ^ got to go.

11. Don't use *maybe* before a verb.

    may
    It ~~maybe will~~ rain later.

PART 1   Find the grammar mistakes with the underlined words, and correct them. Not every sentence has a mistake. If the sentence is correct, write **C**.

EXAMPLES: You must ~~to~~ stop at a red light.

You have to stop at a red light.   C

1.   We're not permitted use our books during the test.

2.   In my country, I couldn't traveled without permission from the government.

3.   When she can leave?

4.   What must I write on this application?

5.   She has to taking her daughter to the doctor now.

6.   What I should do about my problem?

7.   You not supposed to talk during the test.

8.   We're not allowed to take food into the computer lab.

9.   He can't have a dog in his apartment.

10.   Could I use your pen, please?

11.   I rather walk than drive.

12.   You'd better hurry. It's late.

13.   I got to talk to my boss about a raise.

14.   We maybe will buy a house.

15.   She might buy a new car next year.

16.   I may have to go home early tonight.

17.   He can speak English now, but he can't spoke it five years ago.

PART 2   This is a conversation between two friends. Choose the correct expression in parentheses ( ) to complete the conversation.

A.   I'm moving on Saturday. (*Could*/ *May*) you help me?
        (example)

B. I (*should / would*) like to help you, but I have a bad back. I went to my
(1)
doctor last week, and she told me that I (*shouldn't / don't have to*) lift
(2)
anything heavy for a while. (*Can / Would*) I help you any other way besides
(3)
moving?

A. Yes. I don't have enough boxes. (*Should / Would*) you help me find some?
(4)

B. Sure. I (*have to / must*) go shopping this afternoon. I'll pick up some boxes
(5)
while I'm at the supermarket.

A. Boxes can be heavy. You (*would / had*) better not lift them yourself.
(6)

B. Don't worry. I'll have someone put them in my car for me.

A. Thanks. I don't have a free minute. I (*couldn't / can't*) go to class all last
(7)
week. There's so much to do.

B. I know what you mean. You (*might / must*) be tired.
(8)

A. I am. I have another favor to ask. (*Can / Would*) I borrow your van on
(9)
Saturday?

B. I (*should / have to*) work on Saturday. How about Sunday? I (*must not /
(10)   (11)
don't have to*) work on Sunday.

A. That's impossible. I (*'ve got to / should*) move out on Saturday. The new
(12)
tenants are moving in Sunday morning.

B. Let me ask my brother. He has a van too. He (*must / might*) be able to let
(13)
you use his van. He (*has to / should*) work Saturday too, but only for half
(14)
a day.

A. Thanks. I'd appreciate it if you could ask him.

B. Why are you moving? You have a great apartment.

A. We decided to move to the suburbs. It's quieter there. And I want to have
a dog. I (*shouldn't / 'm not supposed to*) have a dog in my present apartment.
(15)
But my new landlord says I (*might / may*) have a dog.
(16)

B. I (*had / would*) rather have a cat. They're easier to take care of.
(17)

CLASSROOM ACTIVITIES

1. A student will read one of the following problems out loud to the class, pretending that this is his or her problem. Other students will ask for more information and give advice about this problem.

EXAMPLE:

My mother-in-law comes to visit all the time. When she's here, she always criticizes everything we do. I told my wife that I don't want her here, but she says, "It's my mother, and I want her here." What should I do?

A. How long do you think she will stay?
B. She might stay for about two weeks or longer.
C. How does she criticize you? What does she say?
B. She says I should help my wife more.
D. Well, I agree with her. You should help with housework.
B. My children aren't allowed to watch TV after 8 o'clock. But my mother-in-law lets them watch TV as long as they want.
E. You'd better have a talk with her and tell her your rules.

Problem 1. My mother is 80 years old, and she lives with us. It's very hard on my family to take care of her. We'd like to put her in a nursing home, where she can get better care. Mother refuses to go. What can we do?

Problem 2. I have a nice one-bedroom apartment with a beautiful view of a park and a lake. I live with my wife and one child. My friends from out of town often come to visit and want to stay at my apartment. In the last year, ten people came to visit us. I like to have visitors, but sometimes they stay from two to four weeks. It's hard on my family with such a small apartment. What should I tell my friends when they want to visit?

Problem 3. My best friend is married. Last week I saw her husband in a restaurant with another woman. They looked very romantic together. Do you think I should tell my friend?

Write your own problem to present to the class. It can be real or imaginary. (Suggestions: a problem with a neighbor, your landlord, a teacher or class, a service you are dissatisfied with)

_____

_____

_____

2. Circle a game you like from the list following. Find a partner who also likes this game. Write a list of some of the rules of this game. Tell what you can, cannot, should, have to, and must not do. (If you and your partner are from the same country, you can write about a game from your country.)

| chess | tennis | football | poker | other _____ |
| checkers | baseball | soccer | volleyball | |

EXAMPLE: checkers
You have to move the pieces on a diagonal. You can only move in one direction until you get a king. Then you can move in two directions.

_____

_____

_____

3. Write a vanity license plate that says something about you. Write it on the chalkboard. Other people have to guess what it says about you.

4. Work with a partner from your own country, if possible. Talk about some laws in your country that are different from laws in the United States. Present this information to the class.

EXAMPLE: Citizens must vote in my country. In the U.S., they don't have to vote.
People are supposed to carry identification papers at all times. In the U.S., people don't have to carry identification papers.
In my country, citizens must not own a gun.

DISCUSSION

1. Compare getting a driver's license in the U.S. with getting a driver's license in your native country. Are the requirements the same?

2. How did you find your apartment?

WRITING

1. Write a short composition comparing rules in an apartment in this city with rules in an apartment in your hometown or native country.

2. Write about the differences between rules at this college and rules at a college in your native country. Are students allowed to do things here that they can't do in your native country?

3. Find out what a student has to do to register for the first time at this college. You may want to visit the registrar's office to interview a worker there. Write a short composition explaining to a new student the steps for admission and registration.

OUTSIDE ACTIVITIES

1. Find out what you must do to get one of the following. Report your information to the class.

a. a passport (Call or write to the U.S. Department of State.)
b. a credit card (Get a credit card application from a business or bank.)
c. a library card (Visit your public library.)
d. a marriage license (Call the marriage license department of this county.)

2. Call or write to the Mayor's office or department of housing in your city. Ask if this department can send you a list of rights and responsibilities of renters and landlords.

3. Look at the Sunday newspaper for notices about garage sales or apartment sales. What kind of items are going to be sold? If you have time, go to a sale. Report about your experience to the class.

4. Get a newspaper. Look for the advice column. Read the problems and the advice. Circle the modals. Do you agree with the advice?

Internet Activities

1. Try to find information online about tenants' rights in the city where you live.

2. Find a phone directory online. Look up the names and addresses of moving companies in your city.

3. Find apartments for rent online.

GRAMMAR
Present Perfect
Present Perfect Continuous

CONTEXT
Genealogy
Carol's Search for Her Roots

LESSON FOCUS

We form the present perfect tense with the auxiliary verb *have* or *has* and the past participle.
> I *have studied* English for six months.
> They *have visited* Miami many times.

We form the present perfect continuous tense with *have* or *has*, plus *been*, and the verb + *-ing*.
> She *has been working* for three hours.
> We *have been watching* TV for 45 minutes.

1. Do you know your family's history?
2. Has your family always lived in the same country?

Read the following article. Pay special attention to the present perfect tense.

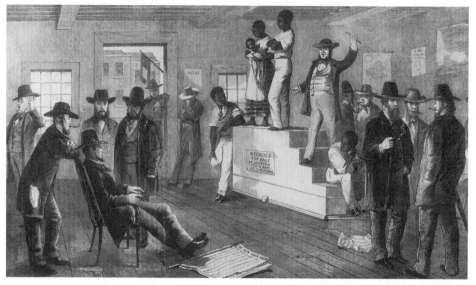

Slave auction

Genealogy

Are you interested in knowing about the history of your family? Many Americans are. *Roots*, a 1977 TV series, showed one man's search to find the history of his family. He learned that his family came from Africa to America as slaves. Ever since this TV series appeared, genealogy **has become** one of America's most popular hobbies. People **have started** to ask themselves: Where does my family come from? How long **has** my family **been** in the United States? Why did they come here? How did they come here? What kind of people were my ancestors?

Until recently, finding a family history was a difficult task. But since the Internet became popular in the 1990s, searching for one's past **has become** a lot easier. Cyndi Howells, from Washington State, quit her job in 1992 and **has worked** on her family history since then. She **has** also **created** a Web site with over 50,000 links to help searchers find their roots. Her site, with about 70,000 visitors a day, **has made** searching for records much easier.

Using the Internet is just a start. Most people have to go to libraries and courthouses to search for family records. They look at census reports, old newspapers (for marriage and death notices), tax records, and land deeds.[1] Early census records are not complete, but since the mid-1800s,

Did you know...?

The LDS Family History Library in Salt Lake City, Utah, has the largest database of genealogy records.

---

[1] A *deed* is a document that shows the owner of a piece of land.

the U.S. Census **has kept** detailed records of family members, their ages, occupations, and place of birth.

How far back can you go in searching for relatives? One Chinese American **has traced** his family history back 2,800 years. Another genealogist **has collected** information about 88,000 relatives. Some people **have** even **found** living relatives that they didn't know about.

But finding this information takes a lot of time. Some people spend all their free time searching for clues that connect them to the past.

9.1 The Present Perfect Tense—Overview

Subject	*Have/Has*	Past Participle	Complement
Genealogy	**has**	**become**	very popular.
The Internet	**has**	**made**	the search easier.
Many people	**have**	**used**	the Internet to find information.
There	**has**	**been**	a lot of interest in genealogy lately.
We	**have**	**been**	in the U.S. for many years.

LANGUAGE NOTES

1. We form the present perfect with the auxiliary verbs *have* or *has* + the past participle. Use *have* with *I, you, we, they.* Use *has* with *he, she, it.*
2. After *there,* we use *have* or *has,* depending on the noun that follows. Use *has* with a singular noun. Use *have* with a plural noun.
   There *has* been a mistake.
   There *have* been some problems.

3. For some verbs, regular and irregular, both the past participle and the past form are the same.

REGULAR VERBS

Base Form	Past Form	Past Participle
study	studied	studied
look	looked	looked

IRREGULAR VERBS

Base Form	Past Form	Past Participle
leave	left	left
understand	understood	understood

4. For some verbs, the past participle is different from the past form.[2]

Base Form	Past Form	Past Participle
become	became	become
come	came	come
run	ran	run
blow	blew	blown
draw	drew	drawn
fly	flew	flown
grow	grew	grown
know	knew	known
throw	threw	thrown
swear	swore	sworn
tear	tore	torn
wear	wore	worn
break	broke	broken
choose	chose	chosen
freeze	froze	frozen
speak	spoke	spoken
steal	stole	stolen
begin	began	begun
drink	drank	drunk
ring	rang	rung
sing	sang	sung
sink	sank	sunk
swim	swam	swum
arise	arose	arisen
bite	bit	bitten
drive	drove	driven
ride	rode	ridden
rise	rose	risen
write	wrote	written
be	was/were	been
eat	ate	eaten
fall	fell	fallen
forgive	forgave	forgiven
give	gave	given
mistake	mistook	mistaken
see	saw	seen
shake	shook	shaken
take	took	taken
Miscellaneous Changes		
do	did	done
forget	forgot	forgotten
get	got	gotten
go	went	gone
lie	lay	lain
prove	proved	proven (or proved)
show	showed	shown (or showed)

[2] For an alphabetical listing of irregular past tenses and past participles, see Appendix M.

EXERCISE 1   Write the past participle of these verbs.

EXAMPLE: eat _____eaten_____

1. go _____
2. see _____
3. look _____
4. study _____
5. bring _____
6. take _____
7. say _____
8. be _____
9. find _____
10. leave _____
11. live _____
12. know _____
13. like _____
14. fall _____
15. feel _____
16. come _____
17. break _____
18. wear _____
19. choose _____
20. drive _____
21. write _____
22. put _____
23. begin _____
24. want _____
25. get _____
26. fly _____
27. sit _____
28. drink _____
29. grow _____
30. give _____

Compare statements, questions, and short answers using the present perfect.

Wh-Word	Have/Has Haven't/Hasn't	Subject	Have/Has Haven't/Hasn't	Past Participle	Complement	Short Answer
		I	have	been	busy.	
		I	haven't	been	available.	
	Have	you		been	tired?	Yes, I have.
Why	have	you		been	busy?	
Why	haven't	you		been	available?	
		Who	has	been	available?	

LANGUAGE NOTES

1. We can make a contraction with the subject pronouns and *have* or *has*.

I have = I've	He has = He's
You have = You've	She has = She's
We have = We've	It has = It's
They have = They've	There has = There's

2. The **'s** in *he's, she's, it's* can mean *has* or *is*. The word following the contraction will tell you what the contraction means.
    She's leaving. = She *is* leaving.
    She's left. = She *has* left.

3. Don't use a contraction with a short *yes* answer.
    Has he left? Yes, he *has*. NOT: Yes, *he's*.

4. To make the negative, put *not* after *have* or *has*. The negative contractions are *haven't* and *hasn't*.
    I *haven't* found any information about my grandfather's family.
    My family *hasn't* been in the U.S. for long.

5. We can add an adverb (*always, never, recently, probably, even*) between the auxiliary verb and the main verb.
    I have *always* wanted to know about my family's history.
    I have *recently* begun to study genealogy.

EXERCISE 2 Fill in the blanks with the missing words of this conversation.

A. Have you _____been_____ in the U.S. for long?
   (example)

B. No. I _____(1)_____ .

A. How _____(2)_____ _____(3)_____ you been in the U.S.?

B. I'_____(4)_____ been here for only six months. I come from Guatemala.

A. I come from Mexico. I've just started to become interested in my family's history. I've _____(5)_____ several magazine articles about genealogy. It's fascinating. Are you interested in your family's history?

B. Of course I am. I'_____(6)_____ _____(7)_____ interested in it for a long time.

A. _____(8)_____ you found out anything interesting?

B. Oh, yes. I've found that some of my ancestors were Mayans and some were from Spain and France. In fact, my great-great grandfather was a Spanish prince.

A. How did you find out so much? Have you ever _____(9)_____ to Spain or France to look at records there?

B. Not yet. I'_____(10)_____ spent many hours on the Internet. I've also _____(11)_____ to libraries to get more information.

A. How many ancestors _____(12)_____ _____(13)_____ found so far?

B. I've _____(14)_____ about 50, but I'm still looking. It'_____(15)_____ been very time-consuming but a lot of fun. My brother in Guatemala is also very interested in genealogy. He _____(16)_____ helped me a lot too. He's started to make a family tree.

A. _____(17)_____ he learned anything interesting?

B. Oh, yes. He'_____(18)_____ found out that he's related to me!!

9.3 Uses of the Present Perfect—Overview

Examples	Explanation
He **has been** interested in genealogy since 1997. I **have been** interested in genealogy for about two years.	The action continues during a period of time that started in the past and includes the present.
I **have gone** to the library three times this month. I **have found** 50 relatives so far.	The action repeats during a period of time that started in the past and includes the present.
Genealogy **has become** an American hobby. Many people **have found** relatives and ancestors by using the Internet.	The action occurred at an indefinite time in the past. It still has importance to a present situation.

EXERCISE 3 Fill in the blanks with the missing words.

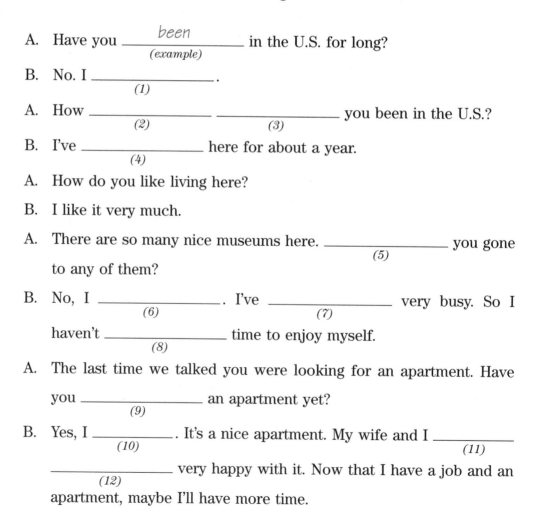

A. Have you ___*been*___ in the U.S. for long?
   (example)

B. No. I _____.
   (1)

A. How _____ _____ you been in the U.S.?
   (2)   (3)

B. I've _____ here for about a year.
   (4)

A. How do you like living here?

B. I like it very much.

A. There are so many nice museums here. _____ you gone
   (5)
   to any of them?

B. No, I _____. I've _____ very busy. So I
   (6)   (7)
   haven't _____ time to enjoy myself.
   (8)

A. The last time we talked you were looking for an apartment. Have
   you _____ an apartment yet?
   (9)

B. Yes, I _____. It's a nice apartment. My wife and I _____
   (10)   (11)
   _____ very happy with it. Now that I have a job and an
   (12)
   apartment, maybe I'll have more time.

A. I'm going to the Art Museum on Saturday. Do you want to go with me?

B. I _____ always _____ to see the Art Museum. I'd
 (13)   (14)

love to go with you. My wife _____ never seen the Art Museum
                                (15)

either. Can she come along too?

A. Of course.

9.4 Continuation from Past to Present

We use the present perfect tense to show that an action or state started in the past and continues to the present.

Examples	Explanation
I **have had** my computer **for** two years.	Use *for* + an amount of time: *for two years, for ten months, for a long time,* etc.
I **have been** interested in genealogy **since** 1997.	Use *since* + date, month, year, etc. to show when the action began: *since April, since 1977, since May 2,* etc.
I **have been** interested in genealogy **since** I saw the TV program "Roots."	Use *since* + a clause to show the start of a continuous action. The verb in the *since* clause is in the simple past tense: *since he found a job, since he saw the TV program, since he came to the U.S.*
How long has your family **been** in the U.S.?	Use *how long* to ask about the amount of time from the past to the present.
We **have always wanted** to know more about our ancestors.	We use the present perfect with *always* to show that an action began in the past and continues to the present.
I **have never gone** to Spain.	We use the present perfect with *never* to show that something has not occurred from the past to the present.

EXERCISE 4   Fill in the blanks with the missing words.

EXAMPLE: I've known my best friend _*since*_ we were in high school.

1. My brother has been in the U.S. _____ 1998.

2. My mother _____ never been in the U.S.

3. How _____ have you been in the U.S.?

4. I've known the teacher since I _____ to study at this college.

5. She's _____ married for two years.

6. She's had the same job _____ ten years.

7. My wife and I _____ known each other since we _____ in elementary school.

8. She'_____ been a student at this college _____ September.

9. I've had my car for three years. _____ long have you _____ your car?

10. I'm interested in art. I'_____ _____ interested in art since I was in high school.

11. _____ always wanted to have my own business.

12. We've never _____ a test on the present perfect.

EXERCISE 5   Write **true** statements using the present perfect with the words given and *for, since, always*, or *never*. Share your sentences with the class.

EXAMPLES: know *My parents have known each other for over 40 years.*

have *I've had my car since 1998.*

want *I've always wanted to learn English.*

1. have _____

2. be _____

3. want _____

4. know _____

EXERCISE 6   Make statements with *always*.

EXAMPLE: Name something you've always thought about.
I've always thought about my future.

1.   Name something you've always enjoyed.

2.   Name a person you've always liked.

3.   Name something you've always wanted to do.

4.   Name something you've always wanted to have.

5.   Name something you've always needed.

6.   Name something you've always been interested in.

7.   Name something you've always thought about.

EXERCISE 7   Make statements with *never*.

EXAMPLE: Name a machine you've never used.
I've never used a fax machine.

1.   Name a movie you've never seen.

2.   Name a food you've never liked.

3.   Name a subject you've never studied.

4.   Name a city you've never visited.

5.   Name a sport you've never played.

6.   Name a food you've never tasted.

EXERCISE 8   Write four sentences telling about things you've always done (or been). Share your sentences with the class.

EXAMPLES: *I've always cooked the meals in my family.*

I've always been lazy.

1.   _____

2.   _____

3.   _____

4.   _____

EXERCISE 9 Write four sentences telling about things you've never done (or been) but would like to. Share your sentences with the class.

EXAMPLES: *I've never studied photography, but I'd like to.*

I've never acted in a play, but I'd like to.

1. _____

2. _____

3. _____

4. _____

9.5 The Simple Present vs. The Present Perfect

Simple Present	Present Perfect
I **am** in the U.S. now.	I **have been** in the U.S. for two years.
She **has** a car.	She **has had** her car since March.
I **love** my job.	I **have** always **loved** my job.
I **don't work** in a restaurant.	I **have** never **worked** in a restaurant.

LANGUAGE NOTES

The simple present refers only to the present time. The present perfect with *for, since, always,* or *never* connects the past to the present.

EXERCISE 10 Read each statement about your teacher. Then ask the teacher a question beginning with the words given. Include *always* in your question. Your teacher will answer.

EXAMPLE: You're a teacher. Have you _____ *always been a teacher* _____?
No. I was an accountant before I became a teacher. I've only been a teacher for five years.

1. You teach English. Have you _____?

2. You work at this college. Have you _____?

3. You think about grammar. Have you _____?

4. English is easy for you. Has English _____?

5. Your last name is _____. Has your last
    name _____?

6. You're interested in foreigners. Have you _____?

7. You live in this city. Have you _____?

8. You're a teacher. Have you _____?

EXERCISE 11 Ask the teacher these questions. If the answer is yes, ask "Have you always . . . ?"

EXAMPLE: Do you like soccer?
Teacher: Yes, I do.
Student: Have you always liked soccer?
Teacher: Yes. I've liked soccer since I was a small child.

1. Are you an American citizen?

2. Do you wear glasses?

3. Do you like to travel?

4. Are you interested in your family history?

5. Are you an optimist?

6. Are you health conscious?

7. Do you save money?

8. Do you think about your future?

Before You Read 1. Do you think it's important to know your family's history? Why or why not?

2. What would you like to know about your ancestors?

Read the following article. Pay special attention to present perfect continuous and present perfect verbs.

Carol's Search for Her Roots

My name is Carol Angelo. I am the second generation of my family born in the U.S. My family came from a small town in the mountains in Southern Italy. I've **been working** on my family tree for two years. It's been fun but **has** sometimes **been** frustrating. I've **been spending** all my free time at a family history library looking for family records. I've also **been spending** a lot of time on the Internet looking at Web sites for information about genealogy. I've **joined** genealogy newsgroups[3], which **have been** a big help. I've **gone** to courthouses to look for public records, such as land deeds and tax records. I've **been reading** old newspapers, checking the obituaries[4] and wedding notices. I've **been searching** old phone books for family names and new phone books online[5] for living relatives in Italy. I was fortunate to find a man in Italy who went to the town where my ancestors were born. He provided me with a lot of information, pictures, and a wonderful book about the town my family came from.

By doing this search, I **have found** that I still have relatives in Italy and here that I didn't know existed. This year, there was a huge family reunion, and I was able to meet some of my relatives for the first time. People came from all over the country and brought old photo albums along with stories. I am in the process of doing a family Web site where we can all exchange information and photos and chat online.

So far I **have** only **found** information from the last couple hundred years; there is much more for me to do. One thing I **have learned** about genealogy is that it is a work in progress that is never finished.

---

[3] A *newsgroup* is a group of people on the Internet who communicate with each other about a similar interest. There are thousands of newsgroups on the Internet.
[4] *Obituaries* are death notices.
[5] *Online* means on the Internet.

9.6 The Present Perfect Continuous

Wh-Word	Have/Has Haven't/ Hasn't	Subject	Have/Has Haven't/ Hasn't	Been + Verb-*ing*	Complement	Short Answer
		Carol	has	been living	in the U.S.	
		She	hasn't	been living	in Italy.	
	Has	she		been living	in New York?	No, she **hasn't**.
How long	**has**	she		been living	in the U.S.?	
Why	**hasn't**	she		been living	in Italy?	
		Who	has	been living	in Italy?	

LANGUAGE NOTES

1. With some verbs (*live, work, study, teach, wear*), we can use either the present perfect or the present perfect continuous with actions that began in the past and continue to the present. There is very little difference in meaning.
    She *has been working* on her family history for two years.
    She *has worked* on her family history for two years.

2. If the action is happening right now, at this minute, it is better to use the present perfect continuous.
    She *is sleeping* now.→ She *has been sleeping* for eight hours.

3. Remember that we do not use the continuous form with nonaction verbs.
    She *has had* a car since she came to the U.S. (NOT: She has been having . . .)
    Some nonaction verbs are: *like, love, have, want, need, know, remember, hear, own, see, seem, understand*.

EXERCISE 12 Write **true** statements using the present perfect continuous with the words given and *for* or *since*. Share your sentences with the class.

EXAMPLE: work ___My brother has been working as a waiter for six years.___

1. study English _____
2. work _____
3. live _____
4. use _____
5. study _____

EXERCISE 13 The following statements refer to the present only. Include the past by changing to a present perfect continuous statement. Use *for* or *since*. Fill in the blanks to make a **true** statement about yourself.

EXAMPLE: I'm studying _____ karate. _____

  I've been studying karate for six years.

1. I live in _____

_____

2. I work in/as _____

_____

3. I attend _____
  (write name of school)

4. The teacher is explaining the present perfect tense.

_____

5. The students are practicing the present perfect continuous.

_____

EXERCISE 14 Read aloud each of the following present tense questions. Another student will answer. If the answer is *yes*, add a present perfect continuous question with "How long have you . . . ?"

EXAMPLE: Do you play a musical instrument?
  A. Do you play a musical instrument?
  B. Yes. I play the piano.
  A. How long have you been playing the piano?
  B. I've been playing the piano since I was a child.

1. Do you drive?

2. Do you work?

3. Do you use the Internet?

4. Do you wear glasses?

5. Do you play a musical instrument?

Ask the teacher questions with "How long . . . ?" and the present perfect continuous form of the words given. The teacher will answer your questions.

EXAMPLE: speak English
A. How long have you been speaking English?
B. I've been speaking English all[6] my life.

1. teach English
2. work at this school
3. live in this city

4. use this book
5. live at your present address

EXERCISE **16** Fill in the blanks in the following conversations.

EXAMPLE: A. Do you wear glasses?

B. Yes, I ___do.___

A. How long ___have___ you ___been wearing___ glasses?

B. I ___'ve been wearing___ glasses since I ___was___ in high school.

1.   A. Do you work in a restaurant?

B. Yes, I do.

A. How long _____ you _____ in a restaurant?

B. I _____ in a restaurant since 1998.

2.   A. Does your father live in the U.S.?

B. Yes, he _____ .

A. How long _____ he been _____ in the U.S.?

B. He _____ in the U.S. since he _____ 25 years old.

3.   A. Are you studying for the test now?

B. Yes, I _____ .

A. How long _____ for the test?

B. For _____ .

[6] We do not use the preposition *for* before *all*.

4. A. Is your teacher teaching you the present perfect lesson?

B. Yes, he _____.

A. _____ long _____ you this lesson?

B. Since _____.

5. A. Are they using the computers now?

B. Yes, _____.

A. How long _____ them?

B. _____ they started to write their compositions.

6. A. Are you studying your family history?

B. Yes, we _____.

A. How long _____?

B. Since we _____.

7. A. _____ your grandparents live in the U.S.?

B. Yes, they _____.

A. How _____ in the U.S.?

B. Since they _____ born.

8. A. _____ you using the Internet?

B. Yes, I _____.

A. How _____?

B. _____ for two hours.

9.7 The Present Perfect with Repetition from Past to Present

We use the present perfect to talk about the repetition of an action in a time period that includes the present.

now

Past ←----┌----x--------x-------x----┼-------------------------→ Future

Carol **has gone** to the library three times this month.

Examples	Explanation
Carol **has used** the Internet five times this week. She **has learned** a lot about her family in the past two years.	We often use a number or an expression that indicates repetition, such as *a lot, several times, a few times.*
So far she **has found** information only for the past couple hundred years. She **has gone** to only one family reunion up to now.	We sometimes use *so far* and *up to now* to mean "including this moment."
How many relatives in Italy **has** she **met**? How much information **has** she **gotten** about her family?	We can ask a question about repetition with *how many* or *how much.*
How many times **has** she **gone** to Italy this year? She **hasn't gone** to Italy **at all** this year.	If the answer is zero, we use a negative verb + *at all.*

LANGUAGE NOTES

1. Do not use the continuous form for repetition.
    She *has gone* to the dentist three times this year.
    NOT: She *has been going* to the dentist three times this year.

2. We use the present perfect when the time period is open and there is a possibility for more repetition to occur. Open time periods include: *today, this week, this month, this year, this semester.* Do not use the present perfect with a past time expression such as *yesterday, last month,* or *last year.* Use the simple past with a past time expression.
    COMPARE:
    I *have seen* two movies this month.
    I *saw* four movies last month.
    He *has been* absent three times this semester.
    He *was* absent five times last semester.

EXERCISE 17 A student is talking to a teacher about her grade. Fill in the blanks with the present perfect tense of the verb in parentheses ( ).

EXAMPLE: S: Why am I failing this course?

T: We ___*have had*___ six tests so far, but you _____ only
   (example: have)   *(1 take)*

four of them. And you _____ two out of those four. Also,
                       (2 fail)

you _____ absent five times. You _____
    (3 be)   *(4 not give)*

me any compositions at all this semester.

S: But I _____ very busy with my job this month. And my mother
         (5 be)

_____ sick this month. I _____ her
   (6 be)   *(7 take)*

to the doctor twice this month.

T: I'm sorry you're having so many problems. But when you're absent, you
need to call me and find out about your assignments and tests.

S: I _____ to call you several times this week, but you never answer.
     (8 try)

T: Most of the time I'm in class. Please call the English office and leave a
message with the secretary.

S: I will.

EXERCISE 18 Ask a *yes/no* question with *so far* or *up to now* and the words given. Another student will answer.

EXAMPLE: you/come to every class
A. Have you come to every class so far?
B. Yes, I have.
   OR
B. No, I haven't. I've missed three classes.

1. we/have any tests

2. this lesson/be difficult

3. the teacher/give a lot of homework

4. you/understand all the explanations

5. you/have any questions about this lesson

EXERCISE 19 Ask a question with "How many . . . ?" and the words given. Talk about this month. Another student will answer.

EXAMPLE: times/go to the post office
A. How many times have you gone to the post office this month?
B. I've gone to the post office once this month.
    OR
I haven't gone to the post office at all this month.

1. letters/write
2. times/eat in a restaurant
3. times/get paid
4. long-distance calls/make

5. books/buy
6. times/go to the movies
7. movies/rent
8. times/cook

EXERCISE 20 Write four questions to ask another student or your teacher about repetition from the past to the present. Use *how much* or *how many*. The other person will answer.

EXAMPLES: *How many cities have you lived in?*

How many English courses have you taken at this college?

1. _____

2. _____

3. _____

4. _____

9.8 The Simple Past vs. the Present Perfect with Repetition

Present Perfect	Simple Past
I **have used** the Internet twice today. *Today is not finished. There's a possibility for more Internet use today.*	I **used** the Internet three times yesterday. *Yesterday is finished. The number three is final.*
I **have gone** to many American cities. *I can still go to other American cities.*	Martin Luther King **went** to many American cities to fight for equality. *He died. He cannot go to another American city.*

LANGUAGE NOTES

1. When we use a past time expression (*yesterday, last week, last year*), the number is final. We must use the simple past tense.

   She *went* to Alaska last summer.

2. If you refer to the experiences of a dead person, you must use the simple past tense because nothing more can be added to that person's experience.

   Marilyn Monroe *starred* in many movies. (She died in 1962.)
   Julia Roberts *has starred* in many American movies.

3. If you are an immigrant in the U.S. and do not plan to live in your native country again, use the simple past tense to talk about experiences in your native country.

   COMPARE:
   In my native country, I *had* five jobs.
   In the U.S., I *have had* two jobs.

4. With present time expressions such as *today, this week* and *this month*, use the present perfect if you think there will be more occurrences in this time period. Use the simple past if you think that the number is final.

   She *has eaten* three cookies today. (She may eat more cookies.)
   She *ate* three cookies today. (Three is probably the final number.)

EXERCISE 21 Fill in the blanks with the simple past or the present perfect to ask a question. Another student will answer.

EXAMPLES: How many cars _____ *have you owned* _____ in the U.S.?
   I've owned two cars in the U.S.

   How many cars _____ *did you own* _____ in your country?
   I owned only one car in my country.

   1. How many apartments _____ in your country?

   2. How many apartments _____ in the U.S.?

   3. How many schools _____ in your country?

   4. How many schools _____ in the U.S.?

   5. How much coffee _____ yesterday?

   6. How much coffee _____ today?

   7. How many jobs _____ in the U.S.?

   8. How many jobs _____ in your country?

   9. How many compositions _____ last semester?

   10. How many compositions _____ this semester?

9.9 The Present Perfect with Indefinite Past Time

We use the present perfect to refer to an action that occurred at an indefinite time in the past that still has importance to the present situation.

```
                                    now
Past ←-----┌--------?-----------------┬------------------------→ Future
           │  Have you ever           │
           │  used the Internet?      │
           └──────────────────────────→
```

Examples	Explanation
Have you ever **used** the Internet? Yes, I **have**. **Have** you ever **gone** to a family reunion? I**'ve gone** to many family reunions. **Has** Carol ever **gone** to Italy? No, she never **has**.	A question with *ever* asks about any time between the past and the present. Put *ever* between the subject and the main verb. We can answer an *ever* question with a frequency response: *a few times, many times, often, never.*
Has Carol **met** her cousin yet? Yes, she **has** already **met** her cousin. **Has** Carol **finished** her study of her family yet? No, she **hasn't finished** it yet. OR No, not yet.	*Yet* and *already* refer to an indefinite time in the near past. Use *yet* in questions and negatives. Use *already* in affirmative statements.
Have you **washed** the dishes yet? Yes. I **have** just **washed** them.	*Just* shows that something happened very recently.

EXERCISE **22** A man (A) is trying to remember where he met a woman (B) whom he sees at a party. Fill in the blanks to complete the conversation.

A. Excuse me. You look familiar. ___*Have*___ we ever ___*met*___ before?
   (*example: meet*)

B. I don't think so.

A. I'm sure I've met you. Have you ever _____ to the University of
   (*1 go*)
   Wisconsin? I was a student there five years ago.

B. No, I _____.
   (*2*)

A. _____ in Milwaukee?
   (*3 ever/live*)

B. No, I never _____ .
      (4)

A. _____ your picture ever _____ in the newspaper?
      (5 be)

B. No, it never _____ .
      (6)

A. What's your name?

B. Betty Shapiro.

A. Are you related to Michael Shapiro?

B. I _____ of him.
      (7 never/hear)

A. _____ Boone School?
      (8 your children/ever/attend)

B. I don't have any children.

A. _____ at First National Bank?
      (9 ever/work)

B. Yes! I work there now. I'm a teller.

A. I work there too! I work in the accounting department. So that's where I know you from.

EXERCISE 23 A mother (M) is trying to give her grown son (S) something to eat. Fill in the blanks to complete the conversation.

M. Do you want something to eat? _____*Have you eaten*_____ yet?
                                        (you/eat)

S. No, thanks. I'm not hungry. I _____ just _____ .
                                   (1 eat)

M. Your father _____ his dinner yet. You can eat
                  (2 not/have)
with him.

S. I _____ you. I'm not hungry.
      (3 already/tell)

M. Have a little dessert, then. I _____ an apple pie.
                                    (4 just/make)

S. It seems I _____ myself clear yet. I'm not hungry!
                (5 not/make)

Answering with Present Perfect	Answering with Simple Past
Have you ever gone to Italy? Yes, I **have gone** there several times.	Have you ever gone to Italy? Yes, I **went** there in 1997.
Have you ever taken a taxi in this city? No. I **have** never **taken** a taxi in this city.	Have you ever taken a taxi in this city? Yes, I **took** a taxi last week.
Have you eaten dinner yet? Yes, I **have eaten** dinner already.	Have you eaten dinner yet? Yes, I **ate** dinner at five o'clock.
Have you written the letter yet? No, I **haven't written** the letter yet.	Have you written the letter yet? Yes, I **wrote** it 15 minutes ago.

LANGUAGE NOTES

A present perfect question can be answered with the simple past tense when a specific time is introduced.

EXERCISE 24 Ask a question with "Have you ever . . . ?" and the present perfect tense of the verb in parentheses ( ). Another student will answer. To answer with a specific time, use the past tense. To answer with a frequency response, use the present perfect tense. (You may work with a partner.)

EXAMPLES: (go) to the zoo
A. Have you ever gone to the zoo?
B. Yes. I've gone there many times.

(go) to Disneyland
A. Have you ever gone to Disneyland?
B. Yes. I went there last summer.

1. (work) in a factory
2. (lose) a glove
3. (run) out of gas[7]
4. (fall) out of bed
5. (make) a mistake in English grammar
6. (tell) a lie
7. (eat) raw[8] fish

[7] To *run out of gas* means to use all the gas in your car.
[8] *Raw* fish is not cooked.

8. (study) calculus
9. (meet) a famous person
10. (go) to an art museum
11. (stay) up all night
12. (break) a window
13. (get) locked out[9] of your house or car

14. (see) a French movie
15. (go) to Las Vegas
16. (travel) by ship
17. (be) in love
18. (write) a poem

EXERCISE 25 Write five questions with *ever* to ask your teacher. Your teacher will answer.

EXAMPLES: *Have you ever gotten a ticket for speeding?*

Have you ever visited Poland?

1. _____

2. _____

3. _____

4. _____

5. _____

EXERCISE 26 Ask a question with *ever* and the words given. Another student will answer.

EXAMPLE: your country/have a woman president
A. Has your country ever had a woman president?
B. Yes, it has. We had a woman president from 1975 to 1979.

1. your country/have a civil war

2. your country's leader/visit the U.S.

3. an American president/visit your country

4. your country/have a woman president

5. you/go back to visit your country

6. there/be an earthquake in your hometown

[9] To get *locked out* of your house means that you can't get in because you left the keys inside.

EXERCISE 27 Ask a student who has recently arrived in this country if he or she has done these things yet.

EXAMPLE: buy a car
A. Have you bought a car yet?
B. Yes, I have.   OR   No, I haven't.   OR   I bought a car last year.

1. find a job
2. make any American friends
3. open a bank account

4. save any money
5. buy a car
6. write to your family

SUMMARY OF LESSON 9

1.   Compare the present perfect and the simple past

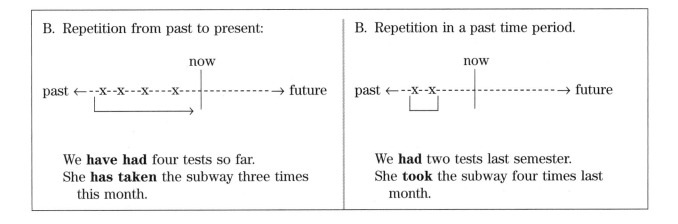

Present Perfect	Simple Past
A. The action of the sentence began in the past and includes the present:	A. The action of the sentence is completely past:
I've **had** my car since May. I've **been** in the U.S. for ten years. How long **have** you **known** the teacher? I've always **wanted** to learn karate.	I **bought** my car last May. I **was** in Thailand for two years before I came to the U.S. When **did** you **meet** the teacher? When I **was** a child, I always **wanted** to ride my bike.
B. Repetition from past to present:	B. Repetition in a past time period.
We **have had** four tests so far. She **has taken** the subway three times this month.	We **had** two tests last semester. She **took** the subway four times last month.

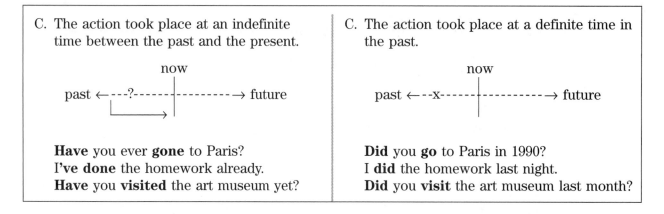

C. The action took place at an indefinite time between the past and the present.	C. The action took place at a definite time in the past.
Have you ever **gone** to Paris? **I've done** the homework already. **Have** you **visited** the art museum yet?	**Did** you **go** to Paris in 1990? I **did** the homework last night. **Did** you **visit** the art museum last month?

2. Compare the present perfect and the present perfect continuous

Present Perfect	Present Perfect Continuous
A. A continuous action (non-action verbs) I **have had** my car for five years.	A. A continuous action (action verbs) **I've been driving** a car for 20 years.
B. A repeated action **I've gone** to the library two times this month.	B. A nonstop action **I've been studying** English for one year.
C. Question with *how many* How many times **have** you **gone** to New York?	C. Question with *how long* How long **has** he **been living** in New York?
D. An action that is at an indefinite time, completely in the past. Carol **has found** a cousin in Italy.	D. An action that started in the past and is still happening. Carol **has been finding** a lot of information about her family.

EDITING ADVICE

1. Don't confuse the *-ing* form and the past participle.

    taking
    She has been ~~taken~~ a test for two hours.

    given
    She has ~~giving~~ him a present.

2. Use the present perfect, not the simple present, to describe an action or state that started in the past and continues to the present.

    had
    He has ^ a car for 2 years.

    have   ed
    How long ~~do~~ you work ^ in a factory?

3. Use *for*, not *since*, with the amount of time.

    for
    I've been studying English ~~since~~ three months.

4. Use the simple past, not the present perfect, with a specific past time.

> *came*
> He ~~has come~~ to the U.S. five months ago.

> *did*
> When ~~have~~ you come to the U.S.?

5. Use the simple past, not the present perfect, in a *since* clause.

> *came*
> He has learned a lot of English since he ~~has come~~ to the U.S.

6. Use correct word order. Put the adverb between the the auxiliary and the main verb.

> *never seen*
> He has ~~seen never~~ a French movie.

> *ever gone*
> Have you ~~gone ever~~ to France?

7. Use correct word order in questions.

> *have you*
> How long ~~you have~~ been a teacher?

8. Use *yet* for negative statements; use *already* for affirmative statements.

> *yet*
> I haven't eaten dinner ~~already~~.

9. Don't forget the verb *have* in the present perfect (continuous).

> *have*
> I been living in New York for two years.

10. Don't forget the *-ed* of the past participle.

> *d*
> He's use a computer many times.

11. Use the present perfect, not the continuous form, with *always*, *never*, *yet*, *already*, *ever*, and *how many*.

> *gone*
> How many times have you ~~been going~~ to Paris?

> *visited*
> I've never ~~been visiting~~ Paris.

PART 1   Find the mistakes with the underlined words, and correct them. Not every sentence has a mistake. If the sentence is correct, write C.

EXAMPLES: I have *had* my car for six years.

We've always wanted to learn English.   C

1. Since I've come to the U.S., I've been studying English.

2. Have you ever eating Chinese food?

3. How long you've been in the U.S.?

4. Have you gone ever to Canada?

5. I've know my best friend since I was a child.

6. She's a teacher. She's been a teacher since ten years.

7. I never gone to Mexico.

8. How long time has your father been working as an engineer?

9. Has he ever gone to Paris? Yes, he went to Paris last year.

10. He works in a restaurant. He been working there since 1995.

11. Have you ever study biology?

12. Have they finished the test yet?

13. She's done the homework yet.

14. I've just won the lottery.

PART 2   Fill in the blanks with the simple past, the present perfect, or the present perfect continuous form of the verb in parentheses ( ).

Conversation 1

A.   _____*Have*_____ you ever _____*studied*_____ computer programming?
        (study)

B.   Yes. I _____ it in college. And I _____ as a
                        (1 study)   (2 work)
        programmer for five years. But my job is boring.

A. _____ you ever _____ about changing jobs?
         (3 think)

B. Yes. Since I _____ a child, I _____ to be an
                (4 be)   *(5 always/want)*

   actor. When I was in college, I _____ in a few plays, but since I
                          (6 be)

   _____, I _____ time to act.
    (7 graduate)   *(8 not/have)*

Conversation 2

A. How long _____ in the U.S.?
           (1 you/be)

B. For about two years.

A. _____ your life _____ a lot since you _____ to
   (2 change)   *(3 come)*
   the U.S.?

B. Oh, yes. Before I _____ here, I _____ with my family. Since
             (4 come)   *(5 live)*

   I came here, I _____ alone.
            (6 live)

A. _____ in the same apartment?
   (7 always/live)

B. No. I _____ three times so far. And I plan to move again at
      (8 move)
   the end of the year.

A. Do you plan to have a roommate?

B. Yes, but I _____ one yet.
        (9 not/find)

PART 3

Fill in the blanks with the simple present, the simple past, the present perfect, or the present perfect continuous form of the verb in parentheses ( ).

Paragraph 1

I _____ the Internet every day. I _____ it for three years.
  (1 use)   *(2 use)*

I _____ to use it when I _____ interested in genealogy.
 (3 start)   *(4 become)*

I _____ on my family tree for three years. Last month, I _____
 (5 work)   *(6 find)*

information about my father's ancestors. My grandfather _____ with us
               (7 live)

now and likes to tell us about his past. He _____ born in Italy, but
             (8 be)

he _____ here when he was very young, so he _____
 (9 come)   *(10 live)*
here most of his life. He doesn't remember much about Italy. I

_____ any information about my mother's ancestors yet.
 (11 not/find)

Paragraph 2

I _____ to the U.S. when a war _____ out in my country.
(1 come)   (2 break)

I _____ in the U.S. for five years. At first, everything _____ very
(3 live)   (4 be)

hard for me. I _____ any English when I _____.
(5 not/know)   (6 arrive)

But I _____ English for the past five years, and now I _____
(7 study)   (8 speak)

it pretty well. I _____ my college education yet, but I
(9 not/start)

plan to next semester.

EXPANSION ACTIVITIES

CLASSROOM ACTIVITIES

1. Form a group of 4–6 students. Find out who in your group has done each of these things. Write that person's name in the blank.

    a) _____ has found a good job.

    b) _____ has been on a ship.

    c) _____ has never eaten Mexican food

    d) _____ hasn't done today's homework yet.

    e) _____ has never seen a French movie.

    f) _____ has taken a trip to Canada.

    g) _____ hasn't been downtown yet.

    h) _____ has acted in a play.

    i) _____ has gone swimming in the Pacific Ocean.

    j) _____ has flown in a helicopter.

    k) _____ has served in the military.

    l) _____ has worked in a hotel.

m) _____ has never been in a church.

n) _____ has never studied chemistry.

o) _____ has taken the TOEFL™ Test.

p) _____ has just gotten a "green card."

q) _____ has made a family tree.

2. Draw your family tree for the past three generations, if you can.

WRITING

1. Write a composition about one of the following:

   How your life has changed (*choose one*):
   a. since you came to the U.S.
   b. since you got married
   c. since you had a baby
   d. since you started college
   e. since you graduated from high school

2. Write about an interesting member of your family. What has he or she done that you think is interesting?

OUTSIDE ACTIVITY

Use the ideas in Exercise 24 to interview an American about his or her experiences. Invite the American to interview you. Tell the class something interesting you found out about the American. Tell the class an interesting question that the American asked you.

Internet Activities

1. On the Internet, find Cyndi Howell's genealogy Web site. Find out about people who have the same last name as yours.

2. Type the word "genealogy" at a search engine. How many Web sites did you find?

3. Look for the LDS Family Center libraries on the Internet. Where are these centers?

GRAMMAR

Gerunds
Infinitives

CONTEXT

Finding a Job
Tips on Résumé Writing
Alexander's Story

LESSON FOCUS

A gerund is formed by putting an *-ing* ending on a verb: *running, swimming, seeing, being.*[1]

> I enjoy *traveling.*

An infinitive is *to* + the base form of the verb: *to run, to swim, to see, to be.*

> I want *to travel* around the world.

[1] Even nonaction verbs like *see* and *be* have a gerund form.

Examples	Use of Gerund
Finding a job is hard.	As subject
I don't enjoy **talking** about myself.	As object
I thought about **changing** my career.	As object of preposition
I got job information **by talking** with my counselor.	In adverbial phrase
I like to **go shopping**.	In expressions with *go*

Before You Read
1. Have you ever had a job interview in the United States?
2. What was your profession in your native country? What profession or job do you have or plan to have in the future?

Read the following article. Pay special attention to gerunds.

Finding a Job

Finding a job in the United States takes specific skills. The following advice will help you find a job.

- Write a good résumé. Describe your accomplishments.[2] Avoid **including** unnecessary information. Your résumé should be one page, if possible.
- Find out about available jobs. One way is by **looking** in the newspaper or on the Internet. Another way is by **networking**. **Networking** means **exchanging** information with anyone you know—family, friends, neighbors, classmates, former coworkers, professional groups—who might know of a job. These people might also be able to give you insider information about a company, such as who is in charge and what it is like to work at their company. According to an article in the *Wall Street Journal*, 94 percent of people who succeed in **finding** a job say that **networking** was a big help.
- Practice the interview. The more prepared you are, the more relaxed you will feel. If you are worried about **saying** or **doing** the wrong thing, practice will help.
- Learn something about the company. You can find information by **going** to the library and **looking** in directories or **finding** the company's Web site. **Finding** information takes time, but it pays off.

Did you know...?

According to the Bureau of Labor Statistics, the fastest growing field is for computer engineers. The growth for this career between 1996 and 2006 is expected to more than double.

[2] *Accomplishments* are the unusual good things you have done, such as awards you have won or projects you have successfully managed.

You can get help in these skills—**writing** a résumé, **networking**, **preparing** for an interview, **researching** a company—by **seeing** a career counselor. Most high schools and colleges have one who can help you get started.

Finding a job is one of the most difficult jobs. Some people send out hundreds of résumés and go on dozens of interviews before **finding** a job. And it isn't something you do just once or twice in your lifetime. For most Americans, **changing** jobs many times in a lifetime is not uncommon.

10.2 Gerund as Subject

Examples	Explanation
Finding a good job takes time.	We can use a gerund or gerund phrase as the subject of the sentence.
Exchanging information with friends is helpful.	A gerund subject takes a singular verb.

LANGUAGE NOTES

1. A gerund phrase is a gerund + a noun: *finding a job, learning English.*
2. We can put *not* in front of a gerund to make it negative.
   Not having a job is frustrating.

EXERCISE 1 Complete each statement with a gerund (phrase) as the subject.

EXAMPLE: _____*Learning a foreign language*_____ takes a long time.

1. _____ is one of the most difficult jobs.

2. _____ is one of the best ways to find a job.

3. _____ is not permitted in this classroom.

4. _____ is difficult for a foreign student.

5. _____ takes a long time.

6. _____ is not polite.

7. _____ makes me feel good.

8. _____ makes me nervous.

9. _____ scares me.

10. _____ is against the law.

EXERCISE 2 Write a list of activities that would improve a person's health. Write a list of habits or activities that are not good for a person's health. (You may work with a partner.)

EXAMPLES: Eating a lot of fruits and vegetables can improve a person's health.
Living in a big city that has a lot of pollution is bad for a person's health.

_____

_____

_____

_____

10.3 Gerund After Verb

Examples	Explanation
Have you considered **going** to a job counselor? Do you appreciate **getting** advice? You can discuss **improving** your skills. You should practice **answering** interview questions.	Some verbs are commonly followed by a gerund (phrase).
I like to **go swimming**. Would you like to **go hiking** with me?	_Go_ + gerund is used in many idiomatic expressions.

LANGUAGE NOTES

1. The verbs below can be followed by a gerund:

admit	discuss	mind	put off
appreciate	dislike	miss	quit
avoid	enjoy	permit	recommend
can't help	finish	postpone	risk
consider	keep	practice	suggest

2. _Go_ + gerund is used in many idiomatic expressions:

go boating	go jogging
go bowling	go sailing
go camping	go shopping
go dancing	go sightseeing
go fishing	go skating
go hiking	go skiing
go hunting	go swimming

3. *I mind* means that something bothers me. *I don't mind* means that something is OK with me; it doesn't bother me.
    Do you mind wearing a suit to work? No, I *don't mind.*

4. *Can't help* means to have no control over something.
    When I see a sad movie, I *can't help* crying.

5. *Put off* means postpone.
    Don't *put off* writing your résumé. Do it now.

EXERCISE 3   Fill in the blanks with an appropriate gerund (or noun) to complete the statement. Share your answers with the class.

EXAMPLE: I don't mind _shopping for food_, but I do[3] mind _cooking it._

1. I usually enjoy _____ during the summer.

2. I don't enjoy _____

3. I don't mind _____, but I do mind

    _____

4. I appreciate _____ from my friends.

5. I need to practice _____ if I want to improve.

6. I often put off _____

7. I need to keep _____ if I want to be successful.

8. People should avoid _____ because it isn't a healthy activity.

EXERCISE 4   Make a list of things that you miss from your native country. You may use nouns or gerunds. Share your list with a partner, a small group, or the entire class.

EXAMPLE: I miss the beautiful parks in my hometown.
I miss taking walks by the sea.

_____

_____

_____

_____

[3] *Do* makes the verb more emphatic. It shows contrast with *don't mind.*

EXERCISE 5 Make a list of suggestions and recommendations for a tourist who is about to visit your native country. Read your list to a partner, a small group, or the entire class.

EXAMPLES: *I recommend taking warm clothes for the winter.*

You should avoid drinking tap water.

1. I recommend:

_____

_____

_____

2. You should avoid:

_____

_____

_____

EXERCISE 6 Tell if you like or don't like the following activities. Explain why.

EXAMPLES: go shopping
I like to go shopping for clothes because I like to try out new styles.

go bowling
I don't like to go bowling because I don't think it's an interesting sport.

1. go fishing   4. go swimming

2. go camping   5. go hunting

3. go jogging   6. go shopping

10.4 Gerund After Preposition

Examples	Explanation
I thought **about going** to a job counselor. She succeeded **in finding** a job.	Some verbs are followed by a preposition. A gerund can be used as the object of the preposition.
They're tired **of working** in a factory. I'm interested **in learning** more about computers.	Some adjectives are followed by a preposition. A gerund can be used as the object of the preposition.

(continued)

Examples	Explanation
I plan **on asking** my friends about jobs. I plan **to ask** my friends about jobs. He's afraid **of losing** his job. He's afraid **to lose** his job.	Some words (*plan, proud, afraid*) can be followed by a preposition + gerund or by an infinitive.

LANGUAGE NOTES

1. These are some common verb + preposition combinations:

care about	adjust to
complain about	look forward to
dream about	object to
forget about	
talk about	depend on (or upon)
think about	insist on (or upon)
worry about	plan on
believe in	
succeed in	

2. These are some common adjective + preposition combinations:

afraid of	accustomed (or used) to
fond of	
proud of	responsible for
tired of	famous for
	good at
concerned about	
excited about	interested in
upset about	(un)successful in
worried about	
sad about	

3. Notice that some expressions contain *to* as a preposition, not as part of an infinitive. COMPARE:
   I'm accustomed *to using* a computer.
   I like *to use* a computer.

4. *Look forward to* means to wait for a future event with pleasure.
   I *look forward to* seeing my sister next month.

5. *Fond of* means to like very much.
   I'm *fond of* gardening.

6. To make a gerund negative, put *not* before the gerund.
   I worry about *not* having enough time to work and study.

7. For a list of verbs and adjectives followed by a preposition, see Appendix H.

Fill in the blanks with a preposition and a gerund (phrase) to make a **true** statement.

EXAMPLE: I plan _____*on going back to my country soon.*_____

1. I'm afraid _____

2. I'm not afraid _____

3. I'm interested _____

4. I'm not interested _____

5. I want to succeed _____

6. I'm not very good _____

7. I'm accustomed _____

8. I'm not accustomed _____

9. I plan _____

10. I don't care _____

EXERCISE 8   Fill in the blanks to complete each statement. Compare your experiences in the U.S. with your experiences in your native country. (You may share your answers with a small group or with the entire class.)

EXAMPLES: In the U.S., I'm afraid of _____*walking alone at night.*_____

In my country, I was afraid of _____*not being able to give my children*_____
a good future.

1. In the U.S., I'm interested in _____

In my native country, I was interested in _____

_____

2. In the U.S., I'm afraid of _____

In my native country, I was afraid of _____

_____

3. In the U.S., I worry about _____

In my native country, I worried about _____

_____

4. In the U.S., I dream about _____

   In my native country, I dreamed about _____

   _____

5. In the U.S., I look forward to _____

   In my native country, I looked forward to _____

   _____

6. In the U.S., I often think about _____

   In my native country, I often thought about _____

   _____

7. In the U.S., people often complain about _____

   In my native country, people often complain about _____

   _____

8. In the U.S., families often talk about _____

   In my native country, families often talk about _____

9. In the U.S., teenagers are usually interested in _____

   In my native country, teenagers are usually interested in _____

   _____

10. American students are accustomed to _____

    Students in my native country are accustomed to _____

    _____

10.5 Gerund in Adverbial Phrase

Examples	Explanation
You should practice interview questions **before going** on an interview. I found my job **by looking** in the newspaper. She took the test **without studying**.	We can use a gerund in an adverbial phrase that begins with a preposition: *by, before, after, without*.

Fill in the blanks to complete the sentences.

EXAMPLE: The best way to improve your vocabulary is by _____*reading.*_____

1. The best way to improve your pronunciation is by _____

2. One way to find a job is by _____

3. It is very difficult to find a job without _____

4. The best way to quit a bad habit is by _____

5. One way to find an apartment is by _____

6. I can't speak English without _____

7. It's impossible to get a driver's license without _____

8. You should read the instructions of a test before _____

EXERCISE **10** Fill in the blanks in the conversation below with the gerund form. Where you see two blanks, use a preposition before the gerund.

A. I need to find a job. I've had ten interviews, but so far no job.

B. Have you thought ____*about*____ ____*going*____ to a job counselor?
              (example)

A. No. Where can I find one?

B. Our school office has a counseling department. I suggest _____
                                                                      (1)
    an appointment with a counselor.

A. What can a job counselor do for me?

B. Do you know anything about interviewing skills?

A. No.

B. Well, with the job counselor, you can talk _____ _____ a
                                                  (2)   *(3)*
    good impression during an interview. You can practice _____
                                                                (4)
    questions that the interviewer might ask you.

A. Really? How does the counselor know what questions the interviewer
    will ask me?

B. Many interviewers ask the same general questions. For example, the interviewer might ask you, "Do you enjoy _____(5) with computers?" Or she might ask you, "Do you mind _____(6) overtime and on weekends?" Or "Are you good _____(7) _____(8) with other people?"

A. I dislike _____(9) about myself.

B. That's what you have to do in the U.S.

A. What else can the counselor help me with?

B. If your skills are low, you can talk about _____(10) your skills. If you don't know much about computers, for example, she can recommend _____(11) more classes.

A. It feels like I'm never going to find a job. I'm tired _____(12) _____(13) and not finding anything.

B. If you keep _____(14), you will succeed _____(15) _____(16) a job. I'm sure. But it takes time and patience.

A. And job hunting skills.

10.6   Infinitives—Overview

Examples	Explanation
I want **to find** a job.	An infinitive is used after certain verbs.
I want you **to help** me.	An object can be added before an infinitive.
I'm happy **to help** you.	An infinitive can follow certain adjectives.
It's important **to write** a good résumé.	An infinitive follows certain expressions with *it*.
He went to a counselor **to get** advice.	An infinitive is used to show purpose.

1. Have you ever written a résumé? What is the hardest part about writing a résumé?
2. Do people in your native country have to write a résumé?

1234 Andersen Avenue
West City, MA 01766
Phone: 555-123-1234 (home)
      555-321-4321 (work)

Tina White

Objective:	To obtain a position in the computer field
Work Experience:	**Acme Computer Services, Inc., Concord, MA** March 1999–Present Computer Sales Manager – Managed computer services department – Created customer database – Exceeded annual sales goals by 20% in 1999
	West Marketing Services, West City MA June 1991–March 1999 Office Manager – Managed 5 sales reps – Implemented new system for accounting records and timely submission of reports to home office – Grew sales contracts for support services by 200% in first two years
Education and Special Training:	**Northeastern Community College—Salem, MA** Associate Degree, Major: Accounting Institute of Advanced Studies—New York, NY Certificate of Completion (3 week course) Financial Management
Computer Skills:	Proficient in use of Windows, Wordperfect, Word, FrameMaker, Lotus 123, and other spreadsheet software programs

Read the following article. Pay special attention to infinitives.

Tips[4] on Writing a Résumé

It's important **to write** a good, clear résumé. A résumé should be limited to one page. It is only necessary **to describe** your most relevant work.[5] Employers are busy people. Don't expect them **to read** long résumés.

You need **to sell** yourself in your résumé. Employers expect you **to use** action verbs **to describe** your experience. Don't begin your sentences with "I." Use past-tense verbs like: *managed, designed, created, developed*. It is not enough **to say** you improved something. Be specific. How did you improve it?

Before taking your résumé to be copied, it is important **to check** the grammar and spelling. Employers want **to see** if you have good communications skills. Ask a friend or teacher **to read** and **criticize** your résumé.

It isn't necessary **to include** references. If the employer wants you **to provide** references, he or she will ask you **to do** so during or after the interview.

Don't include personal information such as marital status, age, race, family information, or hobbies.

Be honest in your résumé. Employers can check your information. No one wants **to hire** a liar.

10.7 Infinitive as Subject

Examples	Explanation
It is important **to write** a good résumé. It takes time **to find** a job. It isn't necessary **to include** all your experience.	An infinitive can be the subject of a sentence. We begin the sentence with *it* and delay the infinitive.
It was hard **for her** to leave her last job. It isn't easy **for me** to sell myself.	Include *for* + noun or object pronoun to make a statement that is true of a specific person.

---

[4] A *tip* is a small piece of advice.
[5] *Relevant work* is work that is related to this particular job opening.

LANGUAGE NOTES

1. We can use an infinitive after these adjectives:

    dangerous   good   necessary
    difficult   great   possible
    easy   hard   sad
    expensive   important   wrong
    fun   impossible

2. There is no difference in meaning between an infinitive subject and a gerund subject.

    It's important *to arrive* on time.
    Arriving on time is important.

EXERCISE 11 Complete each statement with an infinitive phrase. You can add an object, if you like.

EXAMPLES: It's easy _to shop in an American supermarket._

It's necessary _for me to pay my rent by the fifth of the month._

1. It's important _____

2. It's impossible _____

3. It's possible _____

4. It's necessary _____

5. It's dangerous _____

6. It isn't good _____

7. It's expensive _____

8. It's hard _____

EXERCISE 12 Tell if it's important or not important for you to do the following.

EXAMPLE: own a house
            It's (not) important for me to own a house.

1. get a college degree   6. study American history

2. find an interesting job   7. become an American citizen

3. have a car   8. own a computer

4. speak English well   9. have a cell phone

5. read and write English well   10. make a lot of money

EXERCISE 13 Write a sentence with each pair of words below. (You may read your sentences to the class.)

EXAMPLE: hard/the teacher
It's hard for the teacher to pronounce the names of some students.

1. important/us (the students)

   _____

2. difficult/Americans

   _____

3. easy/the teacher

   _____

4. necessary/children

   _____

5. difficult/a woman

   _____

6. difficult/a man

   _____

EXERCISE 14 Write a list of things that are important when you are looking for a job. Write two sentences with a gerund. Write two sentences with an infinitive. (You may work with a partner.)

EXAMPLES: *Wearing nice clothes is important.*
It's important to prepare a good résumé.

1. _____
2. _____
3. _____
4. _____

EXERCISE 15 Write a list of things that a foreign student or immigrant should know about life in the U.S. Use gerunds or infinitives as subjects. (You may work with a partner.)

EXAMPLES: *It is possible for some students to get financial aid.*

Learning English is going to take longer than you expected.

1. _____

2. _____

3. _____

4. _____

10.8 Infinitive After Adjective

Examples	Explanation
I would be happy **to help** you with your résumé. Are you prepared **to make** copies of your résumé?	Some adjectives can be followed by an infinitive.

LANGUAGE NOTES

Adjectives often followed by an infinitive are:

afraid	happy	prepared	ready
glad	lucky	proud	sad

EXERCISE 16 Fill in the blanks.

EXAMPLE: I'm lucky ____*to be in the U.S.*____

1. I was lucky _____

2. I'm proud _____

3. I'm sometimes afraid _____ alone.

4. I'm not afraid _____

5. In my native country, I was afraid _____

6. In the U.S., I'm afraid _____

7. Are we ready _____

8. I'm not prepared _____

10.9 Infinitive After Verb

Examples	Explanation
I need **to find** a new job. I decided **to quit** my old job. I prefer **to work** outdoors. I want **to make** more money.	Some verbs are commonly followed by an infinitive (phrase).

LANGUAGE NOTES

1. We can use an infinitive after the following verbs:

agree	decide	like	promise
ask	expect	love	refuse
attempt	forget	need	remember
begin	hope	plan	start
continue	learn	prefer	try

2. The *to* in infinitives is often pronounced "ta" or, after a **d** sound, "da." *Want to* is often pronounced "wanna." Listen to your teacher pronounce the sentences in the above box.

EXERCISE 17 Ask a question with the words given in the present tense. Another student will answer.

EXAMPLE: like/travel
A. Do you like to travel?
B. Yes, I do. OR No, I don't.

1. want/learn another language

2. plan/take classes here next semester

3. hope/speak English fluently

4. like/write compositions

5. continue/speak your native language at home

6. try/read novels in English

7. plan/move this year

8. need/own a fax machine

9. expect/return to your country

10. need/use a dictionary when you read the newspaper

EXERCISE 18 Write a sentence about yourself, using the words given, in any tense. (You may share your sentences with the class.)

EXAMPLES: like/eat
    I like to eat Chinese food.
    _____

    try/find
    I'm trying to find a job.
    _____

1. like/read
    _____

2. not like/eat
    _____

3. want/visit
    _____

4. decide/go
    _____

5. try/learn
    _____

6. begin/study
    _____

EXERCISE 19 Check (✓) the activities that you like to do. Tell the class why you like or don't like this activity.

chess

1. _____ stay home on the weekends   5. _____ play chess

2. _____ eat in a restaurant   6. _____ dance

3. _____ get up early   7. _____ write letters

4. _____ talk on the phone   8. _____ go to museums

10.10 Gerund or Infinitive After Verb

	Examples
Gerund	I started **looking** for a job a month ago.
Infinitive	I started **to look** for a job a month ago.
Gerund	He continued **working** until he was 65 years old.
Infinitive	He continued **to work** until he was 65 years old.

1. The verbs below can be followed by either a gerund or an infinitive with almost no difference in meaning.

attempt	continue	like	start
begin	deserve	love	try
can't stand	hate	prefer	

2. *Can't stand* means hate or can't tolerate.
    I *can't stand* waiting in a long line.

3. *Try* followed by a gerund is a little different from *try* followed by an infinitive.
    I'll *try to improve* my résumé.
    (*Try* = make an effort)
    If you can't find a job by looking at the want ads, you should *try networking*.
    (*Try* = use a different technique)

EXERCISE 20 Complete each statement using either a gerund (phrase) or an infinitive (phrase). Practice both ways.

EXAMPLES: I started _to learn English four years ago._
                                 (learn)

            I started _studying French when I was in high school._
                                 (study)

1. I started _____ to this school in _____
                  (come)

2. I began _____ English _____
                 (study)

3. I like _____ on TV.
                              (watch)

4. I like _____
                              (live)

5. I like _____
                              (wear)

6. I hate _____
                              (wear)

7. I love _____
                              (eat)

10.11 Object Before Infinitive

Examples	Explanation
Don't expect **an employer to read** a long résumé. I want **you to criticize** my résumé. My boss wants **me to work** overtime. I expected **him to give** me a raise.	We can use a noun or object pronoun (*me, you, him, her, it, us, them*) before an infinitive.

LANGUAGE NOTES

1. We often use an object between the following verbs and an infinitive:

advise	ask	invite	permit	want
allow	expect	need	tell	would like

2. *Help* can be followed by either an object + base form or an object + infinitive.
    He helped me *find* a job.
    He helped me *to find* a job.

EXERCISE 21 Tell if the teacher wants or doesn't want the students to do the following.

EXAMPLES: do the homework
The teacher wants us to do the homework.

use the textbook during a test
The teacher doesn't want us to use the textbook during a test.

1. talk to another student during a test
2. study before a test
3. copy another student's homework
4. learn English
5. speak our native languages in class
6. improve our pronunciation

Tell if you expect or don't expect the teacher to do the following.

EXAMPLES: give homework
I expect him/her to give homework.

give me private lessons
I don't expect him/her to give me private lessons.

1. correct the homework
2. give tests
3. speak my native language
4. help me after class
5. come to class on time

6. pass all the students
7. know a lot about my native country
8. answer my questions in class
9. teach us American history
10. pronounce my name correctly

EXERCISE **23** Complete each statement. Use an object pronoun with an infinitive.

EXAMPLE: My boss doesn't pay me enough money.

I want _____him to give me a raise._____.

1. I have to work on Sundays.

   He expects _____

2. All the workers have to attend a meeting once a week.

   He wants _____

3. We can't talk to each other while we're working.

   He doesn't want _____

4. He promised to give me a vacation soon.

   I expect _____

5. He doesn't treat us with respect.

   I want _____

6. I have to wear a suit and tie every day.

   He expects _____

7. We're thinking of going on strike.

   My boss doesn't want _____

8. We have to eat lunch in 20 minutes.

   He expects _____

9. He never gives me a compliment or word of praise.

   I'd like _____

10. My friend gave me advice. He said, "Quit this job."

    My friend advised _____

EXERCISE 24 Respond to each statement telling what someone wants or doesn't want another person to do.

EXAMPLE: I want a pet, but my landlady doesn't allow it.
            She doesn't want me to have a pet.

1. The landlady is going to raise the rent, and I'm not happy about it.

2. My neighbors' TV is on loud at night, and I can't sleep.

3. The walls are dirty and they need paint. I talked to my landlord about it.

4. My neighbors don't close the front door securely. Anyone can come into the building.

5. My children make a lot of noise, and the woman next door complains about them.

EXERCISE 25 Write sentences to tell what one member of your family wants (or doesn't want) from another member of your family.

EXAMPLES: _I don't want my son to watch so much TV._

            My son wants me to help him with his math homework.

1. _____

2. _____

3. _____

4. _____

10.12 Infinitive to Show Purpose

Examples	Explanation
You can use the Internet **to get** job information. He's working hard and saving his money **to buy** a house.	We use the infinitive to show the purpose of an action. We can also say *in order to*: I am saving my money **in order to** buy a house.

EXERCISE 26 Fill in the blanks with an infinitive to show purpose.

EXAMPLE: I bought the Sunday newspaper _to look for jobs._

1. I called the company _____ an appointment.

2. She wants to work overtime _____ .

3. You should use the Internet _____ jobs.

4. You can use a résumé writing service _____ your résumé.

5. My interview is in a far suburb. I need a car _____ the interview.

6. Use express mail _____ faster.

7. In the U.S., you need experience _____ , and you need a job _____ .

8. I need two phone lines. I need one _____ on the phone with my friends and relatives. I need the other one _____ the Internet.

9. She needs a cell phone _____ while she's out of the house.

10. I'm sending a letter that has a lot of papers in it. I need extra stamps _____ this letter.

11. You should go to the college admissions office _____ a copy of your transcripts.

12. After an interview, you can call the employer _____ that you're very interested in the position.

Before You Read
1. What are some differences in the American lifestyle and the lifestyle in your native country?
2. Are there any small children in your family here? Do they speak English or do they continue to speak your native language?

Read the following story. Pay special attention to *used to*, *be used to*, and *get used to*.

Alexander's Story

I've been in the U.S. for two years. I **used to** study British English, so I had a hard time understanding Americans at first. Without good English skills, I couldn't find a job in my field. Now my English is much better. I'm **used to speaking** English every day in my job, with my neighbors, and even with my children. My children **used to speak** Ukrainian with me all the time when we first arrived, but now that they're in school, they're **used to hearing** and **speaking** English all the time. They also learned English from watching American TV. They're beginning to forget Ukrainian. When I ask them a question in Ukrainian, they answer me in English. It's no problem for me, but my parents don't speak English, and they can't **get used to having** so little communication with their grandchildren.

I **used to be** an engineer in Ukraine. But for the past two years in the U.S., I've been working as a taxi driver. Now that I know enough English, I'm ready to find a job in my field. However, it's been difficult for two reasons. First, I'm **not using to selling** myself at a job interview. In fact, it's uncomfortable for me to say how wonderful I am to a stranger. But my job counselor told me that I have to **get used to** it because that's what Americans do. Second, in my country, I **used to** draw by hand. In the U.S., everything is done by computer. I'm **not used to using** a computer. To improve my skills, I've been taking courses in Computer Aided Design (CAD). My children, however, have grown up with computers, so they're **used to** them and love them.

It has been hard to **get used to** so many new things, but little by little we're doing it.

10.13   *Used To* vs. *Be Used To*

Subject	*Used To*	Base Form	Complement	Comparison to now
Alexander	**used to**	live	in Ukraine.	Now he lives in the U.S.
He	**used to**	be	an engineer.	Now he's a taxi driver.
He	**used to**	study	British English.	Now he studies American English.
He	**didn't use to**	speak	any English.	Now he speaks English pretty well.

(continued)

Subject	*Be/Get Used To*	Gerund/Noun	Complement	Explanation
His children	**are used to**	speaking	English all the time.	It's easy for them.
Alexander	**isn't used to**	selling	himself at an interview.	It isn't his custom.
His children	**are used to**	computers.		Using a computer is no problem for them.
His parents	**can't get used to**	communicating	in English.	It's hard to change their habit.
He	**is getting used to**	American life.		His customs are changing.

LANGUAGE NOTES

1. *Used to* + base form tells about a past habit or custom. This activity has been discontinued. The negative is *didn't use to* + base form.
2. *Be used to* + gerund or noun means *be accustomed to*. Something is a person's custom and not difficult to do. The negative is *be + not + used to* + gerund or noun.
3. *Get used to* + gerund or noun means *become accustomed to*. A person's habit changes. For the negative, we often say *can't get used to*.

EXERCISE 27 This is a list of behaviors that a person had when he was younger and immature. Not that he's older and more mature, he has changed. What do you think his behavior is now? (You may work with a partner.)

EXAMPLE: I used to go to parties on Saturdays with my friends. _Now I stay home on the weekends and study._

1. I used to do my homework at the last minute. _____

2. I used to go to my parents whenever I had a problem. _____

3. I used to ask my parents for money all the time. _____

4. I used to spend money on foolish things. _____

5. I used to give my dirty laundry to my mother. _____

EXERCISE 28 Write four sentences comparing your former behaviors to your behaviors or customs now.

EXAMPLE: *I used to live with my family. Now I live with a roommate.*

I used to worry a lot. Now I take it easy most of the time.

1. _____

2. _____

3. _____

4. _____

EXERCISE 29 Write sentences comparing the way you used to live in your country and the way you live now. Read your sentences to the class.

EXAMPLE: *I used to go everywhere by bus. Now I have a car.*

1. _____

2. _____

3. _____

4. _____

EXERCISE 30 A student wrote about things that are new for her in an American classroom. Fill in the blanks with a gerund. Then tell if *you* are used to or not used to these things.

EXAMPLE: I'm not used to ___*taking*___ multiple-choice tests. In my native country, we have essay tests.

1. I'm not used to _____ at small desks. In my native country, we sit at large tables.

2. I'm not used to _____ the teacher by his/her first name. In my country, we say Professor.

3. I'm not used to _____ in a textbook. In my native country, we don't write in the books because we borrow them from the school.

304 Lesson Ten

4. I'm not used to _____ jeans to class. In my native country, students wear a uniform.

5. I'm not used to _____ and studying at the same time. Students in my native country don't work. Their parents support them.

6. I'm not used to _____ a lot of money to attend college. In my native country, college is free.

7. I'm not used to _____ when a teacher asks me a question. In my native country, students stand to answer a question.

EXERCISE 31 Name four things that you had to get used to in the U.S. (These things were strange for you when you arrived.)

EXAMPLES: I had to get used to ___living in a small apartment.___

I had to get used to ___American pronunciation.___

1. I had to get used to _____

2. I had to get used to _____

3. I had to get used to _____

4. I had to get used to _____

EXERCISE 32 Answer each question with a complete sentence. Practice *be used to* + gerund or noun.

EXAMPLE: What are you used to drinking in the morning?
I'm used to drinking coffee in the morning.

1. What kind of food are you used to (eating)?

2. What kind of weather are you used to?

3. What time are you used to getting up?

4. What kind of clothes are you used to wearing to class?

5. What kind of things are you used to doing every day?

6. What kind of classroom behaviors are you used to?

7. What kinds of things are you used to doing alone?

Gerunds

Examples	Explanation
Working all day is hard.	As the subject of the sentence
I don't enjoy **working** as a taxi driver.	After certain verbs
I **go swimming** once a week.	In many idiomatic expressions with *go*
I'm worried about **finding** a job.	After prepositions
She found a job by **looking** in the newspaper.	In adverbial phrases

Infinitives

Examples	Explanation
I need **to find** a new job.	After certain verbs
My boss wants me **to work** overtime.	After an object
I'm ready **to quit**.	After certain adjectives
It's important **to have** some free time. It's impossible for me **to work** 80 hours a week.	After certain expressions beginning with *it*.
I work **to support** my family.	To show purpose

Gerund or Infinitive—No Difference in Meaning

Gerund	Infinitive
I like **working** with computers. I began **working** three months ago.	I like **to work** with computers. I began **to work** three months ago.
Writing a good résumé is important.	It's important **to write** a good résumé.

Gerund or Infinitive—Difference in Meaning

Infinitive (Past Habit)	Gerund (Custom)
I **used to be** an engineer. Now I'm a taxi driver.	I drive all day. I **am used to driving** all over the city.
I **used to live** in a large house in my country. Now I live in a small apartment.	I can't **get used to living** in a small apartment. I don't like it at all.

EDITING ADVICE

1. Use a gerund after a preposition.

   He read the whole book without ~~use~~ *using* a dictionary.

2. Use the correct preposition.

   She insisted ~~in~~ *on* driving me home.

3. Use a gerund after certain verbs.

   I enjoy ~~to~~ walk*ing* in the park.

   He went ~~to~~ shop*ing* after work.

4. Use an infinitive after certain verbs.

   I decided *to* buy a new car.

5. Use a gerund, not a base form, as a subject.

   ~~Find~~ *Finding* a good job is important.

6. Don't forget to include *it* for a delayed infinitive subject.

   It i~~Is~~ important to find a good job.

7. Don't use the past form after *to*.

   I decided to ~~bought~~ *buy* a new car.

8. After *want, expect, need, advise, ask*, use an object pronoun, not a subject pronoun, before the infinitive. Don't use *that* as a connector.

He wants <u>that I</u> drive.   <i>me to</i>

The teacher expects <u>we</u> do the homework.   <i>us to</i>

9. Use *for*, not *to*, to introduce an object after expressions beginning with *it*.

It's important <u>to</u> me to find a job.   <i>for</i>

It's necessary for <u>he</u> to be on time.   <i>him</i>

10. Use *to* + base form, not *for*, to show purpose.

I called the company <u>for</u> make an appointment.   <i>to</i>

11. Don't put *be* before *used to* for the habitual past.

<u>I'm</u> used to live in Germany. Now I live in the U.S.

12. Don't use the *-ing* form after *used to* for the habitual past.

We used to <u>having</u> a dog, but he died.   <i>have</i>

13. Don't forget the *d* in *used to*.

I use to live with my parents. Now I live alone.   <i>d</i>

LESSON 10 TEST / REVIEW

PART 1   Find the mistakes with the underlined words, and correct them. Not every sentence has a mistake. If the sentence is correct, write **C**.

EXAMPLES: He read the article without <u>use</u> a dictionary.   <i>using</i>

Do you <u>like to play</u> tennis?   **C**

1. <u>Using</u> the Internet is fun.

2. I recommend <u>to see</u> a job counselor.

3. Do you enjoy <u>learning</u> a new language?

4. <u>Save</u> your money is important for your future.

5. It's important <u>to me</u> to know English well.

6. It's impossible <u>for she</u> to work 60 hours a week.

7. Do you <u>go fish</u> with your brother every week?

8. Do you <u>want the teacher to review</u> modals?

9. He got rich <u>by working</u> hard and <u>investing</u> his money.

10. The teacher <u>tried to explained</u> the present perfect, but we didn't understand it.

11. <u>Is</u> necessary to come to class on time.

12. Do you <u>want to watch</u> TV?

13. She <u>use to take</u> the bus every day in her country. Now she has a car and drives everywhere.

14. It's necessary <u>for me have</u> a good education.

15. She came to the U.S. <u>for find</u> a better job.

16. He's interested <u>in becoming</u> a nurse.

17. We're thinking <u>to spend</u> our vacation in Acapulco.

18. We've always lived in a big city. We'<u>re used to living</u> in a big city.

19. I'<u>m used to live</u> with my family. Now I live alone.

20. She's from England. She can't <u>get used to drive</u> on the right side of the road.

21. My mother <u>wants that I call</u> her every day.

22. Are you worried about <u>lose</u> your job?

PART **2** _____ Fill in the blanks in the conversation below. Use a gerund or an infinitive. In some cases, either the gerund or the infinitive is possible.

A. Hi, Molly. I haven't seen you in ages. What's going on in your life?

B. I've made many changes. First, I quit _____*working*_____ in a factory.
(example)

I disliked _____ the same thing every day. And I'm not used to
(1)

_____ on my feet all day. My boss often wanted me
(2)

_____ overtime on Saturdays. I need _____
(3)   (4)

with my children on Saturdays. Sometimes they want me _____
(5)

them to the zoo or to the museum. And I need _____ them
_(6)_

with their homework, too.

A. So what do you plan on _____?
_(7)_

B. I've started _____ to college _____ some general courses.
_(8)_ _(9)_

A. What career are you planning?

B. I'm not sure. I'm interested in _____ with children. Maybe I'll
_(10)_

become a teacher's aide. I've also thought about _____ in a
_(11)_

day-care center. I care about _____ people.
_(12)_

A. Yes, it's wonderful _____ other people, especially children.
_(13)_

It's important _____ a job that you like. So you're starting a
_(14)_

whole new career.

B. It's not new, really. Before I came to the U.S., I used _____ a kinder-
_(15)_

garten teacher in my country. But my English wasn't so good when I came

here, so I found a job in a factory. I look forward to _____
_(16)_

to my former profession or doing something similar.

A. How did you learn English so fast?

B. By _____ with people at work, by _____ TV, and by
_(17)_ _(18)_

_____ the newspaper. It hasn't been easy for me _____
_(19)_ _(20)_

American English. I studied British English in my country, but here I have

to get used to _____ things like "gonna" and "wanna." At first
_(21)_

I didn't understand Americans, but now I'm used to their pronunciation.
I've had to make a lot of changes.

A. You should be proud of _____ so many changes in your life so
_(22)_

quickly.

B. I am.

A. Let's get together some time and talk some more.

B. I'd love to. I love to dance. Maybe we can go _____ together
_(23)_

sometime.

A. That would be great. And I love _____. Maybe we can go
_(24)_

shopping together sometime.

EXPANSION ACTIVITIES

CLASSROOM ACTIVITIES

1. Write a list of five things for each category. Find a partner. Compare your list to your partner's list. See how many things you have in common.

I enjoy:	I'm lazy about:
Example:	Example:
I enjoy talking on the phone.	*I'm lazy about writing compositions.*

2. Write about your job or profession (or future profession). In order to do this job well, what skills are important? What isn't important? Share this information with the class.

Job: _____

It's important:	It isn't necessary:
It's important to know English.	*It isn't necessary to wear formal clothes (like a suit or dress).*

3. Fill in the blanks and discuss your answers in a small group or with the entire class.

   a. Americans are used to _____, but people in my native country aren't.

   b. People in my native country are used to _____, but Americans aren't.

c. If an American goes to live in my native country, he or she will have to

get used to _____ .

4. Compare the work environment in your native country to the work environment in the U.S. Discuss your answers in a small group or with the entire class. (If you have no experience with American jobs, ask an American to fill in his/her opinions about the U.S.)

	My native country	The U.S.
1. Coworkers are friendly with each other at the job.		
2. Coworkers get together after work to socialize.		
3. Arriving on time for the job is very important.		
4. The boss is friendly with the employees.		
5. The employees are very serious about their jobs.		
6. The employees use the telephone for personal use.		
7. Everyone wears formal clothes.		
8. Employees get long lunch breaks.		
9. Employees get long vacations.		
10. Employees call the company if they are sick and can't work on a particular day.		
11. Employees are paid in cash.		
12. Employees often take work home.		

DISCUSSION

1. Compare looking for a job in the United States with looking for a job in your native country.

2. Are the job skills you had in your native country useful in the U.S.?

WRITING

1. Write about (a) a change you made in your life.
   OR
   (b) a change you would like to make in your life.

2. Write a paragraph beginning with "It has been hard for me to get used to

   _____ in the U.S."

3. Write your résumé.

Internet Activities

1. Type "career" in a search engine. See how many "hits" come up.

2. Find some career counseling Web sites. Find a sample résumé in your field or close to your field. Print it out and bring it to class.

3. From one of the Web sites you found, get information on one or more of the following topics:
   - how to write a cover letter
   - how to find a career counselor
   - how to plan for your interview
   - how to network
   - what questions to ask the interviewer

4. See if your local newspaper has a Web site. If it does, find the "help wanted" section of this newspaper.

Lesson Eleven

GRAMMAR
Adjective Clauses

CONTEXT
Personal Ads
Senior Singles

LESSON FOCUS
An adjective clause is a group of words that
describes a noun.

The woman *who saw the accident* reported it to the police.
Do you like the new car *that I bought*?

Before You Read
1. Are you married? How or where did you meet your spouse?[1]
2. How do single people meet in your native country?

Read the following article. Pay special attention to adjective clauses.

Personal Ads

Single people **who are looking for a partner** often use the personal ads in the newspaper or online. They can advertise for the kind of person **they want to meet**, or they can respond to ads **they find in the newspaper or on the Internet**. An ad usually gives a description of the advertiser and his or her hobbies or interests. The advertiser often lists the characteristics **he or she wants to find in a partner**.

Look at the newspaper ad below:

SWM, 35 y.o., 5'8", 165 lbs., enjoys sailing, swimming, fishing, skiing, wants to meet S/DWF 25–34, under 5'5", who enjoys sports and the outdoors. #45112 or Write Box 52.

The person **who wrote this ad** is a 35-year-old (y.o.) single white male (SWM). He would like to meet a single or divorced white female (S/DWF) **who is between the ages of 25 and 34**.

A woman **who answers this ad** can call a phone number and leave a message for the advertiser. Usually this phone call is to a 900 number and can cost from one to several dollars a minute. Or she can send a letter to a box number. The newspaper will forward the letters to the man **who placed the ad**.

People **who write ads** usually use abbreviations to make their ads shorter and less expensive. These are some common abbreviations:

S = Single   W = White
D = Divorced   H = Hispanic
M = Male   B = Black
F = Female   A = Asian

Did you know...?

In 1996, 12 percent of all American adults lived alone.

[1] *Spouse* means husband or wife.

11.1 Adjective Clauses—Overview

Examples	Explanation
She'd like to marry a man **who knows how to cook**. She'd like to have a job **that uses her talents**. The man **whom you married** is very responsible. The job **that I have** gives me a lot of satisfaction.	An adjective clause is a group of words that describes a noun. It follows the noun. Relative pronouns introduce an adjective clause: *who(m)* for people, *which* for things, *that* for people and things.

EXERCISE 1 Tell if the statement is true or false based on the reading on page 316. Write **T** or **F**.

EXAMPLE: This man wants to meet a woman who is under 25 years old.   F

1. The man who wrote the ad is 35 years old.

2. The ad that he placed in the newspaper gives his phone number.

3. He is looking for a woman who is under 5′5″ tall.

4. He doesn't want to meet a woman who has been married before.

5. He wants to meet someone who has the same interests as he does.

6. A woman who answers this ad should be at least 52 years old.

7. A person who writes SWM is a man.

8. Ads that have abbreviations save the advertiser money.

EXERCISE 2 Underline the adjective clauses in the sentences in Exercise 1.

11.2 Relative Pronoun as Subject

A relative pronoun can be the subject of the adjective clause.

He wants to meet a woman. The woman likes sports.

He wants to meet a woman | who / that | likes sports.

```
┌─────────────────────────────────────────────────────────────┐
│   An ad                                 is expensive.         │
│           An ad has a lot of words.                          │
│                  ┌──┐                                         │
│                  │↓ │                                         │
│   An ad  ┌─────┐ has a lot of words is expensive.            │
│          │that │                                             │
│          │which│                                             │
│          └─────┘                                             │
└─────────────────────────────────────────────────────────────┘
```

Language Notes

1. A present-tense verb in the adjective clause must agree in number with its subject.
   The man wants to meet a woman who *likes* sports.
   I know a lot of men who *like* sports.

2. Avoid using an adjective clause when a simple adjective is enough.
   He doesn't want to meet a *woman who is tall.*
   BETTER: He doesn't want to meet a *tall woman.*

EXERCISE 3 Complete each statement with an adjective clause. Make sure that the verb in the adjective clause agrees with its subject.

EXAMPLE: I know some women ___*who don't want to have children.*___

1. (Women) I like men _____

   (Men) I like women _____

2. Students like a teacher _____

3. Teachers like students _____

4. There are a lot of Americans _____

5. There are a lot of people in my native country _____

   _____

EXERCISE 4 Complete each statement with an adjective clause. The subject of the adjective clause is general.

EXAMPLE: People ___*who have a wonderful family*___ are very fortunate.

1. Women _____ are very popular.

2. People _____ aren't usually successful.

318   Lesson Eleven

3. People _____ have trouble finding a spouse.

4. Parents _____ are good.

5. Women _____ have a hard life.

EXERCISE 5 Complete each statement with a verb phrase. The subject contains an adjective clause.

EXAMPLE: People who leave their native countries _*have many new experiences.*_

1. People who gossip _____

2. People who can't read or write _____

3. People who have lost their jobs _____

4. People who exercise regularly _____

5. Students who are absent a lot _____

6. Children who use the Internet all day _____

7. Children who eat too many sweets _____

8. People who have a cell phone _____

9. People who talk on a cell phone while driving _____

10. People who don't get enough exercise _____

11. People who don't have enough time to cook _____

12. Students who have a full-time job _____

11.3 Relative Pronoun as Object

A relative pronoun can be the object of the adjective clause.

He included the hobbies.	He has hobbies.

He included the hobbies | that / which / ∅ | he has.

The woman		likes sports.
	He met her.	

The woman | who(m) / that / ∅ | he met | likes sports.

LANGUAGE NOTES

The correct relative pronoun for people is *whom*. However, in conversation, *who* is often heard. Or the relative pronoun is omitted completely.

FORMAL: The woman *whom* he met likes sports.
INFORMAL: The woman *who* he met likes sports.
INFORMAL: The woman he met likes sports.

EXERCISE 6   In each sentence below, underline the adjective clause.

EXAMPLES: The man she married works as a computer programmer.
Do you know the woman he met?

1. The ad he put in the paper cost him $10.

2. The women whom he met through his ad were all very nice.

3. She's not the kind of person I want to marry.

4. Basketball is a sport he doesn't like.

5. She married a man she met in her biology class.

6. I have a friend I'd like you to meet.

7. The textbook we are using is called *Grammar in Context*.

8. We have to underline the adjective clauses we find.

EXERCISE 7   Complete each statement.

EXAMPLE: People often want things they ___*can't afford.*___

1. We sometimes don't appreciate the things we _____

2. I tell my problems to people I _____

3. I once had a teacher I _____

4. Americans sometimes say things I _____

5. There are many American customs I _____

6. Do you follow the advice your parents _____

EXERCISE **8**   Fill in the blanks to complete the adjective clause.

EXAMPLE: My friend just bought a new car. I don't like the new car ___*she bought.*___

1.   I'm going to return the coat _____ last week. It's too small for me.

2.   Look at the beautiful sweater that Mary _____ today. I wonder where she bought it.

3.   I can't find the card _____ with your phone number on it. Can you give me another one?

4.   The movie I _____ last night was terrific. I highly recommend it to you.

5.   Could you please return the money you _____ last month?

6.   The teacher makes corrections on the students' compositions. The students should read the corrections _____

7.   I'm studying American English now. The English _____ in my country was British English.

8.   Please speak more slowly. I can't understand a word you _____ _____

EXERCISE **9**   Fill in the blanks with appropriate words to complete the conversation.

A.   I don't have enough friends in this country.

B.   Haven't you met any people here?

A.   Of course. But the people ___*I've met*___ here don't have my
                                         (example)
interests.

B.   What are you interested in?

A.   I like reading, meditating, and going for quiet walks. Americans seem to like parties, TV, sports, movies, and going to restaurants. The

interests _____ are so different from mine.
            (1)

B.   You're never going to meet people with the interests _____
                                                                (2)
_____ . Your interests don't include other people. You

should find some interests _____ other people, like tennis
                              (3)
or dancing, to mention only a few.

A. The activities _____ cost money, and I don't have
                          (4)
    a lot of money.

B. There are many parks in this city _____ free tennis
                                                (5)
    courts. If you like to dance, I know of a park district near here

    _____ free dance classes. In fact, there are a lot of things
          (6)

    _____ or very low cost in this city. I can give you a
          (7)
    list of free activities, if you want.

A. Thanks. I'd love to have the list. Thanks for all the suggestions

    _____ .
          (8)

B. I'd be happy to give you more, but I don't have time now. Tomorrow
    I'll bring you a list of activities from the parks in this city. I'm sure

    you'll find something _____ on that list.
                                 (9)

A. Thanks.

EXERCISE **10** We often give a definition with an adjective clause. Work with a
partner to give a definition of the following words by using an
adjective clause.

EXAMPLES: twins
            Twins are brothers or sisters who are born at the same time.

            an answering machine
            An answering machine is a device that takes phone messages.

1. a babysitter   5. a fax machine
2. an immigrant   6. a dictionary
3. an adjective   7. a mouse
4. a verb   8. a coupon

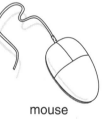

mouse

coupon

1. When you think of single people, what ages do you think of?
2. Do you think senior citizens (65 years old and older) can fall in love?

Read the following article. Pay special attention to adjective clauses beginning with *whose*.

Senior Singles

Florence Lustig

When most of us think of single people, we think of young adults. However, many people who are looking for romance and marriage are seniors. Many people over 65 are single—either because of divorce or death of a spouse.

Florence Lustig, a 72-year-old resident of Florida **whose** husband died six years ago, wanted to meet other singles her age. She looked at singles ads in newspapers, but was discouraged; most of the ads were written by young people. Sometimes she saw an ad for someone her age and answered the ad, but she found she didn't have much in common with the men **whose** ads she answered. She wanted to meet people **whose** age and interests were similar to her own. She looked for groups to join, but couldn't find any that were right for her. So she started her own club. She placed an ad in the local newspapers to look for other senior singles who shared some of her interests, and soon seniors were contacting her. Her group, which she named "Senior Singles, Mix and Mingle," plans all kinds of activities: the members go to concerts, take walks, go to museums, invite speakers.

Did you know...?

Fifty-three percent of women 75 years old and older live alone. Twenty-one percent of men over 75 live alone.

But it will be hard for Florence to find a husband. Because the life expectancy for women is much higher than it is for men (79 for women, 73 for men), most of the people in her group are widows, women **whose** husbands have died. While Florence would like to get married again, she's happy to make new friends so that she doesn't have to go places alone.

11.4   *Whose* + Noun

Whose as Subject of the Adjective Clause

Florence is a Florida resident.

	Her	husband died six years ago.
Florence is a Florida resident	**whose**	husband died six years ago.

Whose as Object of the Adjective Clause

Florence didn't have anything in common with the men.

		their	ads.
	She answered		
Florence didn't have anything in common with the men	**whose**		ads
she answered.			

LANGUAGE NOTES

1. *Whose* is the possessive form of *who*. It substitutes for *his, her, its, their,* or the possessive form of the noun (for example, *the teacher's*).
2. *Whose* + noun can be either the subject or object of an adjective clause.
    SUBJECT
    I have a friend *whose mother* is a widow.
    OBJECT
    The man *whose ad* we saw wants to meet a woman under 34.

EXERCISE **11** Underline the adjective clause.

EXAMPLE: A student <u>whose score is high</u> can take college courses.

1.   A student whose attendance is bad might fail the course.

2.   Students like a teacher whose explanations are clear.

3. The teacher gave an A to the students whose compositions were good.

4. The teacher whose class I took last semester retired.

5. There are some students whose names I can't pronounce.

6. A widow is a woman whose husband has died.

7. The man whose ad we read is looking for an active woman.

8. The woman whose story we read lives in Florida.

EXERCISE 12 Use the sentence in parentheses ( ) to form an adjective clause.

EXAMPLES: The TOEFL™ is a test for students *whose native language isn't English.*
(Their native language isn't English.)

The man *whose wallet I found and returned* gave me a reward.
(I found and returned his wallet.)

1. Students _____ might be able to get financial aid. (Their family incomes are low.)

2. Parents _____ have a lot of expenses. (Their children are in college.)

3. Parents _____ are usually very proud. (Their children graduate from college.)

4. He wants to meet a woman _____ (Her hobbies are the same as his.)

5. There are some students _____ (I don't remember their names.)

6. The students _____ often ask me questions in our language. (I speak their language.)

7. The teacher _____ went to Japan to teach English. (I took his class last semester.)

8. I bought a used book. The student _____ wrote in all the answers. (I bought his book.)

EXERCISE 13 *Part A*: Some women were asked what kind of man they'd like to marry. Fill in the blanks with a response.

EXAMPLE: I'd like to marry a man *whose values are the same as mine.*
              (His values are the same as mine.)

1. I'd like to marry a man _____
   (I can trust him.)

2. I don't want a husband _____
   (He doesn't put his family first.)

3. I want to marry a man _____
   (He makes a good living.)

4. I'd like to marry a man _____
   (I like his family.)

5. I'd like to marry a man _____
   (He's older than I am.)

6. I'd like to marry a man _____
   (He wants to have children.)

7. (Women: Add your own sentence telling what kind of man you'd like to marry, or what kind of man you married.)

_____

Part B: Some men were asked what kind of woman they'd like to marry. Fill in the blanks with a response.

EXAMPLE: I'd like to marry a woman *who knows how to cook.*
              (She knows how to cook.)

1. I'd like to marry a woman _____
   (She has a sense of humor.)

2. I'd like to marry a woman _____
   (I can admire her wisdom.)

3. I'd like to marry a woman _____
   (Her manners are good.)

4. I'd like to marry a woman _____
   (Her mother doesn't interfere.)

5. I'd like to marry a woman _____
   (I have known her for a long time.)

6. I'd like to marry a woman _____
   (She wants to have a lot of kids.)

7. (Men: Add your own sentence telling what kind of woman you'd like to marry, or what kind of woman you married.)

_____

EXERCISE 14 Complete each statement with an adjective clause. You may use *who, whom, that, which,* or *whose* to introduce the adjective clause. (In some cases, no word is necessary to introduce the adjective clause.)

EXAMPLES: I have a neighbor _whose dog barks all the time._

I don't like people _who tell you one thing and do something else._

1. I know a man/woman _____

2. I have a TV/VCR/stereo _____

3. My father is/was a person _____

4. My mother is/was a person _____

5. I would like to buy a car _____

6. I have a neighbor _____

7. I don't like people _____

8. A real friend is a person _____

EXERCISE 15 Fill in the blanks with appropriate words to complete the conversation.

A. I'm getting married next month.

B. Congratulations. Are you marrying the woman __*you met*__ at
   (example)
   Mark's party last year?

A. Oh, no. I broke up with that woman a long time ago. The woman

   _____ is a person _____ in my biology class.
   _(1)_   _(2)_

B. What's her name? I know some of the people who _____ your
                                                    _(3)_
   biology class.

A. Lisa Martin.

B. I think I know her. Is she the young woman _____?
                                               _(4)_

A. Yes. She always gets an A on every test. She's very intelligent.

B. Well, you're a lucky man. Lisa is smart and pretty, too. Are you getting married in church?

A. No. We're going to get married in a house.

B. I didn't know you have a house.

A. We don't. We're going to use a friend's house. The person _____ (5) _____ is an old friend of Lisa's mother. She has a very big house. If the weather is nice, the wedding is going to be outside.

B. My wife and I made plans to get married outside too, but we had to change the plans _____ (6) because it rained that day.

A. That's OK. The woman _____ (7) is more important than the place where we get married. And the life _____ (8) together is more important than the wedding day.

B. You're right about that!

EXERCISE 16 Use the words in parentheses ( ) to form an adjective clause. Then read the sentences and tell if you agree or disagree. Give your reasons.

EXAMPLE: A good friend is a person ___ I can trust. ___
(I can trust her.)

1. A good friend is a person _____ almost every day.
(I see him.)

2. A good friend is a person _____.
(She would lend me money.)

3. A good friend is a person _____.
(He knows everything about me.)

4. A person _____ cannot be my friend.
(He has different political opinions.)

5. A person _____ cannot be my good friend.
(She doesn't speak my native language.)

6. A person _____ cannot be my good friend.
(His religious beliefs are different from mine.)

7. A person _____ cannot be a good friend.
(She lives far away.)

8. I would discuss all the problems _____ with a good friend.
(I have problems.)

Adjective Clauses

1. Pronoun as Subject
    She likes men **who have self-confidence**.
    The man **that arrived late** took a seat in the back.

2. Pronoun as Object
    I'd like to meet the man **(who/m) (that) she married**.
    The book **(which) (that) I'm reading** is very exciting.

3. *Whose* + Noun as Subject
    I have a friend **whose brother lives in Japan**.
    The students **whose last names begin with A or B** can register on Friday afternoon.

4. *Whose* + Noun as Object
    She married a man **whose mother she hates**.
    The student **whose dictionary I borrowed** didn't come to class today.

EDITING ADVICE

1. Use *who*, *that*, or *which* to introduce an adjective clause. Don't use *what*.

    I know a woman ~~what~~ *who* has ten cats.

2. If the relative pronoun is the subject, don't omit it.

    I know a man *who* has been married four times.

3. Use *whose* to substitute for a possessive form.

    I live next door to a couple ~~their~~ *whose* children make a lot of noise.

4. If the relative pronoun is used as the object, don't put an object after the verb of the adjective clause.

    I had to pay for the library book that I lost ~~it~~.

5. Don't use *which* for people.

    The man ~~which~~ *that* bought my car paid me by check.

6. Use subject-verb agreement in all clauses.

I have a friend who live^(s) in Madrid.

People who talks too much bother me.

7. Don't use an adjective clause when a simple adjective is enough.

I don't like long movies.
~~I don't like movies that are long.~~

8. An adjective clause is a dependent clause. It is never a sentence.

who
I sold my car to a man. ~~Who~~ lives on the next block.

9. Put a noun before an adjective clause.

A student w
~~Who~~ needs help should ask the teacher.

10. Put the adjective clause immediately after the noun it describes.

The teacher speaks Spanish (whose class I am taking).

11. Use correct word order in an adjective clause (subject before verb).

my father caught
The fish that ~~caught my father~~ was very big.

12. Don't confuse *whose* (possessive pronoun) and *who's (who is)*.

who's
A woman ~~whose~~ in my math class is helping me study for the test.

LESSON 11 TEST / REVIEW

PART 1   Find the mistakes with the underlined words, and correct them. Not every sentence has a mistake. If the sentence is correct, write C.

EXAMPLES: *who's*
Do you know the man ~~whose~~ standing in the back of the theater?
Could you please return the book I lent you last week?   C

1. The wallet which found my husband has no identification.

2. The coat is too small that I bought last week.

3. I don't know the people that lives next door to me.

4. I have to return the books that I borrowed from the library.

5. I don't like neighbors <u>what make</u> a lot of noise.

6. I don't like the earrings <u>that I bought them</u>.

7. I have a <u>friend lives</u> in Houston.

8. <u>Who</u> speaks English well doesn't have to take this course.

9. I can't understand a word <u>you are saying</u>.

10. I prefer to have an English teacher <u>which speaks</u> my language.

11. The students <u>whose names the teacher calls</u> should stand up.

12. I don't know <u>anyone. Who has</u> a record player any more.

13. We rented an apartment <u>that doesn't have</u> a refrigerator.

14. A couple <u>who's</u> children are small has a lot of responsibilities.

15. I have a friend <u>her</u> brother just graduated from medical school.

16. The student never came back <u>whose dictionary I borrowed</u>.

PART **2**   **Fill in the blanks to complete the adjective clause.**

EXAMPLE: A. You lost a glove. Is this yours?

B. No. The glove ____*that I lost*____ is brown.

1. A. My neighbors make a lot of noise. They play their music every night.

    B. That's too bad. I don't like to have neighbors _____

    _____

2. A. I have a new cat. Do you want to see him?

    B. What happened to the other cat _____
    A. She died last month.

3. A. Do you speak French?
    B. Yes, I do. Why?

    A. The teacher is looking for a student _____
       to help her translate a letter.

4. A. Did you meet your boyfriend by answering a singles ad?

    B. No. I didn't like any of the men _____ from the singles ads.

5. A. Does your last name begin with A?
   B. Yes, it does. Why?

   A. Registration is by alphabetical order. Students _____ can register after two o'clock today.

6. A. I heard you got a good price on the house you bought.

   B. Yes. The woman _____ moved to Alaska.

7. A. Are you planning to marry Charles?

   B. No. He lives with his mother. I want to marry a man _____ lives far away.

8. I found a wallet with $75 and identification. I'm going to contact the person

   _____ .

EXPANSION ACTIVITIES

CLASSROOM ACTIVITIES

1. Tell if you agree or disagree with the statements below. Discuss your answers.

	I agree.	I disagree.
a) People who have different religions can have a good marriage.		
b) People who come from different countries or have different languages can have a good marriage.		
c) Women who marry younger men can be happy.		
d) It's possible to fall in love with someone you've just met.		
e) Young people who want to get married should get the approval of their parents.		
f) A man shouldn't marry a divorced woman who has children.		
g) Couples who have children shouldn't get divorced.		
h) Older women whose husbands have died should try to get married again.		
i) A man should always marry a woman who is shorter than he is.		
j) Couples who live with a mother-in-law usually have problems.		
k) A woman shouldn't marry a man who has a lower level of education.		

2. Bring to class a newspaper with singles ads. In a group, try to read them with the help of your teacher.

3. Write a short definition or description of an object or a person. Read your definition to a small group. The others will try to guess what it is. Continue to add to your definition until someone guesses it.

EXAMPLE:

It's an animal that lives in the water.
Is it a fish?
No, it isn't. It's an animal that needs to come up for air.
Is it a dolphin?
Yes, it is.

4. Write a word from your native language that has no English translation. It might be the name of a food or a traditional costume. Define the word. Read your definition to a small group or to a partner.

EXAMPLE:

A *sari* is a typical Indian dress for women. It is made of a cloth that a woman wraps around her. She wraps one end around her waist. She puts the other end over her shoulder.

5. Bring to class something typical from your country. Demonstrate how to use it.

EXAMPLE:

a samovar
This is a pot that we use in Russia to make tea.

6. Dictionary game. Form a small group. One student in the group will look for a hard word in the dictionary. (Choose a noun. Find a word that you think no one will know.) Other students will write definitions of the word. Students can think of funny definitions or serious ones. The student with the dictionary will write the real definition. Students put all the definitions in a box. The student with the dictionary will read the definitions. The others have to guess which is the real definition.

EXAMPLE:

parapet
Sample definition: A parapet is a small pet that has wings, like a parakeet.
Real definition: A parapet is a low wall that runs along the edge of a roof or balcony.

(The teacher can provide a list of words and definitions beforehand, writing them on small pieces of paper. A student can choose one of the papers that the teacher has prepared.)

DISCUSSION

1. In a small group or with the entire class, discuss what you think of singles ads. Is this a good way to meet a partner? Why or why not?

2. Discuss how single people meet each other in your native culture.

3. Discuss ways you can make friends in a new country.

4. In a small group or with the entire class, talk about the kind of person who makes a good husband, wife, father, mother, or friend.

WRITING

1. Choose one of the following topics and write a paragraph.

   a. I prefer to study English with a teacher who speaks my language.
   b. I prefer to study English with a teacher who doesn't speak my language.

   Give reasons for your preference.

2. Write a paragraph telling how you met your spouse or a new friend.

Internet Activities

1. Find a Web site that has singles ads.

2. Find a Web site for senior citizens. Can you find a senior chat room?

Lesson Twelve

GRAMMAR

Superlatives
Comparatives
Equality
Similarity

CONTEXT

Michael Jordan
Americans' Attitude Toward Soccer
Dennis Rodman and Michael Jordan

LESSON FOCUS

The superlative form shows the top item in a group of three or more.

> New York City is *the biggest* city in the U.S.

The comparative form compares two items.

> Los Angeles is *bigger than* Chicago.

We can show equality.

> Are you *as tall as* your brother?
> Are you and your brother *the same height*?

We can show similarity and difference.

> I'*m like* my father. We're both athletic.
> I *look like* my mother. We both have brown eyes and curly brown hair.

1. Do you like basketball?

2. Did you ever see Michael Jordan play basketball?

Read the following article. Pay special attention to superlative forms.

Michael Jordan

Michael Jordan was **the best known** basketball player of his time. His career started in the early 1980s, when he played college basketball with the University of North Carolina. Although he was not **the tallest** or **the strongest** player, he won the attention of his coach for being an excellent athlete. Probably his **most important** achievement[1] at that time was scoring the winning basket in the 1983–1984 college championship game.

Jordan left college early to join the professional basketball team, the Chicago Bulls. He led the Bulls to **the best** record in professional basketball history. He was voted **the most valuable** player five times. Jordan holds several records: **the highest** scoring average (31.7 points per game) and **the most** points in a playoff game (63).

Many people think that Michael Jordan was **the most spectacular** basketball player of all time. A statue of Jordan in Chicago has these words, "**The best** there ever was. **The best** there ever will be." Jordan retired from basketball in 1999 at the age of 35.

Jordan's popularity with his fans brought him to the attention of advertisers. Jordan is paid a lot of money to have his name appear on sports products and to appear in TV commercials, making him **the highest** paid athlete in the world. He is also one of **the richest** people in the world. *Forbes Magazine* in 1997 said that he earned over 78 million dollars that year.

Did you know...?

When Jordan tried out for the basketball team in high school, he didn't make it on his first try.

12.1 Comparative and Superlative Forms

The chart below shows simple, comparative, and superlative forms of adjectives and adverbs.

	Simple	Comparative	Superlative
One-syllable adjectives and adverbs	tall	taller	the tallest
	fast	faster	the fastest
Exceptions:	bored	more bored	the most bored
	tired	more tired	the most tired

(continued)

---

[1] An *achievement* is something special you do after practice or hard work.

	Simple	Comparative	Superlative
Two-syllable adjectives that end in -*y*	easy	easier	the easiest
	happy	happier	the happiest
Other two-syllable adjectives	frequent	more frequent	the most frequent
	active	more active	the most active
Some two-syllable adjectives have two forms.	simple	simpler	the simplest
		more simple	the most simple
	common	commoner	the commonest
		more common	the most common

NOTE: These two-syllable adjectives have two forms: *handsome, quiet, gentle, narrow, clever, friendly, angry.*

	Simple	Comparative	Superlative
Adjectives with three or more syllables	important	more important	the most important
	difficult	more difficult	the most difficult
-*ly* adverbs	quickly	more quickly	the most quickly
	brightly	more brightly	the most brightly
Irregular adjectives and adverbs	good/well	better	the best
	bad/badly	worse	the worst
	far	farther/further*	the farthest/furthest
	little	less	the least
	a lot	more	the most

*NOTE: *Farther* is used for distances. *Further* is used for ideas.

Compare: I drove *farther* than you did.
 He explained his plan *further.*

(To review spelling rules, see Appendix B.)

EXERCISE 1   Give the comparative and superlative forms of each word.

EXAMPLES: fat   *fatter*   *the fattest*
     important   *more important*   *the most important*

1. interesting _____   _____

2. young _____   _____

3. beautiful _____   _____

4. good _____   _____

5. common _____   _____

6. thin _____   _____

7. carefully _____   _____

8. pretty   _____   _____

9. bad   _____   _____

10. famous   _____   _____

11. lucky   _____   _____

12. simple   _____   _____

13. high   _____   _____

14. delicious   _____   _____

15. far   _____   _____

16. foolishly   _____   _____

12.2   Superlatives

Examples	Explanation
Michael Jordan was **the most popular** basketball player of his time. He became one of **the richest** people in the world. For many years, he was **the most valuable** player.	We use the superlative form to point out the number one item of a group of three or more.

LANGUAGE NOTES

1. Use *the* before a superlative form. Omit *the* if there is a possessive form before the superlative form.

    Jack is *my* tallest friend.

    My *brother's* oldest son is in high school.

2. We sometimes put a prepositional phrase at the end of a superlative sentence.

    in the world   in my family
    in my class   in my country

3. We often say "one of the" before a superlative form. Then we use a plural noun.

    Jordan is *one of the richest people* in the world.

    He was *one of the best athletes* in the world.

4. An adjective clause with *ever* and the present perfect tense often completes a superlative statement.

    Jordan is one of the best athletes *who has ever lived.*

    His last game was one of the most exciting games *I have ever seen.*

5. Superlative forms can be used with adjectives and adverbs.

ADJECTIVES   Michael Jordan was *the best basketball player* on his team.

He was *the most impressive* player on his team.

ADVERBS   He played *the most gracefully*.

He scored *the highest*.

EXERCISE 2   Many people have said that Jordan was the superlative in these categories. Write the superlative form in each blank.

EXAMPLE: He was _____ *the most elegant* _____ athlete.
(elegant)

1. He was _____ athlete.
(popular)

2. He was _____ athlete.
(great)

3. He was _____ athlete.
(powerful)

4. He was _____ athlete.
(graceful)

5. He is _____-known American basketball player
(good)
in the world.

6. He was _____ player.
(valuable)

7. He is one of _____ people in the world.
(rich)

8. He is one of _____-dressed people in the world.
(good)

EXERCISE 3   Write the superlative form of the word in parentheses ( ).

EXAMPLE: Rhode Island is _____ *the smallest* _____ state in the U.S.
(small)

1. Mount Everest is _____ mountain in the world.
(high)

2. Australia is _____ continent in the world.
(small)

3. Smith is one of _____ last names in the U.S.
(common)

4. San Francisco is one of _____ cities in the U.S.
(interesting)

5. California is _____ state in the U.S.
   (populated)

6. *The Simpsons* is one of _____ TV shows in
   the U.S.
   (popular)

EXERCISE 4 Talk about your native country. Talk about the superlative of
each item.

EXAMPLE: popular sport
           Soccer is the most popular sport in my country.

1. big city	6. popular car
2. beautiful city	7. common last name
3. important industry	8. cold month
4. popular sport	9. long river
5. famous athlete	10. large lake

EXERCISE 5 Look at the list of jobs below. Use the superlative form to name
a job that matches each description. You may discuss your
answers in a small group or with the entire class.

EXAMPLE: interesting
           In my opinion, a psychologist has the most interesting job.

psychologist	letter carrier
computer programmer	athlete
high school teacher	actress
factory worker	photojournalist
doctor	firefighter
police officer	politician
engineer	nurse

(you may add other professions)

1. interesting _____

2. dangerous _____

3. easy _____

4. tiring _____

5. dirty _____

6. boring _____

7. exciting _____

8. important _____

9. challenging _____

10. difficult _____

EXERCISE 6 Write a superlative sentence giving your opinion about each of the following items. (You may find a partner and compare your answers to your partner's answers.)

EXAMPLES: big problem in my native country today

The biggest problem in my country today is the civil war.

big problem in the U.S. today

Crime is one of the biggest problems in the U.S. today.

1. good way to find a spouse

_____

2. quick way to learn a language

_____

3. good thing about living in the U.S.

_____

4. bad thing about living in the U.S.

_____

5. terrible world tragedy

_____

EXERCISE 7 Write superlative sentences about your experience with the words given. Use the present perfect form after the superlative.

EXAMPLE: big / city / visit

London is the biggest city I have ever visited.

1. tall / building / visit

_____

---

2. beautiful / actress / see

_____

3. difficult / subject / study

_____

4. far / distant / travel

_____

5. interesting / person / meet

_____

6. bad / American food / eat

_____

7. big / amount of money / spend / on one thing

_____

8. good / vacation / have

_____

9. good / athlete / see

_____

10. interesting/ book / read

_____

11. good / friend / have

_____

12. bad / apartment / have

_____

13. good / time / have

_____

14. big / city / visit

_____

15. hard / job / have

_____

EXERCISE 8 Fill in the blanks.

EXAMPLE: *Swimming across a lake alone at night*

was one of the most dangerous things I've ever done.

1. _____

   is one of the most foolish things I have ever done.

2. _____

   is one of the hardest decisions I have ever made.

3. _____

   is one of the most dangerous things I've ever done.

12.3 Superlatives and Word Order

Examples	Explanation
Michael Jordan was **the most popular** basketball player on his team. In golf, the winner is the person with **the lowest** score.	Put superlative adjectives before the noun.
Michael Jordan played basketball **the most gracefully**. He scored **the highest**. Who played **the most**?	Put superlative adverbs after the verb (phrase). You can put *the most, the least, the best, the worst* after a verb.

EXERCISE 9 Name the person who is the superlative in your family in each of the following categories.

EXAMPLE: works hard
My mother works the hardest in my family.

1. drives well
2. lives far from me
3. speaks English confidently
4. spends a lot of money
5. is well dressed
6. watches a lot of TV
7. worries a lot
8. lives well
9. works hard
10. is athletic
11. is big sports fan
12. is learning English quickly

1. Are you interested in soccer?
2. Who's your favorite athlete?

Read the following article. Pay special attention to comparisons.

Americans' Attitude Toward Soccer

Soccer is by far the most popular sport in the world. Almost every country has a professional league. In many countries, top international soccer players are **as** well-known **as** rock stars or actors. However, in 1994 when the World Cup soccer competition was held in the U.S., there was not a lot of interest in soccer among Americans. Many people said that soccer was boring.

Recently, Americans' attitude toward soccer has been changing. In 1999, when the Women's World Cup was played in the U.S., there was **more** interest than ever before. Little by little, soccer is becoming **more popular** in the U.S. The number of children playing soccer is growing. In fact, soccer is growing **faster** than any other sport. For elementary school children, soccer is now the number two sport after basketball. **More** kids play soccer than baseball. Many coaches believe that soccer is **easier** to play than baseball or basketball, and that there aren't **as many** injuries **as** with sports such as hockey or football.

Interest in professional soccer in the U.S. is still much **lower** than in other countries. The number of Americans who watch professional basketball, football, or hockey is still much **higher** than the number who watch Major League Soccer. However, **the more** parents show interest in their children's soccer teams, **the more** they will become interested in professional soccer.

Did you know...?

American parents spend between $85 and $265 on kids' soccer uniforms and shoes.

EXERCISE 10 Choose the correct word to complete each statement.

EXAMPLE: In the U.S., soccer is *more /(less)* popular than basketball.

1. Football players have *more / fewer* injuries than soccer players.

2. In the U.S., soccer is growing *faster / slower* than any other sport.

3. In 1999, there was *more / less* interest in soccer than in 1994.

4. Professional soccer is *more / less* popular in the U.S. than in other countries.

5. In the U.S., soccer players are *more / less* famous than movie stars.

12.4 Comparisons

Examples	Explanation
Soccer is **more popular** in Mexico than in the U.S. Soccer is growing **faster** than any other sport in the U.S.	We use the comparative form to compare two items. We use *than* before the second item.

LANGUAGE NOTES

1. Omit *than* if the second item of comparison is not included.
   Football is popular in the U.S., but baseball is more popular.
2. In a question, we use *or* instead of *than*.
   What do you like better, soccer *or* basketball?
3. *Much* or *a little* can come before a comparative form.
   Interest in soccer in the U.S. is *much* lower than in other countries.
   I like soccer *a little* better than basketball.
4. When a pronoun follows *than*, the most correct form is the subject pronoun (*he, she, I,* etc.) Sometimes an auxiliary verb follows (*is, are, do, did,* etc.). Informally, many Americans use the object pronoun (*him, her, me,* etc.) after *than* without an auxiliary verb.

   FORMAL
   She is taller than *he (is)*.
   She is older than *I (am)*.

   INFORMAL
   She is taller than *him*.
   She is older than *me*.
5. We can use two comparatives in one sentence to show cause and result.
   The more they practice, *the better* they play.
   The older you are, *the harder* it is to learn a new sport.

6. Comparative forms can be used with adjectives, adverbs, and nouns.

ADJECTIVES In the U.S., basketball is *more popular* than soccer.

Basketball players are *taller* than soccer players.

ADVERBS Interest in soccer is growing *more quickly* than interest in hockey.

One team played *better* than the other team.

NOUNS There is *more* interest in basketball than in soccer in the U.S.

Professional athletes make *more* money than the President.

EXERCISE 11 Fill in the blanks with the comparative form of the word in parentheses ( ).

EXAMPLE: In the U.S., basketball is _____ *more popular than* _____ soccer.
(popular)

1. Los Angeles is _____ New York.
(small)

2. Adults are _____ children.
(responsible)

3. Computers used to be _____ they are today.
(expensive)

4. Computers used to be much _____ they are today.
(big)

5. Adults drive _____ teenagers.
(carefully)

6. Do you think that voice mail is _____ an answering machine?
(good)

7. Police work is _____ teaching.
(dangerous)

8. Children learn languages _____ adults.
(easily)

EXERCISE 12 Compare the people of your native country to Americans (in general). Give your own opinion.

EXAMPLE: tall
Americans are taller than Koreans.

1. polite   5. thin
2. friendly   6. serious
3. formal   7. wealthy
4. tall   8. educated

EXERCISE 13 Compare the U.S. and your native country. Explain your response.

EXAMPLES:
cars
Cars are cheaper in the U.S. Most people in my native country can't afford a car.

education
Education is better in my native country. Everyone must finish high school.

1. rent
2. housing
3. cars
4. education
5. medical care
6. food
7. gasoline
8. the government
9. clothes (or fashions)
10. people

12.5 Comparatives and Word Order

Examples	Explanation
Basketball is **more popular** than soccer in the U.S. Football looks **more dangerous** than soccer.	Put the comparative adjective after the verb *be* (or other linking verbs: *seem, feel, look, sound*).
Jordan played basketball **more gracefully** than any other player. Soccer is growing **faster** than any other sport. My sister likes soccer **more** than I do.	Put the comparative adverb after the verb phrase.
There is **less** interest in hockey than there is in basketball.	You can put *more, less, fewer, better, worse* before a noun.

EXERCISE 14 Put the words in the correct order. Add *than*.

EXAMPLE:
A mouse / smaller / is / a rat

A mouse is smaller than a rat.

turtle

rabbit

1. A turtle / more slowly / moves / a rabbit

_____

2. An elephant / is / bigger / a cow

_____

3. An elephant / longer / lives / a dog

_____

4. A whale / stays under water / a dolphin / longer

_____

5. A shark / has / a sense of smell / a dolphin / better

_____

6. A bear / runs / a person / faster

_____

whale

dolphin

EXERCISE 15 Use a comparative adverb to compare the people of your native country to Americans (in general). Give your own opinion.

EXAMPLE: drive well
Mexicans drive better than Americans.

1. dress stylishly
2. work hard
3. spend a lot

4. live long
5. worry a little
6. live comfortably

7. have freedom
8. have a good life

EXERCISE 16 Compare this school to a school in your native country. Use *better, worse, more, less,* or *fewer* before the noun.

EXAMPLE: classroom/space
This classroom has more space than a classroom in my native country.

1. class/students
2. school/courses
3. teachers/experience

4. library/books
5. school/facilities²
6. school/teachers

EXERCISE 17 *Combination exercise.* Fill in the blanks with the comparative or superlative form of the word in parentheses ( ). Include *than* or *the* when necessary.

EXAMPLES: August is usually ___*hotter than*___ May.
(hot)

January is usually ___*the coldest*___ month of the year.
(cold)

1. November is _____ December.
(short)

---

² *Facilities* are things we use, such as a swimming pool, cafeteria, library, exercise room, or student union.

2. December 21 is _____ day of the year. It
   (short)

has _____ hours of sunlight.
   (few)

3. "Johnson" is one of _____ last names in
   (common)

the U.S.

4. A motorcycle is _____ a car.
   (economical)

5. _____ way to travel is by bicycle.
   (economical)

6. Baseball is one of _____ sports in the U.S.
   (popular)

7. Baseball is _____ soccer in the U.S.
   (popular)

8. What is _____ way to call long distance to your
   (cheap)

hometown?

9. Paris is far from Los Angeles, but Moscow is even _____.
   (far)

10. In my opinion, San Francisco is _____ Detroit.
   (beautiful)

12.6 As . . . As

Examples	Explanation
In the U.S., soccer is not **as** popular **as** basketball. No one plays basketball **as** beautifully **as** Michael Jordan.	We can show that two things are equal or not in some way by using *as adjective/adverb as*.

LANGUAGE NOTES

1. When we make a comparison of unequal items, we put the lesser item first.
   I am not *as tall as* Michael Jordan. (Michael Jordan is taller.)
2. Omit the second *as* if the second item of comparison is omitted.
   Soccer is not *as popular as* football, but
   soccer is *safer*.
3. A very common expression is *as soon as possible*. Some people even say A.S.A.P.
   I'd like to see you *as soon as possible*.
   I'd like to see you *A.S.A.P.*

4. These are some common expressions using *as . . . as.*

as poor as a church mouse
as old as the hills
as quiet as a mouse
as happy as a lark
as sick as a dog
as proud as a peacock
as gentle as a lamb
as stubborn as a mule

mule

peacock

EXERCISE 18 Compare yourself to another person. (Or compare two people you know.) Use the following adjectives and *as . . . as.* You may add a comparative statement if there is inequality.

EXAMPLES:

thin
I'm not as thin as my sister. (She's thinner than I am.)

old
My mother is not as old as my father. (My father is older than my mother.)

1. old	4. patient	7. religious	10. talkative
2. educated	5. lazy	8. friendly	11. athletic
3. intelligent	6. tall	9. strong	12. interested in sports

EXERCISE 19 Use the underlined word to compare yourself to the teacher.

EXAMPLE:

speak Spanish <u>well</u>

The teacher doesn't speak Spanish as well as I do. (I speak Spanish better.)

1. arrive at class <u>promptly</u>

2. work <u>hard</u> in class

3. understand American customs <u>well</u>

4. speak <u>quietly</u>

5. speak English <u>fluently</u>

6. understand a foreigner's problems <u>well</u>

7. write <u>neatly</u>

8. speak <u>fast</u>

Examples	Explanation
Baseball players don't have **as many** injuries **as** football players. I don't have **as much** time for sports **as** you do.	We can show that two things are equal or not equal in quantity by using *as many [count noun] as* or *as much [noncount noun] as*.
I don't play soccer **as much as** I used to. She doesn't like sports **as much as** her husband does.	We can use *as much as* after a verb phrase.

EXERCISE 20 Compare men and women (in general). Give your own opinion. Use *as many as* or *as much as*.

EXAMPLE: show emotion
Men don't show as much emotion as women. (Women show more emotion than men.)

1. earn
2. spend money
3. talk
4. gossip

5. use bad words
6. have responsibilities
7. have freedom
8. have free time

EXERCISE 21 Compare this school and another school you attended. Use *as many as*.

EXAMPLE: classrooms
This school doesn't have as many classrooms as King College.
(King College has more classrooms.)

1. teachers
2. classrooms

3. floors (or stories)
4. English courses

5. exams
6. students

EXERCISE 22 Part A: Fill in the blanks.

1. I drive about ＿＿＿＿＿＿＿ miles a week.

2. I'm ＿＿＿＿＿＿＿ tall.

3. The highest level of education that I completed is ＿＿＿＿＿＿＿

＿＿＿＿＿＿＿ .

(high school, bachelor's degree, master's degree, doctorate).

4. I work _____ hours a week.

5. I study _____ hours a day.

6. I have had _____ tickets while driving my car.

7. I exercise _____ days a week.

8. I'm taking _____ courses now.
   (number)

9. I have _____ siblings.³
   (number)

10. I live _____ miles from this school.
    (number)

Part B: Find a partner and compare your answers to your partner's answers. Write statements with the words given and *(not) as . . . as* or *(not) as much / many as.*

EXAMPLE: drive *I don't drive as much as Lisa.*

1. tall _____

2. have education _____

3. work _____

4. study _____

5. drive carefully _____

6. exercise frequently _____

7. take courses _____

8. have siblings _____

9. live far from school _____

EXERCISE 23 Change these statements so that they use *as . . . as.*

EXAMPLE: The teacher speaks English more fluently than I (do).
            I don't speak English as fluently as the teacher (does).

1. A car costs more than a motorcycle.

   _____

2. Cream has more fat than milk.

   _____

³ *Siblings* are a person's brothers and sisters.

3. Women live longer than men.

_____

4. The teacher speaks English better than I do.

_____

5. Chicago has more people than Miami.

_____

6. Tokyo is more crowded than Los Angeles.

_____

7. In the U.S., baseball is more popular than soccer.

_____

8. Football players have more injuries than soccer players.

_____

EXERCISE 24 Make one or more comparisons for each of the following. Then find a partner. Compare your answers to your partner's answers.

EXAMPLE: public transportation in this city/in my hometown

The buses are cleaner in my hometown than in this city.

or

The buses in this city are not as crowded as the buses in

my hometown.

1. American women/women in my native country

_____

2. medical care in the U.S./in my native country

_____

3. American teachers/teachers in my native country

_____

4. learning English in the U.S./learning English in my native country

_____

12.8 *The Same . . . As*

Examples	Explanation
PATTERN A: A soccer ball isn't **the same shape as** a football. Michael Jordan was on **the same team as** Dennis Rodman.	We can show that two things are equal or not equal in some way by using *the same [noun] as*.
PATTERN B: A soccer ball and a football aren't **the same shape**. Jordan and Rodman were on **the same team**.	Omit *as* in Pattern B.

LANGUAGE NOTES

We can make statements of equality with many nouns, such as *team, shape, color, value, religion, nationality*.

EXERCISE 25 Talk about two relatives or friends of yours. Compare them using the words given.

EXAMPLE: age
My mother and my father aren't the same age.
OR
My mother isn't the same age as my father. (My father is older than my mother.)

1. age	4. nationality
2. height	5. religion
3. weight	6. (have) level of education

EXERCISE 26 Make a **true** affirmative statement or negative statement with the words given.

EXAMPLES: the same nationality
I'm not the same nationality as the teacher. I'm Colombian, and the teacher's American.

the same color
My shoes and my purse are the same color. They're both brown.

1. the same color	4. the same shape
2. (have) the same value	5. the same price
3. the same size	6. (speak) the same language

Equality with Nouns or Adjectives

Noun	Adjective	Examples
height	tall, short	He's not **the same height as** his brother. His brother is **shorter**.
age	old, young	He's not **the same age as** his wife. His wife is **older**.
weight	heavy, thin	She's not **the same weight as** her mother. She is **thinner**.
length	long, short	This shelf is not **the same length as** that shelf. This shelf is **shorter**.
price	expensive, cheap	This car is not **the same price as** that car. This car is **cheaper**.
size	big, small	These shoes are not **the same size as** those shoes. These shoes are **smaller**.

LANGUAGE NOTES

1. For equality with nouns, use *the same . . . as*.
    She's *the same age as* her husband.
2. For equality with adjectives and adverbs, use *as . . . as*.
    She's *as old as* her husband.

EXERCISE 27 Change the following to use the comparative form.

EXAMPLE: Lesson 11 is not the same length as Lesson 12.

Lesson 11 is _____*shorter.*_____

1. I am not the same height as my brother.

    My brother is _____ .

2. You are not the same age as your husband.

    You are _____ .

3. I am not the same height as a basketball player.

    A basketball player is _____ .

4. My left foot isn't the same size as my right foot.

    My right foot is _____.

5. My brother is not the same weight as I am.

    My brother is _____.

Before You Read 1. Have you ever heard of Dennis Rodman?
2. Can you name two players from the same sport team who are very different?

Dennis Rodman

Read the following article. Pay special attention to similarities and differences.

Dennis Rodman and Michael Jordan

Dennis Rodman and Michael Jordan became famous playing basketball for the Chicago Bulls. Although they both were great players from the **same** team, they are very **different**.

Jordan and Rodman don't **act alike**. Jordan always **acts like** a gentleman. Rodman's conduct has been very **different**. Once, he hit a referee. Another time, he kicked a photographer. Rodman was often late for practice or missed practice completely.

These two men don't **dress alike** at all. Jordan is known for his elegant style of dress. Rodman is known for dying his hair many different colors, wearing many earrings, and appearing in outrageous[4] clothing.

The family backgrounds of these two basketball stars are quite **different**. Jordan came from a stable family. He had a close relationship with his father. In high school, he was already recognized for his talents as a basketball player and went on to college basketball. Rodman, on the other hand, was raised without a father. He didn't play basketball in high school. When he left school, he went to work as a janitor.

Even though these two men are very **different**, together they led the Chicago Bulls to victory.

Dennis Rodman	Michael Jordan
6'8" tall	6'6" tall
Born in 1961	Born in 1963
Had several brief marriages	Married for a long time, a family man
Hair dyed many colors	Shaves his head
Nickname: "The Worm"	Nickname: MJ or Air Jordan
worm	
Was short in high school	Was tall in high school
Tried wrestling for a while	Tried baseball for a while

12.10 Similarity with *Like* and *Alike*

Examples	Explanation
PATTERN A: Jordan doesn't **dress like** Rodman. Jordan doesn't **act like** Rodman.	We can show that two things are similar (or not) by putting *like* after the verb.
PATTERN B: Jordan and Rodman don't **dress alike**. Jordan and Rodman don't **act alike**.	Use *alike* in Pattern B.

[4] *Outrageous* clothing is extreme, shocking, or totally different from what people normally wear.

LANGUAGE NOTES

1. We often use the sense perception verbs (*look, sound, smell, taste, feel, seem*) with *like* or *alike*.
   Jordan doesn't *look like* Rodman.
   They don't *look alike* at all.

2. Compare affirmative and negative sentences with a verb + *like*.
   I *look like* my father.
   I *don't look like* my mother.

EXERCISE 28 Make a statement with the words given.

EXAMPLE: taste/Pepsi/Coke
Pepsi tastes like Coke (to me).
OR
Pepsi and Coke taste alike (to me).

1. taste/diet cola/regular cola

2. taste/milk in the U.S./milk in my native country

3. look/an American classroom/a classroom in my native country

4. sound/Asian music/American music

5. feel/polyester/silk

6. smell/cologne/perfume

7. look/salt/sugar

8. taste/salt/sugar

9. act/Michael Jordan/Dennis Rodman

10. dress/Jordan/Rodman

11. act/American teachers/teachers in my native country

12. dress/American teenagers/teenagers in my native country

EXERCISE 29 Fill in the blanks. In some cases, more than one answer is possible.

EXAMPLE: Players on the same team dress _____*alike*_____.

1. Twins _____ alike.

2. Americans don't _____ like people from England. They have different accents.

3. My daughter is only 15 years old, but she _____ an adult. She's very responsible and hard-working.

4. My son is only 16 years old, but he _____ an adult. He's tall and has a beard.

5. Teenagers often wear the same clothing. They like to _____ .

6. Soccer players don't look _____ football players at all.

7. Do you think I'll ever _____ an American, or will I always have an accent?

8. Children in private schools usually wear a uniform. They _____ alike.

9. My children learned English very quickly. Now they _____ like Americans. They have no accent at all.

10. Dogs don't _____ cats at all. Dogs are very friendly. Cats are more distant.

12.11 *Be Like*

Examples	Explanation
PATTERN A: Dennis Rodman **is like** Michael Jordan in some ways. They both became rich, famous athletes. Dennis Rodman **is** not **like** Michael Jordan in other ways. Jordan is polite; Rodman is often impolite.	We use *be like* to show that two things are similar in some ways.
PATTERN B: Rodman and Jordan **are alike** in some ways. They both became rich, famous athletes. Dennis Rodman and Michael Jordan **are** not **alike** in other ways.	Use *alike* in Pattern B.

LANGUAGE NOTES

1. We use *be like* to show a similarity or dissimilarity in internal characteristics, not appearance.

   COMPARE:

   Rodman *isn't like* Jordan. Rodman is impolite. (characteristic)

   Rodman *doesn't look like* Jordan. Rodman looks outrageous. (appearance)

2. Compare affirmative and negative statements with *be like*.
    I *am like* my father.
    I *am not like* my mother.

EXERCISE 30 Ask a question with the words given. Use *be like*. Another student will answer.

EXAMPLE: you/sister
A. Are you like your sister?
B. Yes. We're alike in many ways. We're both interested in art.
   We both like to cook.
   OR
   No. I'm not like my sister at all. She's shy, and I'm outgoing.

1. an English class in the U.S./an English class in your native country

2. your house (or apartment) in the U.S./your house (or apartment) in your native country

3. the weather in this city/the weather in your hometown

4. food in your country/American food

5. women's clothes in your native country/women's clothes in the U.S.

6. a college in your native country/a college in the U.S.

7. American teachers/teachers in your native country

8. American athletes/athletes in your native country

12.12   Same or Different

Examples	Explanation
PATTERN A: Football is not **the same as** soccer. Football is **different from** soccer.	We can show that two things are the same (or not) by using *the same as*. We show that two things are different by using *different from*.
PATTERN B: Football and soccer are not **the same**. Football and soccer are **different**.	Omit *as* and *from* in Pattern B.

LANGUAGE NOTES

You will hear some Americans say *different <u>than</u>*.

EXERCISE 31 Tell if the two items are the same or different.

EXAMPLES: boxing, wrestling
Boxing and wrestling are different.

fall, autumn
Fall is the same as autumn.

1. borrow, lend

2. big, large

3. my book, the teacher's book

4. my last name, my mother's last name

5. Washington, D.C., Washington State

6. L.A., Los Angeles

7. 2 + 5, 5 + 2

8. a mile, a kilometer

9. two quarts, a half gallon

10. an ESL course, a regular English course

11. the Chicago Bulls, the Chicago Bears

12. football and rugby

EXERCISE 32 Combination Exercise. Fill in the blanks in the following conversation.

EXAMPLE: A. I heard that you have a twin brother.

B. Yes, I do.

A. Do you look _____*alike*_____?
                    (example)

B. No. He _____ look _____ me at all.
              (1)   *(2)*

A. But you're twins.

B. We're fraternal twins. That's different _____ identical twins who
                                                (3)

have the _____ genetic code. We're just brothers who were born
            (4)

at _____ time. We're not even the same _____. I'm
        (5)   (6)
much taller than he is.

A. But you're _____ in many ways, aren't you?
                    (7)

B. No. We're completely _____. I'm athletic, and David is
                                (8)
not interested in sports at all. He's a much _____ student
                                                        (9)
than I am. He's much more _____ our mother, who loves to
                                  (10)
read and learn new things, and I _____ our father, who's
                                          (11)
athletic and loves to build things.

A. What about your character?

B. I'm outgoing and he's very shy. Also we don't dress _____ at all.
                                                                (12)
He likes to wear neat, conservative clothes, but I prefer torn jeans
and T-shirts.

A. From your description, it _____ like you're not even from the
                                    (13)
same family.

B. We have one thing in common. We were both interested in _____
_____ girl at school.
    (14)

A. What happened?

B. She didn't want to go out with either one of us!

EXERCISE **33** *Combination exercise.* This is a conversation between two
women about marriage and children. Fill in the blanks using
the word in parentheses ( ) to make a comparative or
superlative statement.

A. Do you think it's ___*better*___ to get married when you're young
                          (good)
or wait until you're in your thirties?

B. If you plan to have children, I think you should get married when
you're young. Women in their thirties don't have _____
                                                          (1 energy)
_____ younger women.

A. But women in their thirties are _____ women in their
                                            (2 mature)
twenties. Also, they're _____.
                                (3 responsible)

B. What do you think is _____ age to get married?
   (4 good)

A. About 24 for women and 28 for men.

B. Do you think the husband should always be _____ the wife?
   (5 old)

A. In my country, that's the custom. But I don't think it makes sense

   because women live _____ men.
   (6 long)

B. I have three sisters. My _____ sister married a man five
   (7 old)

   years _____ she is. I don't think it's a problem. My
   (8 young)

   husband and I are _____. We're both 27.
   (9 age)

A. Is your husband handsome?

B. I think he's _____ man in the world.
   (10 handsome)

A. Do you have any children?

B. We have one daughter. She's two years old. Do you want to see her

   picture? She looks just[5] like her father. They both have _____
   (11 eyes)

   _____ and _____, but her hair is not
                       (12 smile)

   _____ his hair.
   (13 curly)

A. She's a beautiful girl.

B. Thank you. Of course, I think she's _____
   (14 beautiful)

   girl in the world.

SUMMARY OF LESSON 12

1. Simple, Comparative, and Superlative Forms

SHORT WORDS
   California is a **large** state.
   Texas is **larger** than California.
   Alaska is the **largest** state in the U.S.

LONG WORDS
   A small car is **economical**.
   A motorcycle is **more economical** than a car.
   A bicycle is the **most economical** way to travel.

---

[5] *Just,* in this case, means *exactly.*

2. Other Kinds of Comparisons
    She looks **as young as** her daughter.
    She speaks English **as fluently as** her husband.
    She is **the same age as** her husband.
    She and her husband are **the same age**.
    She works **as many hours as** her husband.
    She doesn't have **as much time as** her husband.
    She works **as much as** her husband.

3. Comparisons with *Like*
    She**'s like** her mother. (She and her mother **are alike**.) They're both
        shy.
    She **looks like** her sister. (She and her sister **look alike**.) They're
        identical twins.
    Coke **tastes like** Pepsi. (They taste **alike**.)
    Western music doesn't **sound like** Asian music. (They don't **sound
        alike**.)

4. Comparisons with *Same* and *Different*.
    Her job is **different from** her husband's job.
    Her job is **the same as** her husband's job.

EDITING ADVICE

1. Don't use a comparison word when there is no comparison.

    New York is a ~~bigger~~ city.

2. Don't use *more* and *-er* together.

    He is ~~more~~ older than his teacher.

3. Use *than* before the second item of comparison.

    He is younger ~~that~~ *than* his wife.

4. Use *the* before a superlative form.

    The Nile is *the* longest river in the world.

5. Use a plural noun in the phrase "one of the [superlative] [nouns]."

    Chicago is one of the biggest ~~city~~ *cities* in the U.S.

6. Use the correct word order.

    She ~~more speaks~~ *speaks more* than her husband.

    I have ~~time more~~ *more time* than you.

7. Use *be like* for similar character. Use *look like* for a physical similarity.

He ~~is~~ look $\overset{s}{\wedge}$ like his brother. They both have blue eyes and dark hair.

He is ~~look~~ like his sister. They are both talented musicians.

8. Don't use *the* and a possessive form together.

My ~~the~~ youngest son likes soccer.

9. Use the correct negative for *be like* and *look like*.

I'm ~~not~~ $\overset{don't}{}$ look like my father.

LESSON 12 TEST / REVIEW

PART 1

Find the mistakes with the underlined words, and correct them. Not every sentence has a mistake. If the sentence is correct, write **C**.

EXAMPLES: She ~~is~~ look $\overset{s}{\wedge}$ like her sister. They both have curly hair.

A house in the suburbs is much more expensive than a house in the city.   C

1. I am the same tall as my brother.

2. New York City is the larger city in the U.S.

3. That man is smarter that his wife.

4. The youngest student in the class has more better grades than you.

5. A big city has crime more than a small town.

6. I have three sons. My oldest son is married.

7. I visited many American cities, and I think that San Francisco is the more beautiful city in the U.S.

8. New York is one of the largest city in the world.

9. My uncle is the most intelligent person in my family.

10. She faster types than I do.

11. Texas is one of the biggest <u>state</u> in the U.S.

12. He <u>more carefully drives</u> than his wife.

13. Paul is one of the youngest <u>students</u> in this class.

14. She is richer than her best friend, but her friend is happier <u>than</u>.

15. <u>Your the</u> best grade this semester was A −.

16. She <u>isn't look</u> like her sister at all. She's short and her sister is tall.

PART 2   Fill in the blanks.

EXAMPLE: Pepsi is ___*the same*___ color ___*as*___ Coke.

1. She's 35 years old. Her husband is 35 years old. She and her husband are _____ age.

2. She earns $30,000 a year. Her husband earns $35,000. She doesn't earn as _____ her husband.

3. The little girl _____ like her mother. They both have brown eyes and curly black hair.

4. My name is Sophia Weiss. My teacher's name is Judy Weiss. We have _____ last name.

5. Chinese food is different _____ American food.

6. A dime isn't the same _____ a nickel. A dime is smaller.

7. She is as tall as her husband. They are the same _____

8. I drank Pepsi and Coke, and I don't know which is which. They have the same flavor. To me, Pepsi _____ like Coke.

9. She _____ like her husband in many ways. They're both intelligent and hard-working. They both like sports.

10. A. Are you like your mother?

    B. Oh, no. We're not _____ at all! We're completely different.

11. Please finish this test _____ possible!

12. Borrow and lend don't have _____ meaning. Borrow means take. Lend means give.

13. Dennis Rodman doesn't act _____ Michael Jordan.

14. My two sisters look _____ . In fact, some people think they're twins.

CLASSROOM ACTIVITIES

1. Work with a partner. Find some differences between the two of you. Then write five sentences that compare you and your partner. Share your answers in a small group or with the whole class.

    EXAMPLES:
    I'm taller than Alex.
    Alex is taking more classes than I am.

2. Form a small group (about 3–5 people) with students from different native countries, if possible. Make comparisons about your native countries. Include a superlative statement. (If all the students in your class are from the same native country, compare cities in your native country.)

    EXAMPLES:
    Cuba is closer to the U.S. than Peru is.
    China has the largest population.
    Cuba doesn't have as many resources as China.

3. Work with a partner. Choose one of the categories below, and compare two examples from this category. Use any type of comparative method. Write four sentences. Share your answers with the class.

1. countries	5. cities	9. sports
2. cars	6. animals	10. athletes
3. restaurants	7. types of transportation	
4. teachers	8. schools	

    EXAMPLE:
    animals
    A dog is different from a cat in many ways.
    A dog can't jump as high as a cat.
    A dog is a better pet than a cat, in my opinion.
    A cat is not as friendly as a dog.

    1. _____

    2. _____

    3. _____

    4. _____

4. Compare the U.S. and your native country. Tell if the statement is true in the U.S. or in your native country. Form a small group and explain your answers to the others in the group.

	My country	The U.S.
People have more free time.		
People have more political freedom.		
Families are smaller.		
Children are more polite.		
Teenagers have more freedom.		
People are friendlier.		
The government is more stable.		
Health care is better.		
There is more crime.		
There are more poor people.		
People are generally happier.		
People are more open about their problems.		
Friendship is more important.		
Women have more freedom.		
Schools are better.		
Job opportunities are better.		
Athletes make more money.		
Children have more fun.		
People dress more stylishly.		
Families are closer.		
People are healthier.		

4. Game—Test your knowledge of world facts
Form a small group. Answer the questions below with other group members. When you're finished, check answers. (Answers are at the bottom of the next page.) Which group in the class has the most correct answers?

1. Which athlete said, "I'm the greatest"?
   Michael Jordan   Pele   Muhammad Ali   Dennis Rodman

2. Where is the tallest building in the world?
   New York City   Chicago   Tokyo   Kuala Lampur

3. What country has the largest population?
   The U.S.   India   China   Russia

4. Which country has the largest area?

The U.S.   China   Canada   Russia

5. What is the tallest mountain in the world?
   Mt. McKinley   Mt. Everest   Mt. Kanchenjunga   Mt. Lhotse

6. Which state in the U.S. has the smallest population?
   Alaska   Wyoming   Rhode Island   Vermont

7. What is the longest river in the world?
   The Mississippi   The Missouri   The Nile   The Amazon

8. What is the biggest animal?
   the elephant   the rhinoceros   the giraffe   the whale

9. What is the world's largest island?
   Greenland   New Guinea   Borneo   Madagascar

10. What country has the most time zones?
    China   Russia   the U.S.   Canada

11. What is the world's largest lake?
    Lake Superior   Lake Victoria   The Caspian Sea
    The Aral Sea

12. Which planet is the closest to the Earth?
    Mercury   Venus   Mars   Saturn

13. Where is the world's busiest airport?
    Chicago   New York   Los Angeles   London

14. Which is the most popular magazine in the U.S.?
    Time   *Sports Illustrated*   *TV Guide*   *People Weekly*

15. What language has the largest number of speakers?
    English   Chinese   Spanish   Russian

16. Which country has the most neighboring countries?
    China   Russia   Saudi Arabia   Brazil

The answers are: 1. Ali   2. Kuala Lumpur   3. China   4. Russia
5. Mt. Everest   6. Wyoming   7. The Nile   8. the whale
9. Greenland   10. Russia   11. the Caspian Sea   12. Mars
13. Chicago   14. *TV Guide*   15. Chinese   16. China. (It has 16
neighboring countries.)

1. Do athletes in your native country make a lot of money?

2. Do children in your native country participate in sports? Which sports?

3. Are Michael Jordan and Dennis Rodman well known in your native country? What other American athletes are well known in your native country?

WRITING

Write a short composition comparing one of the sets of items below:

- two stores where you shop for groceries
- watching a movie on a VCR and at a movie theater
- two friends of yours
- you and your parents
- football and soccer (or any two sports)
- clothing styles in the U.S. and your native country
- life in the U.S. (in general) with life in your native country
- your life in the U.S. with your life in your native country
- the American political system with the political system in your native country
- schools (including teachers, students, classes, etc.) in the U.S. with schools in your native country
- American families with families in your native country

OUTSIDE ACTIVITY

Interview an American. Get his or her opinion about the superlative of each of the following items. Share your findings with the class.

prestigious job
beautiful city in the U.S.
popular TV program
terrible tragedy in American history
big problem in the U.S.
handsome or beautiful actor
good athlete

Internet Activities

1. Find an article about Michael Jordan on the Internet. Print the article and circle some interesting facts.

2. Find an article about an athlete that you admire. Print the article and circle some interesting facts.

GRAMMAR
Passive Voice

CONTEXT
Jury Duty

LESSON FOCUS

The verb in some sentences is in the active voice.
My brother *saw* the movie.

The verb in some sentences is in the passive voice.
The movie *was seen* by millions of Americans.

1. Have you ever been to court?
2. Have you ever seen a courtroom in a movie or TV show?

Read the following article. Pay special attention to the passive voice.

Jury Duty

All Americans **are protected** by the Constitution. No one person can decide if a person is guilty or innocent. Every citizen has the right to a trial by jury. When a person **is charged** with a crime, he **is considered** innocent until the jury decides he is guilty.

Most American citizens **are chosen** for jury duty at some time in their lives. How **are** jurors **chosen**? The court gets the names of citizens from lists of taxpayers, licensed drivers, and voters. Many people **are called** to the courthouse for the selection of a jury. From this large number, twelve people **are chosen**. The lawyers and the judge ask each person questions to see if the person is going to be fair. If the person has made any judgment about the case before hearing the facts presented in the trial, he **is not selected**. If the juror doesn't understand enough English, he **is** not **selected**. The court needs jurors who can understand the facts and be open-minded. When the final jury selection **is made**, the jurors must raise their right hand and promise to be fair in deciding the case.

Sometimes a trial goes on for several days or more. Jurors **are** not **permitted** to talk with family members and friends about the case. In some cases, jurors **are** not **permitted** to go home until the case is over. They stay in a hotel and **are** not **permitted** to watch TV or read newspapers that give information about the case.

After the jurors hear the case, they have to make a decision. They go to a separate room and talk about what they heard and saw in the courtroom. When they are finished discussing the case, they take a vote.

Jurors **are paid** for their work. They receive a small amount of money per day. Employers must give a worker permission to be on a jury. Being on a jury is a very serious job.

13.1 The Passive Voice—Overview

Examples	Explanation
The jurors **are chosen** from lists. They **are not permitted** to discuss the case. My sister **was selected** to be on a jury. She **was paid** for jury duty.	The passive voice uses a form of *be* + the past participle. The passive voice is used when the subject receives the action of the verb.

LANGUAGE NOTES

1. The verb in passive voice shows that the subject receives the action. The verb in active voice shows that the subject performs the action of the verb. COMPARE:

    (a) Ms. Smith *paid* her employees at the end of the week. (ACTIVE)
    (b) Ms. Smith *was paid* for being a juror. (PASSIVE)

    In sentence (a), Ms. Smith paid something. In sentence (b), Ms. Smith didn't pay anything. Somebody paid Ms. Smith.

2. Sometimes the performer of the action is included after a passive verb. Use *by* + noun or object pronoun before the performer.

    I was helped *by the lawyer*.
    My sister was helped *by him* too.

3. Usually a performer is not included in a passive sentence.

    I *was chosen* to be on a jury.
    We *were told* to wait on the first floor.

EXERCISE 1 Read the following sentences. Decide if the underlined verb is active (A) or passive (P).

EXAMPLES: I received a letter from the court. **A**

I was told to go to court on May 10. **P**

1. The jury voted at the end of the trial.

2. The jurors received $20 a day.

3. Some jurors were told to go home at noon.

4. Not every juror will be needed.

5. Twelve people were selected for the jury.

6. The judge told the jurors about their responsibilities.

7. My sister has been selected for jury duty three times.

8. I was paid for jury duty.

9. A juror must be at least 18 years old and an American citizen.

10. The judge and lawyers ask a lot of questions.

11. Did you receive a paycheck?

12. Where were you told to go?

13. Were you given information about the case?

14. What did the judge tell the jury?

The Passive Voice—Forms and Tenses

Tense	Active	Passive (*Be* + Past Participle)
Simple Present	They **take** a vote.	A vote **is taken**.
Simple Past	They **took** a vote.	A vote **was taken**.
Future	They **will take** a vote.	A vote **will be taken**.
	They **are going to take** a vote.	A vote **is going to be taken**.
Present Perfect	They **have taken** a vote.	A vote **has been taken**.
Modal	They **must take** a vote.	A vote **must be taken**.

LANGUAGE NOTES

1. The passive voice can be used with different tenses and with modals. The past participle remains the same for every tense. Only the form of *be* changes.
2. An adverb can be placed between the auxiliary verb and the main verb.

   Jurors are *always* paid.
   Non-citizens are *never* selected for jury duty.
3. Never use *do*, *does*, or *did* with the passive voice.

   They aren't permitted to talk to outsiders about the case. (NOT: don't permitted)
   Were you chosen for jury duty? (NOT: did you chosen)
4. If two verbs in the passive voice are connected with *and*, do not repeat *be*.

   We *were taken* to a room and *shown* a video about the court system.

EXERCISE **2**   Change to the passive voice. (Do not include a *by*-phrase.)

ACTIVE

They chose him.

PASSIVE

He was chosen.
(example)

1. They will choose him.

   _____

2. They always choose him.

   _____

3. They can't choose him.

   _____

4. They have never chosen us.

   _____

5. They didn't choose her.

   _____

6. Did they choose her? _____

7. They shouldn't choose her. _____

8. Why did they choose me? _____

EXERCISE 3   Change to the active voice.

PASSIVE

A decision will be made soon by the jury.

ACTIVE

The jury will make a decision soon.
(example)

1. A decision has been made by the jury. _____

2. A decision is usually made by the jury. _____

3. A decision must be made by the jury. _____

4. A decision was made by the jury. _____

5. A decision can't be made by the jury. _____

6. A decision isn't made by him. _____

7. Was a decision made by her? _____

8. When will a decision be made by us? _____

9. A decision was probably made by him. _____

10. How was a decision made by them? _____

EXERCISE 4   Fill in the blanks with the passive voice of the verb in parentheses ( ). Use the present tense.

EXAMPLE: Jurors ___*are chosen*___ from lists.
                         (choose)

1. Only people over 18 years old _____ for jury duty.
                                              (select)

2. Questionnaires _____ to American citizens.
                              (send)

3. The questionnaire _____ out and _____ .
                              (fill)   (return)

4. Many people _____ to the courthouse.
                          (call)

5. Not everyone _____ .
                          (choose)

6. The jurors _____ a lot of questions.
                       (ask)

7. Jurors _____ to discuss the case with outsiders.
   (not/permit)

8. Jurors _____ a paycheck at the end of the day for their
   (give)
   work.

EXERCISE **5** Fill in the blanks with the passive voice of the verb in
parentheses ( ). Use the past tense.

EXAMPLE: I ___*was sent*___ a letter.
                (send)

1. I _____ to go to the courthouse on Fifth Street.
   (tell)

2. My name _____.
   (call)

3. I _____ a form to fill out.
   (give)

4. A video about jury duty _____ on a large TV.
   (show)

5. The jurors _____ to the third floor of the building.
   (take)

6. I _____ a lot of questions by the lawyers.
   (ask)

7. I _____.
   (not/choose)

8. I _____ home before noon.
   (send)

EXERCISE **6** Fill in the blanks with the passive voice of the verb in
parentheses ( ). Use the present perfect tense.

EXAMPLE: We ___*have been given*___ a lot of information.
                (give)

1. The explanation _____ many times.
   (repeat)

2. Many articles about the courts _____.
   (write)

3. Many people _____ for jury duty.
   (choose)

4. I _____ for my work.
   (pay)

5. The check _____ at the door.
   (leave)

6. The money _____ in an envelope.
   (put)

7. Your name _____.
   (call)

8. Your missing car _____.
   (find)

EXERCISE 7 Students are concerned about their final exam. The teacher is giving them advice about taking the final exam next week. Fill in the blanks with the passive voice of the verbs in parentheses ( ).

EXAMPLE: The final exam ____*will be given*____ in Lecture Hall C on Friday.
(will give)

1. You don't need to bring your own paper. You _____
    (will/give)
    paper by the teacher.

2. The composition _____ in pen, not pencil.
    (should/write)

3. You will also have a multiple-choice grammar test. A pencil
    _____ for this test because it _____
    (must/use)   (will/score)
    electronically.

4. A dictionary _____ for your composition.
    (can/use)

5. Your paper _____ on organization, spelling, and
    (will/grade)
    correct grammar.

6. Talking during the test _____.
    (will/not/permit)

7. The papers _____ at 10 o'clock.
    (will/collect)

8. After the final exam, your grades _____ to you by
    (will/send)
    mail.

13.3 Using the Passive Voice without a Performer

Active Voice	Passive Voice
a) The lawyers **presented** the case yesterday.	b) The case **was presented** well.
c) The judge **gave** the jurors instructions.	d) The jurors **were given** instructions before the trial.
e) The judge and lawyers **choose** the jurors.	f) People who don't understand English **are** not **chosen**.
	g) The jurors **are paid** for their work.
	h) The criminal **was arrested**.
	i) English **is spoken** in the U.S.

LANGUAGE NOTES

We use the passive voice when it is not important or necessary to mention who performed the action. It may not be necessary because:

- We are shifting the emphasis from the performer to the receiver of the action. (a→b, c→d, e→f)
- It is not important to know who performed the action. (g)
- The performer is obvious. (h)
- The action is done by everyone or people in general. (i)

EXERCISE 8   Fill in the blanks with the passive voice of the underlined verbs. Use the same tense.

EXAMPLE: The jury <u>took</u> a vote. The vote ___*was taken*___ after three hours.

1. The lawyers <u>asked</u> a lot of questions. The questions _____ to find facts.

2. The court <u>will pay</u> us. We _____ $20 a day.

3. They <u>told</u> us to wait. We _____ to wait on the second floor.

4. They <u>gave</u> us instructions. We _____ information about the law.

5. People <u>pay</u> for the services of a lawyer. Lawyers _____ a lot of money for their services.

6. You <u>should use</u> a pen to fill out the form. A pen _____ for all legal documents.

7. They <u>showed</u> us a film about the court system. We _____ the film before we went to the courtroom.

8. <u>Did</u> they <u>send</u> you a letter? _____ the letter _____ by registered mail?

9. <u>Does</u> the judge <u>allow</u> you to talk about the case? _____

   you _____ to go home at the end of the day?

10. <u>Did</u> the lawyers <u>choose</u> you? No, I (not) _____ because I don't understand enough English.

13.4 Using the Passive Voice with a Performer

Active	Passive
Einstein **developed** the theory of relativity.	The theory of relativity **was developed** by Einstein.
James Earl Ray **killed** Martin Luther King, Jr.	Martin Luther King, Jr., **was killed** by James Earl Ray.
Mozart **composed** *The Magic Flute*.	*The Magic Flute* **was composed** by Mozart.
Shakespeare **wrote** *Romeo and Juliet*.	*Romeo and Juliet* **was written** by Shakespeare.

LANGUAGE NOTES

1. When the sentence has a strong performer (a specific person), we can use either the active or passive voice. The active voice puts more emphasis on the person who performs the action. The passive voice puts more emphasis on the action. The active voice is more common than the passive voice when there is a strong performer.
2. We often use the passive voice when the performer *made, discovered, invented, built, wrote, painted,* or *composed* something.
3. Notice the difference in pronouns in an active sentence and a passive sentence. After *by*, the object pronoun is used.

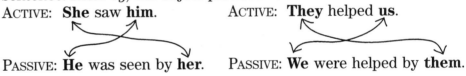

ACTIVE: **She** saw **him**. ACTIVE: **They** helped **us**.

PASSIVE: **He** was seen by **her**. PASSIVE: **We** were helped by **them**.

EXERCISE **9** Change these sentences from active to passive voice. Mention the performer because the performer is a specific person and is important. Use the same tense.

EXAMPLE: Mark Twain <u>wrote</u> *Tom Sawyer*.
Tom Sawyer was written by Mark Twain.

1. John Hancock <u>signed</u> the U.S. Constitution.

_____

2. Stephen King <u>has written</u> many novels.

_____

3. Alexander Graham Bell <u>invented</u> the telephone.

_____

4. Columbus discovered America.

_____

5. The Wright Brothers invented the airplane.

_____

6. Martin Luther King, Jr., led a bus boycott.

_____

7. Congress makes the laws.

_____

8. The President signs a new law.

_____

9. Bill Gates created Microsoft.

_____

10. The judge will make a decision.

_____

EXERCISE 10 The following sentences would be better in passive voice without a performer. Change them. (Use the same tense.)

EXAMPLE: They paid me for jury duty.
             I was paid for jury duty.
             _____

1. They sent me a questionnaire.

_____

2. They have taken us to a separate room.

_____

3. They told us not to discuss the case.

_____

4. They will choose 12 people.

_____

5. Someone has selected your name.

_____

6. They didn't permit us to read any newspapers.

_____

7. They <u>will not select</u> him again for jury duty.

_____

8. They <u>will pay</u> you.

_____

9. They <u>don't allow</u> us to eat in the courtroom.

_____

10. Someone <u>has called</u> my name.

_____

EXERCISE 11 The following sentences would be better in active voice. Change them to active voice. (Use the same tense.)

EXAMPLE: You <u>are loved</u> by me.
I love you.
_____

1. A good time <u>was had</u> by everyone.

_____

2. You <u>are needed</u> by me.

_____

3. My homework <u>was eaten</u> by the dog.

_____

4. You <u>will be helped</u> by her.

_____

5. The photo <u>has been seen</u> by my classmates.

_____

6. Your mother <u>should be helped</u> by you.

_____

7. A lot of money <u>is spent</u> by him.

_____

8. Movies <u>are seen</u> by us every week.

_____

9. The paper <u>was written</u> by me.

_____

10. The grammar <u>is explained</u> by the teacher.

_____

EXERCISE 12 Fill in the blanks with the passive or active voice of the verb in parentheses ( ), using the past tense of the verb in parentheses ( ).

A. Why weren't you at work last week? Were you sick?

B. No. I ___was chosen___ to be on a jury.
(example: choose)

A. How was it?

B. It was very interesting. A man _____ for fighting with a
(1 arrest)
police officer.

A. It sounds like an interesting case.

B. The jury selection was interesting too. But it took half a day to choose
12 people.

A. Why?

B. The judge and lawyers _____ more than 50 people.
(2 interview)

A. Why so many people?

B. Well, several people _____ the judge's questions.
(3 not/understand)
They _____ English very well. And a woman _____
(4 not/speak)   (5 tell)
the judge that she was very sick. The judge _____ her
(6 give)
permission to leave. I don't know why the other people _____

_____.
(7 not/choose)

A. What kind of questions _____ by the judge and lawyers?
(8 you/ask)

B. First the lawyers _____ to see if we could be fair. Some
(9 want)
jurors _____ that they had a bad experience with a police
(10 say)
officer. Those jurors _____.
(11 not/select)

A. Why not?

B. Because the judge probably thought they couldn't be fair in this case.

A. How long did the trial last?

B. Only two days.

A. _____ about the case with your family when you
(12 you/talk)

_____ home the first night?
(13 go)

B. Oh, no. We _____ not to talk to anyone about the case.
   (14 tell)

   When it was over, I _____ my wife and kids about it. It was so
   (15 tell)

   interesting.

A. How long did it take the jurors to make a decision?

B. About two hours. One of the jurors _____ with the other
   (16 not/agree)

   eleven. We _____ about the evidence until she changed her
   (17 talk)

   mind.

A. _____ you for the days you missed work?
   (18 your boss/pay)

B. Of course. He had to pay me. That's the law.

A. Now that you've done it once, you won't have to do it again. Right?

B. That's not true. This was the second time I _____.
   (19 choose)

13.5   Using the Active Voice Only

Active Voice Only	Explanation
An accident **happened** on the corner of Main and First. I **slept** for six hours last night. She **went** home after work. My parents **live** in London. My grandfather **died** 10 years ago.	Some verbs can never be used with the passive voice. These are verbs that have no object. Verbs of this kind are: happen go fall become live sleep come look die seem work stay These are called *intransitive* verbs.

LANGUAGE NOTES

1. Even though *have* is followed by an object, it is not usually used in the passive voice.
   He *has* a car. NOT: A car *is had* by him.
2. Notice that we say *was/were born*. (This is a passive construction.)
   However, *die* is always an active verb.
   Martin Luther King, Jr., *was born* in 1929. He *died* in 1968.

EXERCISE 13 Fill in the blanks with the active or passive of the verb in parentheses ( ). Use the past tense.

EXAMPLE: My grandfather ____*died*____ in 1945.
(die)

My grandfather ____*was killed*____ in the war.
(kill)

1. I heard a noise in the kitchen. What _____?
(happen)

2. A dish _____ off the shelf and broke.
(fall)

3. How many hours _____ last night?
(you/sleep)

4. I _____ by the sound of the garbage trucks.
(awaken)

5. In my country, I _____ with my grandparents.
(live)

6. I _____ by my grandparents.
(raise)

7. She _____ for fifty hours last week.
(work)

8. She _____ $15 an hour for her work.
(pay)

9. I _____ to court last week.
(go)

10. I _____ to be on a jury.
(choose)

11. She is sick, so she _____ home today.
(stay)

12. Martin Luther King, Jr., _____ in 1968.
(kill)

SUMMARY OF LESSON 13

1. Active and Passive Voice

Active	Passive
Sandy **wrote** a book.	A book **was written** by Sandy.
Sandy **will write** a book.	A book **will be written** by Sandy.
Sandy **has written** a book.	A book **has been written** by Sandy.
Sandy often **writes** books.	Books **are** often **written** by Sandy.

2. Uses of the Passive Voice
The passive voice is used without a performer:
- when the emphasis is shifted from the performer to the receiver of the action.

  The court paid me. I **was paid** at the end of the day.
- when the performer is not known or is not important.

  I **was chosen** for jury duty.
- when the performer is obvious.

  The criminal **was taken** to jail.
- when the performer is everybody or people in general.

  English **is spoken** in the U.S.

  Jury duty **is considered** a responsibility of every citizen.

The passive voice is used with a performer:
- when you want to emphasize the receiver of the action more than the performer.

  Romeo and Juliet **was written** by Shakespeare.

EDITING ADVICE

1. Never use *do*, *does*, or *did* with the passive voice.

   wasn't found
   The money ~~didn't find~~.

   were
   Where ~~did~~ the jurors taken?

2. Don't use the passive voice with *happen, die, sleep, work, live, fall, seem*.

   My grandfather ~~was~~ died four years ago.

3. Don't confuse the *-ing* form with the past participle.

   taken
   The criminal was ~~taking~~ to jail.

4. Don't forget the *-ed* ending for a regular past participle.

   ed
   My cousin was select to be on a jury.

5. Don't forget to use *be* with a passive sentence.

   were
   The books found on the floor by the janitor.

6. Use the correct word order with adverbs.

   I was told (never) about the problem.

PART **1**

Find the mistakes with the underlined words and correct them. Not every sentence has a mistake. If the sentence is correct, write **C**.

EXAMPLES:

The same mistake has *been* made many times.

We <u>were told</u> not to say anything.   C

1. Children <u>should taught</u> good behavior.

2. Parents <u>should teach</u> children good behavior.

3. I never <u>was given</u> any information about the test.

4. I <u>have been had</u> my car for three years.

5. The driver <u>was given</u> a ticket for driving without a seat belt.

6. Where <u>did</u> your gloves <u>find</u>?

7. They <u>were find</u> in the back seat of a taxi.

8. Something <u>was happened</u> to my bicycle.

9. This carpet <u>has been cleaned</u> many times.

10. The answers <u>don't written</u> in my book.

PART **2**

Change sentences from active to passive voice. Do not mention the performer. (The performer is in parentheses.) Use the same tense as the underlined verb.

EXAMPLE:

(Someone) <u>took</u> my dictionary.

My dictionary was taken.

1. (People) <u>speak</u> English in the U.S.

2. (You) <u>can use</u> a dictionary during the test.

3. (The police) <u>took</u> the criminal to jail.

4. (People) have seen the President on TV many times.

_____

5. (Someone) will take you to the courtroom.

_____

6. (Someone) has broken the mirror into small pieces.

_____

7. (People) expect you to learn English in the U.S.

_____

8. (They) don't allow cameras in the courtroom.

_____

PART 3

Change the sentences from passive to active voice. Use the same tense.

EXAMPLE: You were told by me to bring your books.
I told you to bring your books.

1. The song *Yesterday* was written and sung by Paul McCartney.

_____

2. You have been told by the teacher to write a composition.

_____

3. Your phone bill must be paid.

_____

4. You are not allowed by the teacher to use your books during a test.

_____

5. The tests will be returned by the teacher.

_____

6. Penicillin was discovered by Fleming.

_____

7. When are wedding gifts opened by the bride and groom?

_____

8. Your missing car was not found by the police.

_____

PART **4**

Fill in the blanks with the passive or active form of the verb in parentheses ( ). Use an appropriate tense.

EXAMPLES: The tests ___will be returned___ tomorrow.
                           (will/return)

The teacher ___will return___ the tests.
                           (will/return)

1. My neighbor had a heart attack and _____ to the hospital
   _____(take)_____
   in an ambulance yesterday.

2. I _____ my neighbor in the hospital tomorrow.
      (will/visit)

3. I _____ the movie *Star Wars* five times.
      (see)

4. This movie _____ by millions of people.
         (see)

5. I _____ a lot of friends.
      (have)

6. I _____ many times by my friends.
      (help)

7. Ten people _____ in the fire last night.
            (die)

8. Five people _____ by the fire department in yesterday's
             (rescue)
   fire.

9. Her husband _____ home from work at six o'clock every
              (come)
   day.

10. He _____ home by his coworker last night.
         (drive)

11. The answer to your question _____ by anyone.
                         (not/know)

12. Even the teacher _____ the answer to your question.
                    (not/know)

EXPANSION ACTIVITIES

CLASSROOM ACTIVITIES

1. Form a small group and compare high school or college graduation ceremonies in your communities or native countries. Discuss the items you checked.

	Yes	No
Special clothes are worn.		
Gifts are given.		
Awards are presented.		
Diplomas are presented.		
The name of each student is called.		

(continued)

	Yes	No
Music is played.		
Songs are sung.		
Speeches are made.		
Parties are given.		
Small children are invited.		

2. Form a small group and tell about how a holiday is celebrated in your native culture. Use the chart below to get ideas.

	Yes	No
Gifts are given.		
The house is cleaned.		
Special clothing is worn.		
The house is decorated with special symbols of the holiday.		
Special food is prepared.		
Stores and businesses are closed.		
Special programs are shown on TV.		
Candles are used.		

3. Form a small group and talk about the legal system in your native country. Use the chart below to get ideas.

	Yes	No
People are treated fairly in court.		
Citizens are selected to be on a jury.		
People are represented by lawyers in court.		
Lawyers make a lot of money.		
Famous trials are shown on TV.		
Punishment is severe for certain crimes.		
The death penalty is used in some cases.		
The laws are fair.		

DISCUSSION

1. Would you like to be on a jury? Why or why not?

2. In a small group, discuss your impressions of the American legal system from what you've seen on TV, from what you've read, or from your own experience.

WRITING

1. Write about an experience you have had with the court system in the U.S. or your native country.

2. Write about a famous court case that you know of. Do you agree with the decision of the jury?

OUTSIDE ACTIVITIES

1. Watch a court movie, such as *The Firm, Witness to the Prosecution, Inherit the Wind, A Time to Kill, To Kill a Mockingbird, Presumed Innocent, Twelve Angry Men, A Civil Action,* or *The Client*. Write your impressions of the American court system after watching one of these movies.

2. Watch a court TV show, such as People's Court or Judge Judy. What do you think of the judge's decisions on these shows?

3. Ask an American if he or she has ever been selected for a jury. Ask him or her to tell you about this experience.

Internet Activity

Look for information about one of these famous American trials:

a) the O.J. Simpson trial

b) the Leopold and Loeb trial

c) the Sacco and Vanzetti trial

d) the Amistad trials

e) the Scopes trial

f) the Rosenberg trial

g) the Bruno Hauptmann trial

Answer these questions about one of the above trials:

- What was the defendant accused of?
- When did the trial take place?
- How long did the trial last?
- Was the defendant found guilty?

Lesson Fourteen

GRAMMAR
Articles
Other/Another
Indefinite Pronouns

CONTEXT
Automatic Teller Machines
Changing the American Dollar
Kids and Money

LESSON FOCUS

The indefinite articles are *a* and *an*. The definite article is *the*.[1]

> She doesn't have *a* computer at home. She uses *the* computers at school.

We have to know if a noun is definite or indefinite,
singular or plural, to use *other* and *another*.

> My computer is old. I have to buy *another* one.
> I have two telephone lines. I use one to talk on the phone. I use *the other* one for my computer modem.

Indefinite pronouns are *one*, *some*, and *any*.

> I don't have a cell phone. I need to get *one*.
> We don't have any more eggs in the house. We need to buy *some*.

[1] For special uses of articles, see Appendix L.

Before You Read   1.   Do you have a cash card (ATM card)? How often do you use it?
2.   Do you have credit cards? Do you use checks?

```
┌─────────────────────────────────┐
│  ▰▱   SAVINGS BANK              │
│ ═══════════════════════════════ │
│  1234 5678 8765 4321            │
│ VALID FROM 11/00 VALID THRU 10/06 │
│  S.B. Fine    ATM / CHECK CARD  │
└─────────────────────────────────┘
```

Read about automatic teller machines. Pay special attention to nouns with and without articles.

Automatic Teller Machines

An automatic teller is a machine that lets you make a deposit or take out cash from your bank account. You use a plastic card that looks like a credit card. You can get an ATM card from the bank where you have your account. When the bank gives you your card, it also gives you a personal identification number (PIN). You should memorize the number. If you lose your card, no one can use it without your special number.

The bank that gave you your card has a machine. However, you don't have to use your card at this bank only. You can use your ATM card in many other banks. There are also machines in other locations: shopping malls, supermarkets, and office buildings, for example.

Can you use your card in every machine? No. On the back of your card, there are symbols. You can use your card only at machines that have these symbols.

If you use a machine that doesn't belong to your bank, you might have to pay a fee. How do you know if the machine you are using belongs to your bank? The screen will tell you if you have to pay a fee and how much it is. You can cancel the transaction if you don't want to pay the fee. You can save money by using machines that are owned by your bank.

People use ATMs for convenience. You can get cash or make a deposit twenty-four hours a day.

The Indefinite Article—Classifying or Identifying the Subject

Examples	Explanation
An ATM is **a** cash machine. A teller is **a** bank worker. Mastercard is **an** American company.	We use the indefinite articles *a* or *an* to classify or define the subject of the sentence.
MasterCard and Visa are credit card companies. My parents are bank workers.	When we classify a plural subject, we don't use an article.

LANGUAGE NOTES

When we classify or identify the subject, we are telling who or what the subject is.

> What's Citibank?
> It's a big American bank.
> Who's Julia Roberts?
> She's an American actress.

EXERCISE 1 Define the following words.

EXAMPLE: A rose _____*is a flower.*_____

1. Gold _____
2. Asia _____
3. A carrot _____
4. Canada _____
5. Chicago _____
6. French and German _____
7. France and Germany_____
8. Volleyball and basketball _____
9. An elephant and a giraffe _____
10. New York and Los Angeles _____

EXERCISE 2 Tell who these people are (or were) by classifying them. (Some of these people were mentioned in previous lessons in this book.) You can work with a partner or in a small group.

EXAMPLE: Martin Luther King, Jr., ____*was an African-American leader.*____

1. Albert Einstein _____

2. Michael Jordan _____

3. Michael Jackson _____

4. Muhammad Ali _____

5. Sammy Sosa and Mark McGwire _____

6. George Washington and Abraham Lincoln _____

7. John Kennedy _____

8. Oprah Winfrey _____

14.2 The Indefinite Article—Introducing a Noun

	Singular Count	Plural Count	Noncount
Affirmative	I have **an** ATM card. There's **a** cash machine near my house.	I have (**some**) checks. There are (**some**) checks on the table.	I have (**some**) cash. There's (**some**) cash on the table.
Negative	I don't have **an** ATM card.	I don't have (**any**) credit cards.	I don't have (**any**) cash.
Question	Do you have **an** ATM card?	Do you have (**any**) credit cards?	Do you have (**any**) cash?

LANGUAGE NOTES

1. We use *a* or *an* to introduce a singular noun into the conversation. We use *some* or *any* to introduce a noncount noun or a plural noun into the conversation.
2. *Some* and *any* can be omitted.
   I don't have *any time* to help you.
   I don't have *time* to help you.

EXERCISE 3   Fill in the blanks with the correct word: *a, an, some, any.*

EXAMPLE: There are ____*some*____ symbols on the back of the card.

1. Do you have _____ account in the bank?

2. Do you have _____ money in your savings account?

3. I have _____ twenty-dollar bill in my pocket.

4. There's _____ ATM machine near my house.

5. I have _____ quarters in my pocket.

6. I have _____ money with me.

7. Do you have _____ credit cards?

8. I don't have _____ change.

14.3 The Definite Article

We use the definite article *the* when the speaker and the listener have the same person(s) or object(s) in mind. The listener knows exactly what the speaker is referring to in the following examples:

Examples	Explanation
The bank gives you *a personal identification number.* You should memorize **the** number. A cash card has *some symbols* on the back. **The** symbols tell you where you can use your card.	A noun is first introduced as an indefinite noun. When referring to it again, the definite article *the* is used.
Don't take **the** money on the table. It's for the rent. **The** credit card on the table expired last May. **The** cash machine is out of order.	The speaker is referring to an object or person that is present.
The sun is not very bright in the winter. There are many problems in **the** world. There are symbols on **the** back of an ATM card. I want to talk to **the** president of the bank.	There is only one in our experience.

(continued)

Examples	Explanation
Where's **the** teacher? I have a question about **the** homework.	The speaker and listener share a common experience. Students in the same class talk about **the** teacher, **the** textbook, **the** homework, **the** chalkboard.
I closed **the** windows and locked **the** door before I left **the** house.	People who live together talk about **the** house, **the** doors, **the** windows, etc. that they share.
I spent **the** money you gave me. I use **the** ATM in the supermarket near my house.	The speaker defines or specifies exactly which one.
I'm going to **the** store after work. Do you need anything? **The** bank is closed. I'll go tomorrow. You should make an appointment with **the** doctor.	We often use *the* with certain familiar places and people when we refer to the one that we usually use: the bank the beach the bus the zoo the post office the train the park the doctor the movies the store

LANGUAGE NOTES

Don't use the definite article with a possessive form.
I use *my* ATM card a lot.

EXERCISE 4   Fill in the blanks with the definite article *the*, the indefinite article *a* or *an*, or quantity words *any* or *some*.

Conversation 1: between two friends

A. Where are you going?

B. To _____*the*_____ bank. I want to deposit _____ check.
       (example)   (1)

A. _____ bank is probably closed now.
     (2)

B. No problem. I have _____ ATM card. There's _____ ATM
                           (3)   (4)

    on _____ corner of Wilson and Sheridan.
       (5)

A. I'll go with you. I want to get _____ cash.
                              (6)

Later, at the ATM . . .

B. Oh, no. _____ ATM is out of order.
       (7)

A. Don't worry. There's _____ ATM in _____ supermarket near
    (8)   (9)
my house.

Conversation 2: between two students at the same school

A. Is there _____ cafeteria at this school?
       (1)

B. Yes, there is. It's on _____ first floor of this building.
          (2)

A. I want to buy _____ cup of coffee.
         (3)

B. You don't have to go to _____ cafeteria.
            (4)
There's _____ coffee machine on this floor.
     (5)

A. I only have a one-dollar bill. Do you have _____ change?
                     (6)

B. There's _____ dollar-bill changer next to _____ coffee
       (7)   (8)
machine.

Conversation 3: between two students (A and B) in the same class and,
      later, the teacher (T)

A. Where's _____ teacher? It's already 7:00.
       (1)

B. Maybe she's absent today.

A. I'll go to _____ English office and ask if anyone knows where
        (2)
she is.

B. That's _____ good idea.
      (3)

A few minutes later . . .

A. I talked to _____ secretary in _____ English office. She
        (4)   (5)
said that _____ teacher just called. She's going to be about 15
       (6)
minutes late. She had _____ problem with her car.
           (7)

Ten minutes later . . .

A. Here's _____ teacher.
     (8)

T. I'm sorry I'm late.

B. Did you fix _____ problem with your car?
         (9)

T. I didn't have time. I left _____ car at home and took _____
                               (10)   (11)
taxi to school.

14.4 Making Generalizations

We can make a generalization about the subject.

No Article	Noncount Noun/ Plural Noun	Verb	Complement
	Money	can't buy	happiness.
	Credit cards	are	made of plastic.

Indefinite Article	Singular Count Noun	Verb	Complement
A	credit card	is	made of plastic.

We can make a generalization about the object.

Subject	Verb	Object (Count Noun)
I	don't eat	bananas.

Subject	Verb	Object (Noncount Noun)
I	don't drink	coffee.

LANGUAGE NOTES

1. To make a generalization about a noncount subject, don't use an article.
2. To make a generalization about a countable subject, use *a* or *an* + a singular noun, or no article + a plural noun. The idea is the same, singular or plural.
3. Don't use an article to make a generalization about the object of the sentence. Use the plural form for count nouns.
   > I don't eat *strawberries*.
   > I don't eat *sugar*.
4. Do not use *some* or *any* with generalizations. COMPARE:
   > I ate *some beef* for dinner. (an indefinite quantity)
   > *Beef* comes from a cow. (a generalization)

5. If you use *the* before count or noncount nouns, you are making the noun specific. COMPARE:

Money can't buy happiness.
The money on the table is mine.
A dog is a friendly animal.
The dog in the next apartment barks all the time.
Love is a wonderful feeling.
The love my mother gives me is something very special.

EXERCISE 5 Decide if the statement is general (true of all examples of the subject) or specific (true of the pictures on this page or of specific objects that everyone in this class can agree on). Fill in the blanks with *a, the,* or Ø (for no article).

EXAMPLES:

The dog is standing.

_A_ dog has four legs.

_Ø_ elephants have big ears.

The elephants are hungry.

The sun is bigger than _the_ moon.

1. _____ women generally live longer than men.

2. _____ women are talking on the phone.

3. _____ window is broken.

4. _____ window is made of glass.

5. _____ children are playing.

6. _____ children can generally learn a foreign language faster than adults.

7. _____ coffee is hot.

8. _____ coffee contains caffeine.

9. _____ sugar is on the shelf.

10. _____ sugar is sweet.

11. _____ cows give milk.

12. _____ cows are eating grass.

13. _____ salt contains a lot of sodium.

14. _____ salt is in the cabinet.

15. _____ teachers make less money than _____ doctors in the U.S.

16. _____ teacher is trying to teach us about articles now.

EXERCISE 6 Tell if you like the following or not. For count nouns (C), use the plural form. For noncount nouns (NC), use the singular form.

EXAMPLES: coffee (NC)
I like coffee.

apple (C)
I don't like apples.

1. tea (NC)   5. milk (NC)   9. potato (C)
2. corn (NC)   6. orange (C)   10. egg (C)
3. peach (C)   7. cookie (C)
4. potato chip (C) 8. pizza (NC)

EXERCISE 7 Fill in the blanks with *the, a, an, some, any,* or Ø (for no article). (In some cases, more than one answer is possible.)

A. Where are you going?

B. I'm going to __*the*__ post office. I need to buy _____ stamps.
   (example)   (1)

A. I'll go with you. I want to mail _____ package to my parents.
                                        (2)

B. What's in _____ package?
              (3)

A. _____ shirts for my father, _____ coat for my sister,
     (4)   (5)

   and _____ money for my mother.
        (6)

B. You should never send _____ money by mail.
                            (7)

A. I know. My mother never received _____ money that I sent in
                                        (8)

   my last letter. But what can I do? I don't have _____ checking
                                                        (9)

   account.

B. You can buy _____ money order at _____ bank.
                  (10)   (11)

A. How much does it cost?

---

400   Lesson Fourteen

B. Well, if you have _____ account in _____ bank, it's usually
    (12)   (13)
    free. If not, you'll probably have to pay a fee.

A. What about _____ currency exchange on Wright Street? Do they
                   (14)

    sell _____ money orders?
           (15)

B. Yes.

A. Why don't we go there? We can save _____ time. It's on
                                            (16)

    _____ same street as _____ post office.
       (17)   (18)

EXERCISE 8 Fill in the blanks with *the, a, an, some, any,* or ∅ (for no
article). (In some cases, more than one answer is possible.)

A. What would you like for lunch? How about _*some*_ soup?
                                              (example)

B. That sounds good. What are you going to put in _____ soup?
                                                       (1)

A. _____ carrots, _____ rice, _____ onion, and _____
       (2)   (3)   (4)   (5)
    pork.

B. Can you leave out _____ pork? I'm a vegetarian, so I don't
                          (6)

    eat _____ meat.
          (7)

A. I'm going to make _____ egg salad sandwiches. Do you eat
                          (8)

    _____ eggs?
       (9)

B. Yes, I do, but not very often because _____ eggs contain a lot
                                              (10)
    of cholesterol.

14.5 General or Specific with Quantity Words

General	Specific
All children need love.	**All (of) the** children in my building are well-behaved.
Very few Americans speak my language.	**Very few of the** Americans in my math class know where my country is.
Most banks have insurance.[2]	**Most of the** banks in this city are open late on Fridays.
	None of the classrooms at this school has a telephone.

[2] In most banks, an account is insured up to $100,000.

LANGUAGE NOTES

1. We use *all*, *most*, *many*, *some*, *(a) few*, *(a) little* before general nouns. Before specific nouns, we add *of the*.

   Most Americans have a TV.

   Most of the Americans I know have a cell phone.

   NOTE: After *all*, *of* is often omitted: *All the children* in my building are well-behaved.

2. After *none* + plural noun, a singular verb is correct. However, you will often hear a plural verb: None of the classrooms at this school *have* a telephone.

3. When we omit **a** before *few* and *little*, the emphasis is on the negative. We are saying the quantity is not enough. (See Lesson 5, section 5.11 for more information.)

   He has *few* friends. He's lonely.

   He has *a few* friends. He's happy.

EXERCISE 9 Fill in the blanks with *all, most, some,* or *(very) few* to make a general statement about Americans. Discuss your answers.

EXAMPLE: _Most_____ Americans have a car.

1. _____ Americans have educational opportunities.

2. _____ Americans have a TV.

3. _____ American families have more than eight children.

4. _____ Americans know where my country is.

5. _____ Americans shake hands when they meet.

6. _____ Americans use credit cards.

7. _____ Americans are natives of America.

8. _____ American citizens can vote.

9. _____ Americans speak my language.

10. _____ Americans are unfriendly to me.

EXERCISE 10 Fill in the blanks with a quantity word to make a **true** statement about specific nouns. (If you use *none*, change the verb to the singular form.)

EXAMPLES: _All of the_____ students in this class want to learn English.

_None of the students_____ in this class come ^s^ from Australia.

1. _____ students in this class speak Spanish.

2. _____ students brought their books to class today.

3. _____ students are absent today.

4. _____ students want to learn English.

5. _____ students have jobs.

6. _____ students are married.

7. _____ students are going to return to their
native countries.

8. _____ lessons in this book end with a review.

9. _____ pages in this book have pictures.

10. _____ tests in this class are hard.

Before You Read
1. Does American money look different from money in your native country? (size, color, etc.)
2. Is it easy for you to use American dollar bills and coins?
3. Have you noticed that not all American paper money looks the same?

Read the following article. Pay special attention to *other* and *another*.

Changing the American Dollar

Look at the two twenty-dollar bills on this page. You can see that one twenty-dollar bill has a big picture left of the center. **The other** one has a smaller picture in the center.

In 1996, the U.S. began to change the appearance of all bills. The changes began with the hundred-dollar bill. **The other** bills ($50, $20, $10, $5, and $1) are being changed gradually. As the new bills come into use, the old ones are "retired."

Some aspects of the bills will remain the same: size, color, paper, the pictures on the front and back, and the motto "In God We Trust." On one side of the one-dollar bill is a picture of George Washington, the first American president. On **the other side** is the Seal of the United States. **The other** bills have pictures of famous historical places. Benjamin Franklin, whose face appears on the $100 bill, and Alexander Hamilton, whose face appears on the $10 bill, were not American presidents, but **the other** bills have faces of American presidents.

Besides the position and size of the face on the new bills, there are seven **other** changes. One of these changes is the watermark (a hidden picture). Another change is the security thread. Hold a bill up to a bright light, and you will see a vertical thread on the left side and the watermark on the right side (a smaller picture).

Why is the U.S. going through all the trouble and expense of changing these bills? The answer is very simple: the new bills are harder to copy.

Did you know...?

The appearance of American dollars did not change from 1928 to 1996.

14.6   *Another* and *Other*

The other + a singular noun is definite. It means the only one remaining.

X   (X)

One side has a picture of Washington. ⎯⎯⎯⎯⎯⎯⎯⎯⎯⎯⎯⎯⎯⎯|

The other side has the American Seal. ⎯⎯⎯⎯⎯⎯⎯⎯⎯⎯⎯⎯⎯⎯⎯⎯⎯⎯|

The other + a plural noun is definite. It means all the remaining ones.

X   (X X X X X)

The $100 bill was changed first. ⎯⎯⎯⎯⎯⎯⎯⎯⎯⎯⎯⎯⎯|

The other bills are being changed too. ⎯⎯⎯⎯⎯⎯⎯⎯⎯⎯⎯⎯⎯⎯⎯⎯|

(continued)

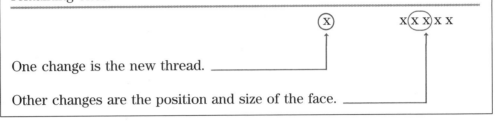

Another + a singular noun is indefinite. It means one of several.

One bill has a picture of Lincoln. _____

Another bill has a picture of Washington. _____

Other + a plural noun is indefinite. It means some, but not all, of the remaining ones.

One change is the new thread. _____

Other changes are the position and size of the face. _____

LANGUAGE NOTES

1. *One* or *ones* can be used in place of the noun.
    The hundred-dollar bill was changed first. The other *ones* are being changed too.
2. When the plural noun or pronoun (*ones*) is omitted, change *other* to *others*.
    The hundred-dollar bill was changed first. The *others* are being changed too.
3. *The* is omitted after a possessive form.
    I'm taking five classes. My math class is easy. My *other* classes are hard.
4. After *some* or *any*, *another* is changed to *other*.
    I'm busy now. Can you come *another* time?
             Can you come *any* other time?
             Can you come *some* other time?
5. *Another* is sometimes used to mean *a different one*.
    This fork is dirty. Please give me *another* one.

EXERCISE 11 Fill in the blanks with *the other, another, the others, others*, or *other*.

EXAMPLE: One side of the one-dollar bill has a picture of George Washington.

_____*The other*_____ side has a picture of the American Seal.

1. Some bills were changed in 1996. _____ bills were changed in 1997.

2. Franklin, on the $100 bill, and Hamilton, on the $10 bill, were not

American presidents. All _____ bills have pictures of American presidents.

3. Franklin was an important person in American history. _____

_____ important people were Thomas Jefferson and John Hancock.

4. One bill has a picture of Lincoln. _____ one has a picture of George Washington.

5. One side of an ATM card has a name and a number. _____ side has symbols.

6. George Washington was an American president. _____ presidents were Lincoln, Roosevelt, and Truman.

7. There were two presidents named Roosevelt. One was Theodore

Roosevelt. _____ was Franklin Roosevelt.

8. We celebrate two Presidents' birthdays in February. One is Lincoln's

birthday. _____ is Washington's birthday.

9. New York is one big city in the U.S. _____ big cities are Philadelphia, Houston, and Detroit.

10. Many cities in the U.S. have warm weather. One city is Miami.

_____ one is San Diego.

11. Do you know the capital of this state? Do you know _____ 49 capitals?

12. Johnson is a common last name in the U.S. _____ common names are Smith, Wilson, and Jones.

13. Some immigrants in the U.S. come from Mexico. _____

immigrants come from Poland. _____ come from Vietnam.

14. There are eight categories of words. Some words are verbs.

_____ are nouns.

15. *Money* is a noncount noun. _____ ones are *love*, *freedom*, and *time*.

16. A present-tense verb has two forms. One is the base form.

_____ is the *-s* form.

17. Some students will get an A in this course. _____ will get a C.

18. If you can't do this exercise today, do it some _____ time.

Before You Read
1. Should parents give children money to spend?
2. At what age do you think children should learn about money?

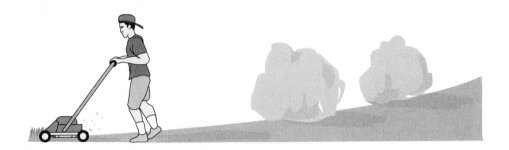

Read the following article. Pay special attention to *one*, *some*, and *any* (indefinite pronouns) and *it* (definite pronoun).

Kids and Money

American kids like to spend money. Many American parents give their children an allowance each week and let their children spend **it** as they please. Other parents expect their kids to earn their money by mowing the lawn, babysitting for younger sisters and brothers, washing the dishes, or cleaning the house. If the child asks for money but he doesn't do his jobs, he doesn't get **any**. This child learns that money "doesn't grow on trees" and that if he needs **some**, he has to do something to get it. Some parents let their kids spend all of the money they get, but others want their kids to save **some** in their own bank account. If the child wants to buy a special toy, he can save his money and pay for **it** himself.

Why do kids need so much money? A lot of marketing on TV and on the Internet is directed at kids. Kids see something new and they want to buy it. Also, kids like to be just like their friends. If their friends have a new doll or game, they want **one** just like it. If their friends have designer blue jeans, they have to have exactly the same kind. If parents say no, kids usually respond, "All of my friends have **one**. I'll die if I don't get **one**." Parents who feel guilty for not spending enough time with their kids often give in to their kids' demands.

Grandparents spoil children too, giving them gifts and generous amounts of cash for birthdays, graduations, and other special occasions.

Did you know...?

In 1997, a typical American ten-year-old got about $14 to spend each week.

14.7 Indefinite Pronouns: *One, Some, Any*

Definite	Indefinite
My daughter has a new doll. Do you want to see **it**?	My daughter has a new doll. Her friend has **one**, too.
He got some money from his grandparents. He wants to spend **it**.	He got some money for his birthday. You got **some**, too. Did you get **any** for your graduation?
I have a young son. I take **him** to the park every day.	I have a son. Do you have **one**?
My son has some video games. He likes to play with **them**.	My son has some video games. Does your son have **any**?

LANGUAGE NOTES

1. We use definite pronouns (*him, her, them, it*) to refer to definite count nouns.
    Last week was my niece's birthday. I gave *her* $25.
2. We use *one* to refer to an indefinite singular count noun.
    My niece doesn't have a Barbie doll. She wants to buy *one*.
3. We use *some* (for statements) and *any* (for negatives and questions) to refer to an indefinite noncount noun or an indefinite plural count noun.
    Did you receive any money for your graduation? Yes, I received *some*.
    Did you receive any gifts for your graduation? No, I didn't receive *any*.
4. We often use *any* and *some* before *more*.
    I need *some* more money.
    I'm not going to give you *any* more.

EXERCISE 12 Tell the person next to you if you have or don't have the following. Then ask this person a question with *one*. The other student will answer.

EXAMPLE: a car
A. I don't have a car. Do you have one?
B. Yes, I do.   OR   No, I don't.

1. a computer
2. a VCR
3. a driver's license
4. a bike
5. a camera
6. a cell phone
7. a cat
8. a library card
9. a microwave oven
10. an answering machine

EXERCISE **13** Tell the person next to you if you have or don't have the following. Then ask this person a question with *any*. The other student will answer.

EXAMPLE: American friends
A. I have some American friends.
   OR
   I don't have any American friends. Do you have any?
B. Yes, I have some.   OR   No, I don't have any.

1. plants in my apartment
2. photos of my family with me
3. American friends
4. questions about this lesson
5. money with me
6. coffee at home
7. fruit at home
8. experience with computer programming

EXERCISE **14** Answer each question. Substitute the underlined words with an indefinite pronoun (*one, some, any*) or a definite pronoun (*it, them*).

EXAMPLES: Do you have a pen with you?
Yes, I have one.

Are you using your pen now?
No. I'm not using it now.

1. Does this school have a library?

2. How often do you use the library?

3. Do you have a dictionary?

4. When do you use your dictionary?

5. Did you buy any textbooks this semester?

6. How much did you pay for your textbooks?

7. Did the teacher give any homework last week?

8. Where did you do the homework?

9. Do you have any American neighbors?

10. Do you know your neighbors?

11. Does this college have a president?

12. Do you know the college president?

13. Did you receive any mail today?

14. What time does your letter carrier deliver your mail?

EXERCISE **15** Combination Exercise. This is a conversation between a teenage girl (A) and her mother (B). Fill in the blanks with *one, some, any, it, them, a, an, the,* or Ø (for no article).

A.   Can I have fifteen dollars?

B.   What for?

A.   I have to buy ____*a*____ poster of my favorite singer.
        (example)

B.   I gave you _____ money last week. What did you do with
                  (1)

       _____?
        (2)

A.   I spent _____ on a CD.
                (3)

B.   No, you can't have _____ more money until next week.
                              (4)

A.   Please, please, please. All of my friends have _____. I'll die if I
                                                              (5)

       don't get _____.
                    (6)

B.   What happened to all _____ money Grandpa gave you for your
                              (7)

       birthday?

A.   I spent _____.
                (8)

B.   What about _____ money you put in the bank after your gradua-
                    (9)

       tion?

A.   I don't have _____ more money in the bank.
                      (10)

B.   You have to learn that _____ money doesn't grow on trees. If
                                (11)

       you want me to give you _____, you'll have to work for it. You
                                    (12)

       can start by cleaning your room.

A.   But I cleaned _____ two weeks ago.
                      (13)

B.   Two weeks ago was two weeks ago. It's dirty again.

A.   I don't have _____ time. I have to meet my friends.
                      (14)

B.   You can't go out. You need to do your homework.

A.   I don't have _____. Please let me have fifteen dollars.
                      (15)

B.   When I was your age, I had _____ job. And I gave my parents
                                    (16)

       half of _____ money I earned. You kids today have _____
                (17)   *(18)*

       easy life.

A. Why do _____ parents always say that to _____ kids?
                (19)   (20)

B. Because it's true. It's time you learn that _____ life is hard.
                (21)

A. I bet Grandpa said that to you when you were _____ child.
                (22)

B. And I bet you'll say it to your kids when you're _____ adult.
                (23)

SUMMARY OF LESSON 14

1. Articles

	Count—Singular	Count—Plural	Noncount
General	*A/An* An orange contains vitamin C.	Ø Article Oranges contain vitamin C. I like oranges.	Ø Article Meat contains cholesterol. I like meat.
Indefinite	*A/An* I ate a cherry.	*Some/Any* I ate (some) cherries. I didn't eat (any) grapes.	*Some/Any* I ate (some) meat. I didn't eat (any) bread.
Specific	*The* The apple on the table is green.	*The* The apples on the table are green.	*The* The meat on the table is fresh.
Classification	*A/An* Boston is a city.	Ø Article Boston and Chicago are cities.	—

2. *Other/Another*

		Definite	Indefinite
Singular		the other book my other book the other one the other	another book some/any other book another one another
Plural		the other books my other books the other ones the others	other books some/any other books other ones others

3. Indefinite Pronouns

> Use *one, some, any* to substitute for indefinite nouns.
> I have *a speaker phone*. Do you have *one*?
> I bought *some apples*. My sister bought *some* too.
> I don't have *any cash*. Do you have *any*?

EDITING ADVICE

1. Use *the* after a quantity word when the noun is definite.

   Most of ^the^ students in my class are from Romania.

2. Be careful with *most* and *almost*.

   ~~Almost~~ *Most of* my teachers are very patient.

3. Use a plural count noun after a quantity expression.

   A few of my friend^s^ live in Canada.

4. *Another* is always singular.

   Some teachers are strict. ~~Another~~ *Other* teachers are easy.

5. Use an indefinite pronoun to substitute for an indefinite noun.

   I need to borrow a pen. I didn't bring ~~it~~ *one* today.

6. *A* and *an* are always singular.

   She has ~~a~~ beautiful eyes.

7. Don't use *there* to introduce a unique, definite noun.

   ~~There's~~ ^T^he Statue of Liberty ^is^ in New York.

8. Use *a* or *an* for a definition or a classification of a singular count noun.

   The Statue of Liberty is ^a^ monument.

412   Lesson Fourteen

PART 1   Find the mistakes with the underlined words, and correct them. Not every sentence has a mistake. If the sentence is correct, write **C**.

EXAMPLES: She has many friends. One of her friends is a doctor. ~~The other~~ *Another* one is a secretary.

Most <u>Americans</u> own a TV.   **C**

1. <u>All of teachers</u> at this college have a master's degree.

2. <u>Some of the animals</u> eat only meat. They are called "carnivores."

3. The students in this class come from many countries. Some of the students are from Poland. <u>Another</u> students are from Hungary.

4. A battery has two terminals. One is positive; <u>another</u> is negative.

5. I'm taking two classes. One is English. <u>The other</u> is math.

6. I lost my dictionary. I need to buy <u>another one</u>.

7. I lost my textbook. I think I lost <u>it</u> in the library.

8. I don't have a computer. Do you have <u>it</u>?

9. <u>Most my teachers</u> have a lot of experience.

10. Cuba <u>is country</u>.

11. <u>Most women</u> want to have children.

12. I have <u>some money</u> with me. Do you have any?

13. <u>Very few of the students</u> in this class have financial aid.

14. I have two brothers. One of my brothers is an engineer. <u>The other my brother</u> is a physical therapist.

15. <u>Almost</u> my friends come from South America.

16. There's the <u>Golden Gate Bridge</u> in San Francisco.

PART 2   Fill in the blanks with *the, a, an, some, any,* or *Ø* (for no article). In some cases, more than one answer is possible.

A.   Do you want to come to my house tonight? I rented _____*some*_____ movies.
                                                   (example)

   We can make _____ popcorn and watch _____ movies together.
                         (1)   *(2)*

B. Thanks, but I'm going to _____ party. Do you want to go with me?
(3)

A. Where's it going to be?

B. It's going to be at Michael's apartment.

A. Who's going to be at _____ party?
(4)

B. Most of _____ students in my English class will be there. Each student
(5)

is going to bring _____ food.
(6)

A. _____ life in the U.S. is strange. In my country, _____ people
(7)   (8)

don't have to bring _____ food to a party.
(9)

B. That's the way it is in my country, too. But we're in _____ U.S. now.
(10)

I'm going to bake _____ cake. You can make _____ special
(11)   (12)

dish from your country.

A. You know I'm _____ terrible cook.
(13)

B. Don't worry. You can buy something. My friend Max is going to buy

_____ crackers and cheese. Why don't you bring _____ salami
(14)   (15)

or roast beef?

A. But I don't eat _____ meat. I'm _____ vegetarian.
(16)   (17)

B. Well, you can bring _____ bowl of fruit.
(18)

A. That's _____ good idea. What time does _____ party start?
(19)   (20)

B. At 8 o'clock.

A. I have to take my brother to _____ airport at 6:30. I don't know if
(21)

I'll be back on time.

B. You don't have to arrive at 8 o'clock exactly. I'll give you _____
(22)

address, and you can arrive any time you want.

PART 3   Fill in the blanks with *other*, *others*, *another*, *the other*, or *the others*.

A. I don't like my apartment.

B. Why not?

A. It's very small. It only has two closets. One is big, but ___*the other*___ is
(example)

very small.

B. That's not very serious. Is that the only problem? Are there _____ (1) problems?

A. There are many _____ (2) .

B. Such as?

A. Well, the landlord doesn't provide enough heat in the winter.

B. Hmm. That's a real problem. Did you complain to him?

A. I did, but he says that all _____ (3) tenants are happy.

B. Why don't you look for _____ (4) apartment?

A. I have two roommates. One wants to move, but _____ (5) likes it here.

B. Well, if one wants to stay and _____ (6) two want to move, why don't you move and look for _____ (7) roommate?

PART **4** _____ Fill in the blanks with *one, some, any, it,* or *them.*

EXAMPLE: I have a computer, but my roommate doesn't have ___*one*___ .

1. Do you want to use my bicycle? I won't need _____ this afternoon.

2. I rented two movies. We can watch _____ tonight.

3. My English teacher gives some homework every day, but she doesn't give _____ on the weekends.

4. My class has a lot of Mexican students. Does your class have _____?

5. I wrote two compositions last week, but I got bad grades because I wrote _____ very quickly.

6. I don't have any problems with English, but my roommate has _____ .

7. I can't remember the teacher's name. Do you remember _____?

8. You won't need any paper for the test, but you'll need _____ for the composition.

9. I went to the library to find some books in my language, but I couldn't find _____ .

EXPANSION ACTIVITIES

CLASSROOM ACTIVITY

1. Fill in the blanks with *all, most, some, a few,* or *very few* to make a general statement about your native country. Then find a partner from a different country, if possible, and compare your answers.

   a. _____ people speak English.

   b. _____ children study English in school.

   c. _____ families own a car.

   d. _____ people are Catholic.

   e. _____ people own a computer.

   f. _____ women work outside the home.

   g. _____ parents have more than five children.

   h. _____ people live in an apartment.

   i. _____ young men serve in the military.

   j. _____ people are happy with the political situation.

   k. _____ people have servants.

   l. _____ people have a college education.

   m. _____ married couples have their own apartment.

   n. _____ old people live with their grown children.

2. Bring in coins and bills from your native country. Form a small group of students from different countries, and show this money to the other students in your group.

DISCUSSION

1. The following sayings and proverbs are about money. Discuss the meaning of each one. Do you have a similar saying in your native language?
   - All that glitters isn't gold.
   - Money is the root of all evil.
   - Friendship and money don't mix.
   - Another day, another dollar.
   - Money talks.
2. Do you think kids should get an allowance from their parents? How much? Does it depend on the child's age? Should the child have to work for the money?

If you have a bank account, get a list of the locations of the ATMs owned by your bank.

Internet Activities

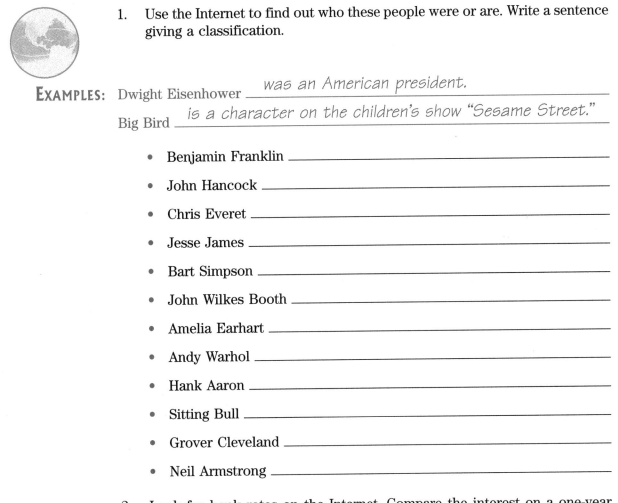

1. Use the Internet to find out who these people were or are. Write a sentence giving a classification.

EXAMPLES: Dwight Eisenhower _____ *was an American president.* _____

Big Bird _____ *is a character on the children's show "Sesame Street."* _____

- Benjamin Franklin _____
- John Hancock _____
- Chris Everet _____
- Jesse James _____
- Bart Simpson _____
- John Wilkes Booth _____
- Amelia Earhart _____
- Andy Warhol _____
- Hank Aaron _____
- Sitting Bull _____
- Grover Cleveland _____
- Neil Armstrong _____

2. Look for bank rates on the Internet. Compare the interest on a one-year CD (certificate of deposit) at two banks.

3. There are nine changes in the new dollar bills. Only a few were discussed in this lesson. Go to the U.S. Treasury Web site to find out what the other changes are.

GRAMMAR

Review of Verb Tenses

Sentence Structure and Word Order

CONTEXT

Letter of Complaint

LESSON FOCUS

We will review the following tenses:

1. The simple present
2. The present continuous
3. The future
4. The simple past
5. The past continuous
6. The present perfect
7. The present perfect continuous

We will review the basic word order for statements and questions.

Before You Read Did you ever complain to a company about a product that you bought or a service that you received? Did you receive any satisfaction as a result of your complaint?

The following is a letter of complaint. Read the letter and identify the tense of each verb. Identify the modals and the infinitives, too.

LETTER OF COMPLAINT

6761 N. Williams
Chicago, IL 60645
July 15, 2001

Jackson Movers
1834 W. Howard St.
Chicago, IL 60626

Dear Mr. Jackson:

I**'m writing** (1) to you to tell you about a problem that **happened** (2) during my move. Two months ago, your movers **moved** (3) me from 7554 N. Oakland to 6761 N. Williams. While they **were carrying** (4) my table upstairs, they **dropped** (5) it and **broke** (6) the corner of the glass top. When I **pointed** (7) it out to them, they **said** (8) that they would speak to the owner about the problem.

I **have been living** (9) in my new apartment for two months already, and so far I **haven't heard** (10) anything from your moving company. I**'m getting** (11) angry because my table **is** (12) still broken. I **want** (13) you **to come** (14) to my house as soon as possible so that you can look at the damage. When you **come** (15) here, you **will see** (16) that the damage is considerable.[1] I **want** (17) you **to take** (18) care of this problem immediately. You **can pay** (19) for the damage or replace the glass top of the table. Please call me when you **receive** (20) this letter so that we can set up an appointment.

I **know** (21) that you **have** (22) insurance. I **have used** (23) your company before, and I **have recommended** (24) your company to many of my friends. However, if you **don't fix** (25) my table, I**'ll never use** (26) your company again. In addition, I**'ll tell** (27) my friends that you **don't take** (28) responsibility for damage.

Sincerely,

Margaret Walters

Margaret Walters

---

[1] *Considerable* means a great amount.

The Seven Patterns:

The Simple Present	
With the base form	With the -s form
I **live** in Chicago.	She **has** a problem with her table.
I **don't live** in New York.	She **doesn't have** a problem with her chair.
Do you **live** on Oakland Street?	**Does** she **have** a problem with the moving company?
No, I **don't**.	Yes, she **does**.
Where **do** you **live**?	What kind of problem **does** she **have**?
Why **don't** you **live** on Oakland Street anymore?	Why **doesn't** she **have** an answer to her problem?
How many people **live** with you?	Who **has** the answer to her problem?

The Present Continuous	
Margaret **is writing** a letter.	I'm **complaining** about the movers.
She **isn't writing** a composition.	I'm **not complaining** about the apartment.
Is she **writing** to her friend?	**Are** you **complaining** about your piano?
No, she **isn't**.	No, I'm **not**.
Why **is** she **writing** a letter?	What **are** you **complaining** about?
Why **isn't** she **writing** a composition?	Why **aren't** you **complaining** by phone?
Who **is writing** a composition?	Who **is complaining** about the movers?

The Simple Present Tense—Uses

Examples	Uses of the Simple Present Tense
Margaret **lives** in Chicago. Chicago **has** a large population.	In a statement of fact
Margaret sometimes **writes** letters. Jackson Moving Co. **moves** people every day. Whenever Margaret **writes** a letter, she **uses** her computer.	With a regular activity

(continued)

Examples	Uses of the Simple Present Tense
Margaret **has** a problem with the moving company now. She **wants** the company to fix her table.	With nonaction verbs (see page 47 for a list of nonaction verbs)
If you **don't fix** my table, I'm never going to use your company again. When Mr. Jackson **receives** the letter, will he call Margaret?	In an *if* or time clause in future statements

The Present Continuous Tense—Uses

Examples	Uses of the Present Continuous Tense
Margaret **is writing** a letter now. She **is typing** the letter on her computer.	With an action that is in progress now, at this moment
Margaret **is waiting** for an answer to her letter. This semester we **are using** *Grammar in Context*.	With an action in a present time period that is not complete
I **am going** to New York on Friday. We **are buying** a new car next month.	With a planned activity in the near future

EXERCISE 1   This is a phone conversation between two students. Fill in the blanks with the present continuous or the simple present form of the verb in parentheses ( ).

A. Hello?

B. Hi. This is Kim.

A. Hi, Kim. What's up?

B. I _____*am looking*_____ for someone to go to the movies with me.
      (example: look)

   What _____ now?
            (1 you/do)

A. I _____ for my test.
         (2 study)

B. _____ to go out for a while and take a break?
      (3 you/want)

A. I can't. I _____ to memorize vocabulary words. I have
              (4 try)
to know 50 words for tomorrow's test.

B. How often _____ a vocabulary test?
            (5 you/have)

A. Once a week.

B. _____ that you have to memorize 50 words a week?
  (6 you/mean)

A. Yes. Every Friday the teacher _____ a vocabulary test.
                    (7 give)

B. I _____ that's terrible.
   (8 think)

A. It's not as bad as it _____ . Every day I _____ ten
                (9 seem)   *(10 learn)*
words. Every Thursday, I _____ my list. And every Friday I
                (11 review)
_____ the test. My vocabulary _____ a lot
  (12 take)   *(13 improve)*
this semester.

B. How _____ new words?
      (14 you/learn)

A. I always _____ them on cards with the translation on the
        (15 write)
back. I _____ my cards whenever I _____ free time.
    (16 study)   *(17 have)*
Someone always gives me a practice test.

B. Who _____ you a practice test?
    (18 give)

A. My roommate usually does.

15.2   The Future

The Seven Patterns:

With *be going to*	With *will*
Margaret **is going to tell** her friends.	Margaret **will tell** her friends.
She **isn't going to use** this company again.	She **won't use** this company again.
Is she **going to send** a letter?	**Will** she **send** a letter?
Yes, she **is**.	Yes, she **will**.
Why **is** she **going to send** a letter?	Why **will** she **send** a letter?
Why **isn't** she **going to use** this company again?	Why **won't** she **use** this company again?
Who **is going to use** this company?	Who **will use** this company?

(continued)

Uses

Will	Be going to	Uses of *will* and *be going to*
Will Mr. Jackson **answer** Margaret's letter?	**Is** Mr. Jackson **going to answer** Margaret's letter?	With a prediction
Registration **will begin** on August 20.	Registration **is going to begin** on August 20.	With a scheduled event
The sun **will set** at 5:47 p.m. tonight.	The sun **is going to set** at 5:47 p.m. tonight.	With a fact about the future
	Margaret **is going to bake** cookies this afternoon.	With a future plan, *be going to* is more common.
I can't help you now. I promise I **will help** you later. If you don't fix my table, I **will** never **use** your company again.		With a promise or a threat, *will* is more common.
A. I'm not strong enough to carry that box. B. **I'll do** it.		With an offer to help, use *will*.

EDITING ADVICE

1. Use the *-s* form when the subject is *he, she, it,* a gerund (verb + *ing*), *everybody,* or *nobody.*

    He ~~have~~ *has* a car.

    Buying a house require*s* a lot of money.

    Everybody need*s* love.

2. Don't use the *-s* form after *does.*

    He doesn't ~~has~~ *have* a car.

    Does he lives in Philadelphia?

3. Always include a form of *be* in a present continuous tense statement.

    She *is* working now.

4. Don't use the present continuous tense for a nonaction verb.

I ~~am~~ knowing my language very well.

5. Use the simple present, not the future tense, after a time word or *if*.

When I ~~will~~ get home, I will call you.

I'll mail the package if I ~~will be~~ *am* at the post office.

6. Don't use *be* with another verb to form the future tense.

Tomorrow I will ~~be~~ look for a job.

7. Include *be* in a future sentence that has no other verb.

He will *be* afraid.

8. Use either *will* or *be going to* for the future. Don't combine them.

She ~~will~~ *is* going to return to her country.

OR *She will return . . .*

9. Use the future tense with *will* for an offer to help.

The phone's ringing. I *'ll* get it.

EXERCISE 2 Find the mistakes with the underlined words, and correct them. Not every sentence has a mistake. If the sentence is correct, write **C**.

EXAMPLES: She usually <u>eating</u> *s* a banana every day.

She <u>will be</u> late for her appointment.   C

1. If you <u>will study</u> here next semester, you will learn a lot.

2. She <u>will be buy</u> a car when she graduates.

3. Walking a few miles a day <u>is</u> good exercise.

4. This semester I <u>studying</u> English and math.

5. Learning a new language <u>take</u> a long time.

6. They <u>are having</u> a beautiful house.

7. Next week <u>I'm leaving</u> on vacation.

8. You <u>will going to</u> learn a lot of English.

9. Before I <u>go</u> home today, I will go to the library.

---

10. <u>Will you angry</u> if I use your car?

11. You can relax. I <u>cook</u> dinner tonight.

12. She <u>needs</u> my help now.

13. Everybody <u>have</u> problems.

14. Nobody <u>knows</u> how I feel.

EXERCISE 3   A student is writing a letter to his friend. Fill in the blanks. Use the simple present, the present continuous, or the future form of the verb in parentheses ( ) to complete this letter.

Dear Ali,

I'm in the school library now. I ___*am waiting*___ for my friend to come
(example: wait)

and meet me. I _____ you this brief letter while I
(1 write)

_____ .
(2 wait)

This semester I _____ 3 courses—English, biology,
(3 take)

and math. I _____ biology, but it's hard for me. Next
(4 like)

week we _____ our first exam. When my friend _____
(5 have)

_____, we _____ together. He _____
(6 arrive) _(7 study)_

_____ more English than I do. Whenever I
(8 know)

_____ some English words, he _____
(9 not/understand) _(10 explain)_

them to me in Arabic. Sometimes we _____ at his house,
(11 study)

but today we _____ in the laboratory. He
(12 study)

_____ me how to do an experiment.
(13 show)

I _____ my friend now. He _____
(14 see) _(15 walk)_

toward me. I _____ you later when I _____ more time.
(16 write) _(17 have)_

Your friend,

Hussein

15.3 The Past Tenses

The Seven Patterns:

With the simple past tense
The movers **broke** the table.
They **didn't break** the mirror.
Did they **break** the glass?
Yes, they **did**.
How **did** they **break** the glass?
Why **didn't** they **break** the mirror?
Who **broke** the mirror?

The Simple Past Tense—Uses

Examples	Uses of the Simple Past Tense
The movers **dropped** the table. They **broke** the glass.	With a past action of little or no duration past ←----x-----┆--------→ future 　　　　　dropped　┆ 　　　　　broke　　┆ 　　　　　　　　　now (above line)
Margaret **lived** on Oakland Street for ten years before she moved.	With a past action of duration that is completely past past ←---▮▮--┆--------→ future 　　　　lived　┆ 　　　　　　now (above line)

The Seven Patterns:

With the Past Continuous Tense
They **were moving** the table.
They **weren't moving** the piano.
Were they **moving** chairs?
Yes, they **were**.
What **were** they **doing** when they dropped the table?
Why **weren't** they **moving** the piano?
Who **was moving** the piano?

Review of Verb Tenses; Sentence Structure and Word Order　　**427**

The Past Continuous Tense—Uses

Examples	Uses of the Past Continuous Tense
Margaret **was writing** a letter at 2 p.m. yesterday.	With a continuous past action that was in progress at a specific time now was writing past ←--▓▓▓▓--|--------→ future ↑ 2 p.m.
While the movers **were moving** the table, they dropped it. They **were carrying** it upstairs when they dropped it.	With the simple past tense, to show the relationship of a longer past action to a shorter one now were moving past ←-- X --|--------→ future ↑ dropped
While Margaret **was washing** the kitchen floor, her husband **was cleaning** the bathroom.	With two past actions that occurred over the same general period of time Action 1: now past ←▓▓▓▓--|--------→ future was washing Action 2: past ←▓▓▓▓--|--------→ future was cleaning

LANGUAGE NOTES

1. You can use either *while* or *when* with a continuous action or state.
   While (or *when*) the movers were moving the table, they dropped it.
2. In a question with two clauses, only the verb in the main clause is in question form.
   What *were the movers doing* when they *dropped* the table?

EXERCISE 4 A student wrote a composition about leaving her country and coming to the U.S. Fill in the blanks with the simple past or the past continuous form of the verb in parentheses ( ).

In 1992, I _____*graduated*_____ from high school in my native country and
_____ (graduate)

_____ to study at the university. I _____ to be
(1 start)   (2 study)

a nurse when a war _____ out. I _____ to leave my country.
(3 break)   (4 have)

I _____ to Germany and _____ there for three years. I
(5 go)   (6 live)

_____ to come to the U.S., so I _____ English in
(7 want)   (8 study)

Germany. Finally, after three years of waiting, I _____ permission to
(9 get)

come to America.

When I _____ in New York, my uncle _____
(10 arrive)   (11 wait)

for me. He _____ me to his house. While we _____ to his
(12 take)   (13 drive)

house, I _____ at the streets of New York. Everything
(14 look)

_____ strange to me. I _____ about so many different
(15 seem)   (16 think)

things when, suddenly, my uncle _____, "Here we are." At that point,
(17 say)

a new life _____ for me.
(18 start)

15.4 The Present Perfect and Present Perfect Continuous

The Seven Patterns:

With the present perfect tense	With the present perfect continuous tense
Margaret **has moved**.	Margaret **has been living** on Williams Street for two months.
She **hasn't moved** out of the city.	She **hasn't been living** alone.
Has she **moved** several times?	**Has** she **been living** with her brother?
Yes, she **has**.	No, she **hasn't**.
How many times **has** she **moved**?	With whom **has** she **been living**?
Why **hasn't** she **moved** out of the city?	Why **hasn't** she **been living** with her brother?
How many people **have moved**?	Who **has been living** with her brother?

(continued)

Uses

Examples	Uses of the Present Perfect Continuous Tense
Margaret **has been living** on Williams Street for two months. She **has been waiting** for an answer to her complaint since May.	With an action that started in the past and continues to the present now past ←- - |░░░░░░| - - - - - → future has been living has been waiting →

Examples	Uses of the Present Perfect Tense
Margaret **has had** a problem with her table since May. The movers **have known** about the problem for two months.	With an action or state that started in the past and continues to the present now past ←- - |░░░░░░| - - - - - → future has had have known →
She **has called** the moving company three times so far.	With an action that repeats in a period of time that includes the present now past ←- -┌x- - -x- - -x- - - - - -┼- - - - - → future has called →
Have you ever **used** Jackson Movers? They **haven't fixed** the table yet.	With an action that occurred at an indefinite time in the past now past ←- -┌- - - - -?- - - - - - -┼- - - - - → future have used haven't fixed ↑

EXERCISE 5 Fill in the blanks with the simple present, the present continuous, the present perfect, the present perfect continuous, or the simple past of the verb in parentheses ( ).

I _____*work*_____ in a restaurant. I _____ at my present job
     (work)   (1 work)

for about two years. But I don't like it. Now, I _____ to find
                                              (2 try)

a new job. I _____ several interviews this month, but I
               (3 have)

_____ a good job yet. However, I _____ hope.
  (4 not/find)   (5 not/lose)

In my native country, I _____ as a bookkeeper, but I can't find
                         (6 work)

this kind of job because I _____ enough English yet.
                        (7 not/learn)

Now my brother-in-law and I _____ about starting our own
                         (8 talk)

business. I _____ to be in business for myself.
      (9 always/want)

EDITING ADVICE 🖉

1. Don't use *was* or *were* + verb to form the past tense.

        lived
   He ~~was live~~ in Detroit from 1988 to 1995.

2. Use the simple past, not the past continuous, when the action has no duration.

        started
   It ~~was starting~~ to rain a few minutes ago.

        lost
   She ~~was losing~~ her purse yesterday.

3. Use the present perfect or the present perfect continuous for an action that started in the past and continues to the present.

        had
   I have ^ my car for three years.

        has been
   She ~~is~~ living in Chicago since March.

4. Include *have* in a present perfect statement.

        have
   They ^ been working for a long time.

---

5. Don't confuse a present participle (*-ing*) with a past participle.

   She has already ~~seeing~~ *seen* that movie.

6. Use the base form, not the past form, after *did*.

   He didn't ~~found~~ *find* his wallet.

   Did you ~~ate~~ *eat* lunch today?

EXERCISE 6 Find the mistakes with the underlined words, and correct them. Not every sentence has a mistake. If the sentence is correct, write **C**.

EXAMPLES: Have you ever ~~being~~ *been* to New York?

Last week we <u>went</u> to see a good movie.   C

1. I dropped the mirror and it <u>was breaking</u>.

2. She <u>was lived</u> in Pakistan when she was a child.

3. I <u>worked</u> at my present job since January.

4. I <u>been watching</u> you for several minutes.

5. <u>I'm studying</u> English since I came to the U.S.

6. She <u>has had</u> her car for three years.

7. I <u>slept</u> when the telephone rang.

8. He didn't <u>knew</u> the answer.

9. Did you <u>bought</u> a car?

10. She's <u>been working</u> for three hours.

EXERCISE 7 Fill in the blanks with the simple present, present continuous, future, simple past, past continuous, present perfect, or present perfect continuous form of the verb in parentheses ( ).

Last week I ____*lost*____ my job. My co-workers and I _____
        (example: lose)   (1 eat)

lunch in the company cafeteria when the boss _____ in and told
                                              (2 come)

me to go to his office. I _____ him to his office. He _____,
                          (3 follow)   (4 say)

"I'm sorry to tell you this, but we have to lay off² three workers. You

_____ here for only six months, less time than the other workers.
　　(5 be)

So I _____ to lay you off." I _____ his office and
　　　(6 decide)　　　　　　　　　　　　(7 leave)

_____ home. I _____ terrible.
　(8 go)　　　　　　(9 feel)

　I _____ for a job now. I _____ the newspaper every
　　　(10 look)　　　　　　　　　　(11 buy)

day and _____ in the help-wanted section, but I _____
　　　(12 look)　　　　　　　　　　　　　　　　　(13 not/find)

a job yet. Yesterday a friend of mine _____ that I see a job
　　　　　　　　　　　　　　　　　　　　(14 suggest)

counselor. I _____ to see her this morning. While I _____
　　　　(15 go)　　　　　　　　　　　　　　　　　　(16 wait)

to see her, I _____ a bulletin board outside her office. I _____
　　　　　(17 notice)　　　　　　　　　　　　　　　　　(18 see)

several interesting ads. I _____ down some information when
　　　　　　　　　　　　(19 write)

she _____ out of her office and _____ herself. She
　　(20 come)　　　　　　　　　　　(21 introduce)

_____ me into her office and _____ me a few phone numbers to
　(22 take)　　　　　　　　　　　(23 give)

call.

　Tomorrow morning, I _____ early. I _____ these
　　　　　　　　　　(24 start)　　　　　　(25 call)

numbers to see if I can get an interview. I _____ I can find a job soon.
　　　　　　　　　　　　　　　　　　(26 hope)

I really _____ the money. When I _____ a job, I _____
　　　(27 need)　　　　　　　　(28 find)　　　　　　(29 save)

my money in case this ever happens again.

15.5　Be

The Seven Patterns:

Present	Past
Margaret **is** angry.	The movers **were** careless.
She **isn't** happy.	They **weren't** careful.
Is she angry at Jackson Movers?	**Were** they irresponsible?
Yes, she **is**.	Yes, they **were**.
Why **is** she angry?	Why **were** they irresponsible?
Why **isn't** she satisfied?	Why **weren't** they careful?
How many customers **are** angry?	Who **was** careful?

(continued)

² To *lay off* a worker means to take away a worker's job because the company doesn't have enough work for everybody. The worker gets *laid off*.

Uses

Examples	Uses of *be*
Margaret **is** angry.	With a description of the subject
Dallas **is** a city. Texas **is** a state. Abraham Lincoln **was** an American president.	With a classification or definition of the subject
Dallas **is** in Texas. Margaret **wasn't** home yesterday.	With a location
She **is** from New York. Where **are** you from?	With a place of origin
How old **is** Margaret? She **is** 35 years old.	With age
Where **were** you born? I **was** born in Peru.	With *born*
Margaret **is** writing a letter. The movers **were** moving the table.	With a continuous tense
There **is** a problem with Margaret's table. There **were** four movers at Margaret's house.	With *there* to introduce an indefinite noun
The furniture **was** moved by the movers.	With passive voice

EDITING ADVICE

1. Every sentence has a verb. Don't omit the verb *be*.

    is
    My doctor ⌃ a very nice woman.

2. Don't confuse *been* and *being*, *seen* and *seeing*, *taken* and *taking*, *given* and *giving*.

    been
    I have never ~~being~~ in New York.

    taken
    She has ~~taking~~ her daughter to the zoo many times.

3. Don't forget *there* when introducing a new noun.

There a
Are a lot of Spanish-speaking people in my building.

4. Use *be*, not *have*, for age.

is
My sister ~~has~~ 22 years old.

5. Don't omit *be* from a passive sentence.

was
My neighbor ᴧ chosen for jury duty last May.

6. Use the correct form of *be*.

were
Where ~~was~~ you yesterday?

EXERCISE 8   Find the mistakes with the underlined words, and correct them. Not every sentence has a mistake. If the sentence is correct, write **C**.

EXAMPLES:
were
Where ̲ ̲y̲o̲u̲ born?

I ̲a̲m̲ ̲s̲t̲u̲d̲y̲i̲n̲g̲ English.   C

1. Where ̲w̲a̲s̲ ̲y̲o̲u̲ born?

2. ̲W̲h̲e̲r̲e̲'̲s̲ Chicago? ̲I̲t̲'̲s̲ in northern Illinois.

3. Have you ever ̲s̲e̲e̲i̲n̲g̲ a French movie?

4. There ̲a̲r̲e̲ a lot of rain in the spring.

5. ̲A̲r̲e̲ a lot of poor people in the world.

6. What ̲w̲a̲s̲ they doing when the fire started?

7. How long have you ̲b̲e̲i̲n̲g̲ in the U.S.?

8. We ̲w̲a̲s̲ watching a movie on TV when the phone rang.

9. ̲S̲h̲e̲ ̲t̲a̲l̲k̲i̲n̲g̲ on the phone now.

10. ̲M̲y̲ ̲s̲i̲s̲t̲e̲r̲ ̲i̲n̲ Poland now.

11. My son ̲i̲s̲ ten years old.

12. The car ̲s̲t̲o̲l̲e̲n̲ last week.

Infinitives

The Seven Patterns:

With Infinitives
She **needs to fix** the table.
She **doesn't need to fix** the chair.
Does she **need to fix** it immediately?
Yes, she **does**.
Why **does** she **need to fix** it?
Why **doesn't** she **need to fix** the chair?
Who **needs to fix** the table?

Uses:

Examples	Explanation
Mr. Jackson **needs to fix** Margaret's table. Margaret **wants to talk** to Mr. Jackson.	An infinitive is used after many verbs.
She wants the **movers to look** at the table. She wants **them to see** the problem.	An object can be placed before the infinitive.
It's impossible to fix the glass top. **It's important** for the moving company **to have** insurance.	An infinitive is used after some expressions beginning with *it*.
We will be **happy to look** at your table. I'm **sorry to bother** you.	Some adjectives are followed by an infinitive.
She **has to leave** early. They**'ve got to go** home. There **were able to find** an apartment.	*To* is part of these expressions: *have to, have got to, be able to, be supposed to, be going to, be allowed to, be permitted to.*
She used a knife **to open** the boxes. I need a pen **to sign** the contract.	*To* is used to show purpose.

1. Use *to*, not *for*, to show purpose.

> I need a map ~~for~~ find your house. *(to)*

2. Use an object pronoun before an infinitive after certain verbs (*want, need, expect*).

> She wants ~~they~~ fix the table. *(them to)*

3. Use the base form after *to*.

> She wants to ~~going~~ home.
> I decided to ~~left~~ early. *(leave)*

4. Use an infinitive after certain adjectives.

> It's important ^ understand your rights. *(to)*
> I'm happy ^ meet you. *(to)*

5. Use an infinitive after certain verbs.

> I need ^ leave early. *(to)*

EXERCISE 9 Find the mistakes with the underlined words, and correct them. Not every sentence has a mistake. If the sentence is correct, write **C**.

EXAMPLES: I need ^ talk to you. *(to)*

I'm happy <u>to see</u> you. **C**

1. I took a course <u>for learn</u> more about computers.
2. She's not <u>able find</u> a job.
3. She wanted <u>to saw</u> the movie yesterday.
4. I have <u>to explain</u> the problem to you now.
5. Are they going <u>to fix</u> the table?
6. She <u>needs to talks</u> with Mr. Jackson.
7. She called Mr. Jackson because she wants <u>he fix</u> the table.

8. She wants him <u>paid</u> for the damage.

9. We're not supposed <u>to talk</u> during the test.

10. My son wants <u>me to help</u> him with his homework.

11. I don't <u>like write</u> letters.

12. She didn't <u>want him to went</u> home.

13. It's <u>important explain</u> the problem.

14. I've <u>got to talk</u> with you.

15. I'm sorry <u>keep</u> you waiting.

16. They want <u>us to visit</u> them.

17. He wanted <u>to drove</u> my car.

18. I'm not <u>able help</u> you.

15.7   Modals

The Seven Patterns:

With Modals
Jackson Movers **should fix** the table. They **shouldn't ignore** the problem. **Should** they **fix** the table soon? Yes, they **should**. When **should** they **fix** the table? Why **shouldn't** they **ignore** the problem? Who **should fix** the table?

EDITING ADVICE

1.   Always use the base form after a modal.

   I must ~~to~~ see a doctor immediately.

   couldn't go
   She ~~can't went~~ to work yesterday because she was sick.

2.   Don't confuse *don't have to* and *must not*.

   must not
   You ~~don't have to~~ steal. It's against the law.

3. Don't confuse *shouldn't* and *don't have to.*

                  shouldn't
      You ~~don't have to~~ talk in a loud voice in the library.

4. Use correct word order with modals.

      Why you can't help me?

5. Use *not* to make the negative of a modal.

          can't
      I ~~don't can~~ type fast.

6. Use *could,* not *can* for a past meaning.

            couldn't go
      I ~~can't went~~ with you to the party last Saturday.

EXERCISE 10 Find the mistakes with the underlined words, and correct them. Not every sentence has a mistake. If the sentence is correct, write **C.**

EXAMPLES:
          should I
      What ~~I should~~ do about the problem?

      Why <u>can't you</u> go to the party?   C

1. She should <u>talks</u> with her counselor.

2. She <u>doesn't can</u> swim very well.

3. You can't <u>to talk</u> during the test.

4. I can <u>writing</u> well now.

5. She should <u>call</u> the moving company.

6. You <u>don't should</u> make a lot of noise in your apartment.

7. It's going to snow a lot tonight. You <u>don't have to</u> drive.

8. The teacher <u>should explain</u> modals again if the students don't understand them.

9. You <u>must not</u> drive without a license.

10. I <u>can't called</u> you last night because I lost your phone number.

Review of Question Formation

Study these statements and related questions with the verb *be*.

Wh- Word	*Be* (+ *n't*)	Subject	*Be*	Complement
Where	**is**	She she?	**is**	in California.
Why	**were**	They they	**were**	hungry. hungry?
Why	**isn't**	He he	**isn't**	tired. tired?
When	**was**	He he	**was**	born in England. born?
How old	is	She she?	**is**	a teenager.
How tall	**is**	She she?	**is**	tall.
		One student Who Which student	**was** **was** **was**	late. late? late?
		Some kids How many kids Which kids	**were** **were** **were**	afraid. afraid? afraid?

Study these statements and related questions with an auxiliary verb (Aux.) and a main verb.

Wh- Word	Aux. (+ *n't*)	Subject	Aux.	Main Verb	Complement
Where	**is**	She she	**is**	**running**. **running**?	
When	**will**	They they	**will**	**go** **go**	on a vacation. on a vacation?
What	**should**	He he	**should**	**do** **do**?	something.
How many pills	**can**	You you	**can**	**take** **take**?	a pill.

(continued)

Wh- Word	Aux. (+ n't)	Subject	Aux.	Main Verb	Complement
		You	can't	drive	a car.
Why	can't	you		drive	a car?
		They	have	lived	in Boston.
How long	have	they		lived	in Boston?
		Someone	should	answer	the question.
		Who	should	answer	the question?
		Some students	have	done	the homework.
		Which students	have	done	the homework?

Study these statements and related questions with a main verb only.

Wh- Word	Do/Does/ Did (+ n't)	Subject	Verb	Complement
		She	watches	TV.
When	does	she	watch	TV?
		My parents	live	in Peru.
Where	do	your parents	live?	
		Your sister	likes	someone.
Who(m)	does	she	like?	
		They	left	early.
Why	did	they	leave	early?
		The car	cost	a lot of money.
How much	did	the car	cost?	
		She	didn't go	home.
Why	didn't	she	go	home?
		He	doesn't like	tomatoes.
Why	doesn't	he	like	tomatoes?
How	do	you	spell	"calendar"?
How	do	you	say	"calendar" in French?
What	does	"calendar"	mean?	
		Someone	has	my book.
		Who	has	my book?
		Someone	took	my pen.
		Who	took	my pen?

(continued)

Wh- Word	Do/Does/ Did (+ n't)	Subject	Verb	Complement
		One teacher	**speaks**	Spanish.
		Which teacher	**speaks**	Spanish?
		Some men	**have**	a car.
		Which men	**have**	a car?
		Some boys	**saw**	the movie.
		How many boys	**saw**	the movie?
		Something	**happened**.	
		What	**happened**?	

EXERCISE 11 Find the mistakes with the underlined words, and correct them. Not every sentence has a mistake. If the sentence is correct, write C.

EXAMPLES: How long ~~they have~~ *have they* been living in the U.S.?

How many times have they gone to Canada?   C

1. How many people came to the party?

2. Was she buy a new car last month?

3. Did she drove to the party?

4. When your father came to the U.S.?

5. What was you doing when the accident happened?

6. What were they doing at 7:30 in the morning?

7. When arrived the airplane?

8. Who arrived on the airplane?

9. Why didn't you call me last night?

10. What you were doing when the teacher arrived?

11. What profession do your husband have?

12. How often he goes for a haircut?

13. What you will do on your vacation?

14. Who know the answer to my question?

15. When will arrive your father from Vietnam?

16. How spell your name?

16. How spell your name?

17. What means "bug"?

18. What language he's speaking now?

19. When will they know the answer?

20. Who has a dictionary?

21. What happened after the accident?

22. Why you can't finish the job?

23. How much does the textbook cost?

24. How you are old?

25. How tall is your father?

EXERCISE **12** Read the letter of complaint to Jackson Movers again. Fill in the blanks with the correct form of the verb in parentheses ( ). In some cases, more than one answer is possible.

I _am writing_ to you to tell you about a problem that _____
(example: write)   (1 happen)

during my move. Two months ago, your movers _____ me from
                                                (2 move)

7554 N. Oakland to 6761 N. Williams. While they _____ my table
                                                    (3 carry)

upstairs, they _____ it and _____ the corner of the glass top.
                (4 drop)   (5 break)

When I _____ it out to them, they _____ that they would
        (6 point)   (7 say)

speak to the owner about the problem.

I _____ in my new apartment for two months already,
  (8 live)

and so far I _____ anything from your moving company.
             (9 not/hear)

I _____ angry because my table _____ still broken.
  (10 get)   (11 be)

I _____ you _____ to my house as soon as possible so
  (12 want)   (13 come)

that you can look at the damage. When you _____ here, you
                                            (14 come)

_____ that the damage is considerable. I _____
(15 see)   (16 want)

you _____ care of this problem immediately. You _____ for
    (17 take)   (18 can/pay)

the damage or replace the glass top of the table. Please call me when you

_____ this letter so that we can set up an appointment.
(19 receive)

I _____ that you _____ insurance. I _____ your
(20 know)   (21 have)   (22 use)
company before, and I _____ your company to many of my
                            (23 recommend)
friends. However, if you _____ my table, I _____
                              (24 not/fix)   (25 never/use)
your company again. In addition, I _____ my friends that you
                                         (26 tell)
_____ responsibility for damage.
      (27 not/take)
Sincerely,

Margaret Walters

EXERCISE 13 Read each statement. Then change the underlined verb to the
negative form to fill in the blanks.

EXAMPLE: Margaret is <u>writing</u> a letter. She ___*isn't writing*___ a letter to a friend.

1. She's <u>been living</u> in her new apartment for two months. She
   _____ in her apartment for very long.

2. Mr. Jackson <u>will receive</u> an angry letter. He _____
   a letter from a happy customer.

3. The movers <u>broke</u> the glass of her table. They _____
   anything else.

4. Margaret usually <u>writes</u> a letter when she's angry. She _____
   _____ a letter when she's satisfied with the service.

5. In 1999, Margaret <u>was living</u> on Oakland Street. She _____
   _____ on Williams Street.

6. Mr. Jackson <u>needs to fix</u> the glass top. He _____
   the rest of the table.

7. She's <u>going to tell</u> her friends about her problem. She _____
   _____ her friends good things about this company.

8. Jackson Movers <u>can ignore</u> the problem. Margaret _____
   _____ the problem.

EXERCISE 14 Read each statement. Then write a question with the words in parentheses ( ). An answer is not necessary.

EXAMPLE: Margaret is angry. (why)

Why is she angry?

1. Margaret moved to a new apartment. (when)

2. She lived in her old apartment for ten years. (how long/in her new apartment) (*Be careful*: The question has a different tense.)

3. She's complaining. (why)

4. Mr. Jackson will receive her letter. (when)

5. She won't use this company again. (why)

6. Someone broke the table. (who)

7. Mr. Jackson should pay Margaret. (how much)

8. Margaret wants him to look at the table. (when)

9. Mr. Jackson hasn't called her. (why)

10. Margaret is going to tell someone about her problem. (whom)

11. Margaret has used this company before. (how many times)

12. She wants Mr. Jackson to do something. (what)

13. While the movers were carrying the table, they dropped it. (where/they/carry/when/they/drop/it)

_____

14. The table cost a lot of money. (how much)

_____

15.9 Sentence Structure and Word Order

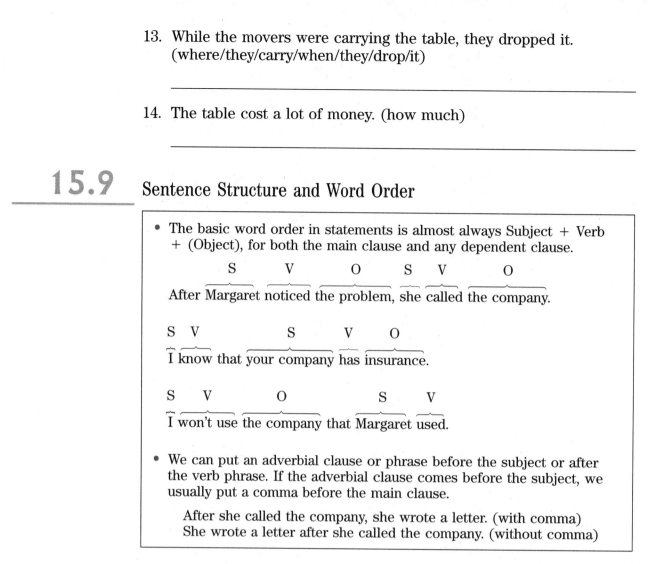

- The basic word order in statements is almost always Subject + Verb + (Object), for both the main clause and any dependent clause.

       S   V   O   S   V   O
  After Margaret noticed the problem, she called the company.

  S V   S   V   O
  I know that your company has insurance.

  S   V   O   S   V
  I won't use the company that Margaret used.

- We can put an adverbial clause or phrase before the subject or after the verb phrase. If the adverbial clause comes before the subject, we usually put a comma before the main clause.

  After she called the company, she wrote a letter. (with comma)
  She wrote a letter after she called the company. (without comma)

EDITING ADVICE ✏

1. Every sentence must have a verb.

                  _is_
   My teacher ˄ very nice.

2. Every verb must have a subject.[3]

   _It is_
   ~~Is~~ important to speak English well.

                               _it_
   He didn't understand the lesson because ˄ was too hard.

   There are
   ~~Are~~ a lot of Asian students at this college.

[3] An imperative sentence omits the subject: _Sit down. Listen to me._

3. Put the subject before the verb in all clauses.

The workers left when ~~was finished the meeting~~. *the meeting was finished*

Everything that ~~said the teacher~~ is true. *the teacher said*

4. An adverbial phrase or clause (time, place, reason) can come before the subject or at the end of the verb phrase. Do not put a phrase between the subject and the verb.

She (once in a while) takes the bus to work.

5. Do not separate the verb from the object.

She speaks (fluently) English.

6. If a compound subject includes *I*, put *I* at the end.

~~I and my brother~~ went to Miami. *My brother and I*

7. Do not start with a pronoun and put the subject at the end. Start with the subject noun.

~~It's very beautiful your car.~~ *Your car is very beautiful.*

8. Do not repeat the subject with a pronoun.

My father ~~he~~ works as an engineer.

9. Put a one-word adverb between the subject and simple verb; after the verb *be*; between the auxiliary verb and the main verb.

She ~~drinks never~~ coffee at night. *never drinks*

I have ~~gone never~~ to Paris. *never gone*

She ~~probably is~~ proud of her son. *is probably*

10. Don't use a double negative in a sentence.

She doesn't have ~~no~~ time to study. *any*

I didn't understand ~~nothing~~. *any*

11. Don't put an object between a modal and a main verb.

I shouldn't ~~ice cream eat~~. *eat ice cream*

EXERCISE 15 Find and correct the mistakes with missing words, extra words, double negatives, and word order. Not every sentence has a mistake. If the sentence is correct, write **C**.

EXAMPLES:

My wife came late because ^she couldn't find a parking space.

After the teacher left, the students began to talk.   C

1. I and my sister went to the movies.

2. Before arrived his father, he was very unhappy.

3. She read very quickly the letter.

4. We from time to time go to a baseball game.

5. She 25 years old.

6. She can't the lesson understand.

7. The class began when the teacher arrived.

8. It's very expensive their house.

9. The car that bought my brother cost $5000.

10. Is very interesting your composition.

11. Are a lot of new books in the library.

12. London a very beautiful city.

13. He didn't go skiing yesterday because was too cold.

14. Every sentence that the student wrote was correct.

15. My wife made dinner when came home from work.

16. Is important to speak English well.

17. I didn't understand nothing the teacher said.

18. I go to bed usually at 11:30.

19. I'm usually tired after work.

20. You should bring always your dictionary to class.

21. I have never met your wife.

22. My wife she is very intelligent.

23. He doesn't have no money for college.

EXPANSION ACTIVITIES

CLASSROOM ACTIVITIES

1. Find a partner. Find out as much as you can about your partner and his or her native country. Tell the class a few interesting things you learned about your partner.

Sample interview:

A. Where are you from?
B. I'm from Colombia.
A. How long have you been in the U.S.?
B. For two years.
A. Are you married?
B. Yes, I am.
A. How long have you been married?
B. For three years.
A. Is your husband studying English too?
B. No, he isn't. He's working.
A. Are you going to return to your country?
B. Only for a vacation. I live here now.

2. Work with a partner. Write five questions to ask your teacher.

Sample questions and answers:

A. How long have you been teaching English?
B. For ten years.
A. What other languages do you speak?
B. French and Polish.
A. Where did you learn Polish?
B. From my parents. They were born in Poland.

WRITING

1. Use the model letter on page 420 to write your own letter. Complain about a product you bought or a service you used. State what the problem is and how you want the company to help you solve it. Write about a situation that is real for you. If you can't think of a real problem, choose one of the imaginary problems below:

a. A mechanic fixed your car. You paid $500, but you still have the same problem.
b. You bought a very expensive shirt. When you washed it, it was ruined. You tried to return it to the store where you bought it, and they told you to write to the manufacturer.
c. The college where you are studying English has decided to cancel all ESL classes because they want to save money. You are angry. Write to the president of the college.
d. You gave your landlord a security deposit. You moved out two months ago, and he hasn't returned your money.

2. Write a letter to a company about a product you like. Tell how long you've been using this product and why you like it.

Interview an American about his or her life. Invite the American to interview you too. Report to the class something interesting you learned about this person.

Internet Activity

Choose a famous person or event that has been in the news recently. Use the Internet to find information about this person or event. Print an article. Circle all the verbs in the article. Identify the tenses.

Appendices

Spelling and Pronunciation of Verbs

Spelling of the *-S* Form of Verbs

Rule	Base Form	*-S* Form
Add *s* to most verbs to make the -s form.	hope eat	hopes eats
When the base form ends in *s*, *z*, *sh*, *ch*, or *x*, add *es* and pronounce an extra syllable, /əz/.	miss buzz wash catch fix	misses buzzes washes catches fixes
When the base form ends in a consonant + *y*, change the *y* to *i* and add *es*.	carry worry	carries worries
When the base form ends in a vowel + *y*, do not change the *y*.	pay obey	pays obeys
Add *es* to *go* and *do*.	go do	goes does

Pronunciation of the *-S* Form
The -s form has three pronunciations.

A. We pronounce /s/ if the verb ends in these voiceless sounds: /**p t k f**/.

    hope—hopes   pick—picks

    eat—eats   laugh—laughs

B. We pronounce /**z**/ if the verb ends in most voiced sounds.

    live—lives   read—reads   sing—sings

    grab—grabs   run—runs   borrow—borrows

C. When the base form ends in *s, z, sh, ch, x, se, ge,* or *ce,* we pronounce an extra syllable, /əz/.

miss—misses	watch—watches	change—changes
buzz—buzzes	fix—fixes	dance—dances
wash—washes	use—uses	

D. These verbs have a change in the vowel sound.

do /**du**/—does /**dʌz**/

say /**sei**/—says /**sɛz**/

Spelling of the *-ing* Form of Verbs

Rule	Base Form	*-ing* Form
Add *ing* to most verbs.	eat go study	eating going studying
For a one-syllable verb that ends in a consonant + vowel + consonant (CVC), double the final consonant and add *ing*.	p l a n | | | C V C s t o p | | | C V C s i t | | | C V C	planning stopping sitting
Do not double final *w, x,* or *y*.	show mix stay	showing mixing staying
For a two-syllable word that ends in CVC, double the final consonant only if the last syllable is stressed.	refér admít begín	referring admitting beginning
When the last syllable of a two-syllable word is not stressed, do not double the final consonant.	lísten ópen óffer	listening opening offering
If the word ends in a consonant + *e*, drop the *e* before adding *ing*.	live take write	living taking writing

Spelling of the Past Tense of Regular Verbs

Rule	Base Form	-ed Form
Add *ed* to the base form to make the past tense of most regular verbs.	start kick	started kicked
When the base form ends in *e*, add *d* only.	die live	died lived
When the base form ends in a consonant + *y*, change the *y* to *i* and add *ed*.	carry worry	carried worried
When the base form ends in a vowel + *y*, do not change the *y*.	destroy stay	destroyed stayed
For a one-syllable word that ends in a consonant + vowel + consonant (CVC), double the final consonant and add *ed*.	s t o p | | | C V C p l u g | | | C V C	stopped plugged
Do not double final *w* or *x*.	sew fix	sewed fixed
For a two-syllable word that ends in CVC, double the final consonant only if the last syllable is stressed.	occúr permít	occurred permitted
When the last syllable of a two-syllable word is not stressed, do not double the final consonant.	ópen háppen	opened happened

Pronunciation of Past Forms That End in *-ed*

The past tense with *-ed* has three pronunciations.

A. We pronounce a /**t**/ if the base form ends in these voiceless sounds: /**p, k, f, s, š, č**/.

jump—jumped	cough—coughed	wash—washed
cook—cooked	kiss—kissed	watch—watched

B. We pronounce a /**d**/ if the base form ends in most voiced sounds.

rub—rubbed	charge—charged	bang—banged
drag—dragged	glue—glued	call—called
love—loved	massage—massaged	fear—feared
bathe—bathed	name—named	free—freed
use—used	learn—learned	

C. We pronounce an extra syllable /**əd**/ if the base form ends in a /**t**/ or /**d**/ sound.

wait—waited	want—wanted	need—needed
hate—hated	add—added	decide—decided

Spelling of Short Comparative and Superlative Adjectives and Adverbs

A. For most short adjectives and adverbs, we add *-er* to make the comparative form and *-est* to make the superlative form.
> old—older—oldest
> tall—taller—tallest
> fast—faster—fastest

B. If the word ends in *-e*, just add *r* or *st*.
> nice—nicer—nicest
> fine—finer—finest

C. For adjectives that end in *-y*, change *y* to *i* before adding *–er* or *–est*.
> happy—happier—happiest
> healthy—healthier—healthiest
> sunny—sunnier—sunniest

NOTE: Do not add *–er* or *–est* to an *-ly* adverb.
> quickly—more quickly—most quickly

D. For one-syllable words that end in consonant-vowel-consonant, we double the final consonant before adding *–er* or *–est*.
> big—bigger—biggest
> sad—sadder—saddest
> hot—hotter—hottest

EXCEPTION: Do not double final *w*.
> new—newer—newest

Spelling Rules for Adverbs Ending in *-ly*

1. Most adverbs of manner are formed by putting *-ly* at the end of an adjective.

Adjective	*Adverb*
careful	carefully
quiet	quietly
illegal	illegally

2. For adjectives that end in *-y*, we change *y* to *i*, then add *-ly*.
> easy—easily
> happy—happily
> lucky—luckily

3. For adjectives that end in *-e*, we keep the *e* and add *-ly*.
> nice—nicely
> free—freely

EXCEPTION:
> true—truly

4. For adjectives that end in a consonant + *-ly*, we drop the *e* and add *-ly*.
> simple—simply
> comfortable—comfortably
> double—doubly

5. For adjectives that end in *-ic*, add *-ally*.
> basic—basically
> enthusiastic—enthusiastically

EXCEPTION:
> public—publicly

APPENDIX D

Metric Conversion Chart

LENGTH

When You Know	Symbol	Multiply by	To Find	Symbol
inches	in	2.54	centimeters	cm
feet	ft	30.5	centimeters	cm
feet	ft	0.3	meters	m
yards	yd	0.91	meters	m
miles	mi	1.6	kilometers	km
centimeters	cm	0.39	inches	in
centimeters	cm	0.32	feet	ft
meter	m	3.28	feet	ft
meters	m	1.09	yards	yd
kilometers	km	0.62	miles	mi

NOTE: 1 foot = 12 inches, 1 yard = 3 feet or 36 inches

AREA

When You Know	Symbol	Multiply by	To Find	Symbol
square inches	in²	6.5	square centimeters	cm²
square feet	ft²	0.09	square meters	m²
square yards	yd²	0.8	square meters	m²
square miles	mi²	2.6	square kilometers	km²

When You Know	Symbol	Multiply by	To Find	Symbol
square centimeters	cm²	0.16	square inches	in²
square meters	m²	10.76	square feet	ft²
square meters	m²	1.2	square yards	yd²
square kilometers	km²	0.39	square miles	mi²

WEIGHT (Mass)

When You Know	Symbol	Multiply by	To Find	Symbol
ounces	oz	28.35	grams	g
pounds	lb	0.45	kilograms	kg

When You Know	Symbol	Multiply by	To Find	Symbol
grams	g	0.04	ounces	oz
kilograms	kg	2.2	pounds	lb

NOTE: 16 ounces = 1 pound

VOLUME

When You Know	Symbol	Multiply by	To Find	Symbol
fluid ounces	fl oz	30.0	milliliters	mL
pints	pt	0.47	liters	L
quarts	qt	0.95	liters	L
gallons	gal	3.8	liters	L

When You Know	Symbol	Multiply by	To Find	Symbol
milliliters	mL	0.03	fluid ounces	fl oz
liters	L	2.11	pints	pt
liters	L	1.05	quarts	qt
liters	L	0.26	gallons	gal

TEMPERATURE

When You Know	Symbol	Do This	To Find	Symbol
degrees Fahrenheit	°F	Subtract 32, then multiply by 5/9	degrees Celsius	°C

When You Know	Symbol	Do This	To Find	Symbol
degrees Celsius	°C	Multiply by 9/5, then add 32	degrees Fahrenheit	°F

Sample temperatures:

Fahrenheit	Celsius	Fahrenheit	Celsius
0	−18	60	16
10	−12	70	21
20	−7	80	27
30	−1	90	32
40	4	100	38
50	10		

APPENDIX E

The Verb *GET*

Get has many meanings. Here is a list of the most common ones:

• get something = receive

   I got a letter from my father.

• get + (to) place = arrive

   I got home at six. What time do you get to school?

• get + object + infinitive = persuade

   She got him to wash the dishes.

- get + past participle = become

get acquainted	get worried	get hurt
get engaged	get lost	get bored
get married	get accustomed to	get confused
get divorced	get used to	get scared
get tired	get dressed	

They got married in 1989.

- get + adjective = become

get hungry	get sleepy
get rich	get fat
get nervous	get dark
get well	get angry
get upset	get old

It gets dark at 6:30.

- get an illness = catch

While I was traveling, I got malaria.

- get a joke or an idea = understand

Everybody except Tom laughed at the joke. He didn't get it.

The boss explained the project to us, but I didn't get it.

- get ahead = advance

He works very hard because he wants to get ahead in his job.

- get along (well) (with someone) = have a good relationship

She doesn't get along with her mother-in-law.

Do you and your roommate get along well?

- get around to something = find the time to do something

I wanted to write my brother a letter yesterday, but I didn't get around to it.

- get away = escape

The police chased the thief, but he got away.

- get away with something = escape punishment

He cheated on his taxes and got away with it.

- get back = return

He got back from his vacation last Saturday.

- get back at someone = get revenge

My brother wants to get back at me for stealing his girlfriend.

- get back to someone = communicate with someone at a later time

I can't talk to you today. Can I get back to you tomorrow?

- get by = have just enough but nothing more

    On her salary, she's just getting by. She can't afford a car or a vacation.

- get in trouble = be caught and punished for doing something wrong

    They got in trouble for cheating on the test.

- get in(to) = enter a car

    She got in the car and drove away quickly.

- get out (of) = leave a car

    When the taxi arrived at the theater, everyone got out.

- get on = seat yourself on a bicycle, motorcycle, horse

    She got on the motorcycle and left.

- get on = enter a train, bus, airplane

    She got on the bus and took a seat in the back.

- get off = leave a bicycle, motorcycle, horse, train, bus, airplane

    They will get off the train at the next stop.

- get out of something = escape responsibility

    My boss wants me to help him on Saturday, but I'm going to try to get out of it.

- get over something = recover from an illness or disappointment

    She has the flu this week. I hope she gets over it soon.

- get rid of someone or something = free oneself of someone or something undesirable

    My apartment has roaches, and I can't get rid of them.

- get through (to someone) = communicate, often by telephone

    She tried to explain the harm of eating fast food to her son, but she couldn't get through to him.

    I tried to call my mother many times, but her line was busy. I couldn't get through.

- get through with something = finish

    I can meet you after I get through with my homework.

- get together = meet with another person

    I'd like to see you again. When can we get together?

- get up = arise from bed

    He woke up at 6 o'clock, but he didn't get up until 6:30.

MAKE and *DO*

Some expressions use *make*. Others use *do*.

Make

make a date/an appointment
make a plan
make a decision
make a telephone call
make a reservation
make a mistake
make an effort
make an improvement
make a promise

make money
make noise
make the bed

Do

do (the) homework
do an exercise
do the dishes
do the cleaning, laundry,
    ironing, washing, etc.
do the shopping

do one's best
do a favor
do the right/wrong thing
do a job
do business
What do you do for a living?
    (asks about a job)
How do you do? (said when
    you meet someone for the
    first time)

Nouns That Can Be Both Count or Noncount

In the following cases, the same word can be a count or a noncount noun. The meaning is different, however.

Noncount	Count
I spent a lot of *time* on my project.	I go shopping two *times* a month.
I have a lot of *experience* with computers.	I had a lot of interesting *experiences* on my trip to Europe.

In the following cases, there is a small difference in meaning. We see a noncount noun as a whole unit. We see a count noun as something that can be divided into parts:

Noncount	Count
There is a lot of *crime* in a big city.	A lot of *crimes* are never solved.
There is a lot of *opportunity* to make money in the U.S.	There are a lot of job *opportunities* in my field.
She bought a lot of *fruit*.	Oranges and lemons are *fruits* that have a lot of Vitamin C.
I don't have much *food* in my refrigerator.	Milk and butter are *foods* that contain cholesterol.
I have a lot of *trouble* with my car.	He has many *troubles* in his life.

Verbs and Adjectives Followed by a Preposition

accuse someone of	(be) familiar with	pray for
(be) accustomed to	(be) famous for	(be) prepared for
adjust to	feel like	prevent someone from
(be) afraid of	(be) fond of	prohibit from
agree with	forget about	protect from
(be) amazed at/by	forgive someone for	(be) proud of
(be) angry about	(be) glad about	recover from
(be) angry at/with	(be) good at	(be) related to
apologize for	(be) grateful to someone for	rely on/upon
approve of	(be) guilty of	(be) responsible for
argue about	(be) happy about	(be) sad about
argue with	hear about	(be) satisfied with
(be) ashamed of	hear of	(be) scared of
(be) aware of	hope for	(be) sick of
believe in	(be) incapable of	(be) sorry about/for
blame someone for	insist on/upon	speak about
(be) bored with/by	(be) interested in	speak to/with
(be) capable of	(be) involved in	succeed in
care about/for	(be) jealous of	(be) sure of/about
compare to/with	(be) known for	(be) surprised at
complain about	(be) lazy about	take care of
(be) concerned about	listen to	talk about
concentrate on	look at	talk to/with
consist of	look for	thank someone for
count on	look forward to	(be) thankful to someone for
deal with	(be) mad about	think about/of
decide on	(be) mad at	(be) tired of
depend on/upon	(be) made from/of	(be) upset about
(be) different from	(be) married to	(be) upset with
disapprove of	object to	(be) used to
(be) divorced from	(be) opposed to	wait for
dream about/of	participate in	warn (someone) about
(be) engaged to	plan on	(be) worried about
(be) excited about	pray to	worry about

Direct and Indirect Objects

1. The order of direct and indirect objects depends on the verb you use.

$$\underset{\text{He told }\underbrace{\text{his friend}}\underbrace{\text{ the answer.}}}{\text{IO} \qquad\qquad \text{DO}}$$

IO   DO

He told his friend the answer.

    DO   IO

He explained the answer to his friend.

2. The order of the objects sometimes depends on whether you use a noun or a pronoun object.

S   V   IO   DO
He gave the woman the keys.

S   V   DO   IO
He gave them to her.

3. In some cases, the connecting preposition is *to;* in some cases, *for.* In some cases, there is no connecting preposition.

She'll serve lunch *to* her guests.
She reserved a seat *for* you.
I asked him a question.

Each of the following groups of words follows a specific pattern of word order and preposition choice.

Group I   **Pronouns affect word order.** The preposition is *to.*

Patterns: He gave a present to his wife. (DO to IO)
He gave his wife a present. (IO/DO)
He gave it to his wife. (DO to IO)
He gave her a present. (IO/DO)
He gave it to her. (DO to IO)

Verbs: | bring | lend | pass | sell | show | teach |
|-------|------|------|------|------|-------|
| give | offer | pay | send | sing | tell |
| hand | owe | read | serve | take | write |

Group II   **Pronouns affect word order.** The preposition is *for.*

Patterns: He bought a car for his daughter. (DO for IO)
He bought his daughter a car. (IO/DO)
He bought it for his daughter. (DO for IO)
He bought her a car. (IO/DO)
He bought it for her. (DO for IO)

Verbs: | bake | buy | draw | get | make |
|-------|-----|------|-----|------|
| build | do | find | knit | reserve |

Group III **Pronouns don't affect word order.** The preposition is *to.*

Patterns: He explained the problem to his friend. (DO to IO)
He explained it to her. (DO to IO)

Verbs: | admit | introduce | recommend | say |
|-------|-----------|-----------|-----|
| announce | mention | repeat | speak |
| describe | prove | report | suggest |
| explain | | | |

Group IV **Pronouns don't affect word order.** The preposition is *for.*

Patterns: He cashed a check for his friend. (DO for IO)
            He cashed it for her. (DO for IO)

Verbs: answer   change   design   open   prescribe
         cash   close   fix   prepare   pronounce

Group V **Pronouns don't affect word order.** No preposition is used.

Patterns: She asked the teacher a question. (IO/DO)
            She asked him a question. (IO/DO)
            It took me five minutes to answer the question. (IO/DO)

Verbs: ask   charge   cost   wish   take (with time)

APPENDIX J

Capitalization Rules

- The first word in a sentence: **M**y friends are helpful.

- The word "I": My sister and **I** took a trip together.

- Names of people: **M**ichael **J**ackson; **G**eorge **W**ashington

- Titles preceding names of people: **D**octor (**D**r.) **S**mith; **P**resident **L**incoln; **Q**ueen **E**lizabeth; **M**r. **R**ogers; **M**rs. **C**arter

- Geographic names: the **U**nited **S**tates; **L**ake **S**uperior; **C**alifornia; the **R**ocky **M**ountains; the **M**ississippi **R**iver

  NOTE: The word "the" in a geographic name is not capitalized.

- Street names: **P**ennsylvania **A**venue (**A**ve.); **W**all **S**treet (**S**t.); **A**bbey **R**oad (**R**d.)

- Names of organizations, companies, colleges, buildings, stores, hotels: the **R**epublican **P**arty; **H**einle and **H**einle **P**ublishers; **D**artmouth **C**ollege; the **U**niversity of **W**isconsin; the **W**hite **H**ouse; **B**loomingdale's; the **H**ilton **H**otel

- Nationalities and ethnic groups: **M**exicans; **C**anadians; **S**paniards; **A**mericans; **J**ews; **K**urds; **E**skimos

- Languages: **E**nglish; **S**panish; **P**olish; **V**ietnamese; **R**ussian

- Months: **J**anuary; **F**ebruary

- Days: **S**unday; **M**onday

- Holidays: **C**hristmas; **I**ndependence **D**ay

- Important words in a title: **G**rammar in **C**ontext; **T**he **O**ld **M**an and the **S**ea; **R**omeo and **J**uliet; **T**he **S**ound of **M**usic

  NOTE: Capitalize "the" as the first word of a title.

Glossary of Grammatical Terms

- **Adjective** An adjective gives a description of a noun.

    It's a *tall* tree.   He's an *old* man.   My neighbors are *nice*.

- **Adverb** An adverb describes the action of a sentence or an adjective or another adverb.

    She speaks English *fluently*.   I drive *carefully*.

    She speaks English *extremely* well.   She is *very* intelligent.

- **Adverb of Frequency** An adverb of frequency tells how often the action happens.

    I *never* drink coffee.   They *usually* take the bus.

- **Affirmative** means *yes*.

- **Apostrophe** '

- **Article** The definite article is *the*. The indefinite articles are *a* and *an*.

    I have *a* cat.   I ate *an* apple.   *The* President was in New York last weekend.

- **Auxiliary Verb** Some verbs have two parts: an auxiliary verb and a main verb.

    He <u>*can't*</u> study.   We <u>*will*</u> return.

- **Base Form** The base form of the verb has no tense. It has no ending (*-s* or *-ed*): *be, go, eat, take, write*

    I didn't *go* out.   He doesn't *know* the answer.   You shouldn't *talk* loud.

- **Capital Letter** A B C D E F G . . .

- **Clause** A clause is a group of words that has a subject and a verb. Some sentences have only one clause.

    She speaks Spanish.

Some sentences have a **main clause** and a **dependent clause.**

MAIN CLAUSE	**DEPENDENT CLAUSE (reason clause)**
She found a good job	because she has computer skills.
MAIN CLAUSE	**DEPENDENT CLAUSE (time clause)**
She'll turn off the light	before she goes to bed.
MAIN CLAUSE	**DEPENDENT CLAUSE (*if* clause)**
I'll take you to the doctor	if you don't have your car on Saturday.

- **Colon :**

- **Comma ,**

- **Comparative Form** A comparative form of an adjective or adverb is used to compare two things.

    My house is *bigger* than your house.

    Her husband drives *faster* than she does.

- **Complement** The complement of the sentence is the information after the verb. It completes the verb phrase.

  He works *hard*.   I slept *for five hours*.   They are *late*.

- **Consonant** The following letters are consonants: *b, c, d, f, g, h, j, k, l, m, n, p, q, r, s, t, v, w, x, y, z.*

  NOTE: *y* is sometimes considered a vowel.

- **Contraction** A contraction is made up of two words put together with an apostrophe.

  He's my brother.   *You're* late.   They *won't* talk to me.
  (*He's = he is*)   (*You're = you are*)   (*won't = will not*)

- **Count Noun** Count nouns are nouns that we can count. They have a singular and a plural form.

  1 pen / 3 pens   1 table / 4 tables

- **Dependent Clause** See **Clause**.

- **Direct Object** A direct object is a noun (phrase) or pronoun that receives the action of the verb.

  We saw *the movie*.   You have *a nice car*.   I love *you*.

- **Exclamation Mark !**

- **Hyphen -**

- **Imperative** An imperative sentence gives a command or instructions. An imperative sentence omits the word *you*.

  Come here.   *Don't be* late.   Please *sit* down.

- **Indefinite Pronoun** An indefinite pronoun (*one, some, any*) takes the place of an indefinite noun.

  I have a cell phone. Do you have *one*?

  I didn't drink any coffee, but you drank *some*. Did he drink *any*?

- **Infinitive** An infinitive is *to* + base form.

  I want *to leave*.   You need *to be* here on time.

- **Linking Verb** A linking verb is a verb that links the subject to the noun or adjective after it. Linking verbs include *be, seem, feel, smell, sound, look, appear, taste.*

  She *is* a doctor.   She *seems* very intelligent.   She *looks* tired.

- **Modal** The modal verbs are *can, could, shall, should, will, would, may, might, must.*

  They *should* leave.   I *must* go.

- **Negative** means *no*.

- **Nonaction Verb** A nonaction verb has no action. We do not use a continuous tense (*be* + verb *-ing*) with a nonaction verb. The nonaction verbs are: *believe,* *cost, care, have, hear, know, like, love, matter, mean, need, own, prefer, remember, see, seem, think, understand, want*

• **Noncount Noun** A noncount noun is a noun that we don't count. It has no plural form.

> She drank some *water.*   He prepared some *rice.*   Do you need any *money*?

• **Noun** A noun is a person (*brother*), a place (*kitchen*) or a thing (*table*). Nouns can be either count (*1 table, 2 tables*) or noncount (*money, water*).

> My *brother* lives in California. My *sisters* live in New York. I get *mail* from them.

• **Noun Modifier** A noun modifier makes a noun more specific.

> *fire* department   *Independence* Day   *can* opener

• **Noun Phrase** A noun phrase is a group of words that form the subject or object of the sentence.

> *A very nice woman* helped me at registration.
>
> I bought *a big box of candy.*

• **Object** The object of the sentence follows a verb or a preposition.

> He bought *a car.*   I saw *a movie.*   She travels with *me.*

• **Object Pronoun** Use object pronouns (*me, you, him, her, it, us, them*) after the verb or preposition.

> He likes *her.*   I saw the movie. Did you see *it*?

• **Parentheses** ( )

• **Paragraph** A paragraph is a group of sentences about one topic.

• **Participle, Present** The present participle is verb + *-ing.*

> She is *sleeping.*   They were *laughing.*

• **Period** .

• **Phrase** A group of words that go together.

> *Last month* my sister came to visit.
>
> There is a strange car *in front of my house.*

• **Plural** Plural means more than one. A plural noun usually ends with *-s.*

> She has beautiful *eyes.*

• **Possessive Form** Possessive forms show ownership or relationship.

> *Mary's* coat is in the closet.   *My* brother lives in Miami.

• **Preposition** A preposition is a short connecting word: *about, above, across, after, around, as, at, away, back, before, behind, below, by, down, for, from, in, into, like, of, off, on, out, over, to, under, up, with.*

- **Pronoun** A pronoun takes the place of a noun.

  I have a new car. I bought *it* last week.

  John likes Mary, but *she* doesn't like *him*.

- **Punctuation** Period . Comma , Colon : Semicolon ; Question Mark ? Exclamation Mark !

- **Question Mark** ?

- **Quotation Marks** " "

- **Regular Verb** A regular verb forms its past tense with *-ed*.

  He *worked* yesterday.   I *laughed* at the joke.

- **Sense-Perception Verb** A sense-perception verb has no action. It describes a sense.

  She *feels* fine.   The coffee *smells* fresh.   The milk *tastes* sour.

- **Sentence** A sentence is a group of words that contains a subject[1] and a verb (at least) and gives a complete thought.

  Sentence: She came home.

  Not a sentence: When she came home

- **Simple Form of Verb** The simple form of the verb has no tense; it never has an *-s*, *-ed*, or *-ing* ending.

  Did you *see* the movie?

  I couldn't *find* your phone number.

- **Singular** Singular means one.

  She ate *a sandwich*.   I have one *television*.

- **Subject** The subject of the sentence tells who or what the sentence is about.

  My sister got married last April. *The wedding* was beautiful.

- **Subject Pronoun** Use subject pronouns (*I, you, he, she, it, we, you, they*) before a verb.

  They speak Japanese.   *We* speak Spanish.

- **Superlative Form** A superlative form of an adjective or adverb shows the number one item in a group of three or more.

  January is the *coldest* month of the year.

  My brother speaks English the *best* in my family.

- **Syllable** A syllable is a part of a word that has only one vowel sound. (Some words have only one syllable.)

  change (one syllable)   after (af·ter = 2 syllables)

  look (one syllable)   responsible (re·spon·si·ble = 4 syllables)

---

[1] In an imperative sentence, the subject *you* is omitted: *Sit down. Come here.*

- **Tag Question** A tag question is a short question at the end of a sentence. It is used in conversation.

    You speak Spanish, *don't you?*

    He's not happy, *is he?*

- **Tense** A verb has tense. Tense shows when the action of the sentence happened.

    SIMPLE PRESENT: She usually *works* hard.

    FUTURE: She *will work* tomorrow.

    PRESENT CONTINUOUS: She *is working* now.

    SIMPLE PAST: She *worked* yesterday.

- **Verb** A verb is the action of the sentence.

    He *runs* fast.   I *speak* English.

    Some verbs have no action. They are linking verbs. They connect the subject to the rest of the sentence.

    He *is* tall.   She *looks* beautiful.   You *seem* tired.

- **Vowel** The following letters are vowels: *a, e, i, o, u. Y* is sometimes considered a vowel (for example, in the word *mystery*).

APPENDIX L

Special Uses of Articles

No Article	Article

Personal names:
    John Kennedy
    Michael Jackson
	The whole family:
	    the Kennedys
	    the Jacksons

Title and name:
    Queen Elizabeth
    Pope John Paul
	Title without name:
	    the Queen
	    the Pope

Cities, states, countries, continents:
    Cleveland
    Ohio
    Mexico
    South America
	Places that are considered a union:
	    the United States
	    the former Soviet Union
	    the United Kingdom
	Place names: the _____ of _____
	    the Republic of China
	    the District of Columbia

Mountains
    Mount Everest
    Mount McKinley
	Mountain ranges:
	    the Himalayas
	    the Rocky Mountains

Islands:
    Coney Island
    Staten Island
	Collectives of islands:
	    the Hawaiian Islands
	    the Virgin Islands
	    the Philippines

No Article	Article

Lakes:
    Lake Superior
    Lake Michigan
	Collectives of lakes:
	    the Great Lakes
	    the Finger Lakes

Beaches:
    Palm Beach
    Pebble Beach
	Rivers, oceans, seas, canals:
	    the Mississippi River
	    the Atlantic Ocean
	    the Dead Sea
	    the Panama Canal

Streets and avenues:
    Madison Avenue
    Wall Street
	Well-known buildings:
	    the Sears Tower
	    the World Trade Center

Parks:
    Central Park
    Hyde Park
	Zoos:
	    the San Diego Zoo
	    the Milwaukee Zoo

Seasons:
    summer   fall
    spring   winter
    Summer is my favorite season.
NOTE: After a preposition, *the* may
be used.
    In (the) winter, my car runs
        badly.
	Deserts:
	    the Mojave Desert
	    the Sahara Desert

Directions:
    north   south
    east   west
	Sections of a piece of land:
	    the Southwest (of the U.S.)
	    the West Side (of New York)

School subjects:
    history
    math
	Unique geographical points:
	    the North Pole
	    the Vatican

Name + *college* or *university:*
    Northwestern University
    Bradford College
	The University (College) of _____
	    the University of Michigan
	    the College of DuPage County

Magazines:
    Time
    Sports Illustrated
	Newspapers:
	    the *Tribune*
	    the *Wall Street Journal*

Months and days:
    September
    Monday
	Ships:
	    the *Titanic*
	    the *Queen Elizabeth*

Holidays and Dates
(Month + Day)
    Thanksgiving
    Mother's Day
    July 4
	The day of (month)
	    the Fourth of July
	    the fifth of May

Diseases:
    cancer
    polio
    AIDS
    malaria
	Ailments:
	    a cold
	    a headache
	    a toothache
	    the flu

No Article	Article

Games and sports:
    poker
    soccer
	Musical instruments, after *play:*
	    the drums
	    the piano
	NOTE: Sometimes *the* is omitted.
	    She plays (the) drums.

Languages:
    French
    English
	The _____ language:
	    the French language
	    the English language

Last month, year, week, etc. = the one before this one:
    I forgot to pay my rent last month.
    The teacher gave us a test last week.
	The last month, the last year, the last week, etc. = the last in a series:
	    December is the last month of the year.
	    Summer vacation begins the last week in May.

In office = in an elected position:
    The president is in office for four years.
	In the office = in a specific room:
	    The teacher is in the office.

In back/front:
    She's in back of the car (1).
	In the back/the front:
	    He's in the back of the bus (2).

(1)

(2)

APPENDIX M

Alphabetical List of Irregular Verb Forms

Base Form	Past Form	Past Participle	Base Form	Past Form	Past Participle
be	was/were	been	choose	chose	chosen
bear	bore	born/borne	cling	clung	clung
beat	beat	beaten	come	came	come
become	became	become	cost	cost	cost
begin	began	begun	creep	crept	crept
bend	bent	bent	cut	cut	cut
bet	bet	bet	deal	dealt	dealt
bind	bound	bound	dig	dug	dug
bite	bit	bitten	do	did	done
bleed	bled	bled	draw	drew	drawn
blow	blew	blown	drink	drank	drunk
break	broke	broken	drive	drove	driven
breed	bred	bred	eat	ate	eaten
bring	brought	brought	fall	fell	fallen
broadcast	broadcast	broadcast	feed	fed	fed
build	built	built	feel	felt	felt
burst	burst	burst	fight	fought	fought
buy	bought	bought	find	found	found
cast	cast	cast	fit	fit	fit
catch	caught	caught	flee	fled	fled

Base Form	Past Form	Past Participle	Base Form	Past Form	Past Participle
fly	flew	flown	shut	shut	shut
forbid	forbade	forbidden	sing	sang	sung
forget	forgot	forgotten	sink	sank	sunk
forgive	forgave	forgiven	sit	sat	sat
freeze	froze	frozen	sleep	slept	slept
get	got	gotten	slide	slid	slid
give	gave	given	slit	slit	slit
go	went	gone	speak	spoke	spoken
grind	ground	ground	speed	sped	sped
grow	grew	grown	spend	spent	spent
hang	hung	hung[2]	spin	spun	spun
have	had	had	spit	spit	spit
hear	heard	heard	split	split	split
hide	hid	hidden	spread	spread	spread
hit	hit	hit	spring	sprang	sprung
hold	held	held	stand	stood	stood
hurt	hurt	hurt	steal	stole	stolen
keep	kept	kept	stick	stuck	stuck
know	knew	known	sting	stung	stung
lay	laid	laid	stink	stank	stunk
lead	led	led	strike	struck	struck/stricken
leave	left	left	strive	strove	striven
lend	loaned/lent	loaned/lent	swear	swore	sworn
let	let	let	sweep	swept	swept
lie	lay	lain	swim	swam	swum
light	lit/lighted	lit/lighted	swing	swung	swung
lose	lost	lost	take	took	taken
make	made	made	teach	taught	taught
mean	meant	meant	tear	tore	torn
meet	met	met	tell	told	told
mistake	mistook	mistaken	think	thought	thought
pay	paid	paid	throw	threw	thrown
prove	proved	proven/proved	understand	understood	understood
put	put	put	upset	upset	upset
quit	quit	quit	wake	woke	woken
read	read	read	wear	wore	worn
ride	rode	ridden	weave	wove	woven
ring	rang	rung	weep	wept	wept
rise	rose	risen	win	won	won
run	ran	run	wind	wound	wound
say	said	said	withdraw	withdrew	withdrawn
see	saw	seen	wring	wrung	wrung
seek	sought	sought	write	wrote	written
sell	sold	sold			
send	sent	sent			
set	set	set			
shake	shook	shaken			
shed	shed	shed			
shine	shone/shined	shone			
shoot	shot	shot			
show	showed	shown/showed			
shrink	shrank	shrunk			

The past and past participle of some verbs can end in -ed or -t. Americans generally prefer the -ed form:

burn	burned or burnt
dream	dreamed or dreamt
kneel	kneeled or knelt
learn	learned or learnt
spill	spilled or spilt
spoil	spoiled or spoilt

[2] *Hanged* is used as the past form to refer to punishment by death. *Hung* is used in other situations: She *hung* the picture on the wall.

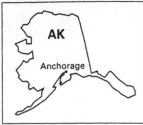

The United States of America

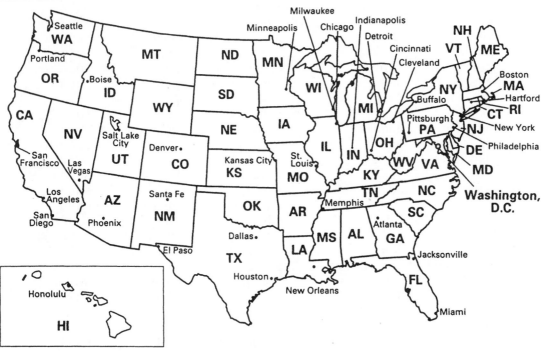

AL	Alabama	IN	Indiana	NE	Nebraska	SC	South Carolina
AK	Alaska	IA	Iowa	NV	Nevada	SD	South Dakota
AZ	Arizona	KS	Kansas	NH	New Hampshire	TN	Tennessee
AR	Arkansas	KY	Kentucky	NJ	New Jersey	TX	Texas
CA	California	LA	Louisiana	NM	New Mexico	UT	Utah
CO	Colorado	ME	Maine	NY	New York	VT	Vermont
CT	Connecticut	MD	Maryland	NC	North Carolina	VA	Virginia
DE	Delaware	MA	Massachusetts	ND	North Dakota	WA	Washington
FL	Florida	MI	Michigan	OH	Ohio	WV	West Virginia
GA	Georgia	MN	Minnesota	OK	Oklahoma	WI	Wisconsin
HI	Hawaii	MS	Mississippi	OR	Oregon	WY	Wyoming
ID	Idaho	MO	Missouri	PA	Pennsylvania	DC*	District of Columbia
IL	Illinois	MT	Montana	RI	Rhode Island		

*The District of Columbia is not a state. Washington D.C. is the capital of the United States. Note: Washington D.C. and Washington state are not the same.

North America

Alaska

CANADA

U. S. A.

Hawaii

MEXICO

Puerto Rico

Index